STANLEY FISH ON PHILOSOPHY, POLITICS, AND LA

Fish's writings on philosophy, politics, and law comprise numerous books and articles produced over many decades. This book connects those dots in order to reveal the overall structure of his argument and to demonstrate how his work in politics and law flows logically from his philosophical stands on the nature of the self, epistemology, and the role of theory. Michael Robertson considers Fish's political critiques of liberalism, critical theory, postmodernism, and pragmatism before turning to his observations on political substance and political practice. The detailed analysis of Fish's jurisprudence explores his relationships to legal positivism, legal formalism, legal realism, and critical legal studies, as well as his debate with Ronald Dworkin. Gaps and inconsistencies in Fish's arguments are fully explored, and the author provides a description of Fish's own positive account of law and deals with the charge that Fish is an indeterminacy theorist who undermines the rule of law.

MICHAEL ROBERTSON is an associate professor of law in the Faculty of Law at the University of Otago, New Zealand, where he teaches courses in jurisprudence, legal theory and law & society.

STANLEY FISH ON PHILOSOPHY, POLITICS, AND LAW

How Fish Works

MICHAEL ROBERTSON

CAMBRIDGE
UNIVERSITY PRESS

CAMBRIDGE
UNIVERSITY PRESS

University Printing House, Cambridge CB2 8BS, United Kingdom

Cambridge University Press is part of the University of Cambridge.

It furthers the University's mission by disseminating knowledge in the pursuit of education, learning and research at the highest international levels of excellence.

www.cambridge.org
Information on this title: www.cambridge.org/9781107427372

First published 2014
First paperback edition 2016

A catalogue record for this publication is available from the British Library

Library of Congress Cataloguing in Publication data
Robertson, Michael Spencer, 1952– author.
Stanley Fish on philosophy, politics and law : how Fish works / Michael Robertson.
pages cm
ISBN 978-1-107-07474-3 (Hardback)
1. Fish, Stanley Eugene.   2. Law–Philosophy.   3. Political science–Philosophy.   I. Title.
K230.F57 R63014
340′.1–dc23   2014014330

ISBN 978-1-107-07474-3 Hardback
ISBN 978-1-107-42737-2 Paperback

Additional resources for this publication at www.cambridge.org/9781107074743

For Vicki Evans and Rick Norris

CONTENTS

Short titles of books by Stanley Fish   x

Introduction   1

PART I: **Philosophy**   5

1 **The nature of the self**   7
Kant's conception of the self   7
Fish's critique of Kant's conception of the self   9
Fish's conception of the self   11

2 **Epistemology**   16
Foundationalism   16
Fish's critique of foundationalism   18
Fish's anti-foundationalism   21
Facts, reasons, and beliefs   40

3 **The role of theory**   48
Three orthodox claims about the role of theory   48
Fish's rejection of the claim that theory can transcend
the limitations of local contexts   50
Fish's rejection of the claim that all local practices
presuppose some theory   53
Fish's rejection of the claim that theory has a special role in
guiding or reforming other practices   55
Fish's account of the contingent consequences of theory   70

PART II: **Politics**   79

4 **Political theory**   81
Fish's critique of liberal political theory   81
Fish's critique of anti-foundationalist political theories:
critical theory, postmodernism, and pragmatism   108

5   **Political substance**   139
     Fish's claim that there is no necessary connection between his
     philosophical analysis and any substantive political positions   139
     Fish's own substantive political positions   139
     The objection that some substantive political positions do
     follow from Fish's philosophical analysis   144

6   **Political practice**   154
     Fish's different senses of "politics"   154
     Fish on political practice   156

     PART III: **Law**   177

7   **Legal positivism**   179
     The impossibility of the unconstrained legal actor   179
     Fish's rejection of the separation of law and morality/politics   183
     Legal positivist responses to Fish   186

8   **Legal formalism**   206
     The textualist version of legal formalism   206
     Fish's critiques of textualism   213
     More on Fish's intentionalism   228

9   **The Fish/Dworkin debate**   251
     Fish's critique of Dworkin's fear of an unconstrained legal actor   253
     Fish's critique of Dworkin's hope for an independent
     constraint upon interpretation   259
     Fish's critique of Dworkin's hope that philosophy can provide
     coherence and guidance for law   264
     How does Fish's analysis of Dworkin fit with Fish's intentionalism?   269
     Dworkin's critique of Fish's rejection of unconstrained legal actors   273
     Dworkin's critique of Fish's analogizing judging to the instinctive
     performances of athletes   281

10   **Fish's positive account of law**   287
     Law's disorder   287
     Law's jobs   290
     Law's two stories   295
     Law's amazing trick   299
     Rewriting in law   301

11   **Change and indeterminacy in law**   305
     Arguments for the claim that Fish is an indeterminacy theorist   305

Does the ability to recontextualize entail indeterminacy?   308
Consequences of the constraints on achieving
recontextualization in law   311
Three implications of Fish's analysis   315

12 **Legal realism and critical legal studies**   320
Legal realism   320
Critical legal studies   327

Conclusion   335
Index   339

SHORT TITLES OF BOOKS BY STANLEY FISH

Stanley Fish, *Is there a text in this class? The authority of interpretive communities* (Cambridge, MA: Harvard University Press, 1980) will be referred to as *Text*.

Stanley Fish, *Doing what comes naturally. Change, rhetoric, and the practice of theory in literary and legal studies* (Durham, NC: Duke University Press, 1989) will be referred to as *Doing*.

Stanley Fish, *There's no such thing as free speech and it's a good thing, too* (New York, NY: Oxford University Press, 1994) will be referred to as *No free speech*.

Stanley Fish, *Professional correctness. Literary studies and political change* (Oxford: Clarendon Press, 1995) will be referred to as *Professional*.

Stanley Fish, *The trouble with principle* (Cambridge, MA: Harvard University Press, 1999) will be referred to as *Trouble*.

Stanley Fish, *How Milton works* (Cambridge, MA: Belknap Press, 2001) will be referred to as *Milton*.

Stanley Fish, *Save the world on your own time* (New York, NY: Oxford University Press, 2008) will be referred to as *Save*.

INTRODUCTION

Stanley Fish lists his areas of expertise as "the American academy, the nature and history of professionalism, the theory and history of disciplines, sixteenth- and seventeenth-century English Literature, Freud, literary theory, legal theory, philosophy of language, contract law, first amendment jurisprudence, affirmative action, the jurisprudence of church and state, [A]nglo-American liberalism, university administration, the teaching of composition, American television shows."[1] This covers an impressive sweep of terrain, and he is not just a minor laborer in these disparate vineyards. He is a prominent authority on Milton, and he has made contributions to the other listed areas in a series of books and articles that have attracted much academic commentary. He has lectured in law schools as well as English departments. He has been a university administrator as well as a university professor. He has a blog in the digital edition of *The New York Times* and appears on television and the public lecture circuit. He was the model for the Morris Zapp character in three of David Lodge's comic novels about academic life. In summary, he is a major contemporary thinker with an influence beyond the academy and beyond the shores of his homeland.

This book focuses on Fish's work in philosophy, politics, and law and does not attempt to cover all of the territory that he does. This limited focus nevertheless deals with incendiary material that has produced an intense negative reaction in most of his readers. He is accused of being a relativist and a skeptic who denies that we can have access to objective reality. He is said to hold that texts have no fixed meanings and that the rule of law is illusory. He is charged with being a conservative who denies the possibility of progressive political change. His critics are outraged by his declarations that theory, interdisciplinarity, and multiculturalism do

---

[1] Stanley Fish, "One more time" in G. Olson and L. Worsham (eds.), *Postmodern sophistry: Stanley Fish and the critical enterprise* (Albany: State University of New York Press, 2004), 265–6.

1

not exist. In response, Fish insists that his critics are outraged because they persistently misunderstood what his position is. "I keep saying the same thing and getting misunderstood in the same way," he complains.[2] Again and again, he tries to show that nothing negative follows from his position once it is correctly understood, but the lesson never seems to take.

Why would there be such a consistent failure to understand what Fish is saying in the areas that this book covers? It is not because he writes in a dense and impenetrable style with a confusing technical vocabulary. Fish's writing style is one of the reasons to read him. It is very clear and entertaining, with little technical terminology and a wealth of everyday (often humorous) examples to illustrate his points. The content of his writings, however, partially explains his readers' difficulties. He contradicts orthodoxy not just here and there, but everywhere, and seems to delight in doing so. The titles of some of his essays display this polemical spirit: "Liberalism doesn't exist," "Truth but no consequences: Why philosophy doesn't matter," "There's no such thing as free speech and it's a good thing, too," "You can only fight discrimination with discrimination," "Boutique multiculturalism," "Being interdisciplinary is so very hard to do," "Why we can't all just get along." And it is not just any old piece of conventional wisdom that he rejects. He claims that some of the deepest hopes of Western culture are impossible dreams – the forum of neutral principle, the unity of knowledge, the brotherhood of man, achieving an open mind, transcending the limitations of the local to grasp the universal and the timeless, resolving disputes through reason alone, and similar matters. Given the overwhelming unorthodoxy of his positions, it is unsurprising that most of his readers have difficulty absorbing them.

A second factor that helps to explain his readers' difficulties is structural. His output dealing with philosophy, politics, and law consists of many articles written over three decades. In these articles he works out different aspects of his position, but he has never consolidated all of this material together in a way that displays the underlying coherence and linkages. (The books that he has published in these areas mainly collect a number of his already published articles.) In these articles, he often relies on arguments that he has made previously but which he does not recapitulate. Nor does he typically separate out his philosophical, political, and legal analyses. Instead one article can touch upon each topic to varying degrees. Also he is typically writing in response to a particular author or position, and what he

---

[2] *The New Yorker* magazine profile, June 11, 2001, 71.

calls the resulting "angle of lean"[3] shapes the way his argument is presented more than the need to provide a coherent overview of his position. Consequently he presents us with a series of snapshots of bits of the edifice, but he does not provide us with a synoptic view of the whole. This fragmentation means that one has to read a lot of Fish, and connect a lot of dots, to appreciate what he is doing. Those who only sample a few of his articles will therefore find it difficult to understand him well.

Some of those commenting on Fish's work have noted these problems. A reviewer of *The trouble with principle* observed that "Fish's prose style is clean and lucid. But his argument is so intricate, demanding, and, at times, counterintuitive that many readers may fail to grasp its full sweep."[4] Another commentator complained that "Professor Fish has never provided an organized, coherent summary of his position on these issues; rather, like a sniper, he must be placed by tracing back the trajectory of his many shots aimed at adversaries (or those of his anti-foundationalist allies who occasionally slip up)."[5] A reviewer of *Doing what comes naturally* lamented that "[o]ne might wish for an essence of Fish: a short book that would set forth the argument in its general form, then demonstrate the kind of application it has to the different fields under consideration."[6] My goal is to provide a book that will meet such concerns and render Fish's position more accessible. My project will involve ranging over the body of his work and assembling, like a giant intellectual jigsaw puzzle, the pieces in a way that reveals the underlying structure, and how the various pieces support each other. I will separate out his philosophical, political, and legal arguments for separate treatments and then show their interconnections. I will move beyond the polemical titles of his articles to a close reading that seeks to make plain each step in his argument and that dispels the initial sense that his position is too unorthodox to be plausible. While this will present Fish's position in a way foreign to him, and which lacks his stylistic flair, it has the merit of making clear the underlying architecture of his position. This is why I have subtitled the book *How Fish works*, cheekily adapting the title of one of Fish's own books, *How Milton works*.

---

[3] *Doing*, 32.

[4] Richard Delgado, "Where's my body? Stanley Fish's long goodbye to law" 99 *Michigan Law Review* (2001) 1381.

[5] Daryl Levinson, "The consequences of Fish on the consequences of theory" 80 *Virginia Law Review* (1994) 1653.

[6] Peter Brooks, "Bouillabaisse" 99 *Yale Law Journal* (1990) 1147.

My project thus has a positive thrust, rather than a negative one. I have tried to advance an interpretation that makes the best of Fish's texts, rather than one that pounces upon and emphasizes problems. When problems have arisen, I have tried to find solutions that fit within the framework of Fish's position. Fish mentions the injunction of St. Augustine to engage in "diligent scrutiny until an interpretation contributing to the reign of charity is produced,"[7] and I have tried to be such a charitable reader. However, in a few instances I have identified problems with Fish's position that have resisted my charitable efforts, and I have highlighted these.

Because the main focus of the book is getting clear about what Fish's arguments are, other philosophers, political theorists, and legal theorists will only play subordinate roles, even if their contribution to the topic under discussion is more important than Fish's.[8] Fish is aware of these other writers, as evidenced by occasional footnotes, but he does not make extensive references to them, and it is unclear whether he has been greatly influenced by them. In fact, Fish notes that "many of the people whom I now regularly cite in essays are people that I read *after* most of the views that found my work were already formed."[9]

Ultimately, my conclusion will be that Fish's critics generally get him wrong and that consequently his original and valuable contributions to philosophy, politics, and law have been underappreciated, even as they garner notoriety. I want to make his important contributions more accessible and more clearly understood, so that even if the reader is not convinced, at least he or she will have a correct version of Fish's arguments against which to direct a critique.

One of the central themes of this book is that Fish's work in philosophy, politics, and law is strongly interrelated. His critiques of various political theories shape his jurisprudence, and both his jurisprudence and his political work flow logically from his philosophical commitments. Consequently Part I is the foundation of the book and should not be skipped, even if the reader is more interested in politics or law. Indeed, I would argue that the philosophical matters dealt with in Part I are the key to understanding Fish's work in all of the many fields noted at the beginning of this introduction.

[7] *Trouble*, 265.
[8] For a sustained effort to place Fish's work in the context of other relevant authors, see Peter Schanck, "Understanding postmodern thought and its implications for statutory interpretation" 65 *Southern California Law Review* (1991) 2505.
[9] *No free speech*, 292.

PART I

Philosophy

Stanley Fish's philosophical work focuses on the nature of the self, epistemology, and the role of theory. The chapter on the nature of the self is the shortest but possibly the most important because the positions that Fish develops in the following two chapters draw out the logical implications of his conception of the self. And since Fish's philosophical positions determine his political and legal analyses, his conception of the self can serve as the polestar guiding us safely through his work without foundering on the rocks of error and incomprehension.

1

The nature of the self

Human beings at first sight appear to be very diverse. We see a profusion of ethnicities, cultures, religions, and languages. Physical attributes and diets and entertainments vary greatly, as do morals, political structures, and family arrangements. Some philosophers do not accept this diversity at face value, however, and seek an enduring self that is separate from the variable and contingent attributes that people exhibit in different times and places.

Kant's conception of the self

Some religious philosophers conceived of this enduring self as a spirit or soul, but the eighteenth-century Enlightenment philosopher Immanuel Kant is credited with originating the conception of the essential self as an autonomous rational will that is separate from any of the contingent attributes that a person exhibits.[1] These attributes are inessential because the underlying rational self is always able to stand apart from them, evaluate them, and choose to affirm or change them. If the choice is to change them, then this is like changing a suit of clothes. Only accidental attributes of the self change, leaving the essential self as it was. Human beings could thus differ greatly with respect to the secondary attributes that socialization or deliberate choice establish while at the same time they shared the same essential nature as autonomous rational wills.

Stanley Fish argues that this Kantian conception of the self remains the dominant one within the Western liberal tradition. As an example of this, he offers John Rawls's project in *A theory of justice*[2] of seeking to find principles for ordering society that all members can accept, even though

---

[1] See, for example, Michael Sandel, *Democracy's discontent* (Cambridge, MA: Belknap Press, 1996), 11–17 and Margaret Radin, *Contested commodities* (Cambridge University Press, 1996), 34–40 and ch. 5 ("Personhood and the dialectic of contextuality").
[2] John Rawls, *A theory of justice* (Cambridge, MA: Belknap Press, 1971).

they may have different partisan commitments or "comprehensive doctrines." Rawls suggests the following thought experiment: Imagine an
"original position" in which selves who know nothing about their contingent secondary attributes (they are behind "a veil of ignorance") reason
about what principles they should choose to order society. The results of
this process will be neutral principles that cannot be biased in favor of any
partisan viewpoint, and so these principles can without unfairness be
applied to everybody, regardless of their local commitments. However,
as Fish points out, Rawls's procedure relies upon the Kantian conception
of the self, because Rawls assumes that it is possible to abstract away all
of the secondary attributes of a person and still have something left,
namely a rational self capable of engaging in political discussion and
freely choosing principles for ordering society:

> The trick is to regard social, political, and institutional investments
> as cosmetic. One sees how it is done when Rawls describes reasoning
> in the original position as proceeding "in accordance with the enumer-
> ated restrictions on information." The restrictions are the sum of what
> you are not allowed to know under the veil of ignorance – everything
> from name, rank, and serial number to matters of gender, class and race
> to memberships in churches and political parties to "various native
> endowments such as strength and intelligence." By referring to these
> as restrictions on *information*, Rawls makes it clear that in his view
> the characteristics they remove from inspection are not essential to
> the person, who is what he is with or without these identifying marks
> of merely social relations: he is an agent with a capacity to imagine a
> condition of justice and a vision of the good; and it is this capacity,
> rather than any realization it happens to have, that defines him. Those
> who have this capacity, even if they realize it in different ways, are the
> same; and a person who realizes it differently at different times in his
> life is also the same.[3]

Similarly, Fish sees the Kantian conception of the self at work in the
liberal principle mandating tolerance of cultural differences (described by
Fish as "boutique multiculturalism"):

---

[3] *Trouble*, 10–11. See also Michael Sandel, *Justice* (New York, NY: Farrar, Straus and
Giroux, 2009), 214–5: "Kant's idea of an autonomous will and Rawl's idea of a hypothetical agreement behind a veil of ignorance have this in common: both conceive the moral
agent as independent of his or her particular aims and attachments. When we will
the moral law (Kant) or choose the principles of justice (Rawls), we do so without
reference to the roles and identities that situate us in the world and make us the particular
people we are."

[A] boutique multiculturalist does not and cannot take seriously the core values of the cultures he tolerates. The reason he cannot is that he does not see these values as truly "core" but as overlays on a substratum of essential humanity. That is the true core, and the differences that mark us externally – differences in language, clothing, religious practices, race, gender, class, and so on – are for the boutique multiculturalist no more than what Milton calls in his *Areopagitica* "moderate varieties and brotherly dissimilitudes that are not vastly disproportional." We may dress differently, speak differently, woo differently, worship or not worship differently, but underneath (or so the argument goes) there is something we all share (or that shares us) and that something constitutes the core of our identities. Those who follow the practices of their local culture to the point of failing to respect the practices of other cultures – by calling for the death of an author whose writings denigrate a religion or by seeking to suppress pornography because it is offensive to a gender – have simply mistaken who they are by identifying with what is finally only an accidental aspect of their beings.[4]

Fish's critique of Kant's conception of the self

Notwithstanding the importance and pervasiveness of the Kantian conception of the self in the liberal tradition, Fish rejects it as not simply flawed but impossible. His claim is that if you deprive a self of the material that comes from being embedded in particular local contexts, then you do not end up with an essential self, rather you end up with no self at all. "[W]e cannot possibly start with a clean slate and still be somebody capable of starting."[5] His argument for this claim is that such a stripped-down abstract self without values, beliefs, goals, organizing categories of thought, etc., would be empty of the very content it needs to exist and function. Rather than being completely autonomous and rational, it would be unable to think or choose anything at all. A being with all local content removed would no longer be a human being, who "must always be somewhere (in a context) in order to be something (a self); and if it is never anywhere, if it stands free of all confining hierarchies and roles, it is nothing."[6] Furthermore, Fish claims:

> A mind so open that it was anchored by no assumptions, no convictions of the kind that order and stabilize perception, would be a mind without gestalt and therefore without the capacity of keeping anything in.

---

[4] *Trouble*, 57.

[5] Stanley Fish, "Intention is all there is: A critical analysis of Aharon Barak's Purposive interpretation in law" 29 *Cardozo Law Review* (2008) 1135.

[6] *Doing*, 428.

> A consciousness not shored up at one end by a belief (not always the same one) whose negation it could not think would be a sieve. In short, it would be empty.[7]

It is not only Rawls's project that is rendered impossible by this objection. Fish's objection also undermines any project that, in the name of freedom or open-mindedness or critical self-reflection, encourages the essential self to detach itself from all of its contingent local content and subject that content to rational scrutiny. The goal would be to identify which of our values and beliefs we should choose to retain and which we should reject as the mere products of ideology or socialization. But Fish argues that this project is impossible because a self separated from all of its values and beliefs would be unable to evaluate anything:

> The problem with this strategy is simply that one cannot follow it; moreover, even if we could somehow follow it, the condition of being free from ideological control would be wholly disabling because there would be nothing either to be free *with* or *for*. There would be nothing to be free *with* because were every preconception, acquired belief, assumed point of view, opinion, bias, and prejudice removed from the mind, there would be nothing left with which to calculate, determine, and decide; and there is nothing left to be free *for*, because a mind divested of all direction – a mind not already orientated toward this or that purpose or plan or agenda – could not recognize any reason for going in one direction rather than another, or, for that matter, for going in any direction at all.[8]

In short, all of our local commitments cannot be made the object of rational thought and subject to an autonomous will, because some already-in-place and unquestioned local commitments are a *precondition* for any thought and judgment.[9]

Fish has another, more striking and polemical, way of making his objection to the Kantian conception of the self. As well as arguing that no human being would exist if everything that was the product of some local

---

[7] *No free speech*, 117.
[8] *Doing*, 518. See too 394: "The demand for self-consciousness is a demand for a state of consciousness in which nothing has yet been settled and choices can therefore be truly rational. But if all concepts or constructs remained to be chosen, there would be nothing— no criteria, no norms of measurement, no calibration of value—with which or within which the choosing could be done; indeed, there would be no chooser, for if the question of direction were totally open the mind (such as it is) would be incapable of going in any direction at all if only because it would be unable to recognize one. To put the matter baldly, already-in-place interpretive constructs are a condition of consciousness."
[9] *Trouble*, 158.

context were abstracted away, Fish also argues that the only type of being that *could* exist free of any local context would be God.[10] It is only God who does not see the world from a partial, angled, biased perspective but who sees it entire and completely; it is only God who is not the product of local tradition or history or politics; it is only God who is not tied to a particular time and place; it is only God who does not depend upon categories learned from family, or school, or professional community, etc. The Kantian conception of the self is thus revealed to be the impossible desire to be like God. Fish concludes:

> [N]ot only is there no one who could spot a transcendent truth if it happened to pass through the neighborhood, but it is difficult even to say what one would be like. Of course we would know what it would *not* be like: it would not speak to any particular condition, or be identified with any historical production, or be formulated in the terms of any national, ethnic, racial, economic, or class traditions. In short, it would not be clothed in any of the guises that would render it available to the darkened glasses of mortal – that is, temporally limited – man. It is difficult not to conclude either (a) that there are no such truths, or, (and this is my preferred alternative) (b) that while there are such truths, they could only be known from a god's eye view. Since none of us occupies that view (because none of us is a god), the truths any of us find compelling will all be partial, which is to say they will all be political."[11]

Fish's conception of the self

The outlines of Fish's alternative conception of the self have already been revealed by his critiques of the Kantian conception.[12] Fish insists that a human self is necessarily embedded in some thick local context: "Human beings are always in a particular place; that is what it means to be human; to be limited by what a specific coordinate of space and time permits

---

[10] Sometimes Fish says "God," and sometimes he says "a god" when making this argument. See *Text*, 390 n. 2; *Doing*, 430; *No free speech*, 39, 74, 224, 241; *Trouble*, 113, 239; *Professional*, 8, 72, 104.

[11] *No free speech*, 8.

[12] For analyses of Fish's conception of the self that differ from mine, see Pierre Schlag, "Fish v. Zapp: The case of the relatively autonomous self" 76 *Georgetown Law Journal* (1987) 37 and Drucilla Cornell, "'Convention' and critique" 7 *Cardozo Law Review* (1986) 682, 689–91. Gavin Bryne agrees with my account of Fish's conception of the self, but he suggests that Fish got it from Heidegger. See his "The self and strong legal theory: A Heideggerian alternative to Fish's scepticism" 19 *The Canadian Journal of Law and Jurisprudence* (2006) 3–12.

us to see until we move on to another coordinate with its equally (if differently) limited permission."[13] It is as a result of being locally embedded that selves acquire a particular contingent content (beliefs, values, projects, organizing categories, paradigms, narratives, etc.) and are thereby "constituted, formed, made into what they are."[14] Rather than the true self being what remains when this contingent content is taken away, Fish asserts that the self is *nothing but* this contingent content. There is no separate self beneath these attributes, which is related to them in some way: "[T]here is no *relationship* between us and our beliefs; rather, there is an identity. The operations of my consciousness and the shape of my beliefs are not two entities somehow 'relating' to one another but one entity called by different names."[15]

Fish argues that what the local context provides gives structure and content to our consciousness and so simultaneously constrains and enables us. It is not something we think *with*, but something we think *within*. Our most basic beliefs are not something that we hold, rather they hold and constitute us.[16]

> It is these assumptions and categories that have been internalised in the course of training, a process at the end of which the trainee is not only possessed *of* but possessed *by* a knowledge of the ropes, by a tacit knowledge that tells him not so much what to do, but already has him doing it as a condition of perception and even of thought. The person who looks about and sees, without reflection, a field already organized by problems, impending decisions, possible courses of action, goals, consequences, desiderata, etc., is not free to choose and originate his own meanings because a set of meanings has, in a sense, already chosen him and is working itself out in the actions of perception, interpretation, judgment etc., he is even now performing.[17]

It follows that a human self can never transcend the local context. It cannot rise above its locally acquired content or stand to the side of it or hold it more loosely.[18] It can move from being embedded in one local context to being embedded in another (and so can play different roles or undergo conversions), but it cannot rise above any local context at all.

> In my story, agents are always and already situated, and efforts either to transcend that situation or understand its features down to the ground

---

[13] *Professional*, 81. See too 74–5.   [14] *Doing*, 19.   [15] *Trouble*, 280.
[16] Examples of Fish making these claims can be found in *Text*, 320; *Doing*, 326, 360, 386–7; *Trouble*, 284; *Milton*, 32; Stanley Fish, "Holocaust denial and academic freedom" 32 *Valparaiso University Law Review* (2001) 514.
[17] *Doing*, 127–8.   [18] Ibid., 346, 350; *No free speech*, 20, 251–2.

are always doomed to failure ... [T]he realm of the historical and
the particular provides us with the light by which we see, but it cannot light
the way to a realm beyond itself or even cast a light on its own foundations.[19]

For Fish, "local contexts" are provided by communities or institutions
such as families, tribes, churches, professions, academic disciplines, etc.
They preserve and transmit the clusters of beliefs, values, and projects that
constitute human selves and structure their thoughts and perceptions.

> When I use words like "institution" or "community" I refer not to a
> collection of independent individuals who, in a moment of deliberation,
> *choose* to employ certain deliberative strategies, but rather to a set of
> practices that are defining of an enterprise and fill the consciousness of the
> enterprise's members.[20]

Consequently Fish describes the self "not as an independent entity but
as a social construct whose operations are delimited by the systems of
intelligibility that inform it ... Selves are constituted by the ways of
thinking and seeing that inhere in social organizations."[21] He says that
"institutional history is the very ground of consciousness,"[22] and talks of
"membership in a community from whose (deep) assumptions one takes
one's very identity."[23] Because the self is formed out of what institutions
or communities provide, for Fish the self is best understood as "a moving
extension"[24] of those institutions or as "community property":

> [An interpretive community is] not so much a group of individuals who
> shared a point of view, but a point of view or way of organizing experience
> that shared individuals in the sense that its assumed distinctions, categor-
> ies of understanding, and stipulations of relevance and irrelevance were
> the content of the consciousness of community members who were
> therefore no longer individuals, but, insofar as they were embedded
> in the community's enterprise, community property.[25]

His focus is upon "the competent member of the enterprise" or "fully
situated members of a community."[26] That is, people who have had their
thinking and perceiving structured by institutional training and who
therefore stand in need of no additional constraints.

> It follows, then, that the fear of solipsism, of the imposition by the
> unconstrained self of its own prejudices, is unfounded because the self

---

[19] *Milton*, 562.   [20] *Professional*, 14.   [21] *Text*, 335–6.   [22] *Doing*, 389.
[23] *No free speech*, 214.   [24] *Doing*, 13. See too 82; *Text*, 334–5.
[25] *Doing*, 141. See too *Text*, 14.   [26] *Doing*, 388, 372.

does not exist apart from the communal or conventional categories of thought that enable its operations (of thinking, seeing, reading). Once one realizes that the conceptions that fill consciousness, including any conception of its own status, are culturally derived, the very notion of an unconstrained self, of a consciousness wholly and dangerously free, becomes incomprehensible.[27]

Fish does not accept the standard liberal dichotomy of a free self that stands opposed to the forces of constraint and convention represented by social institutions and communities. His conception of the self is thoroughly social, and he rejects hyper-individualistic accounts of the self that obscure its institutional origin.

> But I have no real interest in individual identity, and, indeed, individual identity is a casualty of my theorizing and my textual analyses, both of which are concerned with the life of institutions and tend to turn individuals into an extension of that life. (That is how far I am from the subjectivist position . . . attribute[d] to me.)[28]

Because Fish gives such an important role to institutions in shaping, constraining, and enabling individuals, it is unsurprising that he is keen to investigate how particular institutions function. In particular, he is very interested in universities (and their various disciplines) and law. He is interested in what their distinctive jobs are, how they sustain themselves, change, face challenges, etc.

Finally, Fish is well aware that people are locally embedded in complex ways. We all belong to many different communities and institutions.[29] But, as we shall see in Chapter 3, he insists that we are not free to mix and match the commitments that come with these roles as we please. If the consciousness of an actor has been structured and enabled by a particular institution's values, goals, assumptions, and categories, then it is impossible for that actor genuinely to occupy that institutional role free of those commitments.[30] Fish argues that the institutional context that is currently dominant will determine the point of view and the operative

---

[27] *Text*, 335. See too 320; *Doing*, 11, 12–3, 83–4, 127–8, 322–3, 346, 365–6, 386–9.

[28] Stanley Fish, "One more time" in G. Olson and L. Worsham (eds.), *Postmodern sophistry: Stanley Fish and the critical enterprise* (Albany: State University of New York Press, 2004), 293. See too Gary Olson, *Justifying belief. Stanley Fish and the work of rhetoric* (Albany: State University of New York Press, 2002), 139.

[29] See, for example, *Doing*, 30–1.

[30] The situation where the person is not genuinely occupying the institutional role, but only pretending to do so in order to advance the goals of some other practice, will be dealt with in Chapter 9.

background beliefs and values of the competent practitioner. When that same person later comes to occupy a different institutional role, the imperatives and concerns of the new role will supplant the previous one. It is thus possible to detach oneself from the commitments that come with one form of embeddedness but only in order to be gripped by the commitments that come with another form of embeddedness. What is not possible, according to Fish, is for the self to be detached from *any* form of embeddedness.

2

Epistemology

Foundationalism

Just as Fish critiques and rejects the currently dominant conception of the self, so he critiques and rejects the currently dominant epistemology, and for very similar reasons. Fish understands this epistemology to make the claim that humans can achieve direct and unmediated perception of things in the world that have their own characteristics independently of any human beliefs or practices. On this account, any genuine human knowledge must be based upon an accurate apprehension of these independently existing things. Such genuine knowledge has foundations in the world as it is apart from us. By contrast, claims to knowledge or truth based only upon human beliefs and practices that cannot be shown to rest on these independently existing foundations are ungrounded and defective. Fish calls this epistemology "foundationalism."

> By foundationalism I mean any attempt to ground inquiry and communication in something more firm and stable than mere belief or unexamined practice. The foundationalist strategy is first to identify that ground and then so to order our activities that they become anchored to it and are thereby rendered objective and principled. The ground so identified must have certain (related) characteristics: it must be invariant across contexts and even cultures; it must stand apart from political, partisan, and "subjective" concerns in relation to which it must act as a constraint; and it must provide a reference point or checkpoint against which claims to knowledge and success can be measured and adjudicated. In the long history of what [Jacques] Derrida has called the logocentric tradition of Western metaphysics, candidates for the status or position of "ground" have included God, the material or "brute fact" world, rationality in general and logic in particular, a neutral-observation language, the set of eternal values, and the free and independent self.[1]

[1] *Doing*, 342–3.

Accounts have differed on the nature of the independent reality that is the foundation for human knowledge. For Plato the ultimate extra-human reality was the Forms, of which the things found in everyday life were mere imperfect instances. In the Christianized West that followed the ancient civilizations, God was the ultimate external reality and foundation of knowledge. With the Enlightenment and the beginning of the industrial revolution in the eighteenth century, metaphysical accounts of the external foundations for knowledge came under challenge. The surge of confidence in the powers of human reason and the scientific method that the Enlightenment represented gave foundationalism the positivistic shape that is dominant today. For positivism, understood in its most general sense, accurate perceptions of empirical facts are the foundations of knowledge.[2] The influence of the positivistic version of foundationalism has spread beyond the natural sciences to the humanities and social sciences. The focus upon observable facts in the world as the basis for knowledge can also be found in philosophy (English empiricism and logical positivism[3]), psychology (behaviorism), and, as we shall see in Part III, law (legal positivism).

The promise of foundationalism is that objective knowledge can be achieved by humans if it is based on accurate perceptions and under-standings of an extra-human reality, whether that reality is physical or metaphysical. But as we have already noted in Chapter 1, human beings are found located in particular communities and cultures that have different beliefs about, and experiences of, the world. This gives rise to two problems for foundationalism – distortion and limitation. The problem of distortion arises because peoples' different beliefs, values, preferences, etc., can bias their perceptions and conceptions of reality. Wishful thinking, or willful blindness, or tunnel vision, or closed-mindedness can result in humans failing to register accurately the nature of the world. We often see such distortion afflicting others, and this leads to the concern that we ourselves might be similarly affected without being aware of it. The problem of limitation arises because the accidents of birth and history can give us a rich exposure to some things but only

---

[2] See Nicola Abbagnano, "Positivism" in Paul Edwards (ed.), vol. VI *The Encyclopedia of Philosophy* (New York, NY: Macmillan Publishing Co., 1967), 414: "The characteristic theses of positivism are that science is the only valid knowledge and facts the only possible object of knowledge . . . It opposes any kind of metaphysics and, in general, any procedure of investigation that is not reducible to scientific method."

[3] See *Doing*, 477–8 where Fish describes the efforts of Rudolf Carnap, an important member of the Vienna Circle of logical positivists.

at the cost of leaving us ignorant of many others. If we are to attain knowledge of universal norms or principles not tied to particular contexts, we have to find a way of seeing beyond our limited vantage point.

The foundationalist solution to the problems of distortion and limitation is to find methods for separating ourselves – if only temporarily – from the local commitments that cause the problems:

> In other words, what the clearheaded man is cleared of (or from) is his own head, the repository of the "local and temporary views" that have fallen to him . . . by virtue of the accidents and limitations of his education, professional training, political affiliations, etc. Once cleared of these views he can then turn an impartial eye on all positions, including his own, and begin to determine which of them "are rationally warranted, reasonable, or defensible."[4]

So the scientific method involves bracketing one's local commitments, holding them at arm's length, and not allowing them to distort one's observations of the world's characteristics. Or, if one cannot put the local commitments to one side completely, one at least becomes aware of them and makes allowances for them.[5] Ultimately, the goal of the scientific method is to find a way of describing the world that is purely neutral and so purged of the distorting influence of local commitments.[6] The foundationalist response to the problem of limitation is to use reason or revelation as a lever to lift us above the local level, and thus achieve a vantage point from which universal principles and norms can be ascertained.

Fish's critique of foundationalism

The foundationalist solution to the twin problems of distortion and limitation just described – detaching oneself from the beliefs and values that come with being locally embedded – requires a particular kind of self:

> What is required is a self that has no interests "of its own" or has set them aside in favor of something larger; for only that selfless self will be able to

---

[4] Ibid., 438. See too 142–3, 230–1, 474; Stanley Fish, "Holocaust denial and academic freedom" 32 *Valparaiso University Law Review* (2001) 515 (hereafter cited as Fish, "Holocaust denial"); *Milton* 56.

[5] See Fish's discussion of Stephen Toulmin and the scientific method at *Doing*, 436–41. There is also a discussion of the scientific method and its originator, Francis Bacon, in Stanley Fish, "French theory in America," a review of Francois Cusset, *French theory: How Foucault, Derrida, Deleuze, & co. transformed the intellectual life of the United States* (Minneapolis: University of Minnesota Press, 2008) in his *New York Times* Opinionator Blog for April 6, 2008.

[6] *Doing*, 474–5.

espy and embrace a piece of rationality or truth that is itself independent
of any interest ... These are strong words, and they show us what is at
stake ... the protection and nourishing of a set of related and finally
equivalent acontextual entities. First, there is a truth that exists independently of any temporal or local concern; and then there is knowledge about
this truth, a knowledge that is itself dependent on no particular perspective but has as its object this same transperspectival truth; and finally, and
most importantly, there is a self or knowing consciousness that is under
the sway of no partial vision, and is therefore free (in a very strong sense)
first to identify and then to embrace the truth to which a disinterested
knowledge inescapably points.[7]

But this is exactly the kind of self that Fish argued in Chapter 1 was
impossible. The local commitments that this project wants to bracket or
transcend in order to get access to the true foundations of knowledge are,
we have seen Fish argue, preconditions for the very existence of a self,
and so the foundationalist project is impossible for the same reason that
the Kantian conception of the self is impossible. We cannot put all of
our contingent local commitments to one side, either in order to uncover
an essential self, or in order to see what the world looks like independently of them, because some local commitments have to be in place
in order for us to exist as conscious beings able to perceive anything
at all.

In Fish's account, our local commitments do not *distort* perception of
the world as foundationalists fear; rather they are what *enable* perception
of the world. Take local commitments away and you would not have
accurate perception of a foundational reality, rather you would have no
perception, Fish argues: "Selves that are progressively emancipated from
social divisions, hierarchies, and roles would be selves ... without a core
of assumptions in relation to which the shape of things (physical, mental,
moral) came into immediate and unreflective view.[8] Because local
commitments have to be in place in order for us to be conscious beings
able to perceive anything, the world always has a shape for us that is
structured by our local commitments: "Perception is never innocent of
assumptions, and the assumptions within which it occurs will be responsible for the contours of what is perceived."[9]

---

[7] Ibid., 220–1   [8] Ibid., 427.

[9] Ibid., 78. See too 82: "What can be seen will be a function of the categories of vision that
already inform perception, and those categories will be social and conventional and not
imposed upon us by an independent world" and ibid., 146: "[T]he mind is informed by
assumptions that limit what it can even notice."

Fish sometimes uses words like "angled," "partisan," "non-neutral," and "biased" to describe the situation of perceiving the world while locally embedded, but he does not mean by these words that our perception of the world is defective: "Bias is just another word for seeing from a particular perspective as opposed to seeing from no perspective at all, and since seeing from no perspective at all is not a possibility, bias is a condition of consciousness and therefore of action."[10] Fish similarly argues that an embedded self cannot rise above local commitments and identify universal principles beyond the limited horizon of concrete human practices.[11] Neither reason nor revelation can allow us to transcend our necessarily context-bound existences. He is not saying that religion is impossible or that God does not exist, only that our understanding of God and His commands (either via authoritative text or revelation) is always mediated (and so enabled and shaped) by categories that derive from a form of local embeddedness. "[A]s the history of biblical interpretation shows, even God's word must appear in some socially constructed and authorized form."[12]

In summary, Fish rejects the foundationalist epistemological claim that it is possible for us to apprehend accurately things in the world (physical or metaphysical) as they are, uncontaminated by any distorting or limiting human taint, if only we apply the correct method (neutral observation, neutral reason, religious revelation, etc.).[13] He also rejects as impossible the foundationalist desire to achieve a perception of reality that is "direct" or "undistorted" in a strong sense: "perception is always mediated (and therefore objects are never available directly)."[14] According to Fish, "there are no unmediated facts nor any neutral perception and . . . everything we know and see is known and seen under a description or as a function of some paradigm."[15] Since humans are necessarily embedded beings, it is impossible for us even to conceive of "Reality As It Is" outside any embedded position (e.g., God's experience of the world).

---

[10] Ibid., 176.   [11] Ibid., 13.

[12] No free speech, 196. Because we cannot gain unmediated access to God, "the permanence that underwrites and finally mitigates temporal instability is not something we can apprehend, and, as Paul explains elsewhere (notably in the eleventh chapter of Hebrews) we must therefore take it on faith, defined famously as 'the substance of things hoped for, the evidence of things not seen.'" Professional, 8.

[13] A nice summary of Fish's objections to foundationalist epistemology can be found in Fish, "Holocaust denial," 517.

[14] Doing, 83.   [15] Ibid., 326.

Any of the questions Dworkin might put to Rorty – Is genocide wrong? Do mountains exist? Does water boil at a certain temperature? – can be answered firmly and without metaphysical reservation (even by persons aware that the answers could change if the systems of knowledge and predications within which we "naturally" move change). The question that cannot be answered about any of these matters is: is this so in Reality As It Is? – is this really so, where by "really" is meant "independently of any of the ways of knowing and predicating and verifying available to us as human beings." Rorty's answer to that question, and it is also mine, is not "no," but, rather, the question doesn't make any sense because no sense can give given to the category "independently of the ways of knowing, predicating, and verifying available to us as human beings."[16]

Fish's anti-foundationalism

Protagoras said that "man is the measure of all things."[17] William James said that "the trail of the human serpent is . . . over everything." [18] Clifford Geertz said that "man is an animal suspended in webs of significance he himself has spun."[19] Fish agrees with these and similar authors,[20] and asserts that it is the human condition always to live in a world that is given shape, order, and significance by humanly generated categories, beliefs, and values that we hold (or that hold us) because we are embedded in particular communities.[21] This is why, in the previous section of this chapter, he rejected as incoherent any epistemology that declares

---

[16] Stanley Fish, "Theory minimalism" 37 *San Diego Law Review* (2000) 766 (hereafter cited as Fish, "Theory minimalism"). See too Stanley Fish, "One more time" in G. Olson and L. Worsham (eds.), *Postmodern sophistry: Stanley Fish and the critical enterprise* (Albany: State University of New York Press, 2004), 291 (hereafter cited as Olson and Worsham [eds.], *Postmodern sophistry*); *Doing*, 158–9.

[17] *Doing*, 480; Stanley Fish, "Foreword" in Gary Olson, *Justifying belief. Stanley Fish and the work of rhetoric* (Albany: State University of New York Press, 2002), xiii (hereafter cited as Olson, *Justifying belief.*) For more on the link between the ancient Greek sophists and modern anti-foundationalists (including Fish), see Steven Mailloux, "Measuring justice: Notes on Fish, Foucault, and the law" 9 *Cardozo Studies in Law & Literature* (1997) 1.

[18] *Trouble*, 305.

[19] Clifford Geertz, "Thick description: Toward an interpretive theory of culture" in *The interpretation of cultures* (New York, NY: Basic Books, 1973), 5.

[20] For Fish's lists of fellow anti-foundationalists, see *Doing*, 225, 321, 345, 500 and *No free speech*, 56–7.

[21] Fish acknowledges that his anti-foundationalism has similarities to pragmatism and also postmodernism, but as we shall see in Part II, he takes issue with the claims of some postmodernists and pragmatists. More importantly, it is likely that Fish's anti-foundationalism originated in his study of *premodern* religious authors, rather than any *postmodern* philosophical authors. Fish states that he derives many of his

that this human element can be stripped away to allow us access to "Reality As It Is." We cannot base knowledge, truth, and facts on such an unavailable foundation, but Fish does not conclude that we therefore cannot have access to knowledge, truth, and facts. Human communities have developed methods for ascertaining facts about the world, and it is these practices and the institutions devoted to pursuing them that will lead us to the truths we seek. We do not have to look outside the human realm to find truth (an impossibility for us anyway), for the resources that will reveal it are already available to us.

> Anti-foundationalism teaches that questions of fact, truth, correctness, validity and clarity can neither be posed nor answered in reference to some extracontextual, ahistorical, nonsituational reality, or rule, or law, or value; rather, anti-foundationalism asserts, all of these matters are intelligible and debatable only within the precincts of the contexts or situations or paradigms or communities that give them their local and changeable shape ... Entities like the world, language, and the self can still be named; and value judgments having to do with validity, factuality, accuracy, and propriety can still be made; but in every case these entities and values, along with the procedures by which they are identified and marshalled, will be inextricable from the social and historical circumstances in which they do their work. In short, the very essentials that are in foundationalist discourse opposed to the local, the historical, the contingent, the variable, and the rhetorical, turn out to be irreducibly dependent upon, and indeed to be functions of the local, the historical, the contingent, the variable and the rhetorical. Foundationalist theory fails, lies in ruins, because it is from the very first implicated in everything it claims to transcend.[22]

Objectivity, facts, truth, knowledge, etc., are therefore all still possible in Fish's account, but they are made possible by beliefs and traditions of

---

distinctive positions from his long study of Milton and Augustine. See *No free speech*, 272, 291–2; Stanley Fish, "Foreword" in Olson, *Justifying belief*, xvi–xx. The epistemological position that Fish ascribes to Milton in *Milton*, especially pages 23–4, 25, 26, 28, 30, 32, 41–2, 44–5, 53, 56–8, 79, 105–6, is one he adopts and defends in his own work, in which examples taken from Milton's writings appear often. See too H. Aram Veeser, "Extirpating for fun and profit" in Olson and Worsham (eds.), *Postmodern sophistry*, 211–4 where the influence on Fish of sixteenth- and seventeenth-century writers is noted.

[22] *Doing*, 344–5. For other general descriptions of anti-foundationalism, see *Doing*, 225, 321, 347, 436; *No free speech* 39. For a sympathetic account of Fish's anti-foundationalist epistemology, see Peter Schanck, "Understanding postmodern thought and its implications for statutory interpretation" 65 *Southern California Law Review* (1991) 2542–8, 2560–4 (hereafter cited as Schanck, "Understanding postmodern thought").

inquiry that do not rest on extra-human foundations. "[T]he issue is not the removal of objectivity, but the determination of the point of view from which objectivity (what is real, perspicacious, undoubted, worth dying for) will reveal itself."[23]

Fish is well aware that those captivated (or captured) by the foundationalist picture of truth and knowledge find it difficult to understand or even hear his position.[24] Because they are convinced that an objective apprehension of reality can only be understood in foundationalist terms, they typically misunderstand his rejection of foundationalism as a rejection of objective reality itself, or as an embrace of skepticism and relativism.[25] For foundationalists, if truth and knowledge rest upon local practices and beliefs, which are themselves the products of history, politics, and persuasion, then Fish has not delivered genuine truth and knowledge but only an ersatz version of them. Fish's facts and truths are not absolute but only relative to different local contexts. Fish has not given us knowledge of the world but only a view of it through culturally specific spectacles – a view that must always be inadequate and therefore defective. Fish's facts and truth are not stable and permanent but instead transient and shifting – as local contexts change, so will they. In summary, Fish's epistemology seems weak and second-best compared to the stronger and more satisfying foundationalist offering.

Fish makes a number of responses to the difficulty that foundationalists have in understanding him. One response is that just because

---

[23] *Doing*, 20. See too 29–30; *No free speech*, 290–1.

[24] *No free speech*, 290; Stanley Fish, "Truth but no consequences: Why philosophy doesn't matter" 29 *Critical Inquiry* (2003) 412 (hereafter cited as Fish, "Truth but no consequences"); Stanley Fish, "A reply to J. Judd Owen" 93 *The American Political Science Review* (1999) 927–8 (hereafter cited as Fish, "Reply to Owen").

[25] See, for example, Torben Spaak, "Relativism in legal thinking: Stanley Fish and the concept of an interpretative community" 21 *Ratio Juris* (2008) 164–70; Richard Weisberg, "Fish takes the bait: Holocaust denial and post-modernist theory" 14 *Law and Literature* (2002) 131; Georgia Chrysostomides, "Doing the unnatural – Stanley Fish's theory of interpretation" (2000) *UCL Jurisprudence Review* 181–2 (hereafter cited as Chrysostomides, "Doing the unnatural"); Gavin Bryne, "The self and strong legal theory: A Heideggerian alternative to Fish's scepticism" 19 *The Canadian Journal of Law and Jurisprudence* (2006) 19–23. (Byrne cites articles of mine as supporting his claim that Fish's position entails skepticism and extreme relativism. I argue against Byrne's reading of Fish (and me) in the present chapter.) A list of earlier critics of Fish's epistemology is provided in Schanck, "Understanding postmodern thought" 2546 n167. Schanck's account of Fish's response to critics who charge him with relativism is at 2547–8.

something is socially constructed and potentially revisable, it does not follow that it is unstable or transient or insubstantial.[26] His argument is for the social construction of reality, not the social construction of an illusion.[27] Revising or replacing things that are socially constructed requires work of the same kind as that which put the existing formation in place, and the work required may be beyond the powers of people for a very long time. Thus Fish talks of a "victory (*temporary, although it may stand for hundreds of years*) by one of the contending parties whose norms will be for a while the ones that can be unproblematically invoked."[28] He also talks of a "political victory (*which can last a moment or a millennium*)"[29] and says that the deconstruction of an established understanding "may not happen for *a very long time, long enough to feel like forever.*"[30] The facts and knowledge that local commitments make perspicuous and certain can therefore be very stable and secure. I shall return to this point in Part III.

Fish's response to the charge that his epistemology is weak and second-best when compared to the more full-blooded foundationalist account is that there is no better epistemological position available for humans than that which anti-foundationalism describes. Foundationalism is not a possible alternative to anti-foundationalism, because foundationalism does not describe anything a human being could experience. If in-place local commitments are a precondition for any human perception (as well as thought and action), as he has argued, then it is not possible for humans to perceive reality as it is independent of any local commitments. A being who could perceive reality without any local commitments in place could only be God, who is not limited by history, time, and space.[31] Once foundationalism is exposed as the impossible desire to experience reality as God does, it drops out of the picture as something with which anti-foundationalism could be unfavorably compared. (You cannot have a contest if one of the competitors will never show up.)

Fish's strategy here is to reveal foundationalism to be a mirage and to show us that we have been held captive by a picture that can never be realized. He is not urging us to change our use of terms like "objectivity"

---

[26] *Doing*, 236; *No free speech*, 190–1, 240–1, 290–1, 301; *Professional*, 74ff.; *Trouble*, 295.
[27] *No free speech*, 211. For Fish accepting a description of himself as a "social construction-ist." see 289–90.
[28] *Trouble*, 124. Emphasis added.   [29] *No free speech*, 4. Emphasis added.
[30] Ibid., 191. Emphasis added.   [31] Ibid., 39.

from a strong sense to a weak sense. He is not saying that because you cannot reach the foundations you crave, you must make do with second-best. He is making the stronger claim that the foundations you crave are impossible for human beings. Humans cannot even conceive of what attaining such foundations would be like, because they cannot conceive of God's experience of the world. Consequently, when the idea of foundationalism evaporates, we are deprived of nothing, and left exactly where we were before. "[T]he unavailability of an absolutely objective vantage point, of a god's eye view, doesn't take anything away from us."[32] Fish's argument purports to reveal the sense of objectivity that is the only one possible for us, the one we have always been operating with, whether we were aware of it or not.

> Rothstein tells us ... that "postmodernists challenge assertions that truth and ethical judgment have any objective validity." Well, it depends on what you mean by "objective." If you mean a standard of validity and value that is independent of any historically emergent and therefore revisable system of thought and practice, then it is true that many postmodernists would deny that any such standard is or could ever be available. But if by "objective" one means a standard of validity and value that is backed up by the tried-and-true procedures and protocols of a well-developed practice or discipline – history, physics, economics, psychology, etc. – then such standards are all around us, and we make use of them all the time without any metaphysical anxiety.[33]

So Fish's position is that just because our judgments cannot be given grounds of the impossible sort that foundationalists yearn for, it does not follow that our judgments are groundless. Nor are those actually available grounds defective or deficient.[34]

---

[32] *Save*, 140.

[33] Ibid., 139. See too Fish, "Truth but no consequences," 407; Fish, "Reply to Owen," 926; Stanley Fish, "Evidence in Science and Religion, Part Two" in his *New York Times* Opinionator Blog for April 9, 2012: "I am not laying waste to objective truth claims; like everyone else I make them all the time and, when I am asked to, I defend them. But any defense I offer will not proceed by citing unmediated and unchallengeable evidence, but by citing evidence that appears to me to be conclusive given the features of the world as I see it and the force of arguments I unproblematically affirm, at least for now. In short, I rely on the world that has been delivered to me by the traditions of inquiry and demonstration I currently have faith in. That is what objectivity means, going with the best arguments and bodies of evidence one has at the moment. A more severe definition of objectivity that would require a measure of validity outside any tradition of inquiry or paradigm or episteme or habitus is simply uncashable."

[34] Fish, "Theory minimalism," 766–7; *Trouble*, 125, 294; *Professional*, 72.

Fish's response to the charge of being a skeptic or a relativist is that he is not guilty because nobody could be guilty. He claims that neither skepticism nor relativism is a possibility for beings that cannot detach themselves from, or hold at arm's length, the deep local beliefs and values that constitute them. Both skepticism and relativism are versions of the same impossible project that we have already met before in other forms – the project of transcending our locally embedded condition.

> [R]adical skepticism is a possibility only if the mind exists independently of its furnishing, of the categories of understanding that inform it; but if, as I have been arguing, the mind is constituted by those categories, there is no possibility of achieving the distance from them that would make them available to a skeptical inquiry. In short, one cannot, properly speaking, be a skeptic, and one cannot be a skeptic for the same reason that one cannot be a relativist, because one cannot achieve the distance from his own beliefs and assumptions that would result in their being no more authoritative for him than the beliefs and assumptions held by others.[35]

For Fish, our inability to be skeptics or relativists is not due to limits on our mental powers, like our inability to remember all of the numbers in the phone book, but it is due to our nature as embedded selves. That is, his claim is ontological, not psychological.

As necessarily embedded beings, we cannot subject all of our beliefs to skepticism because we cannot achieve an Archimedean position outside of our beliefs from which we could scrutinize them all.[36] Moreover, if local commitments are a precondition of any human perception, thought, and action, then whenever we doubt some of our beliefs, there will always be other beliefs in place enabling and structuring this activity that cannot be doubted:

> Booth declares that it is possible to protect oneself from one's "prejudgments" by putting on a "true shield" in the form of a "healthy tentativeness about oneself and one's responses." The trick, he says, is "in developing a habit of great skepticism about one's own hypotheses." It would indeed be a trick if it were possible (and in a weak sense, of course, it is possible), but again any skepticism one "developed" would have a content; that is, it would be made up of questions ("are there really no exceptions to this rule whose validity I am assuming?"), tests ("is there anything that would falsify this thesis?"), cautions ("don't rush to premature conclusions on the basis

---

[35] *Text*, 360–1. See too 319–21; *Doing*, 370–1; *No free speech*, 41; Fish, "Truth but no consequences," 414–5; Fish, "Reply to Owen," 927–8.

[36] See *Text* 360–1 where Fish briefly mentions Descartes's project of systematic doubt. I shall return to Descartes when I deal with the role of philosophy in Chapter 3.

of inadequate evidence."), all of which would presuppose some set of already-in-place distinctions, hierarchies, values, definitions, which could not themselves be the object of "skepticism" because they formed the taken-for-granted background against and within which skepticism acquired its present shape.[37]

So Fish's anti-foundationalism does not deny that we can have doubts about the truth of particular knowledge claims or beliefs; it just claims that such doubts are always local and contextual, rather than universal and general, as with skepticism.

> Schlag's mistake can be seen by considering the nature of the "doubts" he considers "requisite," the doubts he thinks too few of us ever entertain. They are cosmic doubts, not doubts about this or that, but doubts about the entire cognitive structure within which "this" or "that" emerge as objects of inquiry. That form of doubt is not available to situated beings, and therefore it cannot be a criticism of anyone, or of the forms thought habitually has, that such wholesale doubt is absent. This does not mean that doubts of all kinds do not arise, only that they arise in ordinary contexts – when some expectation has been disappointed, some person has performed badly, or some experiment has not turned out well.[38]

Such local doubts are resolved by having recourse to the established methods and traditions judged to be appropriate for the particular context in which the doubt has arisen. Unlike the skeptic, the anti-foundationalist assures us that we have all of the resources we need to achieve knowledge of the world, make new discoveries, correct erroneous beliefs, and so on.[39]

Relativism, unlike skepticism, does not deny that knowledge is possible for humans; it just says that knowledge is never universal and trans-contextual. According to the relativist, what is accepted as true differs between communities and shifts over time even within the same community as assumptions and traditions of inquiry change. Consequently, we can never assert any truth with complete and aggressive certainty; we must always accept it provisionally and tentatively. We must always endorse it subject to the reservation that it will not be absolutely true for all times and places. Relativism is what Dennis Patterson is charging anti-foundationalism with supporting in this passage:

> [T]he anti-foundationalist spirit [is] the aspiration to throw off all accounts of knowledge as resting upon an edifice and to replace them with perspectives or points of view. Inspired by the idea that we cannot

---

[37] *Doing*, 440.   [38] Fish, "Theory minimalism," 772.
[39] *No free speech*, 10; Fish, "Holocaust denial," 513.

study "the phenomenon itself" apart from a language of description, the possibility of objectivity in judgment is sacrificed in favor of a perspectival epistemology.[40]

Indeed, many anti-foundationalists do endorse relativism, as we shall see when we come to examine postmodernism more closely in Part II. But Fish is distinctive because he holds that neither skepticism's instruction to doubt all of our beliefs and values, nor relativism's instruction to assert their truth only locally not universally, can be carried out. A self that is constituted by local commitments is a self for whom some beliefs and values are presently foundational and so they cannot be held more tentatively or with greater awareness of their provisional and socially constructed nature. If, as Fish put it in Chapter 1, there is no relationship between myself and my deep beliefs but rather an identity,[41] then certainty and absolute unwavering conviction about some things is a necessary and unavoidable feature of human existence, even though the commitments that occupy that foundational position may change over time:

> It is thus a condition of human life always to be operating as an extension of beliefs and assumptions that are historically contingent, *and yet to be holding those beliefs and assumptions with an absoluteness that is the necessary consequence of the absoluteness with which they hold – inform, shape, constitute – us.*[42]

It is thus inevitable that human beings will make assertions about facts, and judgments about values (ethical, aesthetic, etc.), that are absolute and unreserved and unqualified. Fish does not disparage this as many anti-foundationalists do. He does not describe such assertions and judgments as mistakes, or delusions, or false consciousness. "There are no cynics in my scenario ... [T]o have a conviction is to believe that what it commits you to is true not only for you but for everyone, including those who, for whatever reasons (blindness, error, perversity) are not presently persuaded of it."[43] So rather than being a skeptic and a relativist who seeks to deprive us

---

40 Dennis Patterson, "The poverty of interpretive universalism: Toward the reconstruction of legal theory" 72 *Texas Law Review* (1993) 4–5. For another piece charging anti-foundationalists with relativism, see Eric Blumenson, "Mapping the limits of skepticism in law and morals" 74 *Texas Law Review* (1995) 523.

41 *Trouble*, 280.

42 *Doing*, 246 (emphasis added). See too 18, 323–4, 335, 383–4, 432–3, 435, 523–4; *Text* 319–20, 359–60, 361–2, 364–5, 370.

43 *Trouble*, 206. See too *Doing*, 245, 467; *No free speech*, 117.

of absolute truths and unshakable judgments, Fish's anti-foundationalism asserts that we can never be without absolute truths and unshakable judgments.

> The question sometimes put to me – "If what you are saying is true, what is the point of teaching or arguing for anything?" – misses my point, which is not that there is no perspective within which one may proceed confidently but that one is always and already proceeding within just such a perspective because one is always and already proceeding within a structure of beliefs. The fact that a standard of truth is never available independently of a set of beliefs does not mean that we can never know for certain what is true but that we *always* know for certain what is true (because we are always in the grip of some belief or other), even though what we certainly know may change if and when our beliefs change."[44]

Of course, our strong truth claims will be backed up by deploying historically produced vocabularies and methods of verification. That is, our methods of proving our truth claims are always local; we have no algorithm or mechanism that is guaranteed to get everybody to accept the absolute and universal truths that we have identified. If some people disagree with us because they do not share our local commitments and traditions of truth-finding, we cannot show them the error of their ways by pointing out the "brute facts" to them, or by showing them how "neutral reason" supports our positions. This is because, according to anti-foundationalists, facts and reason themselves depend upon local commitments, which will differ. (I will return to these claims later in this chapter and in Part II.) We may be able to persuade other people to change their minds, which would be a contingent rhetorical success, but if we cannot, the fact that others disagree with us is no reason for us to doubt the correctness of the truths we have identified, either psychologically or logically. Error and ignorance have long been unfortunate facts of life.[45]

---

[44] *Text*, 364–5. See too *No free speech*, 39, 41.

[45] See Stanley Fish, "Postmodern Warfare" in *Harper's Magazine*, July 2002, 37: "The problem is not that there is no universal—the universal, the absolutely true, exists, and I know what it is. The problem is that you know, too, and that we know different things, which puts us right back where we were a few sentences ago, armed with universal judgments that are irreconcilable, all dressed up and nowhere to go for an authoritative adjudication. What to do? Well, you do the only thing you can do, the only honest thing: you assert that your universal is the true one, even though your adversaries clearly do not accept it, and you do not attribute their recalcitrance to insanity or mere criminality—the desired public categories of condemnation—but to the fact, regrettable as it may be, that they are in the grip of a set of beliefs that is false. And there you have it, because

Fish is therefore not saying that we cannot assert universal truths; he is just saying that we cannot identify such truths uncontroversially:

> I would not be misunderstood. I am not saying that there are no universal truths or no values independent of particular perspectives. I am saying that whatever universal values and independent truths there may be (and I believe in both), they are not acknowledged by everyone and no mechanism exists that would result in their universal acceptance ... [H]ere is a point that is often missed, the independence from each other of two assertions thought to be contradictory: (1) I believe X to be true and (2) I believe that there is no mechanism, procedure, calculus, test, by which the truth of X can be necessarily demonstrated to any sane person ... The claim that something is universal and the acknowledgment that I couldn't necessarily prove it are logically independent of each other. The second does not undermine the first.[46]

Notwithstanding all of his efforts, foundationalist misunderstandings of Fish's anti-foundationalist position remain common. Recently, Fish has acknowledged that this is partly his fault, because he has sometimes described his anti-foundationalism in ways that aid and abet such misunderstandings:

> I have too often surrendered to the temptation of making flamboyant statements that are rhetorically effective but misleading at best and downright mistakes (to which I myself at times become captive) at worst ... The result is an argument that appears to go in two different directions, depending on whether I am peddling a weak antifoundationalism that asserts the ubiquity of mediation ("everything comes to us under a description") but draws no moral or marching order or negative conclusion about truth from the assertion, or a strong antifoundationalism in whose wake truth, fact, evidence, conviction and a lot of other things become problems and puzzles. I have usually wanted to do the first, but more than occasionally put things in a way that allowed – no, encouraged – others to read me as doing the second. To a certain extent, it is a matter of how generous a commentator is inclined to be.[47]

---

the next step, the step of proving the falseness of their beliefs to everyone, including those in their grip, is not a step available to us as finite situated human beings."

[46] *Save*, 140–1. See too Stanley Fish, "One more time" in Olson and Worsham (eds.), *Postmodern sophistry*, 274; Fish, "Reply to Owen," 927; Stanley Fish, "The case against universalism" in Olson, *Justifying belief*, 128–9.

[47] Stanley Fish, "One more time" in Olson and Worsham (eds.), *Postmodern sophistry*, 281–2. An example of the kind of passage Fish is apologizing for might be *No free speech*, 57: "Merely to state this view is to see the problems it presents to 'traditional' thinking: notions of objectivity, accuracy, verisimilitude no longer provide the comfort and guidance they once did, for they are now not absolute judgments, but judgments relative

Thus far, I have presented the negative argument for anti-foundationalism – showing that foundationalism is impossible because it requires a self that can separate itself from all of its contingent local commitments. The positive argument for anti-foundationalism is to expose the background work done by these contingent local commitments in delivering to the foreground of our consciousness the items that we experience as unproblematically given.[48] However, this will not be an easy matter because, according to anti-foundationalism, the background role played by local commitments in enabling and structuring any human perception, thinking, and acting is typically going to be unnoticed. "One sees a poem or a tort, but the immediacy of the perception is produced by a stage-setting – by the behind-the-scenes network of interdependent and mutually defining practices – which at once escapes our attention and determines its content. (We don't see 'it,' but what 'it' enables us to see)."[49] Nevertheless, Fish does seek to make part of the "behind-the-scenes network" visible to us in a number of different contexts.

Everyday life

In order to make even the simplest of assertions or perform the most elementary action, I must already be proceeding in the context of innumerable beliefs which cannot be the object of my attention because they are the content of my attention: beliefs on the order of the identity of persons, the existence of animate and inanimate entities, the stability of objects, in addition to the countless beliefs that underwrite the possibility and intelligibility of events in my local culture – beliefs that give me, without reflection, a world populated by streets, sidewalks and telephone poles, restaurants, figures of authority and figures of fun, worthy and unworthy tasks, achievable and unachievable goals, and so on. The descriptions of what assumptions must already be in place for me to enter an elevator, or stand in line in a supermarket, or ask for the check in a restaurant would fill volumes, volumes that would themselves be intelligible only within a set of assumptions they in turn did not contain.[50]

---

to differing and competing vocabularies or paradigms; and a whole host of distinctions—between fact and value, norm and deviation, reason and rhetoric, centre and periphery, truth and politics—become, if not untenable, at least *disputable* in any of their proffered forms."

[48] For passages where Fish stresses the importance of the background in producing the foreground, see *No free speech*, 131, 153–4; *Trouble*, 286; *Doing*, 459.

[49] *Professional*, 76.   [50] *Doing*, 326–7.

Similarly, it is background beliefs, not simply the bare words used, that make the signs we meet in daily life clear and compelling:

> As a frequent flyer, I have been amused by the efforts of airlines to police their lavatories. In particular, I've noticed the now almost desperate search for a sign whose wording will make absolutely and explicitly clear what should and should not be flushed down the toilet. The latest (and doomed) effort goes something like this: "Only toilet paper and tissue should be deposited in the toilet." How long will it be, I wonder, before flight attendants and maintenance men begin to find bodily waste, liquid and solid, deposited in the most inconvenient places, if only by wags who recognize and testify to the folly of thinking that language can be made so explicit as to preclude interpretation. Of course, one could add faeces and urine to the list of proper things to deposit, but that would only fuel the game, not stop it. What stops the game when it is stopped (as it almost always is) is not the explicitness of words, but the tacit assumptions (concerning what toilets are for, and, on an even more basic level, what is and is not waste in a post-agricultural society) within which the words immediately take on an unproblematic (though interpretively produced) shape.[51]

And it is background beliefs that cause us to understand (or misunderstand) other people in our transactions with them:

> Consider . . . a cartoon that appeared some time ago in the *New Yorker*. It shows a man seated in a chair, staring morosely at a television set. Above him stands a woman, presumably his wife, and she is obviously speaking to him with some force and conviction. The caption reads, "You look sorry, you act sorry, you say you're sorry, but you're not sorry." . . . What the woman is able to hear depends upon her assumption of the kind of man her husband is; she constructs an image of him (has been constructing it for a long time), and that image controls her sense of his intentions and produces what is for her the obvious literal meaning of his utterance, and also of his facial expression and physical gesture.[52]

The crucial but unnoticed role in our everyday lives of enabling backgrounds can also be highlighted when we are placed in situations where they no longer do their invisible work. People who move through life serenely at home can suddenly find themselves flummoxed when they are called upon to do so in a foreign country where the in-place background understandings are different. Phone systems,

---

[51] Ibid., 302.   [52] Ibid., 80. Fish also refers to this cartoon at 43.

transportation systems, and plumbing fixtures that were intuitive and simple to negotiate at home suddenly become incomprehensible and irrational.

Campus life

In *Is there a text in this class?*, Fish makes the point a number of times that the facts apprehended by university students in the course of their on-campus activities are only available to them because they have internalized an institution-specific set of assumptions, goals, and practices:

> You might think that when you're on campus (a phrase that itself requires volumes) that you are simply walking around on the two legs God gave you; but your walking is informed by an internalized awareness of institutional goals and practices, of norms of behavior, of lists of do's and don't's, of invisible lines and the dangers of crossing them; and, as a result, you see everything as *already* organized in relation to those same goals and practices. It would never occur to you, for example, to wonder if the people pouring out of that building are fleeing from a fire; you *know* that they are exiting from a class (what could be more obvious?) and you know that because your perception of their actions occurs within a knowledge of what people in a university could possibly be doing and the reasons they could have for doing it (going to the next class, going back to the dorm, meeting someone at the student union).[53]

Similarly, Fish reports that when a student in one of his classes raised his hand, and he asked the class what this student was doing, they all replied that the student was asking permission to speak. But Fish points out that this fact could only be seen by someone who was already in possession of a background knowledge of what was involved in being a university student and whose seeing was therefore immediately structured by this background. With a different background in place, Fish says, the same gesture could be seen as a man pointing to the light, or calling attention to an object on the ceiling about to fall, or asking permission to go to the bathroom, or suffering from a disease, or making a political salute, or engaging in a muscle improving exercise, or trying to kill flies.[54]

---

[53] *Text*, 330. See too *Doing*, 53: "The 'facts' of a baseball game, of a classroom situation, of a family reunion, of a trip to the grocery store, of a philosophical colloquium on the French language are only facts for those who are proceeding within a prior knowledge of the purposes, goals, and practices that underlie those activities."

[54] *Text*, 333, 334.

> The point is the one I have made so many times before: it is neither the case that the significance of Mr. Newlin's gesture is imprinted on its surface where it need only be read off, or that the construction put on the gesture by everyone in the room was individual and idiosyncratic. Rather, the source of our interpretive unanimity was a structure of interests and understood goals, a structure whose categories so filled our individual consciousnesses that they were rendered as one, immediately investing phenomena with the significance they *must* have, given the already-in-place assumptions about what someone could possibly be intending by (a word or gesture) in a classroom.[55]

Finally, Fish describes an experiment in which he left a reading assignment from a linguistics class on the board and told the next poetry class that the list of authors' names was a poem.[56] The students were able to interpret the "poem" with ease, and Fish sees this as illuminating the way in which textual meaning comes to be apprehended because of background beliefs already in place (about the characteristics that poems possess, for example), rather than the observation of some independently existing features of the text. He anticipates the objection that what the second class did with the list of names from the first class was a mistake and so generates no general lessons about the apprehension of textual meaning. His response is that *whatever* the true facts about what is on the board are held to be, they will presuppose an in-place background, just as the apprehension of the poem did.

> That is, it requires just as much work, and work of the same kind, to see this as an assignment as it does to see it as a poem. If this seems counterintuitive, it is only because the work required to see it as an assignment is work we have already done, in the course of acquiring the huge amount of background knowledge that enables you and me to function in the academic world. In order to know what an assignment is, you must first know what a class is (know that it isn't an economic grouping) and know that classes meet at specified times for so many weeks, and that one's performance in class is largely a matter of performing between classes.[57]

Fish next anticipates that a positivist foundationalist might try to resist this line of argument by pointing to a more basic level of uninterpreted "brute facts" (perhaps even "sense data") that depends upon no background being in place, but he blocks this move in the same way:

[55] Ibid., 333. See too *Doing*, 82.
[56] This is described in *Text*, ch. 14 ("How to recognize a poem when you see one").
[57] Ibid., 329.

Of course, one might want to argue that there is a bedrock level at which these names constitute neither an assignment nor a poem but are merely a list. But that argument too falls because a list is no more a natural object – one that wears its meaning on its face and can be recognized by anyone – than an assignment or a poem. In order to see a list, one must already be equipped with the concepts of seriality, hierarchy, subordination, and so on, and while these are by no means esoteric, they are nonetheless learned, and if there were someone who had not learned them, he or she would not be able to see a list. The next recourse is to descend still lower (in the direction of atoms) and to claim objectivity for letters, paper, graphite, black marks on white spaces, and so on; but these entities too have palpability and shape only because of the assumption of some or other system of intelligibility.[58]

In every case, Fish argues, what is claimed to be a neutral and objective description of the bare empirical reality facing the students turns out to depend upon an already-in-place background of socially constructed material.

Law

A thick strand of contemporary legal scholarship is devoted to uncovering the background moral and political assumptions that sit beneath "black-letter" law and account for its shape. Critical legal studies, critical race theory, and feminism have all been active in this project. Fish is also interested in highlighting the background that delivers legal rules, interpretations, and decisions (although, as we shall see in Part III, his project is different from critical legal theory).

The persuasiveness of [a contractual interpretation] is not the product merely of the arguments it explicitly presents, but of the relationship between those arguments, and other, more tacit, arguments – tantamount to already-in-place beliefs – that are not so much being urged as they are traded on. It is this second, recessed, tier of arguments – of beliefs so much a part of the background that they are partly determinative of what will be heard as an argument – that does much of the work of fashioning a persuasive story and, therefore, does much of the work of filling in the category of "plain and clear" meaning.[59]

In these next two passages, Fish points to the role played in legal interpretation by background understandings of law's values and purposes:

---

[58] Ibid., 331. [59] *No free speech*, 153–4.

The enterprise of law, for example, is by definition committed to the ahistoricity of its basic principles, and workers in the field have a stake in seeing the history of their own efforts as the application of those principles to circumstances that are only *apparently* new (i.e., changed). That is why a judge will do almost anything to avoid overturning a precedent ... In short, the very point of the legal enterprise requires that its practitioners see continuity where others, with less of a stake in the enterprise, might feel free to see change.[60]

Legal texts might be written in verse or take the form of narratives or parables (as they have in some cultures); but so long as the underlying rationales of the enterprise were in place, so long as it was understood (at a level too deep to require articulation) that judges give remedies and avoid crises, those texts would be explicated so as to yield the determinate or settled result the law requires.[61]

The same point can be given a finer focus: constitutional interpretation is enabled and shaped by background beliefs about what a constitution is supposed to do.

If there are debates about what the [American] Constitution means, it is not because it is a certain *kind* of text, but because for persons reading (constituting) it within the assumption of different circumstances, different meanings will seem obvious and inescapable. By "circumstances" I mean, among other things, the very sense one has of what the Constitution is *for*. Is it an instrument for enforcing the intentions of the framers? Is it a device for assuring the openness of the political process? Is it a blueprint for the exfoliation of a continually evolving set of fundamental values? Depending on the interpreter's view of what the Constitution is for, he will be inclined to ask different questions, to consider different bodies of information as sources of evidence, to regard different lines of inquiry as relevant or irrelevant, and, finally, to reach different determinations of what the Constitution "plainly" means.[62]

Science

It may seem that the natural sciences can deliver objective facts that do not depend upon a background of socially constructed beliefs, but Fish asserts that his analysis applies here as well. Scientists, too, only see the facts they do because of a shared background that they have internalized in the course of their professional training. That background constituted

---

[60] *Doing*, 157.   [61] Ibid., 138.   [62] Ibid., 129.

them as scientists, and it shapes and limits what they see.[63] Fish often defends this claim by referring to the work of the historian of science Thomas Kuhn, who in *The structure of scientific revolutions* seeks to demonstrate that even the facts disclosed by physics and chemistry depend upon socially constructed paradigms.[64] When the paradigms change, some facts cease to be seen by scientists, and different facts come into view.[65]

> Kuhn challenges [the orthodox model of scientific inquiry] by introducing the notion of a paradigm, a set of tacit assumptions and beliefs within which research goes on, assumptions which rather than deriving from the observation of facts are determinative of the facts that could possibly be observed . . . What this means is that science does not proceed by offering its descriptions to the independent judgment of nature; rather, it proceeds when the proponents of one paradigm are able to present their case in a way that the adherents of other paradigms find compelling. In short, the "motor" by which science moves is not verification or falsification, but persuasion.[66]

So the natural sciences depend upon backgrounds that are just as socially constructed as the enabling backgrounds of literary critics and lawyers according to Fish.

Why then is science seen as a practice that is more likely to produce objective facts or truths than law or literary criticism? For Fish, the explanation is not that the natural sciences rest upon solid extra-human foundations while law and literature rest only upon an unstable foundation of human practices. Rather the difference is due to sociological and historical factors. Fish notes that scientists currently exhibit a greater

---

[63] See, for example, Fish's analysis of the running man at *Doing*, 60–1.

[64] Thomas Kuhn, *The structure of scientific revolutions* (Chicago, IL: University of Chicago Press, 1970; hereafter cited as Kuhn, *Scientific revolutions*). For examples of Fish drawing on Kuhn's work, see *Doing*, 125–6, 143, 486–8.

[65] See Kuhn, *Scientific revolutions* 116–7: "Can it conceivably be an accident, for example, that Western astronomers first saw change in the previously immutable heavens during the first half-century after Copernicus' new paradigm was first proposed? The Chinese, whose cosmological beliefs did not preclude celestial change, had recorded the appearance of many new stars in the heavens at a much earlier date . . . The very ease and rapidity with which astronomers saw new things when looking at old objects with old instruments may make us wish to say that, after Copernicus, astronomers lived in a different world." Fish echoes this at *Doing*, 462: "When our beliefs change—when the assumptions within which the possibilities of seeing, saying, and acting emerge are no longer what they were—the category of the obvious and perspicuous—of that of which we are *aware*—will have changed too."

[66] *Doing*, 487.

degree of unanimity with respect to their background commitments than the practitioners of other disciplines do – although this is a contingent sociological fact and not something demanded by the subject matter of the disciplines. "In a discipline that can be said to display scientific objectivity – for example science or at least some corners of it – potentially disputable premises are simply not in dispute for reasons of history, disciplinary politics, societal expectations, etc."[67] Science only recently attained its present status as a "prestige discourse" after it had displaced religion, which had held that status for centuries previously, and that displacement was due to contingent historical factors – the Protestant reformation, the rise of commerce following the discovery of the new world, the rise of liberalism, the Enlightenment, etc.

> [T]he difference between the rhetoric of science – the rhetoric of proof, deduction, and mathematical certainty – and other rhetorics in modern society is a difference between a prestige discourse, a discourse that has for historical reasons become associated with the presentation of truth, and the discourses that will for a time measure themselves against it. I am not saying that these differences are illusory or that they don't have real consequences, only that their reality and their consequentiality are historical achievements – achievements fashioned on the anvil of argument and debate – and that as historical achievements they can be undone in much the same way as they were achieved.[68]

Logic

Do the abstract realms of logic provide universal truths that do not depend upon a background of contingent commitments being in place? Is logic completely acontextual? Consider the syllogism, All As are Bs, X is an A, therefore X is a B. This is certainly very abstract and does not refer to a specific context, but an anti-foundationalist would argue that it is still the case that for this syllogism to be intelligible, a background of contingent beliefs about the world must already be in place. William James made this argument in the chapter of his book *Pragmatism* entitled "The one and the many." He notes that for logic to exist, there had to be a prior belief in place that

---

[67] *No free speech*, 205. See too 201–2.
[68] *Doing*, 298. See too *Trouble*, 216–7. Fish applies the same analysis to mathematics. See *Trouble*, 270–1.

things exist in kinds, there are many specimens of each kind, and what the "kind" implies for one specimen, it implies also for every other specimen of that kind. We can easily conceive that every fact in the world might be singular, that is, unlike any other fact and sole of its kind. In such a world of singulars our logic would be useless, for logic works by predicating of the single instance what is true of all of its kind. With no two things in the world alike, we should be unable to reason from our past experiences to our future ones.[69]

An anti-foundationalist would deny that whether "things exist in kinds" or we have "a world of singulars" is a matter of brute fact that the world impresses upon our sensory and cognitive facilities. (That would be the positivistic version of foundationalism.) Instead, an anti-foundationalist would insist, as Fish does, that "[w]hat can be seen will be a function of the categories of vision that already inform perception, and those categories will be social and conventional and not imposed upon us by an independent world."[70] So according to this argument, even logic is not acontextual and universal – it too presupposes certain background local commitments and contingent assumptions.

The role of contingent background beliefs in logic is also highlighted by Fish when he considers the rule against self-contradiction. He notes that in order for that rule to apply, a finding has to be made that contradictory propositions have indeed been asserted. But, Fish insists, the existence of a contradiction is not a brute fact simply given to us by the world. A contradiction, like any other fact, only comes into view by virtue of an already-in-place background. One cannot simply invoke

> supposedly abstract – i.e., contentless – logical operations like the "law of contradiction"; for just what is and is not a contradiction will vary depending on the distinctions already in place; a contradiction must be a contradiction between something and something else and the shape of those somethings will always be the product of an interpretive rather than a formal determination.[71]

The background commitments of different interpretive communities can increase or decrease their perception of contradictions. As we shall see in

---

[69] William James, *Pragmatism and other essays* (New York, NY: Washington Square Press, 1968), 62.

[70] *Doing*, 82.

[71] *No free speech*, 136. Steven Winter mistakenly thinks that Fish is committed to a hard-edged version of the law against contradiction and "has no patience with fluidity." See Steven Winter, "Bull Durham and the uses of theory" 42 *Stanford Law Review* (1990) 652–3.

Part III, law has a deep commitment to the coherence and stability of its basic principles, and this has the effect of making lawyers less inclined to see contradictions in the law. (We shall also see that lawyers have many devices to finesse what others might see as contradictions.) Once again we find that logic is not purely acontextual and universal but depends upon background contingent beliefs being in place.

Facts, reasons, and beliefs

Fish's epistemology boldly reverses the conventional understanding that relegates beliefs to a subordinate position. For foundationalists, beliefs can float free of the external foundations upon which any genuine knowledge must rest. Beliefs are subjective and are therefore epistemologically inferior to objective facts. All beliefs must therefore subject themselves to the scrutiny of fact and reason and must yield in the event of a conflict.

> [I]f one defines knowledge as that which exists independently of any particular perspective, belief – which is another word for perspective – becomes a bar to its achievement. In this view beliefs are the property of partisan agendas and if one is to resist their appeal . . . one must distance oneself from them and neutralize their force.[72]

Foundationalists have faith that disagreements between those with different beliefs can in principle be resolved by appealing to something that stands outside any particular partisan viewpoint. For positivists, there are empirical or "brute" facts that all parties must accept, even if they disagree about their significance or consequences. For more rationalist philosophers, there is reason as a neutral umpire that can be applied to partisan disputes and which can compel resolutions that all must accept (unless they are irrational).

However, in Fish's epistemology, belief has a more complex and more important role to play. His general anti-foundationalist position is that there can be no human thought or perception without a background of local beliefs, etc., already in place that enables and structures that experience. It follows that background local beliefs enable and structure our experience of facts and our conception of reason. Therefore such background beliefs cannot be inferior things that are subject to the scrutiny

---

[72] *Doing*, 519.

of facts, reason, and evidence, because these beliefs determine what we understand facts, reason, and evidence to be.[73]

> It is often claimed that reason is what is left when belief, preconception, and prejudice have been set aside or discounted, but reason cannot operate independently of some content ... and that content will reflect some belief or attitude that will inform whatever outcome reason dictates ... I am aware that in so arguing I am asserting the identity of two entities that are often distinguished and even opposed, reason and belief ... In [the standard view] beliefs are the property of partisan agendas and if one is to resist their appeal, an appeal that amounts to nothing less than coercion, one must distance oneself from them and neutralize their force. It is my contention that this is precisely what one cannot possibly do and still remain a "one," a being with a capacity for action.[74]

There is therefore no neutral, universal reason, only modes of reasoning enabled and structured by the contestable background beliefs of different groups. "It follows then that persons embedded within *different* discursive systems will not be able to hear the other's reasons *as* reasons, but only as errors or even delusions."[75] The same anti-foundationalist analysis applies to facts. The positivist distinction between empirical facts (which all should apprehend in the same way) and interpretations of these facts (which can vary with partisan viewpoint) is untenable, Fish argues, because facts too are "interpretive." That is, facts come to have their "brute" and obvious shape only when a certain background of deep contingent commitments is already in place. "That's the way it is with evidence; it doesn't just sit there unadorned and unencumbered asking for your independent evaluation; it sits in the midst of a structure (of belief and conviction) that precedes it and colors one's reception of it."[76] Disagreements between those with different deep background beliefs therefore cannot be resolved by appealing to the facts. "Difference is a condition that cannot be overcome by attaching ourselves to a bedrock level of social/empirical fact because that level, along with the facts seen as its components, is itself an interpretive construction."[77] Fish endorses Kuhn's claim that when scientists operating within different

---

[73] Olson, *Justifying belief*, 80–4; Gary Olson and Lynn Worsham, "Rhetoric, emotion, and the justification of belief" in Olson and Worsham (eds.), *Postmodern sophistry*, 143–56.

[74] *Doing*, 518–9. See too *No free speech*, 203; *Trouble*, 216, 247–8, 255, 284. I will deal with reason in more detail in Part II.

[75] *No free speech*, 136. See too *Trouble*, 269–70.

[76] Fish, "Holocaust denial," 502. See too 508–9.

[77] *No free speech*, 215. See too *Doing*, 55–6, 153.

paradigms generate conflicting accounts, one cannot resolve the disagreement by having recourse to the facts, because facts are paradigm-specific. Consequently, the disagreement regarding accounts will be reproduced, rather than resolved, at the level of facts.[78]

Because, in Fish's analysis, there are no facts or reasons that stand *outside* of all local and partisan background beliefs, there is no method available that all must accept for the resolution of disagreements. Those who are similarly embedded can see the same facts as obvious, the same evidence as compelling, the same reasoning as cogent, but those whose deep local commitments are different will see different facts, feel different evidence to be conclusive, and be swayed by different reasoning.[79] Different communities will therefore be opaque to each other to the extent that their deep beliefs diverge. If the backgrounds provided by local embeddedness are vastly different, no communication at all will be possible. Ludwig Wittgenstein has a pithy way of making this point: "If a lion could talk, we could not understand him."[80] This analysis of disagreement obviously has implications for politics that I will consider in Part II, but for now I want to consider some of the examples that Fish offers in support of his analysis.

Fish provides a number of examples of how people gripped by different deep background beliefs perceive different facts[81] and employ different conceptions of reason and evidence. One of his examples is the contest between Holocaust deniers and mainstream historians. The mainstream historians insist that the historical facts are all on their side and that the deniers have no grounds for their views and are therefore irrational. Fish is strongly opposed to the Holocaust deniers, and offers advice on how to smite them, but he recognizes that the Holocaust deniers do not simply ignore facts and reason. Rather, they see the facts and employ the reasoning that flows from their deep beliefs, just as the mainstream historians do.

> [Deborah] Lipstadt knows before she even encounters it that any argument denying or diminishing the Holocaust is specious and that the so-

---

[78] *Doing*, 487.   [79] Fish, "Reply to Owen," 926.
[80] Ludwig Wittgenstein, *Philosophical investigations* (Oxford: Basil Blackwell, 1958), §223. For Wittgenstein the notion of a "form of life" plays the same role that shared deep background beliefs play for Fish.
[81] In Michael Robertson, "Picking positivism apart. Stanley Fish on epistemology and law" 8 *Southern California Interdisciplinary Law Journal* (1999) 422–4, I presented an example of my own when I considered how death is perceived by people differently embedded.

called evidence it invokes is not really evidence at all but strained ration-
alization and downright fabrication; that is why she dismisses Holocaust
denial as "the apotheosis of irrationalism." And on the other side, her
opponents know that any evidence supposedly supporting the myth of the
Holocaust proceeds from the vast and well funded machinery of a Zionist
conspiracy, and that in truth, in the words of Mark Weber, the myth's
"underpinnings in the world of historical fact are non-existent – no Hitler
order, no plan, no budget, no gas chambers, no autopsies of gassed
victims, no bones, no ashes, no skulls, no nothing." Neither party reaches
its conclusion by sifting the evidence on the way to determining the truth
of the matter; rather, each begins with a firm conviction of what the truth
of the matter is, and then from inside the lens of that conviction receives
and evaluates (the shape of the evaluation is assured) the assertion of
contrary truths.[82]

The reason that Holocaust deniers need to be defeated, Fish argues, is not
because they do not care about facts and reason but because by virtue of
our deep beliefs we are absolutely certain that their deep beliefs are wrong
and dangerous, and so the facts and reasoning they advance are without
any weight for us.[83]

The most extended example that Fish provides of groups with different
deep constituting beliefs perceiving different facts and operating with
different conceptions of rationality and evidence is the contest between
strong religious believers and secular liberals. Relying upon arguments
provided by St. Augustine and John Milton,[84] Fish accepts that reason is
not superior to belief, because reason can only operate if background
beliefs are already in place. It follows that secular reasoning and religious
reasoning will exhibit exactly the same formal structure – each will rest
upon (different) deep beliefs or local commitments.

On the one side, there is the assumption (and conviction) that the truth of
things is revealed (although darkly) by an all-powerful, all-seeing,
and benevolent deity; on the other, there is the assumption (and conviction) that the truth of things can be discovered by the application of
disinterested procedures that start with empirically observed particulars
and ascend, by means of experimentation and tests, to the level of the
general.[85]

Secular liberalism cannot distinguish itself epistemologically from fundamentalist religion by saying that it is based on reason while the other is

---

[82] Fish, "Holocaust denial," 500–1.   [83] Ibid., 502.
[84] *Trouble*, 243–8, 263–7; *Milton*, 56–8; Fish, "Holocaust denial," 501.
[85] Stanley Fish, "Academic freedom: How odd is that?" 88 *Texas Law Review* (2009) 174.

based on faith, because "both are faiths, that is, ways of reasoning whose cogency and intelligibility depend on assumptions not open to question. Or, if you prefer, both are rationalities, that is, directions for producing evidence and conclusions undergirded by a full and coherent account of what the world is really like."[86] Neither stands opposed to mere belief, because each will have beliefs at its root. Moreover, the different beliefs or faiths at the root of each tradition will cause members of each to experience different facts and reasoning as obviously true.

> [E]vidence is never independent in the sense of being immediately apprehensible; evidence comes into view (or doesn't) in the light of some first premise or "essential axiom" that cannot itself be put to the test because the protocols of testing are established by its presumed authority. A "creationist parent whose child is being taught ... evolution" protests not in the name of religion and against the witness of fact; he protests in the name of fact as it seems indisputable to him given the "central" truth "that God is real." Given such a "starting point and the methodology" that follows from it, "creationism is as rational an explanation as any other"; and from the other direction, you might say that given the assumption of a material world that caused itself ... evolution is as faith-dependent an explanation as any other. This is not to debunk rationality in favor of faith but to say that rationality and faith go together in an indissoluble package: you can't have one without the other.[87]

As we saw when discussing relativism earlier, Fish's philosophical anti-foundationalism does not disable him from making firm and unqualified judgments in non-philosophical contexts. Therefore Fish can assert both that secular and religious ways of reasoning have the same epistemological structure (they both rely upon background beliefs that account for their different trajectories, and there is no neutral position from which they could be evaluated) and also that this formal similarity does not mean that they are equivalent in any real-life situation. In any such situation, depending on which background beliefs form the content of your

---

[86] *Trouble*, 216. See too 263; *No free speech*, 136; Olson, *Justifying belief*, 76–9.

[87] *Trouble*, 255. See too 199: "If you tell a serious Christian that no one can walk on water or rise from the dead or feed five thousand with two fishes and five loaves, he or she will tell you that the impossibility of those actions for mere men is what makes their performance so powerful a sign of divinity. For one party the reasoning is: 'No man can do it and therefore Christ didn't do it.' For the other the reasoning is: 'Since no man could do it, he who did it is more than a man.' For one party, falsification follows from the absence of a plausibly empirical account of how the purported phenomena could have occurred; for the other, the absence of a plausibly empirical account is just the point, one that does not challenge the faith but confirms it."

consciousness, some factual claims will be self-evident and some will be laughable, some reasoning will be conclusive and some will be crazy.[88]

> Epistemology-wise (an ugly but useful coinage), the vocabularies and premises of science, religion, liberal humanism, communitarianism, and so on are on a par, each one an orthodoxy to itself, fully equipped with dogma, criteria for evidence, founding texts, exemplary achievements, heroes, villains, goals, agendas, and all the rest. Politics-wise, these visions of life will never be on a par but always exist in some hierarchical relationship of precedence or subordination to which it would be foolish not to pay serious practical attention.[89]

Finally, I need to consider Fish's account of how our beliefs can change. Change is a very important topic in any study of Fish's work, because many of his critics charge him with being unable to account for it. Given its importance, I shall deal with the topic of change frequently in this book.[90] For now, I want to emphasize how the higher status given to background beliefs in Fish's epistemology does not prevent him from acknowledging that our beliefs can be challenged and changed. First, we must keep in mind his distinction between "the first or ground-level beliefs that give us our world" – the beliefs that are "so deep as to be invisible" – and the more surface or foreground beliefs, which can be "invoked within a highly dramatic, even spectacular, situation."[91] In contrast to the deep constituting beliefs, the surface or foreground beliefs are the ones that we think *about*, rather than those we think *within*. Fish acknowledges that it is a routine occurrence for these surface or foreground beliefs to be scrutinized and critiqued and changed. He only insists that any scrutiny that our surface beliefs undergo is not achieved by holding them up against brute facts or an unmediated reality or an external foundation. Rather the tests and procedures that we use to do this are themselves the product of our deeper background beliefs.

> This is not to say that in an anti-foundationalist world one lacks mechanisms for confirming or disconfirming beliefs, or hunches; it is just that such mechanisms (authoritative documents, the pronouncements of

---

[88] Ibid., 247–8.   [89] Ibid., 218.
[90] See the end of Chapters 3 and 5 and all of Chapter 11.
[91] *Doing*, 327, 328. See too *Trouble*, 284: "In short, beliefs emerge historically and in relation to the other beliefs that are already the content of our consciousness"; *Doing*, 146: "[B]eliefs are not all held at the same level or operative at the same time." For an example of a critic failing to note this aspect of Fish's account of belief, see Chrysostomides, "Doing the unnatural" 182–3.

revered authorities, standards of measurement, and so on) do not stand
apart from the structure of one's beliefs *but are items within it.*[92]

So it is a mistake to think that strong religious believers are mindless
zealots who will never allow any facts or reasons to change their beliefs,
Fish says. They can be swayed by facts and reasons, but these must be
internal to their system of beliefs and not external to it.

> When [Richard] Neuhaus declares that essential Christian truth claims
> would be in very deep trouble "were a corpse to be identified beyond
> reasonable doubt as that of Jesus of Nazareth," it depends on what he
> means by "reasonable doubt." If he means the kind of doubt an empiric-
> ally minded non-believer might have, then the doubt is a foregone
> conclusion since it is implicit in the way he (already) thinks. "A virgin
> birth? A God incarnate? Give me a break!" But if Neuhaus means a
> reasonable doubt a Christian might have, then it would have to be a
> doubt raised by tensions internal to Christian belief, and not by tensions
> *between* Christian belief and some other belief system . . . It will take more
> than a body, or carbon dating, or "identifying marks" to shake a faith
> which is not built on that kind of evidence in the first place . . . No believer
> will find his faith shaken by evidence that is evidence only in the light of
> assumptions he does not share and considers flatly wrong.[93]

Second, Fish accepts that background beliefs can also change, just as
surface beliefs can. Indeed, Fish argues that such changes are inevitable.

> Beliefs, if I may use a metaphor, are nested, and on occasion they may
> affect and even alter one another and so alter the entire system or network
> they comprise. Even though the mind is informed by assumptions that
> limit what it can even notice, among those is the assumption that one's
> assumptions are subject to challenge and possible revision under certain
> circumstances and according to certain procedures when they are set
> in motion by certain persons. What this means is that the mind is not
> a static structure, but an assemblage of related beliefs any one of which
> can exert pressure on any other in a motion that can lead to self-
> transformation.[94]

We can expect, though, that such changes will be less common than
changes to our more surface beliefs, because the deep beliefs that give
shape to thought are not easily made the subject of thought, nor are they
easily shifted if they are highlighted and challenged. Indeed, the normal
reaction to such a challenge will be outrage and incredulity:

---

[92] *Trouble*, 306. See too *No free speech*, 136.
[93] *Trouble*, 268. See too Fish, "Reply to Owen," 926.   [94] *Doing*, 146.

> In general that vulnerability does not touch the heart of the enterprise – the values so defining of its purpose that to question them is literally unthinkable, or the texts to which members of the enterprise pledge allegiance – but there are times when a challenge goes that deep. And at those times the guardians of orthodoxy rise up in a combination of outrage and incredulity – outrage at the very fact of an assault on truths so perspicuous that no one could, or should, deny them; incredulity at the spectacle of intelligent, credentialed men and women who seem unaccountably to have forgotten what everyone knows and shouldn't have to say.[95]

What then can bring about a change in deep beliefs? When he addresses this issue, Fish is at pains to stress that there is no general answer. Beliefs, including deep beliefs, can be changed by anything. Sometimes an individual's deep beliefs can be changed abruptly, as in a religious conversion experience. Sometimes the assumptions that define a particular institution change over a longer time, as when a new scientific paradigm gradually comes to be accepted by those working within a field, bringing with it changes to what Thomas Kuhn calls "normal science." Sometimes the background assumptions of a whole culture change over a very much longer time, as when religious belief faded in importance for Western civilization over many centuries in the shift from the medieval world to the modern world.

> Change is produced when a vocabulary takes hold to the extent that its ways of elaborating the world become normative and are unreflectively asserted in everyday practices. Occasionally this can happen when a community self-consciously rejects one theory in favor of another, as when within two years of Noam Chomsky's *Syntactic structures* almost every linguist was thinking in terms of transformations, kernel sentences, recursive functions, etc. . . . [M]ore often change just creeps up on a community as a vocabulary makes its unsystematic way into its every corner.[96]

However it happens, when deep background beliefs change it is not just a matter of a few opinions changing but of a more fundamental change in gestalt. One may see the world in a completely new way, or be "born again." Old certainties disappear, leaving not confusion and doubt, but new certainties that are experienced as progress, rather than as just change.[97]

---

[95] *Trouble*, 52.

[96] *Doing*, 24. On pages 24–5, Fish gives feminism as an example of a change in deep background beliefs that occurred in this more gradual and unsystematic way.

[97] *Text*, 361–2, 364; *Doing*, 150–60.

3

The role of theory

Fish's account of the role of theory in our lives and culture is deflation-ary.[1] This is not because he thinks that theory is frivolous and unworthy of serious attention. As we have seen in the previous chapters of Part I, Fish takes philosophical debates on certain issues very seriously, and he participates in them enthusiastically. Instead, we will find that the limited role that Fish gives to theory follows from his conception of the self and his insistence on the autonomy of practices.

Three orthodox claims about the role of theory

According to Fish, the orthodox story about theory makes three claims. The first is that theory can allow us to transcend the limitations of the contexts into which we happen to be born and socialized. Theory can allow us to achieve a viewpoint that is not hostage to some local set of beliefs or values and so allow us to become aware of principles, values, and norms that are universal and/or neutral.

> The theory of the kind I am interested in – grand theory, overarching theory, general theory, independent theory – claims to abstract away from the thick texture of particular situations with their built-in investments, sedimented histories, contemporary urgencies, and so on, and move toward a conceptual place purified of such particulars and inhabited by large abstractions – fairness, equality, neutrality, equal opportunity, autonomy, tolerance, diversity, efficiency – hostage to the presuppositions of no point of view or agenda but capable of pronouncing judgment on any point of view or agenda.[2]

---

[1] For useful general accounts of Fish on theory, see Gary Olson, *Justifying belief. Stanley Fish and the work of rhetoric* (Albany: State University of New York Press, 2002), 36–45 (hereafter cited as Olson, *Justifying belief*); Daryl Levinson, "The consequences of Fish on the consequences of theory" 80 *Virginia Law Review* (1994) 1653.

[2] Stanley Fish, "Theory minimalism" 37 *San Diego Law Review* (2000) 762 (hereafter cited as Fish, "Theory minimalism"). See too *Trouble*, 2–3.

The second claim is that all of our everyday practices presuppose some theory.

> The idea, then, is that whatever the surface configurations of our actions, *at bottom* we are being guided by principles of the kind that philosophy takes as its special province. Thus it is to philosophy that we should look to get a perspective on those principles and on the actions we perform in everyday life.[3]

The third claim is that theory has a special role in reforming the everyday practices that we perform.[4]

> [T]heory can be seen as an effort to govern practice in two senses: (1) it is an attempt to *guide* practice from a position above or outside it, and (2) it is an attempt to *reform* practice by neutralizing interest, by substituting for the parochial perspective of some local or partisan point of view the perspective of a general rationality to which the individual subordinates his contextually conditioned opinions and beliefs.[5]

When the three claims are combined, a very central role for theory is staked out. Theory can allow us to escape the limitations of our current embedded position; it can give us access to universality and neutrality; it can guide and improve our current local practices. Thus we arrive at "philosophy's age-old claim to be the master art underlying all the other arts."[6]

> Each discipline wants to label itself "Good For All Ills" in the manner of the elixirs sold at country fairs by quack doctors. At least one discipline has at times nearly pulled it off. Philosophy has often managed to convince workers in other fields that whatever abilities may apparently be required to excel at a particular task, the true ability, underlying all others, is philosophical. Basically the assertion is that philosophy is not a discipline – a particular angled project – but a natural kind, that it is another name for clear thinking and as such no less relevant to the task, say, of shoemaking than to the task of explicating Kant.[7]

However, Fish rejects all of these claims.

---

[3] *Doing*, 333. See too Stanley Fish, "Truth but no consequences: Why philosophy doesn't matter" 29 *Critical Inquiry* (2003) 389 (hereafter cited as Fish, "Truth but no consequences").

[4] For examples of this orthodox claim being made with respect to law, see Steven Winter, "Bull Durham and the uses of theory" 42 *Stanford Law Review* (1990) 639; Andrew Goldsmith, "Is there any backbone in this Fish? Interpretive communities, social criticism, and transgressive legal practice" 23 *Law & Social Inquiry* (1998) 373 (hereafter cited as Goldsmith, "Backbone").

[5] *Doing*, 319. See too 23, 25, 371.   [6] *No free speech*, 228.   [7] *Professional*, 89.

Fish's rejection of the claim that theory can transcend the limitations of local contexts

If human beings are necessarily embedded beings, as we have seen Fish argue in Chapter 1, then the goal of theory – the goal of attaining "a perspective . . . unattached to any local point of view, comprehensive doctrine, partisan agenda, ideological vision, or preferred state of political arrangements"[8] – can never be achieved. It is theory of this type, which I will call "strong theory,"[9] that Fish is referring to when he says that "there can be no such thing as theory."[10]

> The argument *against* theory is simply that this substitution of the general for the local has never been and will never be achieved. Theory is an impossible project which will never succeed. It will never succeed simply because the primary data and formal laws necessary to its success will always be spied or picked out from within the contextual circumstances of which they are supposedly independent.[11]

This sounds startling, but Fish is quick to insist that no bad consequences follow from his analysis. If strong theory has never existed, then it has never been doing anything for us, and so its absence will not cause us any problems. The only place where the non-existence of strong theory could have consequences is among those who practice theory. Some theory projects purport to be strong theory, but if strong theory is impossible, these projects cannot be accepted at face value.[12] Fish gives a number of examples of such purported strong theory projects, the most important of which for him is liberal political theory, which will be discussed more fully in Part II. For now, we need only note Fish's assertion that, notwithstanding its claim to have arrived at neutral principles and procedures that stand outside the partisan fray, liberal political theory is actually advancing a substantive partisan agenda and so is a covert participant in the fray.

> [M]y target is never liberalism in the sense of a set of particular political positions on debated issues; rather my target is Liberalism with a capital L, that is, liberalism as an effort to bracket metaphysical or religious views – the sources of intractable endless disputes – so that public questions can

---

[8] Fish, "Theory minimalism," 761.
[9] Michael Robertson, "What am I doing? Stanley Fish on the possibility of legal theory" 8 *Legal Theory* (2002) 368 (hereafter cited as Robertson, "What am I doing?").
[10] *Doing*, 14.   [11] Ibid., 320. See too 378.
[12] Fish, "Truth but no consequences," 397. See too *Professional*, 107.

be considered in terms that will be accessible to, and appear reasonable to, everyone, despite the evident plurality of what Rawls calls "comprehensive doctrines." With respect to this project (which is the project of theory or philosophy in general; liberalism is just one relatively recent name for it) my position is first that it is impossible ... [T]herefore when someone urges a conclusion that follows from the setting aside of comprehensive doctrines, it is really a conclusion that follows from a comprehensive doctrine that, at least for the moment, dare not speak its name and is in hiding. The requirement that comprehensive doctrines be set aside is not merely unattractive, or immoral, or inadvisable; it is not something anyone can do, and since it is not something anyone can do, nothing follows from it.[13]

Fish claims that Jürgen Habermas is also attempting to engage in impossible strong theory:

> Habermas, after all, is the philosopher of the "ideal speech situation" (identified by him as the desirable form of the public forum), a situation inhabited by participants who leave behind the points of view and senses of interest and desires for particular outcomes attached to their local and partisan existence and enter the room intent only on offering propositions that have a claim to universal validity and can be tested against similar claims in a communal effort to arrive at general truths ... Habermas's conversation is not labeled "ideal" for nothing; it requires ... the shedding of all the baggage of belief, interest, desire, aspiration that ... is inseparable from the condition of being human. It is not that the ideal conversation is a bad idea; it is an impossible idea.[14]

Fish admits "that what I intend by 'theory' may seem to some to be excessively narrow."[15]

> Why exclude from the category "theory" much that has always been regarded as theory – works such as W. J. Harvey's *Character in the Novel*, or Barbara Herrnstein Smith's *Poetic Closure* or William Empson's *Seven Types of Ambiguity* – works whose claims are general and extend beyond the interpretation of specific texts to the uncovering of regularities that are common to a great many texts?[16]

His response is that such texts,

---

[13] *Trouble*, 285–6.

[14] Ibid., 122, 131. For other critiques of Habermas by Fish, see *Trouble*, 132–3, 306; *Doing*, 450–5, 498–9; Stanley Fish, "Holocaust denial and academic freedom" 32 *Valparaiso University Law Review* (2001) 515 (hereafter cited as Fish, "Holocaust denial"), and especially Fish, "Truth but no consequences," 397ff.

[15] *Doing*, 378.　　[16] Ibid., 325.

rather than standing apart from practice and constituting an abstract picture of its possibilities, would be derived from practice and constitute a report on its current shape or the shape it once had in an earlier period ... The result, in short, would be *empirical generalizations* rather than a general hermeneutics.[17]

That is, these examples of what I will call "local theory"[18] do not pretend to transcend any local context but instead are performed *within* a particular local context. Local theory is a practice (involving abstraction and generalization) that is performed by those who assume an already-in-place background, and their performance is enabled and structured by that background.[19] As Christopher Norris put it, "[t]heory is perfectly acceptable to Fish so long as it entertains no delusions of grandeur, no ambition to exist on a separate plane from the beliefs, discourses, and practices which make up an ongoing cultural consensus."[20] Indeed, in Fish's analysis, local theory is the only kind of theory that could exist.

Notwithstanding this, Fish is at times so fixated on the task of demonstrating that strong theory is impossible that he dismisses local theory as being without much interest. He even suggests that admitting the existence of theory other than strong theory just muddies the waters.

> A theory, in short, is something a practitioner consults when he wishes to perform correctly, with the term "correctly" here understood as meaning independently of his preconceptions, biases, or personal preferences. To be sure, the word "theory" is often used in other, looser ways, to designate high-order generalizations, or strong declarations of basic beliefs, or programmatic statements of political or economic agendas, or descriptions of underlying assumptions. Here my argument is that to include such activities under the rubric of theory is finally to make everything theory, and if one does that there is nothing of a *general* kind to be said about theory.[21]

But elsewhere, Fish does devote more attention to local theory, and it is a good thing, too, because his deflationary project requires it. Even if strong theory is impossible, and only local theory can exist, local theory might be enough to support the second claim that all local practices

---

[17] Ibid.   [18] Robertson, "What am I doing?" 370.

[19] I take it to be local theory that Brook Thomas is defending in "Stanley Fish and the uses of baseball: The return of the natural" 2 *Yale Journal of Law & the Humanities* (1990) 59 (hereafter cited as Thomas, "Fish and the uses of baseball").

[20] Christopher Norris, "Law, deconstruction, and the resistance to theory" 15 *Journal of Law and Society* (1988) 184.

[21] *Doing*, 378. See too 325–6.

presuppose some theory and the third claim that theory is in a special position to reform other practices. If so, then a lot of theory's prestige and centrality will have been preserved, and Fish's deflationary project will have been blunted. But Fish has a number of responses to any such moves to maintain theory's special status.

Fish's rejection of the claim that all local practices presuppose some theory

It might seem surprising that Fish rejects the second claim that all local practices presuppose some theory, because such a pervasive role for theory appears to be entailed by his own anti-foundationalism. As we have already seen, he argues that any human perception, thought, and action presupposes an already-in-place background of beliefs, goals, values, etc. But does not this essential background for any practice constitute a local theory? No, says Fish,

> because beliefs are not theories. A theory is a special achievement of consciousness; a belief is a prerequisite for being conscious at all. Beliefs are not what you think *about* but what you think *with*, and it is within the space provided by their articulations that mental activity – including the activity of theorizing – goes on. Theories are something you can have – you can wield them and hold them at a distance; beliefs have *you*, in the sense that there can be no distance between them and the acts they enable.[22]

That is, theory does not stand behind and enable local practices because theory itself is just another local practice. Like any other practice, theorizing requires its own enabling background of beliefs, goals, values, and so on. On Fish's account, the already-in-place background commitments are not theories; they are what make foreground activities like theorizing possible.

The reason for Fish's rejection of the claim that all local practices presuppose some theory is once again his conception of the embedded self. According to Fish's analysis, an embedded self has had its consciousness shaped and enabled as a result of becoming a competent member of some community. Such a person therefore has no need of a theory to tell them how to perform as a member of that community, because they will

---

[22] Ibid., 326. See too 327–8 where Fish tries to make this distinction between beliefs and theories more concrete by means of an example.

always be "doing what comes naturally" as a result of that embeddedness. "The internalized 'know-how' or knowledge of 'the ropes' that practice brings is sufficient unto the day and no theoretical apparatus is needed to do what practice is already doing, that is, providing the embedded agent with a sense of relevancies, obligations, directions for action, criteria, etc."[23] This is one of the points Fish seeks to make with his example of the baseball player, Dennis Martinez. Fish argues that Martinez needs no theory to tell him how to do his job, because as a professional baseball player the know-how he needs has already been absorbed over many years of playing the game. It will always and already be structuring what he sees and thinks and does when he is on the field.

> What Martinez is saying to Berkow is something like this: "Look, it may be your job to characterize the game of baseball in terms of overriding theories, but it's my job to play it; and playing it has nothing to do with following words of wisdom ... and everything to do with already being someone whose sense of himself and his possible actions is inseparable from the kinds of knowledge that words of wisdom would presume to impart."[24]

Nor does Fish's "doing what comes naturally" analysis only apply to activities where there is no time for reflection while performing the practice, such as sports.[25] The same analysis would apply to the perform- ance of a competent practitioner where there *is* time for extended thought, such as playing chess or painting a portrait or drafting a contract. These practitioners, too, will be acting as "moving extensions" of the training and the background shared by a particular community – acting in a manner that requires no theory to produce it, even if it involves reflective pauses, doubts, false starts, etc. "[E]ven if [a literary critic] has doubts as to what interpretive direction he should take, those doubts are themselves discipline- specific, capable of being entertained only by those already embedded in the interpretive landscape literary studies presuppose."[26] Being embedded does not mean seeing only one option that is followed without thought; it can involve seeing a number of enterprise-specific possibilities that would only be visible to one who looked with practice-shaped eyes. These possibilities would then be evaluated and compared by employing enterprise-specific criteria of better and worse (a difficult process that

---

[23] Ibid., 388. See too ch. 6 ("Fish v. Fiss")   [24] Ibid., 373.

[25] I shall return to this point in more detail when discussing the Fish/Dworkin debate in Chapter 9.

[26] Stanley Fish, "Interpretation is not a theoretical issue" 11 *Yale Journal of Law & the Humanities* (1999) 514 (hereafter cited as Fish, "Interpretation is not a theoretical issue").

might take some time). So reflective activity, too, is a manifestation of (and is given shape and direction by) an institutionally shaped consciousness.

Finally, just as there is no need for a theory to tell embedded actors what to do, so there is no need for a theory to tell them what not to do, Fish argues. That is, there is no need for a theory to impose constraints upon the activities of embedded agents, because the same things that enable them – the local commitments that constitute the self – will simultaneously constrain them.

> [Thomas] Haskell must assume, falsely, that inquiry is a willful activity in need of an external constraint. In fact, inquiry is only possible if constraints – the constraints of some particular discipline or interpretive community – are already in place and have been internalized by the inquirer who proceeds within them. Constraints, in short, are constitutive of inquiry – were there none in place, inquiry would be directionless – and need not be sought in some external authority.[27]

This, as we shall see in more detail when we get to law in Part III, is the essence of Fish's disagreement with Ronald Dworkin. Dworkin thinks that judges need a theory to tell them the right thing to do and to constrain them from doing the wrong thing. Fish thinks they need no theory and no constraints other than what already comes with being a competent member of the interpretive community of judges and lawyers.

> Dworkin ... underestimates the complexity of the internal structure of practice, and ... it is this underestimation that leads him into a futile and unnecessary search for constraints that practice, properly understood, already contains. This is not to say (as Dworkin does) that practice, at least in some forms, is inseparable from theory, but that (1) competent practitioners operate within a strong understanding of what the practice they are engaged in is *for*, an understanding that generates without the addition of further reflection a sense of what is and is not appropriate, useful, or effective in particular situations; and that (2) such a sense is not theoretical in any interestingly meaningful way.[28]

Fish's rejection of the claim that theory has a special role in guiding or reforming other practices

Fish has a complex series of arguments that respond to the third orthodox claim that theory has a special role in reforming other practices. His ultimate conclusion will be that local theory has no such special role.

---

[27] Fish, "Truth but no consequences," 408 n16. [28] *No free speech*, 224–5.

It can sometimes affect other practices but only in a contingent fashion that does not distinguish it from the mass of other things in the world that sometimes affect practices.

Abstract theory is empty and so cannot guide

Fish's first deflationary argument against local theory having any special role in reforming other practices starts with the fact that any theory necessarily involves some abstraction from concrete particulars. But, Fish argues, the more abstract a local theory becomes, the more it is emptied of content, and the less guidance it can offer in particular contexts.[29] I will call highly abstract forms of local theory "detached theory."[30] For Fish, philosophy is a prime example of detached theory. It is a kind of theory that has deliberately distanced itself from everyday contexts and so can have no guidance to offer to people performing within those other contexts.

> [Philosophy] has been assigned, or has assigned itself, the task of asking and answering certain questions, questions like "What is the nature of justice?" "Are individuals autonomous?" "Is there one truth or are there many truths?" "Is the mind independent of the body?" "What is the relationship between belief and reason?" Both the manner of posing these questions and the acceptable ways of trying to answer them are functions of the history (again disciplinary) in the context of which they have been experienced as urgent. That kind of urgency – theoretical or philosophical urgency – is not what is felt by those persons confronting the real-life problems for which this general form of inquiry is supposed to provide solutions. It doesn't and couldn't, because as a *general* form of inquiry, it proceeds (and this is especially true of the branch of moral philosophy that dominates political theory) by abstracting away from particular situations and stripping from them the specificity and detail the come along with situatedness. The promise is that once this process of abstraction has made everything clear, you will be able to use its answers to order the specific situations from which it moved so resolutely away. But the promise can never be redeemed because the answers so derived are empty of substantive content – substantive content is what the abstracting process flees – and therefore they have no purchase whatsoever on the real-life issues to which you would apply them.[31]

---

[29] *Trouble*, 4.   [30] Robertson, "What am I doing?" 372.
[31] *Trouble*, 286–7. See too *Professional*, 89–90; Fish, "Theory minimalism," 763, 773; *Trouble*, 289; *Doing*, 433–4.

Descartes's famous project of methodical doubt in his *Meditations* is an example of the kind of detached theory that Fish would argue is without consequences for everyday practices. Doubts about whether you turned the oven off before you left the house or whether raising the minimum wage increases unemployment occur in particular contexts, and in those contexts what needs to be done to resolve those doubts is usually clear. But this is very different from the doubts philosophers engage in, which abstract away from any particular context and apply generally to any possible knowledge claim. Philosophers ask questions like: "How can I know that I am not currently dreaming, or hallucinating, or a brain in a vat?" or "I have been wrong about things I was sure of before, so how can I know that I am not wrong about what I am currently sure of?" Fish says that considering such skeptical arguments and the responses to them can be an enjoyable exercise in a philosophy seminar, and he himself joins in,[32] but he insists that once you stop doing philosophy and re-enter everyday contexts, the in-place backgrounds that enable you to perceive and act in those contexts will grip you with undiminished force.

> Doubts can be provoked by almost anything, but they cannot be provoked by some theory or anti-theory, even if you find it persuasive. This is because, to make my original point once again, the persuasiveness of a theory exists on so general a level that the only doubt it provokes is doubt about the soundness of some rival theory pitched at a similarly general level. The rest of the world, the world we live in when we are not being theoreticians or anti-theoreticians, will not be touched by that kind of general, all-encompassing doubt, although it can certainly be touched by the doubts we experience in a thousand everyday moments.[33]

But Fish must face an objection here: How can detached theory, such as philosophy, even exist according to his analysis? Is not the goal of abstracting completely away from local contexts the goal of strong theory, and hasn't Fish declared strong theory to be impossible? Is Fish falling into a contradiction here? No, because Fish is careful to stress that abstracting away from everyday contexts does not lift you outside *all* local contexts (which would be strong theory). Instead it locates you within the confines of one specialized and unusual context – the discipline of philosophy. Philosophy is just a type of local theory. Those who do philosophy are embedded within a particular academic discipline, with

---

[32] See for example *Text*, 360–1 and *Doing*, 440 where Fish himself engages in this exercise by considering the limits to Cartesian doubt.

[33] Fish, "Theory minimalism," 772.

its own distinctive history, projects, revered authorities, modes of reasoning, values, institutional structures, etc. All practices, as we have seen, require an already-in-place background, and philosophy is no different.

> This holds too even for those contexts in which the realm of the normative is the primary focus – philosophy seminars where the community effort is precisely to discover and formulate intersubjectively recognized and mutually shared norms of agreement and validity. For that too is a mundane, pragmatic space, the space of philosophy, not as a natural kind, but as an academic/institutional discipline with its own special history, traditions, exemplary achievements, canonical problems, honored and scorned solutions, holy grails, saints and sinners. Those who work (usually professionally but not exclusively so) within that history and tradition join in the search for context-transcending norms because that is what the local, professional, pragmatic context they belong to directs them to do, in the hope (never to be realized) that if they do it, they will, in an act of noblesse oblige, provide normative help to all of us who are not philosophers. The mistake – made by Habermas in spades but made by many others, too – is to think that normative philosophy is not a local, pragmatic practice like any other, but is a special practice in which the local and pragmatic have been left behind.[34]

According to Fish, if theory is to stop being detached and is to have consequences outside the practice of philosophy itself, it must become less abstract and acquire some content by being filled with some partisan substance. That is, theory can only be consequential if it incorporates that which it seeks to define itself against – the local, concrete, particular, and limited.

> When faced with opposing courses of action ... one can ask of the contenders, "Which is most responsive to the imperative of fairness?" or "which most conduces to the achievement of equality?" or "which will promote the greatest diversity?" The trouble with such questions (or so my argument goes) is that you will not be able to answer them without fleshing out your favorite abstraction with some set of the particulars it supposedly transcends. If you are determined to go with the alternative that is fairest, you will first have to decide whether by "fairness" you mean fairness to everyone independently of his or her achievements, failures, crimes, citizenship, gender, sexual orientation, or fairness inflected by at least some of the considerations in my non-exhaustive list. If "equality" is your lodestar, then you will have to decide whether you mean equality of

---

[34] Fish, "Truth but no consequences," 403. See too *Doing*, 333–4, 371, *Trouble*, 286, *Professional*, 89.

access (a strongly procedural notion) or equality of opportunity (which will take into substantive account the current situation and past history of those on whom equality is to be conferred). And, if "diversity" is your watchword, you will have to decide whether under its umbrella you wish to include pedophiles and Neo-Nazis; if you do not, you will have to think of reasons – and those reasons will inevitably be particular and historical – for excluding them. And if you refuse this task and, when asked "What do you mean by fairness or equality or diversity?" merely repeat the words as if they were a mantra, your interlocutor will rightly complain that you have given him no direction, that if the abstraction is not thickened and provided with content, there is no way to get from it to the real-world dilemma he faces, or – it is the same thing – there are so many ways that the choosing of any one them will be arbitrary.[35]

So the first step in making theory consequential is to ensure that it contains enough local content to enable it to speak to the concrete non-philosophical situations we are concerned with. But this filling of abstractions with content can never be a neutral, technical procedure. All such content will be contestable and will reflect one particular partisan point of view. In other words, the exercise will be political, in a broad sense, and will require rhetorical or persuasive skills.[36] Efficacious local theory can be open about its partisan substance,[37] but it is more common for local theory that has ceased to be detached theory to deny its partisan substance and to present itself instead as being strong theory. Fish thinks this is typical of political philosophy. I will call such theory "sham theory,"[38] and as we shall see in Part II, sham theory's uncashable claim to be neutral, or principled, or universal can sometime help make it more effective in advancing its hidden partisan substance.

But filling abstract theory with some partisan substance by means of skillful rhetorical/political work is not by itself sufficient to make theory consequential. This brings us to the next argument in Fish's deflationary project of breaking down the third orthodox claim that theory has a special role in guiding and reforming other practices. Once filled with substance, theory would only be guaranteed to affect other practices if those other practices were compelled to dance to the tune of, or at least listen to, theory. But they are not, Fish claims, because all practices are

---

[35] Fish, "Theory minimalism," 762. See too 763; *Trouble*, 2–4, 287; Stanley Fish, "A Reply to J. Judd Owen" 93 *The American Political Science Review* (1999) 925 (hereafter cited as Fish, "Reply to Owen").
[36] *Trouble*, 289. [37] See the discussion in ibid., 291–2.
[38] Robertson, "What am I doing?" 369.

separate and autonomous, and so no practice stands in need of guidance by another. In particular, no practice stands in need of guidance by the practice of philosophy.

The autonomy of practices

Fish's thesis of the autonomy of practices brings together two themes that we have already encountered: The importance of institutions (Chapter 1), and the necessity for a particular in-place background to enable any practice (Chapter 2). One reason for the autonomy of practices, Fish argues, is that different institutions have distinct jobs or tasks.

> [Y]ou can't make sense of – or evaluate – the arguments and actions of disciplinary agents unless you have identified and held fast to the institutional purpose in relation to which those arguments and actions have been produced. I call this thesis "the thesis of the distinctiveness of tasks." The location of that distinctiveness is not in the medium in which the task is prosecuted (both legal and literary analysts take words as their objects) or the resources at their disposal (everyone uses metaphors, analogies, ironies, even allegories), but in the purposive context that allows a practitioner to know that he or she is doing this and not that – critiquing an opinion and not explicating a poem – and this distinctiveness obligates a critic to assess what the practitioner has done in relation to that context and not some other.[39]

For Fish, an institution must focus on its unique job and not be seduced into trying to do some other institution's job, or into allowing some other institution to do its job. If it is so seduced, then both the institution and the special objects of its attention will be lost.[40] Fish devotes whole books to the importance of respecting the distinct institutional tasks of various university disciplines. *Professional correctness* warned those academics engaged in literary studies not to change their professional practice to include partisan politics because that would not be expanding literary studies but losing it.[41] *Save the world on your own time* gave the same warning to all university academics, a warning he summarized in his contribution to *Postmodern sophistry*:

---

[39] Fish, "Interpretation is not a theoretical issue," 512. See too *Professional*, 19; *No free speech*, 23.

[40] *Professional*, 65–6, 70, 137; *No free speech*, 23, 222–3.

[41] Gary Olson describes and analyzes Fish's argument here in Olson, *Justifying belief*, ch. 1.

[T]asks, academic and otherwise, only retain their distinctiveness if they are sharply defined so that those who take them up know pretty much (there are always borders being pushed out and contracted) what the job is and so that others will look to them whenever there is a call for that particular job to be done. No one is forced to be a literary critic or a student of epistemology, but if that is the line of work you have chosen, you should stick to it and not try to expand it to the point where it loses its shape and you lose your sense of purpose, having exchanged its saving narrowness for the heady (but impossible) purpose of doing everything. Do your job, don't try to do someone else's job (for which you won't have the qualifications anyway), and don't let anyone else do your job. And if you don't want to give a reading of *King Lear* or a critique of Kant's critiques, but want to save the world, get out of the academy and go into politics or social work.[42]

So one reason for the autonomy of practices, according to Fish, is that institutions each have their distinctive jobs to do, and the concerns of those engaged in one institutional job need have no relevance for those engaged in a completely different job.

Fish's anti-foundationalist epistemology provides a second reason for the autonomy of practices. As we saw earlier, because different groups of people will be constituted and enabled by different backgrounds, it follows that they will not automatically have anything useful to say to each other, or even be comprehensible to each other. Even people in the same community or culture, when they are engaged in different institutional tasks that depend on different background beliefs, values, purposes, categories, modes of reasoning, criteria for evaluation, etc., will find that what is most significant and central to them is often of no interest or relevance to those engaged in a different task. This is true even when it is the *same* person who engages at different times in different institutional tasks. Fish says such a person would be "one (physically defined) man who took on alternate tasks and was, as he moved from one to the other, alternate persons. As one person he would see the centrality of X and the appeal of Y; as another X and Y would never come into view, or if they did come into view, they would be beside his present point."[43] The autonomy of practices on this epistemological analysis is thus a necessary consequence of the different backgrounds that enable

---

[42] Stanley Fish, "One more time" in G. Olson and L. Worsham (eds.), *Postmodern sophistry: Stanley Fish and the critical enterprise* (Albany: State University of New York Press, 2004), 288 (hereafter cited as Olson and Worsham [eds.], *Postmodern sophistry*).

[43] *Professional*, 138. See too 69–70, 81–2.

the different practices (a background that will include a shared understanding within the relevant community of what the unique jobs of the
practice are).

Fish gives a number of examples of the autonomy of practices at work.
In all of them, the practitioners of one discipline do not grasp or see the
relevance of what the practitioners of another discipline are doing,
because each discipline is enabled by a different background and is doing
a different job. He notes that

> [c]ritics of Thomas Kuhn think it a mark against him that his work is not
> taken seriously by scientists, but as Collins makes clear, one cannot
> *be* a scientist and take Kuhn seriously, "for science would not make
> sense as an institution unless it were normally the case that acting
> scientifically meant acting as though the sociology of science were not
> true." ... Everything about the two practices – their respective facts,
> discovery procedures, mechanisms of justification, and so on – is differ-
> ent, and the attempt to unite them will result only in confusion and a loss
> of focus.[44]

That is, advancing an anti-foundationalist history of science and performing as a competent scientist are two different and autonomous
practices with no connection between them. It is because law is an
autonomous practice that Fish responds sympathetically to Ernest Weinrib's argument that law's "immanent rationality" cannot be understood
from the "extrinsic vantage point" of some other discipline, such as
science or economics.[45]

Even when one practice seems to have achieved insights into another,
Fish says that the first practice is only seeing in the second practice things
that are relevant to the first practice's tasks and values. It does not
understand the second practice in terms of its own distinctive tasks and
values.

> Those who complain, as many frequently do, that the materials of their
> discipline have been "distorted" or "trivialized" or "made into a meta-
> phor" by workers in some other discipline are both right and wrong: from
> the perspective they occupy, the relevance of the materials has been
> slighted; but those who are looking around for help see the materials
> as relevant to quite another set of purposes and therefore do not see
> *them* at all.[46]

---

[44] *No free speech*, 24. See too Stanley Fish, "One more time" in Olson and Worsham (eds.),
Postmodern sophistry, 273.
[45] *Professional*, 20ff.   [46] Ibid., 137–8.

As this passage suggests, the autonomy of practices claim leads directly to Fish's startling position that the project of interdisciplinarity is impossible.[47]

> The second casualty of my argument is the hope that we can put all the jobs of work – all the so-called disciplines – together and form one large and unified field of knowledge (call it cultural studies) to replace the fractured and fragmented knowledges now given us by separate departments and schools. This is the hope of interdisciplinary studies when it becomes a religion – when it becomes an agenda called "interdisciplinarity" – and it is dashed when one realizes that different forms of disciplinary work, rather than being co-partners in a single teleological and utopian task, are engaged in performing the particular tasks that would pass away from the earth were they to lose themselves in the name of some grand synthesis, be it the discipline of all disciplines or the truth of all lesser and partial truths.[48]

The goal of interdisciplinarity is to escape from narrow, artificial disciplinary categories and to achieve a larger viewpoint that either transcends all particular disciplines or combines a number of particular disciplines into a more comprehensive apprehension of reality. But a viewpoint that transcends all disciplines is strong theory, which is impossible, while a viewpoint that combines a number of disciplines is also impossible, according to Fish, because different disciplines have different enabling backgrounds and tasks and so cannot be merged into a larger unity. It is a mistake, he says, to think that

> the interdisciplinary map provides a metaphysically superior perspective in the light of which any or all things can be better viewed, as opposed to a *different* perspective in the light of which something can be viewed that could not have been viewed from some other angle. I do not mean by the

---

[47] Given the importance given by many to interdisciplinary work, Fish's claim that it is impossible has been strongly criticized. See, for example, Goldsmith, "Backbone" 417–21; Thomas, "Fish and the uses of baseball" 84ff.

[48] *Professional*, 73. See too 135–41; *No free speech*, 23–4, 223–4, ch. 14, 254; Fish, "Interpretation is not a theoretical issue," 513; Stanley Fish, "Theory's hope" 30 *Critical Inquiry* (2004) 375–7. The neo-pragmatist philosopher Richard Rorty takes a similar position in "Pragmatism as polytheism" in Morris Dickstein (ed.), *The revival of pragmatism. New essays on social thought, law, and culture* (Durham, NC: Duke University Press, 1998), 28. He writes that anti-foundationalism "frees us from the responsibility to unify all our beliefs into a single world view. If our beliefs are all parts of a single attempt to represent a single world, then they must all hang together fairly tightly. But if they are habits of action, then, because the purposes served by action may blamelessly vary, so may the habits we develop to serve those purposes."

word "angle" to suggest a partial opening on a full reality that would be
the sum of all angles. An angle is not an open window, but a mould; it
does not bring light to an antecedently existing reality, but form to a
reality that fades when it is replaced by another.[49]

I shall return to the topic of interdisciplinarity in more detail at the end
of this chapter.

The autonomy of theory means that it has no necessary consequences for other practices

If different practices are autonomous because they are doing different
tasks and are enabled and structured by different in-place backgrounds,
then no practice need be affected by what goes on in another practice,
according to Fish. In particular, no non-philosophical practice need be
affected by what goes on in the discipline of philosophy. It follows that
the third orthodox claim about the role of theory must be incorrect:
theory does not guide or reform other practices.

Fish introduces this deflationary account of theory's role by using some
simple examples. I have already referred to Chapter 17 of *Doing what
comes naturally* called "Dennis Martinez and the uses of theory," where
Fish argues that although theoretical accounts of baseball exist, and can
be useful material for those engaging in practices such as describing
and commentating upon baseball games, the actual performance of the
game by players is not governed by or even connected to such theories.
The players, being embedded agents (or "situated members of a community"), do not need theories to tell them how to perform their distinctive
institutional tasks. Instead their practice is enabled and structured by an
already-in-place background that is not something a player like Martinez
consults when he wants to know what to do but is something that
constitutes him as the person he is.[50] Fish then makes the same point with
an example drawn from industrial research. He refers to an account of
how a research and development team came up with an improved
paintbrush by experimenting with the idea that a brush could be thought

---

[49] *Professional*, 80. See too 137: "Objects, including texts, come into view *within* the
vocabularies of specified enterprises (law, literature, economics, history, etc.) and in
relation to the *purposes* of which that enterprise is the instantiation. The application of
the vocabularies of different enterprises to an object will not bring out facets of the
object's 'complexity' or ineffable thingness, but rather will constitute different objects."
See also *No free speech*, 211.

[50] *Doing*, 372–4.

of as a kind of pump. The process of developing this new brush was not generated by a theory of "pumpoids," but it was later presented in this way for the purposes of winning grant money. Fish argues that here, just as in the baseball situation, theory did not generate or guide the practice, although a theory about the practice can be a useful component in the performance of a completely distinct task.[51]

> First, what [these examples] together suggest is that performing an activity – engaging in a practice – is one thing and discoursing on that practice another. Second, the practice of discoursing on practice does not stand in a relationship of superiority or governance to the practice that is its object ... Even if the practitioners happen to be in possession of a theory of the activity in which they are now engaged, the shape of that activity is not the result of the application of that theory. They do not use their account of what they are doing (assuming they have one) in order to do it. They can, however, use their account of what they are doing to do something else, to perform as a play-by-play analyst or apply for a grant. What is at stake here are two uses of the word "use": on the one hand, "use" in the sense of "making use of" as a component of a practice; on the other, "use" in the sense of using in order to generate a practice. It is in the first sense that baseball analysts and grant applicants use theory, and it is in the second sense that no one (this, at least, is my thesis) uses theory. That is, no one follows or consults his formal model of the skill he is exercising in order to properly exercise it.[52]

These examples drawn from baseball and product development may seem trivial, but the claim that the practice of local theory and the practice of non-theoretical activities are distinct and autonomous has greater bite when it is applied to the aspirations of the highly abstract form of local theorizing called philosophy. Notwithstanding "philosophy's age-old claim to be the master art underlying all the other arts,"[53] Fish says it has no application to other practices at all. Philosophy is just one particular type of practice, a form of local theory with its own enabling background and distinctive tasks, which has nothing to say to those engaged in other practices with different institution-specific tasks and enabling backgrounds. We have previously seen Fish argue that philosophy's extreme abstraction means that it can have nothing to say to those wanting to perform non-philosophical practices in concrete contexts (unless philosophy has smuggled in the very local content it

[51] Ibid., 374–6.
[52] Ibid., 377. See too *No free speech*, 219; Fish, "Truth but no consequences," 414.
[53] *No free speech*, 228.

claims to have transcended). Now we see that his general thesis of the autonomy of practices leads to the same result.

> The relevance of philosophy to every aspect of human culture has been assumed for so long that it now seems less an assertion or an argument than a piece of plain common sense. But it is, in fact, an argument, and one whose content is the debatable proposition that almost everything we do is a disguised and probably confused version of philosophy. That proposition will begin to seem less plausible if we remember that philosophy is not the name of a natural kind but of an academic discipline and, moreover, of a discipline whose traditions are so special as to constitute a prima facie denial of its territorial ambitions. Philosophy is that area of inquiry in which one asks questions about the nature of knowledge, truth, fact, meaning, mind, action, and so forth, and gives answers that fall within a predictable range of positions called realism, idealism, relativism, pragmatism, materialism, mentalism, Platonism, Aristotelianism, Kantianism, etc. Of course, other areas of inquiry are similarly well developed and articulated and come complete with their own array of positions, problems, solutions, and decorums.[54]

It is because other practices "come complete with their own array of positions, problems, solutions, and decorums" that they have no need to receive guidance and improvement from the practice of philosophy – a practice that is deliberately very detached from practical concerns. "It is hard to imagine why agents genuinely committed to a practice would hand over responsibility for judging it to some other practice, especially to a practice that takes place almost exclusively in college classrooms."[55] It follows that knowing a person's position on some philosophical issue will give you absolutely no clue as to how they will act when they are not doing philosophy and are acting in some other context. For Fish, a person's actions in these other contexts will be explained by matters such as the deep background commitments that are engaged and the empirical facts that are established by sources and procedures that are accepted as authoritative in that context, not by the answers a person would give to the kinds of questions asked in philosophy seminars.

> To summarize the argument thus far: considerations on the metaphysical level and considerations on the quotidian, mundane level are independent of one another; you can't get from one to the other; the conclusions you come to when doing metaphysical, normative work (if you are one of the very few people in the world who perform it) do not influence or constrain you when you are concluding something about a mundane

[54] *Doing*, 333–4. See too 371, 435; *Trouble*, 293–4.   [55] *Doing*, 398.

matter; and the fact that you have concluded something about a mundane matter and said so in a form like "that P" commits you to no normative/theoretical presuppositions. The two levels of consideration are different practices or, if you prefer, different games; and your ability or inability to play the one says nothing about your ability or inability to play the other.[56]

At this point, an objector might seek to resist Fish's deflationary arguments regarding philosophy by turning them against Fish himself. If philosophy has no necessary consequences for any other practices, it would follow that Fish's own detailed anti-foundationalist argument can have no effects outside philosophy. But surely, the objector might continue, accepting anti-foundationalism does have effects: We must comport ourselves differently in the world once we realize that all of our truths and norms are merely socially constructed.[57] But Fish emphatically denies that his anti-foundationalism, or any of his philosophical positions, has consequences outside the precincts of philosophy:

> I am a pragmatist in the sense that if you were to ask me a series of questions (Could we find independent grounds for our practices and convictions? Are we progressing toward a clearer sight of something called Reality? Could we identify moral imperatives that would be appropriate to any and all situations? Do texts have plain and perspicuous meanings?), I would give answers (no, no, no, and no) that place me in the pragmatist camp, rather than in the realist camp, or the proceduralist camp, or the strict-constructionist camp. But that would be it; nothing else would follow, no method or style of lawyering or judging. In short, my pragmatism is a badge of identification in the philosophy game, not a recipe for action or a way of deciding between alternative paths in particular situations.[58]

Fish would reply to the objector that one does not become an anti-foundationalist by experiencing the socially constructed nature of the world, because no such experience is possible for embedded beings

---

[56] Fish, "Truth but no consequences," 396–7. See too 389–90, 408–10; *Trouble*, 295; *No free speech*, 180–2; Stanley Fish, "One more time" in Olson and Worsham (eds.), *Postmodern sophistry*, 284; Fish, "Holocaust denial," 522–3.

[57] This claim will be dealt with in more detail when I consider anti-foundationalist political theories in Chapter 4.

[58] Fish, "Theory minimalism," 773. See too 776: "If it has been my argument that theses on the level of general philosophy do not dictate answers or strategies on the level of practical behavior, it must be the case that no form of behavior follows from that argument, which is itself general. Indeed, if there is anything I have said here that moves you in some direction, if after hearing me you go away in possession of something useful, I will have failed."

"whose perspective is not general (that would be a contradiction in terms), but partial (although that partiality can never be experienced as such and those who think it can unwittingly reinstate the objective viewpoint they begin by repudiating)."[59] One becomes an anti-foundationalist by becoming convinced that there are fatal deficiencies in the arguments defending the epistemological position known as foundationalism. Anti-foundationalism would only be developed and defended by someone who was already an embedded member of the community of professional and amateur philosophers, someone who was engaging with a set of problems and projects that were part of the Western philosophical tradition. Anti-foundationalism is a move within the philosophy game and is addressed to other participants in that practice. It has nothing to say to those who are not playing that game and who would not understand the point of asserting it. Fish rejects

> the assumption that the theory you have about fact, truth, evidence, justification, and so on, is a part, and a crucial part, of the equipment you bring with you when you enter the world (and leave off theorizing) ... [W]ere that assumption true, it really would matter which of the range of theories – realist, foundationalist, antifoundationalist, conventionalist, pragmatist, relativist, nihilist – you held. But the assumption is false because of what it itself assumes: that ordinary mundane actions are performed within, or in the company of, beliefs about their underpinnings or lack thereof. But ordinary mundane actions are not underwritten or accompanied by any metaphysical beliefs and receive both their shape and warrant from the pragmatic contexts that call them into being ... Your confidence in the methods of historical research does not flow from your assent to a foundational argument about the bottom line reality of facts, but from the training you received in graduate school, training that taught you how to find archives, how to read them, and what to do with the data you derive from them.[60]

More particularly, we have already seen in Chapter 2 that Fish rejects the charge, implicit in the objector's claim, that if someone is an anti-foundationalist then one must be a relativist who is precluded from asserting absolute and universal truths in non-philosophical contexts. Fish argues over and over again that a commitment to anti-foundationalism in philosophy has no consequences for our ability to make absolute and universal claims in non-philosophical contexts:

---

[59] *No free speech*, 223–4.
[60] Fish, "Truth but no consequences," 408–9. See too 389–90, 410; *Doing*, 21, 381–2; Fish, "Reply to Owen," 929.

[T]he conventionalist theorist, no less than his realist counterpart, is wholly informed by whatever conventions now structure his consciousness and perception, and his conviction that conventions cover the field and are the source of everything he knows will not shake or even be seen to have a bearing on whatever convictions and pieces of knowledge those conventions have now delivered.[61]

I may, in some sense, *know* that my present reading of *Paradise Lost* follows from assumptions that I did not always hold and may not hold in a year or so, but that "knowledge" does not prevent me from knowing that my present reading of *Paradise Lost* is the correct one.[62]

If you believe that your convictions have their source not in ultimate truths or foundations but in contingent traditions of inquiry and are therefore revisable, that belief, in and of itself, will not render you disposed to revise your convictions or turn you into a person who enters into situations provisionally and with epistemic modesty.[63]

You may know (in the sense that you have certain answers to some traditional philosophical questions) that the urgencies you feel, the values you resonate to, the facts you affirm, are contextually produced and therefore revisable, but that knowledge neither loosens the hold of those urgencies, values, and facts nor provides instructions (or even reasons) for their revision.[64]

[A]nti-foundationalist thought deprives us of nothing; all it offers is an alternative account of how the certainties that will still grip us when we are persuaded to it come to be in place.[65]

The assertion that there is no Absolute to invoke is made at the level of philosophical argument and does not preclude declaring the absolute truth about a matter as you now see it.[66]

In summary, local theory is the only kind of theory that can exist, and local theory (including the very abstract type known as philosophy) is not a deep or master practice sitting beneath all other practices but is simply one autonomous practice among others. As an autonomous practice, local theory has its special jobs and enabling backgrounds, but other practices do as well, and this means that the work of theorists is largely (a qualification explained in the next section) irrelevant for them. No practice waits upon news from the precincts of theory before it can proceed. According to Fish, the practitioners of other disciplines are led

---

[61] *Doing*, 383. See too 245, 323–4, 325, 431–2.   [62] *Text*, 359.
[63] *Trouble*, 300. See too 280.   [64] *No free speech*, 197. See too 248–9.   [65] *Doing*, 26.
[66] Fish, "Theory minimalism," 774. See too 766–8, 771–2; Fish, "Truth but no consequences," 393, 407–8, 411, 413–4, 416.

astray and tied up in unnecessary knots when they fail to appreciate this and so think that they have to do philosophy as well as their own practice, or think that philosophical victories must affect their own practice. For example, he argues that it is a mistake for historians to fear that they are precluded from making authoritative statements about objective historical facts if anti-foundationalism is held to be a superior epistemology to foundationalism.[67] Similarly, those engaged in literary studies need not fear that the truth of anti-foundationalism will have consequences for their ability to assert the truth about what particular texts mean.[68] Historians and English literature scholars need not dance to the tune of theory (philosophical, literary, or any other) because their autonomous practices are produced by the hands-on training they received and the deep background beliefs about values, goals, evidence, and authorities that they absorbed in the course of becoming competent members of their respective interpretive communities. It is this training and background that will give them the guidance and constraints and possibilities for change that theory was thought necessary to provide.

Fish's account of the contingent consequences of theory

One type of consequentiality for theory is trivial. Since grappling with philosophical problems is a practice carried out within specialized institutions, the theories or philosophical positions that people endorse can have consequences for their status and careers within those institutions.[69] But if one is concerned with consequences for precincts beyond various university departments, it might seem from what has gone before that Fish is precluded from admitting any. Indeed, his thesis of the autonomy of practices seems to turn all practices into separate silos that are insulated against influences from outside practices that might change them.[70] We therefore need to return to what Fish means by the autonomy of practices in greater detail so that we can see how he rebuts this concern and how he can give theory a contingent role in changing other practices.[71]

---

[67] No free speech, ch. 15; Fish, "Holocaust denial"; Trouble, 302–5; Fish, "Truth but no consequences," 395, 409.

[68] Doing, 288, 324, 334–5; Fish, "Truth but no consequences," 410, 411.

[69] Doing, 336–7.   [70] See Goldsmith, "Backbone" where this criticism is advanced.

[71] For an alternative account of Fish's description of the consequences of theory, see Peter Schanck, "Understanding postmodern thought and its implications for statutory interpretation" 65 Southern California Law Review (1991) 2555–8.

First, Fish denies that his account of the autonomy of practices turns them into hermetically sealed silos:

> This ... is to mistake the nature of autonomy, which is not a matter of refraining from commerce but of stamping whatever is imported or appropriated with a proprietary imprint. While it is true that disciplines do not originate much of what appears in their operations, it is not the materials they traffic in that makes for their distinctiveness, but the underlying purpose or point in the context of which those materials acquire a disciplinary intelligibility. Autonomy ... requires the incorporation of foreign elements, which once appropriated – seen in the light of the discipline's underlying point or purpose – are no longer foreign. Autonomy is a social or political achievement (rather than something initially given), and it can only maintain itself by reconfiguring itself in the face of the challenges history puts in its way.[72]

Fish's argument is that the autonomy of a practice is not achieved by separating it from other practices and ensuring that no foreign material enters it; rather it is achieved by claiming exclusive jurisdiction over some task that society wants done. Once the autonomy of a practice is understood in this way, there is no problem with incorporating new material into the practice, as long as this is done in order to perform the job the practice has claimed as its own. Even if the incorporation of new material alters the practice over time, this does not challenge the autonomy of the practice, according to Fish, as long as the practice has been constant in its pursuit of its distinctive job. So rather than seeking to seal a practice hermetically against outside influences, Fish insists that a practice will constantly be assimilating and incorporating new material in order to find new grist for its particular mill. Thus any distinct practice

> is an engine of change because its assumptions are not a mechanism for shutting out the world but for organizing it, for seeing phenomena as already related to the interests and goals that make the community what it is. The community, in other words, is always engaged in doing work, the work of transforming the landscape into material for its own project; but that project is then itself transformed by the very work it does.[73]

For example, literary scholars typically focus their professional attention on novels, short stories, plays, and poems, but Fish notes that some have sought to expand the scope of their enterprise to encompass new material, such as "diplomatic communiqués, political statements, legal documents,

---

[72] *No free speech*, 22. See too 23–4 and 220.
[73] *Doing*, 150. See too 151–3; *No free speech*, 195, 220; *Professional*, 24.

presidential addresses, advertising, popular culture, television news, bill-boards, restaurant menus, movie marquees," etc.[74] The purpose of this expansion, however, is to find in these materials yet more examples of literary criticism's own distinctive categories and values, even if those who produced this material originally had no inkling of them.

For our present purposes, the most important way in which a practice can incorporate new material is by borrowing concepts or modes of analysis from some other practice. The autonomy of practices means that the borrowing practice sees the thing borrowed as having a role to play in its own distinctive institutional project; it does not see (or see as relevant) the roles the thing borrowed played in the discipline that was the material's original home. Consequently, the borrowing practice can and will ignore as irrelevant any protests from practitioners of the home discipline that the borrowers have failed to understand properly the thing borrowed and may even be misusing it.[75] That which is borrowed does not guide or instruct those carrying out the borrowing, rather it is given a bit part in a drama entirely scripted by the borrowing practice and so the autonomy of the borrowing practice is preserved.

> The core sense of a disciplinary purpose is not destroyed by the presence in the field of bits and pieces and sometimes whole cloths from other fields because when those bits and pieces enter, they do so in a form demanded by the definitions, distinctions, convention, problematics, and urgencies already in place.[76]

For example, law borrowed the notions of insanity from medicine and oath taking from religion although in neither case is the concept used in the same way as in its original home.

> Insanity, for example, is a concept that has a home outside the law. But when lawyers (as opposed to psychiatrists) invoke it, they turn it into something that links up with legal categories. It is defined as an inability to tell right from wrong, not a definition that would recommend itself to the medical community. The law is autonomous when it turns everything into its own stuff so that even when it incorporates concepts from elsewhere they are emptied of their empirical content and given the content the law's internal imperatives require.[77]

> The reason [for the continued use of oath taking in law even after belief in God faded] is that oath taking and swearing to tell the truth are

---

[74] *Professional*, 90.   [75] Ibid., 137–8.   [76] *No free speech*, 220. See too 238–9.
[77] Stanley Fish, "Empathy and the Law," *New York Times* Opinionator Blog, May 24, 2009.

components in a social practice (of Anglo-American law) that has its own traditions, purposes, consequences, and public functions; within that practice the meaning of oath taking and of the penalties one risks by swearing falsely is perfectly clear, and it is that (social/institutional) meaning to which oath takers are responsive independently of what they might say (if they would say anything) if asked "what do you think ultimately underwrites oaths?"[78]

Conversely, law can be borrowed by literature or television or film as a component in a practice in which goals and values other than those of law are determinative.[79] Literary criticism is prolific in its borrowing from other disciplines, Fish notes, but it does so in order to pursue the job of literary criticism and is impervious to the imperatives of the quarried discipline, which "is why psychoanalysis in its classic form, discarded by mainstream psychology today, is alive and well and productively so in English departments."[80] Similarly, literature can be borrowed by other practices to advance goals and values different from those of literary criticism. Fish describes how, during World War II, "[i]n a now forgotten interlude in the history of Milton criticism, *Paradise Lost* was appropriated for the purposes of Allied propaganda."[81]

How is this borrowing from other practices different from the interdisciplinarity that Fish has declared to be impossible because of the autonomy of practices? Interdisciplinarity seeks to step outside the narrow disciplinary tasks and enabling backgrounds of particular practices, but "interdisciplinary borrowing" is done by someone who remains deeply embedded within a particular discipline and who is seeking new ways to perform its specific disciplinary tasks.

> I distinguish between interdisciplinary work – the practice of borrowing materials from fields other than your own – and interdisciplinarity – the hope that by moving from field to field and back again you can enlarge the boundaries of your consciousness and become a more clear-sighted human being. The first, I argue, is just business as usual and involves no metaphysical claim; the second depends on such a claim, the claim

---

[78] Fish, "Holocaust denial," 523.

[79] See Fish, "Theory minimalism," 769–71, where Fish analyzes the television program *L. A. Law* in these terms. See too Fish, "Interpretation is not a theoretical issue," 511–3.

[80] *No free speech*, 222. See too *Doing*, 336.

[81] *Professional*, 66–8. He describes how the author's project was "to search Milton's poetry for passages and images that will provide comfort and inspiration to a nation beleaguered by evil forces; he is *not* going to claim that the meanings he finds are the meanings Milton intended; only that the meanings he finds are helpful to the British people in a moment of present crisis."

that one can by an act of will see through the limitations of one's professional practice and come to engage in it without being confined by its imperatives.[82]

So those who describe themselves as engaging in the project of inter-disciplinarity are incorrectly describing their actual practice. In fact, Fish claims,

> either they are engaging in straightforwardly disciplinary tasks that require for their completion information and techniques on loan from other disciplines, or they are working within a particular discipline at a moment when it is expanding into territories hitherto marked as belonging to someone else – participating, that is, in the annexation by English departments of philosophy, psychoanalysis, anthropology, social history, and now, legal theory; or they are in the process of establishing a new discipline, one that takes as its task the analysis of disciplines, the charting of their history and of their ambitions.[83]

The passage just quoted is important because it brings out the fact that interdisciplinary borrowing is not always benign. Fish says that usually "the natural conservatism of disciplines . . . will work to prevent borrowed material from overwhelming the borrower."[84] But sometimes the bor-rower *can* be overwhelmed, and consequently will find itself "annexed" or colonized or swallowed by another practice. When this happens, the tasks and values and enabling background of the foreign practice come to occupy all or some of the territory hitherto occupied by another, which to the extent of the annexation ceases to exist. A borrowed practice can sometimes act like a Trojan horse, which, once it is brought inside, proceeds to undermine the autonomy of the borrowing practice. (In Chapter 12 I will consider whether law has been colonized in this way by economics.)

I have taken pains to explicate Fish's idea of interdisciplinary borrowing because it is here that we find Fish's positive account of the consequentiality of theory: Although other practices do not await guidance and reform from theory, other practices can *borrow* from the autonomous practice of theory and use what is borrowed as a compon-ent in the performance of their own distinctive, non-theoretical tasks. Theory can therefore sometimes have consequences, but they are not the consequences claimed in the orthodox account of theory. Instead of

---

[82] *No free speech*, 23. See too *Professional*, vii–viii, 137.
[83] *No free speech*, 242. See too 238; *Professional*, 83, 106–7.   [84] *No free speech*, 220.

standing in a special and superior relationship to other practices, theory can sometimes have a contingent bit part in those other practices. Any consequences it has will be rhetorical successes that cannot be predicted or guaranteed in advance, nor assured of replication in different contexts. This is the essence of Fish's account of the consequentiality of theory, and his response to those who claim that his analysis leaves no role for theory to produce change. I will now describe his account in more detail.

When a practitioner of one discipline also produces some theory, there are two ways that this can be explained in Fish's analysis. The first possible explanation is that the person has performed two separate practices. They have performed a non-theoretical practice – for example, playing baseball or drafting a contract – and have also engaged in the separate practice of theorizing. Fish does not deny that the same person can perform both practices, only that the two practices remain distinct and autonomous, with different enabling backgrounds and tasks. In such circumstances, theory does not have any consequences. For example, the same person, Ted Williams, can both be a baseball player and also write a book (*The Science of Hitting*) that provides a theoretical account of baseball and how to perform it better, even though on Fish's analysis nobody's baseball practice is generated or improved by Williams's theory.[85] Similarly,

> if you asked a contract lawyer for a "deeper" justification of his routine deployment of certain vocabularies, you might in some cases, but not all, be told the standard story of "classical" contract doctrine, in which two autonomous agents bargain for an exchange of goods or services whose value they are free to specify in any way they like. Such an answer would be equivalent to a theory, and therefore those who were able to give it could fairly be said to have a theory of their practice. This, however, does not mean that the theory would be necessary to, or generative of, that practice. A theoretical account produced on demand might be little more than the rote rehearsal of something learned years ago in law school and have no relationship at all to skills acquired in the interim. Self-identified theoreticians would then be practicing in ways that could not be accounted for by their theory and yet their practice would not be impaired by this lack of fit. Moreover, other lawyers and jurists who were either incapable or uninterested in responding to the demand for theoretical justification might nevertheless be among the most skilled practitioners of a trade.[86]

---

[85] *No free speech*, 228–9, 303; *Doing*, 374 n3.　　[86] *No free speech*, 226.

Why would anybody ever feel the need to do this – to present a theory of a practice as well as perform the practice? I think Fish would say that this results from accepting the erroneous but familiar claim of philosophy to be the master art underlying all other arts. If you believe that theory produces and guides practice, you may feel you are not entitled to perform a practice without also offering a theory or taking account of theoretical debates. Fish noted earlier that this mistake has led historians and literary critics to think that they cannot just engage in their distinctive disciplinary practices but must engage in philosophical debates too, such as the debate between foundationalism and anti-foundationalism. I think Fish would say that these types of cases in which someone both engages in a practice and also offers a theory of the practice result from a failure to appreciate the autonomy of practices. People mistakenly think that they have to perform two practices because one cannot stand on its own and depends on the other.

The second possible explanation of what is happening when a practitioner of one discipline also produces some theory is that the person only performs one practice, the non-theoretical one, but in the course of doing that he or she quarries the practice of theoreticians in order to find material to borrow to achieve the non-theoretical task. They are not attentive to the demands of the theory project itself, rather they are attentive only to the demands of the practice that is doing the borrowing. In such circumstances, theory can have contingent consequences. For example, judging is a non-theoretical practice that routinely borrows from theory to perform its job, according to Fish. Like Dennis Martinez, he says, judges are embedded agents who need no theory to tell them what to do, even when performing as a judge involves extended reflection and weighing up of alternatives.[87] (The alternatives seen, and the criteria for evaluating them, are institution-specific and are delivered by the background acquired in becoming a competent member of the interpretive community of lawyers.) But when writing judgments it will often be rhetorically effective for judges to import theory-talk and use it as a component in the practice of justifying a decision. This is because judging, unlike hitting baseballs, is a practice where theory-talk is regarded as a positive feature of the performance.

> This means that in the course of unfolding an opinion, a judge might well think it pertinent to invoke some legal "principle" such as "a court cannot

---

[87] Doing, 391–2; No free speech, 228–30.

police the bargains of competent private individuals" or, more abstractly, "the law must be color-blind with respect to the safeguarding of rights"; but at the moment of their invocation, such "principles" would be doing rhetorical, not theoretical, work, contributing to an argument rather than presiding over it. Such principles (and there are loads of them) form part of the arsenal available to a lawyer or judge – they are on some shelf in the storehouse of available arguments (the concept is, of course, Aristotelian) – and the skill of deploying them is the skill of knowing (it is knowledge on the wing) just when to pull them off the shelf and insert them in your discourse. Once inserted, they are just like the other items in the storehouse, pieces of verbal artillery whose effectiveness will be a function of the discursive moment; they do *not* stand in a relation of logical or philosophical priority to more humble weapons, although their force will depend to some extent on the reputation they have for being prior.[88]

Fish also is very interested in theory-talk being quarried by those engaged in partisan political projects, but I will defer a detailed discussion of this topic until Chapter 6 on political practice in Part II.

In summary, theory can be consequential outside the precincts of theory itself when "interdisciplinary borrowing" is engaged in by the practitioners of some non-theoretical practice. However, these consequences are not those claimed by the orthodox account of theory. Theory does not have any special or necessary role to play in other practices; it is not guiding and reforming them from a superior position of oversight. Rather it occupies a subordinate position – it is being used as a tool by the other practices. Its relevance and consequentiality will always be contingent, sporadic, and context-dependent. Its consequentiality will be a rhetorical success, not a theoretical one.

> [T]here are all kinds of ways theory can matter, but they are contingent; they will be a function of particular social and political conditions in relation to which a theoretical vocabulary might have a resonance or cachet useful to this or that party. The usefulness of the vocabulary will be the result not of something inherent in it – that is why theory doesn't matter if by "matter" you mean generate agendas or marching orders all by itself – but of the way a particular issue has been framed by partisan agents with an eye on the moment ... So the ways theory matters are innumerable, but they are not necessary – built into theory – and no one or group of them is generalizable; knowing that a theory mattered in a particular way in this or that situation will not be predictive of how it might operate or be made to operate in the next situation.[89]

---

[88] *No free speech*, 227. See generally 198, 224–30; *Doing*, 384–92.

[89] Stanley Fish, "One more time" in Olson and Worsham (eds.), *Postmodern sophistry*, 285. See too Fish, "Truth but no consequences," 410; *Doing*, 25, 154, 331, 338, 340.

So while theory can be consequential, it enjoys no higher status than the multitude of other things that can affect our practices and so have contingent, non-guaranteed consequences.

> Now it is certainly the case that people are on occasion moved to reconsider their assumptions and beliefs and then to change them, and it is also the case that – as a consequence – there may be a corresponding change in practice. The trouble is, such reconsiderations can be brought about by almost anything, and have no unique relationship to something called "theory" . . . The impulse to reexamine the principles underlying one's practice can be provoked, moreover, by something that is not even within the field of practice: by turning forty, or by a dramatic alteration in one's economic situation, by a marriage, or by a divorce. Of course, it can also be provoked by theory – but not necessarily. That is, you could engage in the exercise of foregrounding your assumptions and even come to see that some of them were incompatible with some piece of your practice and, nevertheless, respond with a shrug, and decide to let things be.[90]

[90] *Doing*, 332–3. See too 427; Stanley Fish, "One more time" in Olson and Worsham (eds.), *Postmodern sophistry*, 285.

PART II

Politics

I have organized Fish's writings on politics into three chapters: political theory, political substance, and political practice. In each of these chapters, we will see the philosophical positions established in Part I rigorously applied. Political theory is what engages Fish's energies the most, and so Chapter 4 will be the longest, with substantive sections on liberal political theory and anti-foundationalist political theories. The question of whether some substantive political position is entailed by his philosophical position is dealt with in the short Chapter 5 on political substance (which will consider again the issue of change[1]), and Chapter 6 on political practice will consider Fish's novel description of what successful political actors are really doing.

---

[1] Change was considered in Chapters 2 and 3 and will be considered again in Chapter 11.

4

Political theory

Fish's critique of liberal political theory

Liberalism is the political theory to which Fish devotes most of his critical energy. He finds its main source in the European experience of religious warfare in the sixteenth and seventeenth centuries.[1] In this post-Reformation period, many sovereigns used force to ensure that their subjects conformed to the true religion, but the resulting carnage eventually led many to conclude that it was an error for the state ever to seek to enforce a religious orthodoxy. The general lesson taken from this experience by liberals was that disagreement between people on matters of fundamental belief was ineradicable. Society could not be organized around a shared conception of the good, because enduring and widespread agreement on what constituted the good for human beings would never be achieved. But if political order could not be based on shared deep beliefs, then a way had to be found to achieve political order while leaving deep disagreements in place. The solution to this problem provided by liberal political theory was the identification of principles and procedures that were *neutral* regarding conceptions of the good. Such neutral principles and procedures could be used to regulate contests between partisans of competing conceptions of the good and so prevent society descending into warfare. Moreover, they could do so without injustice or bias toward anybody, because neutral principles and procedures stood outside the political fray and were not the reflection of any group's local commitments or constituting beliefs. They were identified through reasoning that was itself neutral and so they were available to all people, whatever their history or culture. In other words, they were universal.

> Liberalism is a way not so much to avoid conflict (because liberalism is born out of the unhappy insight that conflict cannot be avoided) but to contain it, to manage it, and therefore to find some form of human

---

[1] *No free speech*, 296. See too 17; *Trouble*, 177.

association in which difference can be accommodated and persons can be allowed the practice and even cultivation of their points of view, but in which the machinery of the state will not prefer one point of view to another but will in fact produce structures that will ensure that contending points of view can coexist in the same space without coming to a final conflict.[2]

This distinctive solution of liberal political theory to the problem of political order in the absence of agreement regarding the good has been widely approved of for centuries, but Fish argues that liberal theory falls into error again and again, mainly because it fails to appreciate the implications of the philosophical positions set out in Part I.

Liberalism's inconsistency

Fish claims that liberalism typically turns its back on the premise from which it began. It began with the premise that human disagreement was ineradicable but then asserts the existence of neutral principles and procedures that every (rational) person will agree to. Fish describes this as liberalism's "double move. First, announce that there exists no mechanism capable of adjudicating between competing systems of belief, and then install in a position of privilege just such a mechanism; declare something to be unavailable and then, almost in the same breath, discover it."[3] Fish writes,

> Liberal thought begins with the acknowledgment that faction, difference, and point of view are irreducible; but the liberal strategy is to devise (or attempt to devise) procedural mechanisms that are neutral with respect to point of view and therefore can serve to frame partisan debates in a nonpartisan manner. I put the matter in this way so as to point up what seems to me an obvious contradiction: on the one hand, a strong acknowledgment of the unavailability of a transcendent perspective of the kind provided by traditional Christianity (against whose dogmas liberalism defines itself), and on the other, a faith (curious word to associate with liberalism) in the capacity of partial (in two senses) human intelligences to put aside their partialities and hew to a standard that transcends them.[4]

Fish acknowledges that not everyone in the liberal tradition is guilty of this contradiction. In his analysis of the work of classical liberal political theorists such as Locke and Hobbes, Fish praises Hobbes for recognizing that if disagreement is indeed ineradicable, then there can be no universal

---

[2] *No free speech*, 297. See too *Trouble*, 154, 175.   [3] *Trouble*, 186. See too 169.
[4] *No free speech*, 16.

agreement on procedures or principles either.[5] Hobbes did not flinch
from the implications of his starting point, and he concluded that if
people wanted a peaceful social order, then they had to give someone the
absolute power to resolve disagreements authoritatively, even if those
resolutions were partisan. However, Fish argues that the main thrust of
liberal political theory put its faith in the existence of neutral principles
and procedures that would regulate the actions of all, even the sovereign,
from a non-partisan position.

> For Locke, Kant, Mill, and Rawls (in their different ways), the equality of
> men and of the values they variously espouse points to the rejection of any
> form of absolutism: If no one's view can be demonstrated to be absolutely
> right, no one should occupy the position of absolute authority. For
> Hobbes the same insight into the plurality of values and the unavailability
> of a mechanism for sorting them out implies exactly the reverse: *Because*
> no one's view can be demonstrated to be absolutely right (and also
> because everyone prefers his own view and believes it to be true) someone
> *must* occupy the position of absolute authority. There can be no question
> as to which of these ways of reasoning won the liberal day, but it might be
> said that Hobbes's is the more consistent with the twin premises from
> which both begin, the premise that, first, every church is orthodox to
> itself, and, second, that there is no principled way of adjudicating disputes
> between opposing orthodoxies.[6]

Liberalism's foundationalism

Liberalism is foundationalist, Fish argues, because its search for universal
and neutral principles is a search for foundations of political order that
would be the same for any group, no matter what their constituting local
commitments; foundations that will remain stable and unchanging even
as people's deep beliefs shift. In short, "the project of liberal theory (of
finding an Archimedean point to the side of or above or below sectarian
interest)"[7] is a political manifestation of the same foundationalist desire
that led philosophical positivists to search for "brute facts" and a neutral

---

[5] *Trouble*, 178–86.

[6] Ibid., 180. See too 92. John Gray makes a similar point: "For, taken by itself, the historical
fact of pluralism supports, most naturally and reasonably, the Hobbesian project of
seeking a peaceful *modus vivendi* rather than any Kantian project of framing a liberal
constitution to which all autonomous agents can give their rational assent." John Gray,
"Mill's liberalism and liberalism's posterity" in Guido Pincione and Horacio Spector (eds.),
Rights, equality, and liberty (Boston, MA: Kluwer, 2000), 163.

[7] *Trouble*, 178.

observation language with which to describe them – and it is impossible for the reasons already described in Chapter 2. Fish declares that he sets himself "against liberal categories of thought and against liberalism in general" because "it is the thesis – and dream – of liberalism that conclusions and actions can be justified . . . from a vantage point which is not already hostage to the presuppositions of some partisan agenda."[8] We saw in Chapter 1 that human beings have to be locally embedded in order to perceive, think, and act, and so we cannot have access to principles or procedures that stand apart from all forms of local embeddedness. Such things may be available to God but not human beings, Fish argues. "A foundational practice would be one that derived from absolutely clear and uncontroversial first principles; but whenever such principles are put forward, they turn out to be knowable only within a set of historical circumstances of the kind to which they are supposedly prior."[9]

Liberalism's dichotomies

The organizing categories of liberal thought often take the form of opposed pairs, or dichotomies, such as the following:[10]

Individual vs. Community
Fact vs. Belief
Reason vs. Faith
Truth vs. Rhetoric
Objectivity vs. Subjectivity
Principle vs. Pragmatism
Freedom vs. Constraint

In liberal thought, the items on the left are the valued ones and so one should try to maximize or protect them. By contrast, one should try to avoid or limit the items on the right. Fish's response to such liberal dichotomies is to deconstruct them, with "deconstruction" understood here in this way: "One deconstructs an opposition not by reversing the hierarchy of its poles but by denying to either pole the independence that makes the opposition possible in the first place."[11] That is, Fish is not

---

[8] *Milton*, 562. See too *Trouble*, 285–6.   [9] *No free speech*, 198.
[10] See too *Doing*, 404–8 for Fish's discussion of Roberto Unger's analysis of "liberal antinomies."
[11] *Doing*, 211. I shall return to the topic of deconstruction and its different meanings when I deal with critical theory and postmodernism in the next section of this chapter.

saying that we should stop valuing facts, reason, truth, and so on and instead start valuing what we previously disparaged, such as belief, faith, and rhetoric. Nor is he saying that the items on the left are illusions and only the items on the right really exist. Instead, Fish argues that it is not possible to avoid or limit the items on the right because they are preconditions for the existence of the items on the left.[12]

Fish deconstructs these liberal dichotomies because he believes that they rest upon the conception of the self, the foundationalism, and the conception of theory that we saw him critique in Part I. So in response to the liberal vs. community dichotomy, Fish argued in Chapter 1 that an individual never stands in a relationship of simple opposition to the community because individual selves only come to exist by being embedded within a community. Similarly, as he argued in Chapter 2, if no epistemological foundation free of any human taint is available to us, and if all human perception and thought requires an already-in-place background of socially inculcated local commitments, then fact, reason, truth, and objectivity cannot stand in a relationship of simple opposition to belief, faith, rhetoric, and subjectivity. Also, as we saw in Chapter 3, principle cannot stand in a relationship of simple opposition to pragmatism if any principle being applied in a concrete situation has already been filled with some contestable partisan content and is therefore being used as an instrument to advance some substantive political goal. In all of these examples, Fish maintains, the relationship between the item on the left of the dichotomy and the one on the right is one of interdependence rather than simple opposition.

Fish's reasoning can be made clearer by looking at one liberal dichotomy – freedom vs. constraint – in greater detail. Fish's deconstructive move here is to point out that if all humans are necessarily embedded, then all humans are necessarily constrained, too. But this constraint is not something bad that we should seek to avoid or limit, which is how constraint is understood on the liberal dichotomy. Rather, the constraint that comes with embeddedness is what enables us to be free. It is only if we are so embedded/constrained that alternative choices for action become visible to us, and we are provided with reasons for preferring one

---

[12] This sub-section revisits and reworks some of the material in Michael Robertson, "Deconstructed to death? Fish on freedom" in G. Olson and L. Worsham (eds.), *Postmodern sophistry. Stanley Fish and the critical enterprise* (Albany: State University of New York Press, 2004), 99–126 (hereafter cited as Olson and Worsham [eds.], *Postmodern sophistry*).

rather than another. If we were not so embedded/constrained, we would not be made freer, rather we would be deprived of the preconditions and resources for any free action at all, Fish argues. Freedom therefore presupposes constraint.

> I do not mean that we are never free to act, but that our freedom is a function of – in the sense of being dependent on – some other structure of constraint without which action of any kind would be impossible. This may seem counterintuitive to those who are accustomed to identify freedom with the *absence* of constraints, but, in fact, such a state, if it could be achieved, would produce not free actions, but *no* actions. An action is only conceivable against a background of alternative paths, a background that is already a constraint in that by marking out some actions as possible it renders unavailable others that might emerge as possibilities against a different background. To imagine a world with no background in place, with no prearticulation of the directions one might take, is to imagine a world where there would be literally nowhere to go, where, since every path is the same path, the notion of doing this rather than that – of acting freely – would be empty.[13]

When Fish performs this deconstruction of the liberal freedom vs. constraint dichotomy, he is engaged in the practice of philosophy. At this very abstract level of analysis, all human beings are fully embedded and so all are completely constrained. It is therefore impossible to have actions that are free from all constraints, or thought that is free of all established orthodoxies, which is what liberals desire.

> This is what I mean by . . . the denial of the distinction between making up one's own mind and being coerced. Of course, each of us endorses and acts on just that distinction, but its shape will always be a function of the constraints one has already internalized as the result of being a practice-situated agent. There is no general sense to the concept of making up one's own mind. You make up your own mind with respect to some issue and within some already-in-place notion of what coercion and freedom – also not general but context-specific alternatives – mean in the confines of this practice, with this history, ruled by this purpose. You make up your own mind within the space accorded you by a practice that already commands and fills your mind in most respects; the mind you make up is already coerced, in the sense (not to be lamented but embraced) that it is structured by imperatives and goals it did not originate.[14]

---

[13] *Doing*, 459.
[14] Stanley Fish, "Interpretation is not a theoretical issue" 11 *Yale Journal of Law & the Humanities* (1999) 513–4 (hereafter cited as Fish, "Interpretation is not a theoretical issue").

Similarly, as a philosophical matter, no form of embeddedness is less constraining than any other, and no institutional structure is more freedom-enhancing than any other. As a simple example to help make this counterintuitive point clearer, Fish considers whether a classroom in which student questioning of the teacher is encouraged is less constraining than one in which student participation is forbidden:

> The difference between a classroom in which participation is routine and a classroom in which a student question would constitute an intervention is not a difference between structures less and more constraining, but a difference between types of structures of constraint. If in one structure there is a pressure to refrain from speaking, in the other there is a pressure to refrain from keeping silent.[15]

His broader point is that

> there can be no continuum which differentiates institutions or structures as being more or less constrained, more or less free, because freedom, in whatever shape it appears, is another name for constraint. Rather than a continuum, what we have is an array, an array of structures of constraint, no one of which is more constraining than another, and each of which is differently productive of actions that are, in the only sense the word can have, free. *Depending on which of those structures one inhabits or by which one is inhabited, things will be very different, including one's sense of what is free and what is constrained.*[16]

However, as we have already noted in Chapter 3, Fish holds that philosophy does not travel; what is true at the level of philosophical analysis is of no consequence for other, non-philosophical practices. Thus the philosophical finding that we are all completely embedded and so all equally constrained does not prevent us from being able to distinguish between freedom and constraint in everyday contexts. *Indeed, it is our particular forms of local embeddedness that give the freedom vs. constraint distinction the shape it has in everyday contexts.* Because different forms of local embeddedness with their different background beliefs give the freedom vs. constraint distinction different shapes, the same thing that seems obviously freedom-enhancing to one group can seem freedom-destroying to another group. Consider the sexual revolution of the 1960s. Some saw this as freeing women from traditional rules about appropriate sexual conduct, but others saw this as constraining the ability of women to say

---

[15] *Doing,* 426.

[16] Ibid., 459. Emphasis added. See *Doing,* 422–7 and 458–9 for Fish's critique of Roberto Unger's goal of a social structure that is less constraining and more open to revision.

no to immoral or unwanted sexual advances (because sexual inhibitions and repressions were deemed unhealthy by the new norms).[17] The new norms also operated to constrain patriarchs in their defense of family honor, womanly virtue, and the sanctity of marriage. Consider the end of slavery in the United States after the Civil War. The victorious North saw this as increasing the freedom of the ex-slaves, but the defeated South saw it as violating the rights and freedoms of private property owners and condemning the ex-slaves to new forms of wage-slavery. Liberalism proudly defines itself as a political tradition devoted to increasing individual freedom, but those not committed to liberal background beliefs and values see the advance of liberalism as the advance of new forms of constraint. The successful liberal assault on autocratic monarchy is seen by socialists as the replacement of the tyranny of kings by the even greater tyranny of capital.[18] Authors on the political left like Marx and Foucault search out the hidden or unacknowledged new forms of constraint that liberalism brought with it. Marx looked at the constraints operating behind the supposedly "free labor contract" while Foucault looked at the novel forms of supervision and discipline imposed by institutions such as schools, hospitals, factories, and prisons. Richard Rorty wrote that "[a] large part of Foucault's work – the most valuable part, in my view – consists in showing how the patterns of acculturation characteristic of liberal societies have imposed on their members kinds of constraints of which older, premodern societies had not dreamed."[19] Conservatives, too, argue that the older forms of hierarchy are only replaced by new oppressive forms of power in liberalism (the financier, the bureaucrat, the party politician).[20] Christopher Dawson wrote that in modern liberal societies, "the average man and woman are no more their own masters than in a dictatorship. Their minds are moulded and their opinions are formed insensibly by the mass suggestion and mass propaganda of the press, the radio and the cinema."[21] In short, at the level of everyday life we will always be able to apply the freedom vs. constraint distinction, although the shape this distinction takes will always be a political prize that is won by determining the background beliefs of the community.

---

[17] *Doing*, 420.

[18] Kier Hardie, *From serfdom to socialism* (London: George Allen, 1907), 8–9, 75–6.

[19] Richard Rorty, *Contingency, irony, and solidarity* (Cambridge University Press, 1989), 63 (hereafter cited as Rorty, *Contingency, irony, and solidarity*). See generally 61ff.

[20] Noel O'Sullivan, *Conservatism* (London: J. M. Dent & Sons, 1976), 33–4.

[21] Christopher Dawson, *Beyond Politics* (1939) quoted in O'Sullivan, *Conservatism*, 136.

Liberalism's neutrality

Fish's anti-foundationalist position is that the abstract notion of "neutrality" can only be given content from *within* some locally embedded position; it cannot be identified by stepping *outside* all forms of local embeddedness. "[N]eutrality, like any other abstraction, has meaning only within some particular set of background conditions; as a rule or measure it will always reflect decisions and distinctions it cannot recognize because it unfolds and has its application within them."[22] But since the ways of being locally embedded differ, there is no assurance that humans will agree on what is neutral. This is why the liberal theory project of using reason to discover neutral principles and procedures for ordering political life that all can accept is constantly being frustrated by people who refuse to accept that what liberalism delivers is indeed neutral:

> In reaction to the apparent failure of mankind to identify the one truly meaningful thing around which life might be organized, liberalism sets out to identify the set of truly *non*meaningful things – things that no one will want to die for or kill for – around which life might be organized. The history of liberalism ... is the unhappy discovery that for everything identified as truly nonmeaningful there will be someone for whom it means everything and who will therefore want to dispute or alter or eliminate the convention.[23]

It is because liberalism can never deliver on its strong neutrality claims that Fish declares: "Liberalism doesn't exist."[24] Fish argues that liberal principles and procedures and reasoning will always presuppose some contestable partisan position, i.e., "some particular set of background conditions." Liberal principles and procedures and reasoning will not stand above the fray, rather they will be participants in the fray. Before I expand upon Fish's arguments for these claims, it is important to stress that Fish is not criticizing liberalism for containing contentious substance, for it is his position that things could not be otherwise. His criticism is only of the inaccurate *description* of liberal political practice provided by liberal political theory: "I don't criticize liberals for employing power in an effort to further the truths they believe in – that's what everyone does, necessarily – but for pretending to be doing something else and for thinking there is something else to do."[25]

---

[22] *Trouble*, 172. See too the similar analysis of "impartiality" at *Doing*, 439.
[23] *Trouble*, 270–1. See too 207.   [24] *No free speech*, ch. 10.   [25] *Trouble*, 201.

Liberal neutral principles

The nature of the liberal political theory project requires that the principles it delivers, such as fairness, toleration, mutual respect, freedom from discrimination, freedom of speech, freedom of religion, etc., will be very abstract. Liberal principles have to be abstract because liberalism wants to transcend the particular in order to find something that will apply in all contexts. Liberalism, Fish tells us,

> urges us to enter a perspective wider than that formed by our local affiliations and partisan goals; [it] gestures toward a morality more capacious than the morality of our tribe, or association, or profession, or religion; [it] invites us to inhabit what the legal philosopher Ronald Dworkin calls "the forum of principle," the forum in which our allegiances are not to persons or to wished-for outcomes but to abstract norms that neither respect nor disrespect particular persons and are indifferent to outcomes.[26]

But as we saw in Chapter 3, Fish argues that very abstract principles can get no grip on the concrete situations from which they have so resolutely distanced themselves. "[E]ven if you could come up with a principle that was genuinely neutral . . . it would be unhelpful because it would be empty . . . ; invoking it would point you in no particular direction, would not tell you where to go or what to do."[27] The only way abstract principles can point us in some specific direction, Fish tells us, is if they stop being abstract and become filled with the very partisan substance they purport to have risen above. That is, if they are able to do work in the world, it is only because they are the unadmitted expression of contestable moral and political substantive commitments.

> The problem is that any attempt to define one of these abstractions – to give it content – will always and necessarily proceed from the vantage point of some currently unexamined assumptions about the way life is or should be, and it is those assumptions, contestable in fact but at the moment not being contested or even acknowledged, that will really be generating the conclusions that are supposedly being generated by the logic of principle.[28]

---

[26] Ibid., 2. See too Stanley Fish, "Theory minimalism" 37 *San Diego Law Review* (2000) 761, 764–5 (hereafter cited as Fish, "Theory minimalism").

[27] *Trouble*, 4.

[28] Ibid., 3. See too 4, 12; Gary Olson, *Justifying belief. Stanley Fish and the work of rhetoric* (Albany: State University of New York Press, 2002), 49–51 (hereafter cited as Olson, *Justifying belief*).

Using the terminology I introduced in Chapter 3, liberal theorists are never engaging in strong theory, whatever they claim. They are either producing detached theory that is so abstract that it cannot do any work outside the special context of philosophy seminars or they are producing sham theory: "[W]hat liberalism does in the *guise* of devising structures that are neutral between contending agendas is to produce a structure that is far from neutral but then, by virtue of a political success, has claimed the right to think of itself as neutral."[29]

The bulk of Fish's efforts to expose the hidden partisan substance beneath so-called neutral liberal principles can be found in his discussions of freedom of speech (in Part II of *The trouble with principle* and Chapters 8 and 9 of *There's no such thing as free speech*) and freedom of religion (in Part III of *The trouble with principle*). I will deal with freedom of religion later in this chapter and with freedom of speech in Part III, so for now I will describe some other examples Fish provides.

> It is my contention ... that liberalism doesn't have the content it believes it has. That is, it does not have at its center an adjudicative mechanism that stands apart from any particular moral and political agenda. Rather it is a very particular moral agenda (*privileging the individual over the community, the cognitive over the affective, the abstract over the particular*) that has managed, by the very partisan means it claims to transcend, to grab the moral high ground, and to grab it from a discourse – the discourse of religion – that had held it for centuries.[30]

The liberal "moral agenda" or conception of the good identified by Fish in passages like this one[31] provides the "vantage point of some currently unexamined assumptions about the way life is or should be" from which abstract liberal principles are filled in, or interpreted. So, for example, providing content for the abstract liberal principle of "fairness" requires making choices like these:

> If, for example, I say "Let's be fair," you won't know what I mean unless I've specified the background conditions in relation to which fairness has

---

[29] *No free speech*, 297. See too *Trouble*, 4, 286; Michael Robertson, "What am I doing? Stanley Fish on the possibility of legal theory" 8 *Legal Theory* (2002) 379–83.

[30] *No free speech*, 137–8. Emphasis added.

[31] See *Trouble* 110 where Fish endorses Ronald Beiner's identification (in *What's the Matter With Liberalism?*) of the substantive political agenda beneath liberalism's neutrality claims: "The maximization of social productivity, the organization of social life so as to enhance efficiency and technological control, the privileging of scientific over other forms of knowledge, the favoring of ways of life consistent with maximal individual mobility." See too 272.

an operational sense. Would it be fair to distribute goods equally irre-
spective of the accomplishments of those who receive them, or would it be
fair to reward each according to his efforts? Is it fair to admit persons to
college solely on the basis of test scores and grades, or is it fair to take into
account the applicant's history, including whatever history he or she may
have of poverty and disadvantage? Such questions sit at the center of long-
standing political, economic, and social debates, and these debates will not
be furthered by the simple invocation of fairness, because at some level
the debate is about what fairness (or neutrality or impartiality) really is.[32]

Those classical liberals who value "the individual over the community"
and "the abstract over the particular" will more naturally understand
fairness to require that goods be distributed according to individual effort
and without reference to particular histories of disadvantage suffered by
some communities. Similarly, they will tend to understand the principle of
non-discrimination as prohibiting individual acts of intentional discrimination but not as requiring affirmative action to overcome institutional
structures that have historically operated to discriminate in a more
indirect and impersonal way. As we shall see when we get to Chapter 5
dealing with political substance, Fish thinks that these ways of filling in
or interpreting the "fairness" and "non-discrimination" principles are
typical of liberals because of their background substantive values.

Based on Fish's analysis, liberal principles are not independent and
neutral constraints on politics, because it is politics that fills them with
the content they need in order to do any work. They "do not mark out an
area quarantined from the pull of contending partisan agendas; they are
among the prizes that are claimed when one political agenda is so firmly
established that its vision of the way things should be is normative and
can go without saying."[33] But precisely because liberal principles are very
abstract, and have to be interpreted (i.e., filled with some partisan
content) in order to do any work, they are a resource available to
liberalism's political opponents, too. A liberal principle is "an unoccupied
vessel waiting to be filled by whoever gets to it first or with the most
persuasive force."[34] There is thus no necessary or even reliable linkage
between liberal principles and the substantive political results that
modern liberals favor on contested issues such as civil rights, women's
rights, or gay rights. Non-liberals can quarry liberal political theory and

---

[32] *Ibid.*, 3. See too *No free speech*, 4; Fish, "Theory Minimalism," 762–3; Stanley Fish,
"A reply to J. Judd Owen" 93 *The American Political Science Review* (1999) 925.
[33] *No free speech*, 4.   [34] *Trouble*, 7.

give the principles found there a content that works rhetorically to advance non-liberal outcomes. (I will return to this point in more detail in Chapter 6.)

> Lately, many on the liberal and progressive left have been disconcerted to find that words, phrases, and concepts thought to be their property and generative of their politics have been appropriated by the forces of neo-conservatism. This is particularly true of the concept of free speech, for in recent years First Amendment rhetoric has been used to justify policies and actions the left finds problematical if not abhorrent: pornography, sexist language, campus hate speech. How has this happened? The answer I shall give . . . is that abstract concepts like free speech do not have any "natural" content but are filled with whatever content and direction one can manage to put into them . . . Free speech, in short, is not an independent value but a political prize, and if that prize has been captured by a politics opposed to yours, it can no longer be invoked in ways that further your purposes, for it is now an obstacle to those purposes.[35]

In summary, neutral liberal principles are never neutral in the impossibly strong sense liberals desire, according to Fish. They always presuppose and are given shape by an assumed partisan background. If they are doing work in the world outside philosophy seminars, they have been filled with partisan content by means of successful rhetorical acts. But partisans of any position can seek to perform these rhetorical acts, and therefore the partisan content that will be found within any so-called neutral liberal principle need not be liberal. Moreover, because the story that liberal principles are independent and neutral constraints on political practice has been sold so well, once an abstract liberal principle has been filled with some partisan content, that story will operate to conceal and facilitate the advancement of that content.

> It is because they don't have the constraining power claimed for them (they neither rule out nor mandate anything) and yet have the *name* of constraints (people think that when you invoke fairness you call for something determinate and determinable) that neutral principles can make an argument look as though it has a support higher or deeper than the support provided by its own substantive thrust.[36]

Liberal neutral procedures

Fish's argument against the possibility of neutral procedures is that any procedure will have a structuring effect; it will make some range of

---

[35] *No free speech*, 102.   [36] *Trouble*, 4.

outcomes more likely than others. "[T]he requirement of procedures that are neutral between competing moral agendas cannot be met because, in order even to take form, procedures must promote some rationales for action and turn a blind eye to others."[37] Consequently, choosing to create or maintain any procedure is an implicit approval of the outcomes or patterns it tends to produce. It reflects a conception of the way the world should be and so is inescapably a substantive political choice.

The free market (either in goods and services or in ideas) is often claimed by liberals to be the paradigm of a neutral procedure that does not have a structuring effect or reflect a commitment to some favored outcome. It merely facilitates the free choices and mutually beneficial interactions of people with different conceptions of the good, without bias toward any. Fish's response is that the idea of a free market, like other liberal abstractions, is empty until filled with some content and made operational in some way. However, there are many ways in which this abstract idea can be given flesh, and each way will favor some outcomes and groups and disfavor others. Consequently, the choice of one way to realize the market over another is always a politically charged choice, not a merely technical one.

> The marketplace of ideas is supposed to regulate in a purely formal way the contest between conflicting agendas; "purely formal" means "without regard to content," because the marketplace (sometimes called the forum of public discourse) leans in no particular ideological direction. It works, we are told, only to assure that each party will get its turn at bat. In fact, however, the marketplace has to be *set up* – its form does not exist in nature – and since the way in which it is to be set up will often be a matter of dispute, decisions about the very shape of the marketplace will involve just the ideological considerations it is meant to hold at bay.[38]

Any marketplace of ideas will be structured by ground-rule decisions on matters such as these: Should we exclude from participation those who deliberately lie? That is, should we exclude anyone who ranks his economic or political or professional goals higher than the truth and who would knowingly utter falsehoods to advance them? Even if someone is convinced that they are speaking the truth, should we exclude from participation those who will not accept any evidence or argument, no matter how cogent and compelling, as counting against their truth-claims? That is, should we exclude zealots whose convictions are

---

[37] *No free speech*, 159. See too 114, 297.
[38] *Ibid.*, 16–7. See too 118–9; *Trouble*, 104.

unyielding and dogmatic? Should a properly structured marketplace of ideas provide positive assistance to those with few resources to ensure that their ideas are heard and also prevent those with many resources from drowning out competing viewpoints? Any way in which ground-rule choices like these are made will advantage or disadvantage different groups, and so the ultimate shape of the market will not be neutral in the strong sense required.

What holds true of the marketplace of ideas holds true of the economic marketplace as well (although Fish does not consider this issue in any depth). The different possible property and contract ground rules that could be used to set up an economic market are value-laden and distribute power among groups differently. For example: What (or who) can be owned? Who (or what) can be an owner? What forms of coercion vitiate a free exchange? This argument was made in the early twentieth century by legal realists like Robert Lee Hale and by more contemporary critical legal studies writers such as Duncan Kennedy.[39] Fish nods briefly in this direction when he notes the contestable commitments made by law and economics, notwithstanding its claims to be neutral and scientific: "As many commentators have observed, 'wealth-maximization,' efficiency, Pareto superiority, the Kaldor Hicks test, and other components of the law and economics position are all hostages to metaphysical assumptions, to controversial visions of the way the world is or should be."[40]

Another of Fish's examples of the impossibility of devising neutral procedures can be found in the attempts by colleges and universities to craft admissions procedures that do not discriminate between applicants. Fish claims that any procedure chosen will inevitably advantage some groups and disadvantage others, so the choice is not between a biased procedure and a neutral one but between the different kinds of structured outcomes that will inevitably be produced. And that choice can only be made on the basis of some contentious conception of the good.

> The assumption ... is that discrimination – the favoring of some groups over others – is a deviant practice and that the appropriate response is simply to eliminate it. I challenge that assumption by observing that whenever a policy of "fairness" or "merit" is put into place, those values will have been defined in ways that could be challenged by parties whose concerns were not uppermost in the minds of the policy's drafters ...

---

[39] For a full account of this argument, see Michael Robertson, "Reconceiving private property" 24 *Journal of Law and Society* (1997) 465.

[40] *No free speech*, 212.

> Discrimination is not a deviant practice; it is the practice everyone is always and already engaged in. And when its particular effects are overturned by a plan devised specifically to remove them, that same plan will inevitably produce *new* discriminatory effects felt by persons whose interests are, for the moment, being slighted ... This does not mean that all discriminatory practices are equal; all it means is that one cannot condemn a practice just for being discriminatory (since there are none that are not). Rather, one must consider the effects of a practice and attempt to calculate as best as one can the costs of either allowing it to flourish or moving to curtail it.[41]

In summary, the liberal talk of neutral procedures is just as much sham theory as the liberal talk of neutral principles: "[T]here is no merely procedural realm; and rather than offering a rational alternative to substantive, agenda-driven judgments, procedural rights and rules are merely one form (and that a self-deluding form) that substantive agenda-driven judgments take".[42]

Liberal neutral reason

Fish identifies reason as a key component of liberal political theory. When differences of belief lead to conflict, liberals believe that reason can allow us to rise above partisanship and resolve our differences peacefully. They do not mean just using reason to cobble together an *ad hoc* solution to a dispute, a *modus vivendi* that will have to be reworked or even abandoned when things change. Reason in liberal political theory is given the more ambitious task of transcending local commitments and discovering universal principles for regulating social life that are neutral regarding conceptions of the good. (This is the project of John Rawls in *A theory of justice*). Reason must therefore be a neutral tool that anyone, however embedded, can use, and that can bring us all to the same conclusions.

> Liberals ... believe in the efficacy of procedures – scientific, parliamentary, judicial – designed to protect us from the overhasty judgments we make when we allow our commitments and allegiances to blind us. Liberals believe that the most important of these procedures is the machinery of rationality, of those laws of logic attached to no agenda or vision, but sufficiently general in their scope as to provide a normative perspective from the vantage point of which any agenda or vision can be assessed, and, if necessary, corrected. Liberals believe that communication

---

[41] Ibid., 12. See more generally ch. 5: "You can only fight discrimination with discrimination."

[42] *Trouble*, 146. See too 208; *No free speech*, 18.

and persuasion take place (or should take place) in the context of that rationality and that it is possible to bring anyone – except, perhaps, the mentally impaired – to a clear understanding, so long as he or she is willing to set aside or bracket all biases and preconceptions.[43]

We have already seen in Part I why Fish rejects this account of reason as not simply inaccurate, but impossible. It rests upon the Kantian conception of the self, and it fails to appreciate that reason cannot rise above and sit in judgment of all local partisan beliefs, because reason itself is enabled and structured by a background of local partisan beliefs: "Belief is prior to rationality; rationality can only unfold in the context of convictions and commitments it neither chooses nor approves."[44] "True belief does not emerge from reason's chain; rather true belief – and false belief too – configure reason's chain and determine in advance what will be seen as reasonable and what will be recognized as evidence."[45] That is, you will only see something as relevant evidence, or a line of argument as compelling, if particular background beliefs are already in place. We have seen Fish make this point by comparing strong religious believers and secular liberals at the end of Chapter 2, and here he makes the same point in another context:

> If, (to take a humble literary example) I am given as a reason for preferring one interpretation of a poem to another the fact that it accords with the poet's theological views, I will only hear it as a reason (as a piece of weighty evidence) if it is *already* my conviction that a poet's aesthetic performance could be influenced by his theology; if, on the other hand, I see poetry and theology as independent and even antagonistic forms of life (as did many of those new critics for whom the autonomy of the aesthetic was an article of faith) this fact will not be a reason at all, but something obviously beside the (literary) point.[46]

Because reason is a function of background beliefs, and background beliefs differ, reason will always be a historical product; it cannot be common to all persons whatever their histories and resulting background beliefs.[47] It follows that it can never be neutral in the strong sense required by liberal political theory, and that it depends upon the very biased, partisan substance it defines itself against:

---

[43] *Milton*, 56–7. See too *Doing*, 438; *No free speech*, 17, 134. [44] *Trouble*, 284.

[45] Stanley Fish, "Holocaust denial and academic freedom" 32 *Valparaiso University Law Review* (2001) 501. See too *No free speech*, 203; *Doing*, 518–9.

[46] *No free speech*, 135. See too *Trouble*, 255. [47] *Trouble*, 287; *No free speech*, 17–8.

> [L]iberalism depends on not inquiring into the status of reason, depends,
> that is, on the assumption that reason's status is obvious: it is that which
> enables us to assess the claims of competing perspectives and beliefs . . .
> But what if reason or rationality itself rests on belief? . . . This is in fact my
> view of the matter, and I would defend it by asking a question that the
> ideology of reason must repress: where do reasons come from? The liberal
> answer must be that reasons come from nowhere, that they reflect the
> structure of the universe or at least of the human brain; but in fact reasons
> always come from somewhere, and the somewhere they come from is
> precisely the realm to which they are (rhetorically) opposed, the realm of
> particular (angled, partisan, biased) assumptions and agendas.[48]

But if reason is historicized, how are we to deal with situations where
people employ competing conceptions of what is reasonable – of what
constitutes evidence and who is a reliable authority, etc.? Fish's answer to
this question again displays his commitment to the autonomy of practices. From the abstract perspective of the philosophy seminar room, the
analysis of those gripped by incompatible understandings of reason is
that "the opposition is never between the rational and the irrational but
between opposing rationalities, each of which is equally, but differently,
intolerant."[49] But from the perspective of those engaged in a dispute
about a particular concrete issue, where deep constituting beliefs are
actively engaged, judgments of rationality and irrationality are inescapable: "[W]hat is a reason for you may not be a reason for me and may
even seem irrational, that is, incompatible with the principles that ground
my perception and judgment."[50] Consequently, in everyday life we will
often be presented with "a conflict of conviction that cannot be rationally
settled because it is also and necessarily a conflict of rationalities, and
when there is a conflict of rationalities, your only recourse is, well, to
conflict, since there is no common ground in relation to which dialogue
might proceed."[51]

However, as we shall see in more detail in Chapter 6 on political
practice, abandoning the liberal dream of using a common neutral reason
to resolve disputes peacefully does not mean that we automatically fall into
the liberal nightmare of a Hobbesian war of all against all. Conflict
between groups can take many forms, and in liberal societies that value
peace, the non-violent forms of conflict are preferred. One peaceful way to
win a conflict, given that reason's shape is a function of already-in-place

---

[48] *No free speech*, 135. For extended discussions of reason in the liberal tradition, see *No free
      speech*, ch. 10 and Fish's critique of Stephen Toulmin in *Doing*, 221–5 and 436–9.
[49] *Trouble*, 70.   [50] *No free speech*, 7.   [51] *Trouble*, 255.

background beliefs, is to get your group's beliefs established in that background role. Reason's shape is a political prize, and one of the benefits of winning the prize is that your group's conception of reason becomes established as natural and commonsensical, perhaps for a very long time. If you can convince your opponents to accept the dominance of your conception of reason, you will have ensured for yourself a structural advantage in any future disagreements.

> What this means is that whenever Reason is successfully invoked, whenever its invocation stops the argument and wins the day, the result will be a victory not for Reason but for the party that has managed (either by persuasion or intimidation or legerdemain) to get the reasons that flow from its agenda identified with reason as a general category, and thereby to identify the reasons of its opponents as obviously *un*reasonable. Like "fairness," "merit," and "free speech," Reason is a political entity, and never more so than when its claim is to have transcended politics.[52]

If your opponents refuse to accept the dominance of your conception of reason, and so refuse to play the game by your rules, then the next move is to categorize them as irrational and hence not deserving of serious consideration. Here then is another way to win a conflict of beliefs without violence – you structure important social spaces so that only the rational can enter, and as a result your more intransigent opponents are excluded and marginalized.

> "Tolerance" may be what liberalism claims for itself in contradistinction to other, supposedly more authoritarian views; but liberalism is tolerant only *within* the space demarcated by the operations of reason; any one who steps outside that space will not be tolerated, will not be regarded as a fully enfranchised participant in the marketplace (of ideas) over which reason presides.[53]

Fish holds that liberalism often uses the contingent and rhetorically achieved dominance of its conception of reason to exclude those with non-liberal deep beliefs by labeling them as irrational. Therefore, as a philosophical matter, liberal theory's claims for neutral reason and the open marketplace of ideas cannot be sustained, but that does not mean that Fish disagrees, as a matter of politics, with the exclusions that liberalism achieves in this way. As always with Fish, the autonomy of practices is paramount, and philosophy and politics are distinct and different practices.

---

[52] *No free speech*, 18. See too *Doing*, 224.   [53] *No free speech*, 137. See too *Trouble*, 190.

A liberal neutral principle examined: freedom of religion

Freedom of speech (which will be discussed in Part III) and freedom of religion are the main examples used by Fish to advance his philosophical critique of liberalism's neutrality. With respect to freedom of religion, his argument is that the deep commitments of strong religious believers are incompatible with the deep commitments of liberals, and so liberal societies find ways to hobble strong religious believers and ensure that they cannot undermine or harm liberal societies. This hobbling is not achieved in an open manner that would make the liberals' opposition to strong religious believers obvious, for that would undermine the liberal claim to respect religious freedom. Instead the liberal solution is to uphold the principle of freedom of religion but to fill this abstract principle with a partisan content that operates in a non-obvious way to marginalize and exclude strong religious believers. In short, this liberal principle is not neutral, as claimed, but is rather biased against those who do not share the deep commitments of liberals. "Strong religious believers," for Fish, describes those religious believers whose commitment to their religious beliefs and values is fundamental and trumps any other commitments, including liberal ones. It would not describe those who have accepted liberal beliefs and values and who have adjusted their religious beliefs accordingly. Although any fundamentalist religious believers would have suited his purposes, Fish focuses on conservative Christians, probably because of his long experience as a Milton scholar.

The first step in Fish's argument is to stress the incompatibility between liberal and conservative Christian background beliefs and to point out how this leads to intractable conflict. The difference in background beliefs is usefully summarized by Fish in a passage where he describes the key values of liberals as "autonomy, individual freedom, rational deliberation, civility" and the competing key values of conservative Christians as "obedience, respect for authority and tradition, faith, the community of worship."[54] These opposed values generate three distinctive conflicts: (i) rational deliberation vs. authority and tradition, (ii) freedom of association vs. community of worship, and (iii) civility and tolerance vs. obedience to God's commands.

---

[54] *Trouble*, 272.

Rational deliberation vs. authority and tradition

For liberals, truth is achieved through a process of rational deliberation in which all competing viewpoints are considered and critiqued in a civil fashion. For conservative Christians, God's truth has already been revealed and so we do not need to wait for it to be generated by a merely human process. As Fish quotes John Webster (writing in 1654): "But if man gave his assent unto, or believed the things of Christ ... because they appeared probable ... to his reason, then would his faith be ... upon the rotten basis of human authority."[55] Instead of considering and critiquing God's word, the proper conservative Christian response is to respect God's truths as established by religious authority and embodied in religious tradition. No human challenges or objections can have any force against truths originating from such a high and unimpeachable source.[56]

Conservative Christians therefore reject the crucial assumptions that underpin liberals' commitment to truth as the product of unconstrained rational deliberation and debate in the free marketplace of ideas. These liberal epistemological assumptions are "fallibilism (all points of view are partial and corrigible) and pluralism (the more points of view in play the better)."[57] For the conservative Christian, God's truth is neither partial nor corrigible, and the proliferation of erroneous points of view is of no benefit. This is the basis for the complaints by conservative Christians against their children being taught about other religions in school. For these people, Fish explains, the liberal distinction between exposure and indoctrination has no weight. *The exposure of their children to other false beliefs amounts to indoctrination of the background liberal assumptions of fallibilism and pluralism.*[58]

Freedom of association vs. community of worship

Another conflict stemming from the different deep background beliefs of liberals and conservative Christians is the relationship between the

---

[55] Ibid., 258. [56] Ibid., 196–7.

[57] Ibid., 240. On fallibilism, see too *Trouble*, 189: "[W]hile fallibilism is a component both of Enlightenment thought and of western religion (which usually calls it 'original sin'), it is not the same doctrine in the two traditions. In one it mandates putting everything under the microscope; in the other the microscope – regarded as a prosthetic extension of carnal vision rather than a correction of it – is the object of its distrust and is rejected as a way of knowing in favor of scripture or revelation. One fallibilism says 'Test everything'; the other says 'Believe one thing.'"

[58] *Trouble*, ch. 8 and 197–8.

individual and the community. For liberals, individual freedom is paramount, and the claims on the individual made by the community are a source of danger (oppressive orthodoxy, stultifying conformity, etc.). The individual can freely choose to join a group, but one's right of freedom of association means that one must always be free to leave if one's personal goals or values change. By contrast, the conservative Christian sees the relationship to God and to the community of worship as not being a mere personal preference or a private association that a person can walk away from. Fish notes that "[s]ecular individualism ... tend[s] in crucial moments to trump [the conservative Christian's] preferred rhetoric of a 'religiously informed communitarianism.'"[59] It is for this reason that one conservative Christian has complained that in a liberal society the community of worship

> must inform its members that they can quit at any time and thus it must inform its members that believing along with the rest of the community is not the most fundamental thing of all. Communities thus become half-minded and thus half-hearted ... They become communities founded on prior respect for individual choice and thus become mirror images of the larger liberal society. In this liberal society, communities are not left free: rather they are constrained to become liberal associations."[60]

Civility and tolerance vs. obedience to God's commands

Finding a way for those who disagree about the good to live together in peace is a crucial goal for liberals, and so they insist that civility and toleration be extended toward people of all views. But for conservative Christians, obedience to God's revealed word is the highest good, not peace, civility, or toleration. "[T]he fundamentalist objection to the doctrine of reciprocity [mutual respect, giving the other fellow a hearing] ... is ... that it is *wrong*, that the moral optimum is not everyone talking to one another in a decorous deliberative forum but is, rather, everyone allied to and acting in conformity with the Truth and the will of God."[61] Fish argues that the goal of strong religious believers should not be to ensure that the civility and tolerance guaranteed by the liberal

---

[59] *Trouble*, 222.
[60] Paul Marshall, "Liberalism, pluralism and Christianity: A reconceptualization" 21 *Fides et Historia* (1989) 9, quoted in Rex Ahdar, *Worlds colliding: Conservative Christians and the law* (Aldershot, UK: Ashgate, 2001), 79.
[61] *Trouble*, 203. See too 182 where Fish refers to "true believers whose zeal for their souls and yours overrides or cancels any such fear [of civil chaos]."

marketplace of ideas is extended to their convictions. Rather their goal should be to replace the error-filled babble of that marketplace with a different space in which only the true word of God is heard and obeyed. "To put the matter baldly, a person of religious conviction should not want to enter the marketplace of ideas but to shut it down, at least insofar as it presumes to determine matters that he believes have been determined by God and faith. The religious person should not seek an accommodation with liberalism; he should seek to rout it from the field."[62]

For a liberal, on the other hand, the strong religious believer's focus on unquestioning obedience instead of a process of civil discussion and critique is incomprehensible and frightening:

> For the Mill of *On Liberty*, what "no reasonable person will believe" is that the highest value is the value of obedience. Mill is incredulous before a philosophy according to which "all the goods of which humanity is capable is comprised by obedience," and he is aghast at an ethics that requires nothing of man but "the surrendering of himself to the will of God." . . . This is no way, he complains, to know the truth, which can be known only "by hearing what can be said about it by persons of every variety of opinion."[63]

It is true that some religious people preach toleration for those with other beliefs, but Fish says that such people are not strong religious believers and have instead become a variety of liberal.

> To be sure, those religions that put "openness of mind" at the center of their faith – or rather at the center of their rejection of faith – will be welcomed into the political process and accorded a role in American public life, but only because in their stripped down and soft-edged form they are indistinguishable from other Enlightenment projects and are hardly religions at all.[64]

Once Fish has established a deep incompatibility between the beliefs, values, and goals of liberals and conservative Christians, the next step in the argument is to look closely at the claims by liberals to have found a principled way to accommodate religious fundamentalists within liberal societies. What convincing reasons have liberals given to the devout to curtail their non-liberal aspirations and submit themselves to the discipline of rational scrutiny in the marketplace of ideas? How have the just bounds between church and state been ascertained?

---

[62] Ibid., 250. See too 221, 252, 298.   [63] Ibid., 248.   [64] Ibid., 189. See too 214–5, 297.

> An uncompromising religion would be a threat to liberalism because were it to be given full scope, there would be no designated safe space in which toleration was the rule ... The fact that such strong forms of religious behavior are always putting themselves forward constitutes the greatest challenge to liberal hopes for a principled adjudication of the claims of church and state ... What does the Lockean liberal say to the person whose religion teaches that it is a holy duty to order the affairs of the world by the true faith? What so-called "independent value" could be so persuasively urged that the zealous would retreat from their zeal and leave their deepest beliefs at home?[65]

Liberalism claims that these questions can be answered by using reason to identify universal and neutral principles for organizing society that all will agree to, but as we have seen, Fish argues that this political project is doomed to failure because there can be no context-free principles of the sort foundationalists seek. Consequently, he concludes, the liberal freedom of religion principle is actually filled with a partisan content that operates to disadvantage and limit those committed to strong religious beliefs. This hidden bias against strong religious believers is manifested in two ways, according to Fish. First, liberalism confines religious belief to the margins of social life where its exercise can have little effect on institutional structures, public policy, and the law. Second, forms of religious belief that do not fit themselves within liberal conceptions of reason and truth are categorized as irrational, which enables liberals to dismiss them without a serious hearing. In other words, they are excluded from admission to the liberal marketplace of ideas where only reasoned positions can enter and demand to be taken seriously. I will now examine each of these mechanisms – marginalization and exclusion – in more detail.

Marginalization

The marginalization of strong religious believers by liberalism is achieved through employing a number of distinctions, each of which assigns to religion a limited scope of operation. The main distinction is between the public and the private zones of life. The public zone is conceived to be the area of legitimate state action and compulsion by law, while the private zone is the area of freedom from state coercion. One of liberalism's innovations, compared to previous political traditions, was to limit the scope of legitimate government activity and to expand and protect

[65] Ibid., 178.

the private zone of individual freedom.[66] Religion is one of the things liberalism moved out of the public zone and placed into the private zone. Liberals can thus claim to be acknowledging the importance of individual religious belief by explicitly protecting it from state intrusion, and they can also claim to be neutral regarding religion because all religious beliefs are protected in the same way by the freedom of religion principle.[67]

But this protection of religion through the public/private distinction simultaneously neuters religion and renders it safe for liberal society, Fish argues. Religion is protected only if it accepts that its legitimate place is confined to the private zone and not the public zone where it could direct public policy and legislation. The liberal public/private distinction creates a safe place for religious belief, but that place is limited in size and located far from where the action is.

> [T]he freedom thus gained is the freedom to be ineffectual, the freedom "to be confined to the margins of public life." ... What is not allowed religion under the private/public distinction is the freedom to *win*, the freedom not to be separate from the state but to inform and shape its every action.[68]

Other liberal distinctions do the same marginalizing work, according to Fish. The distinction between belief and action is employed to ensure that even though an inner religious conviction must be protected from state interference, conduct in the world demanded by that conviction can be regulated by the state. "If religion is basically a matter of belief rather than conduct, a restriction on conduct will not be an infringement on religious liberty."[69] The distinction between the expression of an idea and the content of an idea is employed so that the content of religious ideas can be viewed with suspicion even as the ability of a religious believer to express his ideas is lauded as religious tolerance.[70] The effect of all these distinctions is the same: religious belief is protected and honored as long as it accepts a role in liberal society that will not allow it to carry out its

[66] See Michael Robertson, "The limits of liberal rights: Stanley Fish on freedom of religion" 10 *Otago Law Review* (2002) 253–6 for more on the history and novelty of the liberal public/private distinction.

[67] *Trouble*, 177.

[68] Ibid., 254. See too 171, 173, 187. As Fish suggests in this passage, strong religious believers need not reject the freedom of religion principle; instead they could fill this abstract liberal principle with a different partisan content. For example, freedom of religion could be understood as the freedom of the one true religion to flow into every nook and cranny of life without constraint ("the freedom to win").

[69] Ibid., 172. See too 38.   [70] I ibid., 39.

deepest ambitions. "[L]iberalism cannot allow ['Christ is risen'] to have a public life in the sense that it might be put forward as a *reason* for taking this action (going to war, passing a budget, ending affirmative action) rather than another."[71]

The space that liberalism makes available for religious believers is not only limited and off to the side, it is also a space that the religious believer can only inhabit if he is prepared to distort and truncate his beliefs. Fish argues: "[T]o ask a religious person to rephrase his claims in more mainstream terms is to ask that person to cut himself off from the very source of his conviction and to become in effect the opposite of what he is, to become secular."[72] First, religious believers can enter the market-place of ideas only if they abide by the liberal assumptions of fallibilism and pluralism that underpin that market. According to these assumptions, the truth does not come to us in a monolithic and complete form, but instead it has to be constructed out of the many partial and competing viewpoints that enter the marketplace and have to be sifted by critical reason. Religious beliefs that enter this marketplace therefore cannot present themselves as monolithic and complete truths that eliminate the need to consider any other viewpoints. They must offer themselves as just one competing viewpoint among others that might have something valuable to contribute. But this distorts the nature of the religious claim: "Religious devotion is trivialized when its words are admitted into the forum but its claims to be not just one truth but *the* truth are disallowed."[73] Second, religious believers are precluded from justifying their claims in the liberal marketplace of ideas by revelation or divinely authored texts. Those entering the liberal marketplace have to abide by the liberal conception of reason and defend their positions using material that liberals accept as cogent evidence or compelling authority. Of course, it is possible for religious believers to offer justifications for at least some of their positions that fit within secular conceptions of reason. They can refer to social consequences or human rights, instead of the Ten Commandments. But again participation is purchased at the cost of distorting the true religious position to fit within liberal strictures.

Exclusion

If a strong religious believer refuses to comply with these strictures, and insists instead that all must obey God's one revealed truth, Fish says that

---

[71] Ibid., 271.   [72] Ibid., 254.   [73] Ibid., 257.

the believer will be excluded from the liberal marketplace of ideas. In a liberal society that values peace and neutral principles, this exclusion will not be achieved by overt force or heavy-handed censorship. Rather it will be achieved by a piece of ideological sleight of hand – the strong religious believer will be categorized as someone who cannot demand to be taken seriously because they do not meet the basic threshold requirement for our attention. Liberal toleration only extends to those who conform to liberal conceptions of reason. Those who are judged not to conform, such as strong religious believers (and currently racists and homophobes[74]) will find themselves excluded from the marketplace of ideas and will become the objects of intolerance.

> [L]iberalism rests on the substantive judgment that the public sphere must be insulated from viewpoints that owe their allegiance not to its procedures – to the unfettered operation of the marketplace of ideas – but to the truths they work to establish. That is what neutrality means in the context of liberalism – a continual pushing away of orthodoxies, of beliefs not open to inquiry and correction – and that is why, in the name of neutrality, religious propositions must either be excluded from the marketplace or admitted only in ceremonial forms, in the form, for example, of a prayer that opens a session of Congress in which the proposals of religion will not be given a serious hearing.[75]

This exclusion can be achieved in a gentle fashion, by saying that the strong religious believer prefers faith to reason, or it can be achieved in a more pointed fashion, by saying that the strong religious believer is a closed-minded fanatic, or a zealot who is blind to anything that does not accord with his already fixed beliefs. Fish finds an example of the gentle mode of exclusion in the 1915 declaration of principles of the American Association of University Professors, which "denies to religiously based institutions the name of 'university' because 'they do not, at least as regards one particular subject, accept the principles of free inquiry.'"[76] A more hard-edged exclusion can be found in the refusal to allow creationism into the high school science curriculum because it is based only on religious dogma, not on any real evidence.[77] In short, the way the freedom of religion principle operates in liberal societies ensures that "religious values will either be accorded a ceremonial but empty honor or regarded as a trivial expression of individual taste, or condemned as 'an irrational and regressive antisocial force.'"[78] Fish concludes that this

---

[74] Ibid., 44, 130–1, 192–206.   [75] Ibid., 253. See too 187, 188–9, 249.
[76] Ibid., 37. See too 153–4.   [77] I ibid., 259.   [78] Ibid., 173.

principle is not neutral in the strong sense claimed by liberals, and that the liberal marketplace of ideas cannot be open to and tolerant of strong religious viewpoints, if a liberal social order is to be maintained.[79]

Finally, it is crucial to stress that the analysis just described is a *philosophical* critique of the liberal claim that its freedom of religion principle is an example of the neutral principles it seeks. It does not follow from this critique that Fish sympathizes with or endorses the *political* program of strong religious believers. Indeed, it would be quite possible for him both to debunk the neutrality claims of the liberal freedom of religion principle by highlighting the marginalizations and exclusions it achieves, and also to endorse as good politics those very exclusions and marginalizations. I shall expand upon this in Chapter 6.

Fish's critique of anti-foundationalist political theories: critical theory, postmodernism, and pragmatism

Anti-foundationalist theory hope and anti-foundationalist theory fear

Fish has now critiqued an important foundationalist political project, liberalism, but there are also anti-foundationalists who attempt to derive a political project from their epistemological position. One might expect that Fish, as a fellow anti-foundationalist, would be more sympathetic toward such political projects, but he is not. We saw him argue in Part I that no consequences follow from the anti-foundationalist position, other than the giving of different answers to some traditional philosophical questions. His position is therefore that no *political* consequences follow logically from anti-foundationalism, any more than they do from foundationalism.

> [T]here is no relationship between general metaphysical accounts of human practices and the performance of human practices. There is no relationship in any direction. If I am a foundationalist, my founda- tionalism directs me or inclines me to no particular acts, nor does it forbid any. If I am an antifoundationalist (in the sense that when asked certain philosophical questions, I give antifoundationalist answers), my

---

[79] For a similar analysis that cites Fish's work, see Stanley Hauerwas and Michael Baxter, "The kingship of Christ: Why freedom of belief is not enough" 42 *DePaul Law Review* (1992–1993) 107.

anti-foundationalism neither tells me what to do in particular situations nor tells me what I cannot or should not do.[80]

This explains why we can find foundationalism and anti-foundationalism on both sides of the conservative/progressive political divide. Conservative political theorists often use foundationalist rhetoric to argue for the traditional substantive conceptions of the good (moral, aesthetic, and political) they favor. They claim that these conceptions of the good are underwritten by God or Nature. But those arguing for progressive social change also use foundationalist rhetoric to argue for their favored norms when they claim these amount to universal human rights. Conversely, Fish notes, while it is common for those arguing for progressive social change to use anti-foundationalist reasoning (if the world is socially constructed we can change it more easily than we thought), there is nothing about anti-foundationalism that makes it especially congenial to progressive politics.[81] Conservative political theorists can endorse anti-foundationalism, too, as Richard Rorty noted: "No argument leads from a coherence view of truth, an anti-representationalist view of knowledge, and an anti-formalist view of law and morals, to Dewey's left-looking social prophesies. The Heidegger of *Being and time* shared all these views, but Heidegger looked rightward and dreamed different dreams."[82] Fish is also aware of this: "Strongly anti-essentialist theories – theories that argue for the unavailability of a transcontextual point of reference – have also been put to conservative use."[83] But he does not take up anti-foundationalist conservatives as a subject of analysis,

---

[80] Stanley Fish, "Truth but no consequences: Why philosophy doesn't matter" 29 *Critical Inquiry* (2003) 410–1 (hereafter cited as Fish, "Truth but no consequences"). See too *Doing*, 325.

[81] *Doing*, 350–1.

[82] Richard Rorty, "The banality of pragmatism and the poetry of justice" in Michael Brint and William Weaver (eds.), *Pragmatism in law and society* (Boulder, CO: Westview Press, 1991), 92 (hereafter cited as Brint and Weaver [eds.], *Pragmatism*). See too Thomas Grey, "What good is legal pragmatism?" in Brint and Weaver (eds.), *Pragmatism*, 13–4: "Antifoundationalism (or anti-Enlightenment thinking) can take a conservative, Burkean direction. There are no foundations that reason can discover, there is only the wisdom of the past encapsulated in our traditions, traditions which have shown their survival or adaptability value, and which shouldn't be changed by limited human beings with excessive faith in their own powers of understanding." Paddy Ireland gives a fine description of such conservative anti-foundationalist thinking in Paddy Ireland, "Endarkening the mind: Roger Scruton and the power of law" 6 *Social and Legal Studies* (1997) 52–4 and Paddy Ireland, "Reflections on a rampage through the barriers of shame: Law, community and the new conservatism" 22 *Journal of Law and Society* (1995) 189.

[83] *Professional*, 130.

focusing instead on foundationalist conservatives in the context of the "culture wars" in American universities in the last decades of the twentieth century.[84]

Fish would say that all theorists who embrace anti-foundationalism and then seek to derive from it a political program are failing to absorb the lessons learned in Part I. One of those lessons was that a highly abstract philosophical position, like anti-foundationalism, will be unable to offer guidance in the concrete contexts where partisan political positions are contesting, unless it has already taken an undeclared stand on the very substantive questions under dispute. Another lesson was the autonomy of practices. Anti-foundationalism is the product of a philosophical practice, but results achieved within the precincts of one practice cannot simply be imported into a different one, such as politics (or history or law or literary studies, etc.), which has a different enabling background. The beliefs that structure your thoughts and perceptions in non-philosophical contexts will therefore not be threatened or destabilized by your new philosophical position. Procedures and standards that deliver authoritative results in these other practices will not be affected by what goes on in the separate and exotic practice of epistemology, Fish insists.[85]

The lesson from Part I that Fish emphasizes the most in this context, however, is the incoherence of a conception of the self that would allow a human being to detach himself from all of the particular local commitments that structure and enable his consciousness. Fish argues that most of his fellow anti-foundationalists lose sight of this when they derive their political programs, and consequently fall into self-contradiction. If an anti-foundationalist holds that reality, including the self, is always socially constructed, then realizing this truth cannot enable him to cease being socially constructed. Accepting the truth of anti-foundationalism could only allow him to be more tolerant, or open-minded, or critically self-conscious, or free from ideological distortion, or democratically inclined, if it allowed him to escape the constraints imposed by his local embeddedness, but this contradicts anti-foundationalism's basic premise.

> That is, most people who come to the point of talking about critical self-consciousness or reflective equilibrium or being aware of the status of one's own discourse are also persons who believe strongly in the historical and socially constructed nature of reality; but somehow, at a certain

---

[84] He does this in *No free speech*, chs. 1–3 and pages 92–8.
[85] *Doing*, 335; *No free speech*, 248–9; Fish, "Truth but no consequences," 389–90.

moment in the argument, they are able to marry this belief in social constructedness with a belief in the possibility of stepping back from what has been socially constructed or stepping back from one's own self. I don't know how they manage this. I think, in fact, that they manage it by not recognizing the contradiction.[86]

Fish's position is that consistent anti-foundationalists have to accept that they will be just as socially constructed and locally embedded (and so just as constrained, biased, angled, partisan, etc.) after they accept anti-foundationalism as they were before they saw the epistemological light. In short, Fish insists that the truth does not set you free, or more precisely, that seeing the truth of anti-foundationalism does not make you any less gripped by and constituted by your present beliefs.

The failure to understand properly the non-implications of the necessarily embedded or socially constructed self is a surprising point of commonality between most foundationalists and anti-foundationalists, Fish argues. They both tend to make the mistake of believing that anti-foundationalism *does something*, that it has consequences outside the precincts of philosophy. The difference between them is that one group thinks that those consequences are desirable while the other group thinks that they are undesirable. For one group (typically but not always foundationalists), anti-foundationalism has the consequence of leaving us in a relativistic and chaotic world without the possibility of standards and procedures that are common and authoritative. Fish calls this "anti-foundationalist theory fear," and he calls those afflicted by this fear "the intellectual right." For the other group, anti-foundationalism has positive consequences – it can free us from the constraints of our partisan local context and make us freer, or more open and tolerant, or critically self-conscious. Fish calls this "anti-foundationalist theory hope," and he calls those buoyed by this hope "the intellectual left."[87] Both the hope and the fear are illusory, Fish insists, because each group fails to appreciate that the grip of local contexts cannot be transcended (although this failure is more surprising for the anti-foundationalists).

> It is instructive to observe that the myth of the self free from constraints is necessary to the positions of both the intellectual right and left; on the right the myth generates the fear that if public controls are not kept in place the self will go its own way; on the left the myth generates the hope

---

[86] *No free speech*, 295. See too *Doing*, 245, 324, 348–9, 350, 436–8, 584 n 60.

[87] For more on the intellectual right and left, see *No free speech*, 19; *Doing*, 225–31, 442–67, 494–502.

that if public controls can only be removed the self will be able to go its own way. One side fears that anti-foundationalist thought – teaching as it does that all facts and values are social and political constructs – will deprive us of our certainties; the other side hopes that anti-foundationalist thought will deprive us of our certainties.[88]

Progressive anti-foundationalist political theories

Some progressive anti-foundationalists argue that if disadvantaged groups become aware of the socially constructed nature of the values and beliefs that allow others to oppress them then they will be able to free themselves from these ideological shackles. Other progressive anti-foundationalists argue that if reality is always socially constructed then we have to accept that our group's perception of reality cannot claim a higher standing than those of other groups, and so we have to be more tolerant of these groups and less insistent about them conforming to our beliefs and standards. Still other anti-foundationalists argue that if everything is socially constructed then we need to engage in open democratic discussions as to the kind of reality we should be constructing. These "intellectual left" political positions are associated with critical theory, postmodernism, and pragmatism, respectively. I will now examine Fish's arguments for categorizing them all as varieties of an impossible "anti-foundationalist theory hope."

Critical theory

Critical theory has three components. First, there is an attempt to expose and describe the hitherto unnoticed background that enables and structures our experience. Next, there is a claim that some elements of this background operate to harm us in some way. Finally, there is a claim that bringing these negative background elements to critical self-consciousness is an important step in releasing their grip on us and allowing us to change them. These three components do not form an indissoluble unity, for it is possible to engage in the first of the three without proceeding further. Fish reports:

> [I]t is possible to register one of two responses to the crucial insight impelling the work of left-wing intellectuals – the insight that our sense

---

[88] *Doing*, 26. For more on anti-foundationalist theory hope and fear, see *Doing*, 322–3, 345–8, 438, 466, 524, 593 n 13; *No free speech*, 172; Fish, "Truth but no consequences," 415; Olson, *Justifying belief*, 38–40.

of what is obligatory, routine, ordinary, reasonable, authoritative, matter-of-fact, and even possible is grounded neither in nature nor in inevitability but in background conditions and assumptions that have been put in place by interested agents. One response, and the one almost always given, is outrage and horror, more or less equivalent to the discovery of the worm in the apple; and the reaction to that response is, as we have seen, first, indictment and then a call for action designed to free us from the impositions and deceptions to which we have become captive. The other response is less dramatic and takes the form of a project, of new research, in which the goal is to provide a full and analytical map of what have been called the "conditions of possibility," the conditions that underlie what at any point in the history of a society or an institution are taken to be the components of common sense.[89]

The second, "less dramatic" project mentioned in this passage seeks to describe the enabling and structuring background without hoping to change it. This is the project of the sociology of knowledge pioneered by Karl Mannheim and also of one form of deconstruction.[90] But the first project mentioned in this passage is the full-blown project of critical theory, and elsewhere Fish describes how it can seem to grow naturally out of the more modest project:

[O]ne proceeds to expose the contingent and therefore challengeable basis of whatever presents itself as natural and inevitable. So far this is precisely the procedure of deconstruction; but whereas deconstructive practice (at least of the Yale variety) seems to produce nothing but the occasion for its endless repetition, some cultural revolutionaries discern in it a more positive residue, the loosening or weakening of the structures of domination and oppression that now hold us captive. The reasoning is that by repeatedly uncovering the historical and ideological basis of established structures (both political and cognitive), one becomes sensitized to the effects of ideology and begins to clear a space in which those effects can be combated; and as that sensitivity grows more acute, the area of combat will become larger until it encompasses the underlying structure of assumptions that confers a spurious legitimacy on the powers that currently be. The claim, in short, is that the radically rhetorical insight of Nietzschean/Derridean thought can do radical political work; becoming aware that everything is rhetorical is the first step in countering the power of rhetoric and liberating us from its force.[91]

---

[89] *Doing*, 237. See too Stanley Fish, "Theory's hope," 30 *Critical Inquiry* (2004) 377 (hereafter cited as Fish, "Theory's hope").

[90] *Doing*, 226; Karl Mannheim, *Ideology and utopia* (London: Routledge & Kegan Paul, 1960, originally published in English 1936).

[91] *Doing*, 496.

Modern critical theory has deep roots, as Brian Fay describes in his book *Critical social science.* He locates its source in

> a vision of existence which has a deep history in human thought. This vision, which I shall call the self-estrangement theory ... offer[s] an account which not only tries to disclose the essence of humans by depicting them as fallen creatures, but also claims to offer the means by which this fallenness can be overcome. The self-estrangement theory in all of its many versions is one of the primary stories about themselves which humans have constructed in the face of loss, impotence, despair, and death.[92]

This old root has produced many fruits over the centuries, Fay reports:

> The conception of life of which the Platonic, Gnostic, Hebrew, and Christian doctrines (or at least important strains in them) are instances – that is, one which portrays human existence as separated from the sources of energy which are in fact at its core, but about which people are unconscious so that they unwittingly fashion their lives in necessarily self-defeating ways – has been a dominant presence in Western thought. Some of its most important thinkers, for example, Pascal, Kierkegaard, Hegel, Marx, Freud, and Heidegger, have proclaimed one version or another of it. Nor has this conception been limited to the West. Both Hinduism and Buddhism contain expressions of it too.[93]

But after noting this historical variety, Fay concentrates upon "critical social science," which he describes as the

> form of the self-estrangement theory that comes to prominence in the modern period. It is an expression of what I shall call the modern humanist spirit. Critical social science pictures humans as fallen but only in purely secular terms, and as redeemable through their own capacity to transform their lives in radical ways. By means of analysis and effort, humans are thought to be capable of solving their own problems through an enlightened re-ordering of their collective arrangements. This is an expression of the Enlightenment ideal that through reason humans can achieve a form of existence which is free and satisfying to them ... In the broadest terms, critical social science is an attempt to understand in a rationally responsible manner the oppressive features of a society such that this understanding stimulates its audience to transform their society and so liberate themselves.[94]

Fay sees Marx and his followers as providing the most important example of critical social science, with the followers of Freud providing another.[95] From these two sources, Fay argues, come the modern critical

---

[92] Brian Fay, *Critical social science* (Oxford: Polity, 1987), 2. See too 10.   [93] Ibid., 15.
[94] Ibid., 2–3, 4. See too 17, 66–8.   [95] Ibid., 4, 216–7.

theorists of the Frankfurt School (Max Horkheimer, Herbert Marcuse, Theodor Adorno, and Habermas), feminism, critical legal studies, and others whom he lists.[96] These modern critical theorists are also those who Fish has in mind when he talks of the anti-foundationalist "intellectual left."[97]

But although these modern critical theorists typically identify themselves as philosophical anti-foundationalists, Fish says that their political project fails because it does not remain true to anti-foundationalism. Both the sociology of knowledge's descriptive project of fully mapping the background that enables our thoughts and actions and critical theory's political project of breaking free from this background contradict the positions Fish defended in Part I. Critical theory is thus revealed to be a type of the strong theory that Fish declared to be impossible, and the anti-foundationalist theory hope that it manifests is illusory.

> This is the hope and dream of critical self-consciousness, the thesis that ye shall know that what passes for the truth is socially and historically constructed and that knowledge shall set you free. The critically self-conscious agent, the argument goes, is just as embedded as anyone else, but he is *aware* of it and that makes all the difference, or at least the difference that keeps the hope of boundary-breaking behavior alive. This will work, however, only if the knowledge that we are embedded is stored in a part of the mind that floats free of the embeddedness we experience at any one time; but that would mean that at least a part of our mind was not somewhere but everywhere and that would mean that we were not human beings but gods ... Critical self-consciousness, conceived of as a mental action independent of the setting in which it occurs, is the last infirmity of the mind that would deny its own limits by positioning itself in two places at the same time, in the place of its local embodiment and in the disembodied place (really no place) of reflection.[98]

With respect to the purely descriptive project of the sociology of knowledge, Fish argues that if all human thinking, perceiving, and acting presupposes an already-in-place, socially constructed background, then it follows that the activity of looking at your background assumptions *itself* requires a background.

> [I]f you propose to examine and assess assumptions, what will you examine and assess them *with*? And the answer is that you will examine and assess them with forms of thought that themselves rest on underlying

---

[96] Ibid., 4–6.   [97] *Doing*, 442.
[98] *Professional*, 104. See too *Doing*, 245; *No free speech*, 295.

assumptions. At any level, the tools of rational analysis will be vulnerable to the very deconstruction they claim to perform.[99]

But this means that the descriptive project can never attain its goal of a complete map. If there must always be a background that we are thinking *within*, rather than thinking *about*, then there must always be something that is outside the scope of any present act of self-reflection. Any act of self-reflection cannot notice and expose what is enabling its own present activity, Fish argues, and so it is always incomplete.

> The strategy of "making visible what was hidden" can only be pursued within forms of thought that are themselves hidden; the bringing to light of what Edward Said calls "the network of dark agencies that limit, select, shape, and maintain" meaning requires the dark background of a network that cannot be seen because it is within it that seeing occurs. Partiality and parochialism are not eliminated or even diminished by the exposure of their operation, merely relocated.[100]

Alternatively put, a human being can never detach himself from and scrutinize all elements of his socially constructed, enabling background from some Archimedean external position; he can never escape embeddedness.

As we saw when considering beliefs in Chapter 2, Fish is not denying that we can reflect upon, doubt, and criticize some of our beliefs, even our deep background assumptions: "The 'critical attitude' can always be assumed, but its very shape will be a function of a context in relation to which it does not have and could not have any distance."[101] In other words, any such self-reflection is an activity performed *within* an existing context, rather than an activity performed by stepping *outside* an existing context.[102] Because criticism will always be carried out from a particular embedded position, it will be enabled and given a distinctive shape by assumptions that come with that form of embeddedness. It will therefore always be context-specific or enterprise-specific rather than a free-floating capacity.

> [A]ny skepticism one "developed" would have a content; that is, it would be made up of questions ("are there really no exceptions to this rule whose validity I am assuming?"), tests ("is there anything that would falsify this

---

[99] *No free speech*, 18. See too 197; *Doing*, 195–6, 300, 331–2, 440.
[100] *No free speech*, 237. See too 115–6.   [101] Ibid, 197.
[102] Fish, "Truth but no consequences," 402–3; *Professional*, 106; *No free speech*, 303–4; *Doing*, 427.

thesis?"), cautions ("don't rush to premature conclusions on the basis of inadequate evidence."), all of which would presuppose some set of already-in-place distinctions, hierarchies, values, definitions, which could not themselves be the object of "skepticism" because they formed the taken-for-granted background against and within which skepticism acquired its present shape.[103]

Turning now to the critical theory political project, it claims that after self-reflection has exposed the background commitments that enable our practices, this knowledge will allow us to escape the grip of the background commitments that were enabling undesirable practices.

> How do we know that by exposing a given context as interested and politically repressive we have taken a step toward freedom and not merely stepped into another context, no less interested, no less repressive? The answer given by the critical theorists is at once breathtaking and daring: we know that the critical project will finally succeed by virtue of the fact that we have been able to think of it. That is, the insight that the present order of things is neither natural nor inevitable is itself an indication that the totalizing claims of that order can be resisted . . . That is to say, the condition of unfreedom is breached the moment that we can reflect upon it, for that act of reflection occurs in a space not ruled by the presuppositions of the established reality, and therefore begins the process of overthrowing (by seeing through) that reality and potentially of all the other "realities" imposed upon us by the powers that (presently) be.[104]

But Fish throws cold water on this hope for the reasons we have seen in Part I. First, there is the autonomy of practices. Social constructivism is a move made within the practice of philosophy (it is a way of stating the anti-foundationalist position) and has no necessary consequences for non-philosophical practices. Consequently, realizing that everything is socially constructed will have no effect on the rest of our (socially constructed) lives.[105] Second, there is the nature of the self. If the self is always constituted by local commitments, then realizing this fact cannot change the nature of the self and allow it to escape its local commitments.

> [B]eing situated not only means that one cannot achieve a distance on one's beliefs but that one's beliefs do not relax their hold because one "knows" that they are local and not universal. This in turn means that even someone (like me or Fay) who is firmly convinced of the

---

[103] *Doing*, 440. See too 425; *Text*, 354–5; Fish, "Interpretation is not a theoretical issue," 514.
[104] *Doing*, 447–8. See too *Trouble*, 233.   [105] *Doing*, 351, 396; *No free speech*, 197.

circumstantiality of his convictions will nevertheless experience those
convictions as universally, not locally, true.[106]

If it sounds wrong to claim that accepting anti-foundationalism does not
weaken or affect any of your deep local convictions,[107] then perform this
thought experiment. Identify the worst form of reprehensible conduct
you can think of, and then ask yourself whether this conduct becomes
more acceptable to you once you learn why people do it and why you do
not (i.e., you come to see how its despicableness is "socially constructed"
rather than "natural"). If, for example, you abhor honor killings in which
fathers and sons murder wives, mothers, daughters, and sisters, does your
acknowledgment that your abhorrence derives from your particular
cultural background (Western, secular, individualist) and that those
who engage in this practice see it as legitimate because they are embedded within a different culture and history in which notions of family
honor and shame are paramount, make your rejection of this practice
any less emphatic? Fish claims that your deep convictions do not grip
you less strongly, nor are you less confident of their truth, just because
you have a new account of their origins. Conversely, the account of how
others come to see their practices as acceptable does not serve to make
their beliefs more acceptable to you; it only explains the source of their
error. But those who feel the lure of anti-foundationalist theory hope
must hold that the grip of one's background commitments can be
released if one comes to see how they came to be there and what work
they are doing.

Fish notes other problems as well. If the political project of critical
theory begins with the premise that everything is socially constructed,
then it is not possible to make the fact that something is socially constructed into a criticism of it or a reason for changing it. "Although it may
seem paradoxical at first, the conclusion is inescapable: the larger the
scope of social constructedness, the less it matters ... [I]t can hardly be
a criticism of something that it is socially constructed if everything is."[108]
So in response to any argument "that the cultural systems within which
we live and move and have our beings are not natural but constructed
and therefore imposed," Fish replies:

---

[106] *Doing,* 467. See too 245–6.
[107] See, for example, Georgia Chrysostomides, "Doing the unnatural – Stanley Fish's theory
of interpretation" (2000) *UCL Jurisprudence Review* 180–1.
[108] *Professional,* ix.

It is this last – "and therefore imposed" – that is at once incoherent and the source of theory's politicization. It is incoherent because the substitution of the constructed for the natural was supposed to have removed the natural as a baseline category; but when *constructed* becomes an accusation – you say it's *merely* constructed – the natural is restored to just that position.[109]

Yet another kind of self-contradiction in the project appears whenever critical theory claims to be working toward forms of politics that will be free from the ideology present in prior forms:

> Critical self-consciousness is the ability (stifled in some, developed in others) to discern in any "scheme of association," including those one finds attractive and compelling, the partisan aims it hides from view, and the claim is that as it performs this negative task, critical self-consciousness participates in the positive task of formulating schemes of association (structures of thought and government) that are in the service not of a particular party but of all mankind. It need hardly be said that this claim veers back in the direction of the rationalism and universalism that the critical/deconstructive project sets out to demystify.[110]

All of these problems with the political project of critical theory can be discerned, Fish argues, in the work of the "intellectual left" theorists belonging to the critical legal studies movement[111] (Robert Gordon,[112] Duncan Kennedy,[113] Roberto Unger[114]), the Frankfurt School of critical theory (Habermas,[115] Marcuse,[116] Adorno,[117] Horkheimer[118]), and politically engaged literary critics such as Terry Eagleton.[119] He even argues that Brian Fay himself succumbs to the lure of critical self-consciousness at the end of his own book.[120]

It is important to stress what Fish is *not* saying because his point is easily misunderstood. He is not saying that it is impossible for us to shift from one set of background local commitments to another or that deliberate political action to produce this change cannot be successful.

> Nothing I have said should be construed as urging quietism or fatalism; the only option this line of reasoning takes away is the option of stepping back from one's beliefs in order to survey or reform them; absent that

---

[109] Fish, "Theory's hope," 377.   [110] *Doing*, 497.

[111] Peter Schanck, "Understanding postmodern thought and its implications for statutory interpretation" 65 *Southern California Law Review* (1991) 2577–81 (hereafter cited as Schanck, "Understanding postmodern thought").

[112] *Doing*, 226–8, 496–7.   [113] Ibid., 228–30.   [114] Ibid., 419–35.

[115] Ibid., 450–5, 498–9.   [116] Ibid., 442–4, 449.   [117] Ibid., 456–7.

[118] Ibid., 444–5, 447.   [119] Ibid., 494–6.   [120] Ibid., 465–7.

option, one is in the position one was always in, the position of seeing the world as a field of possibilities to be seized by whatever means your situation recommends.[121]

He is not even saying that critical theory-talk can have no role in achieving this change. We have already seen in Chapter 3 that theory-talk can have a contingent, rhetorical role in politics, and I shall return to this theme in Chapter 6. All Fish is saying is that critical theory cannot be playing the role it *claims* to be playing in achieving this change, because that role is impossible. Because local embeddedness is a precondition of human experience, there can be no moment, however brief, in which a self is enabled, by critical theory or anything else, to step *outside* its existing form of embeddedness and be completely free to choose another. Changes in forms of embeddedness always involve lateral shifts from one form to another, with no moment in which the constraints of embeddedness are released. During and after any such change, the person will be just as constrained (although differently so) than he or she was before. The constraints of embeddedness are as comprehensive as they are constant.

> Those who object to my specification of belief as constraint assume that if I were to acknowledge the complexity and instability of belief I would see that its constraints are continually being relaxed as beliefs jostle one another ... Still, the fact that there is nothing monolithic about constraint ... does not mean that they can be thought of as more or less loose, as possibly "leaking" and opening up at the seams or at points of pressure where the possibility of actions or thoughts *not* constrained is waiting to be seized. However nuanced one's talk about constraint and belief and community may get to be, the nuances will never add up to a moment or place where consciousness becomes transparent to itself and can at last act freely. Being embedded means just that, being embedded *always*, and one does not escape embeddedness by acknowledging, as I do, that it is itself a fractured, fissured, volatile condition.[122]

As I have already explained when dealing with the liberal freedom vs. constraint dichotomy in the first section of this chapter, at the level of philosophical analysis no form of embeddedness is freer than another, according to Fish. He makes the same point when dealing with critical theory:

> What the critical theorists call liberation or emancipation is nothing more (or less) than the passing from one structure of constraint to

---

[121] Ibid., 464–5.   [122] Ibid., 32. See too 420.

another, a passing that will always be attended by the "discovery of new possibilities," but of possibilities that will be no less (or more) constrained than those that have been left behind.[123]

As Fish acknowledges in this passage, the passing from one structure of constraint to another can be experienced as freedom-enhancing, but this is because our understanding of what is freedom-enhancing will be a function of the new background in place. When we move to a new form of embeddedness and hence a new understanding of what is freedom-enhancing, we can experience our old way of life as constraining and our new way of life as liberating. But from the abstract philosophical standpoint called anti-foundationalism, Fish insists, the shape of our constraints has simply changed, and as a result we are now permitted to do some news things and prohibited from doing some old things.

> Of course, for the person who has performed the act of revision, the resulting practice will seem larger, more capacious, than the practice he has left behind; but this capaciousness will be evident and palpable only from within the perspective that now becomes his horizon. For another person the new practice will not seem larger at all, but have the aspect of a restriction on the human capacity for growth and self-realization.[124]

Postmodernism

As Fish presents it, at the core of postmodernism is the same anti-foundationalism that he advances:

> Postmodernism is a general and abstract description of the way knowledge is established and challenged. It tells us that any establishing or challenging of knowledge is a historical rather than a transcendent event ... The argument, basically, is that the structures of intelligibility in which we more or less unselfconsciously live – the coherences that seem to present themselves naturally to us as we look at and move about in the world – are not natural at all, are not the result of the world's pre-existing patterns of meaning imprinting themselves on our perception, but are constructed. They are not constructed by anyone in particular (this is not a conspiracy theory), but by traditions of inquiry, practice, and rhetoric that in time become components in our storehouse of common sense.[125]

[123] Ibid., 459–60. See too 229–30, 424–7, 448, 460–3.   [124] Ibid., 420. See too 423.
[125] Save, 134, 135. Postmodernism and anti-foundationalism are linked in No free speech, 56 and in Stanley Fish, "French theory in America," a review of Francois Cusset, French theory: How Foucault, Derrida, Deleuze, & co. transformed the intellectual life of the United States (University of Minnesota Press, 2008) in his New York Times Opinionator

Although postmodernism is today associated with the work of French theorists such as Jacques Derrida, Michel Foucault, Jean-Francois Lyotard, and Jean Baudrillard, Fish points out that its anti-foundationalism has roots that extend back to Nietzsche and even further back to the ancient Greek sophists.[126] Faced with things that appear to be free-standing and self-sufficient (such as individual selves or brute facts or meaningful texts), the anti-foundationalist/postmodern response is to demonstrate how these things actually depend for their existence upon something outside themselves, and so they are not free-standing after all. The activity of highlighting the unnoticed but essential work done by a background in producing what is apprehended as free standing in the foreground is, as noted earlier while discussing critical theory, one of the core meanings of the term "deconstruction," an activity that is closely connected with postmodernist theorists. It involves revealing the socially constructed nature of something and emphasizing how a different background would have resulted in a different thing.[127] Another strain of deconstructionist thought is to call attention to cases where this necessary "outside" contains the very things against which the supposedly self-sufficient item defined itself. The deconstructionist move here is to show that the two poles of a conventional dichotomy are actually interdependent, rather than standing in opposition. As Fish put it earlier: "One deconstructs an opposition not by reversing the hierarchy of its poles but by denying to either pole the independence that makes the opposition possible in the first place."[128]

Although Fish endorses the anti-foundationalist epistemology at the core of postmodernism, and himself engages in deconstructionist analyses of the two types described above, he nevertheless has deep disagreements with

Blog for April 6, 2008 (hereafter cited as Fish, "French theory"). Individual postmodern theorists (such as Derrida) are associated with anti-foundationalism in *Doing*, 225, 321, 345.

[126] *Doing*, 472–3, 480, 494. Fish accepts a description of himself as a "contemporary sophist" at *No free speech*, 281.

[127] *Save*, 135–6. On deconstruction, see generally *Save*, 135–8; *Doing*, 492–4; *Trouble*, 303.

[128] *Doing*, 211. For a more detailed discussion, see the material on deconstructing liberalism's dichotomies earlier in this chapter. This strain of deconstructive thought existed long before the word "deconstruction" was invented. See, for example, *Milton*, 13: "But it is precisely Milton's thesis that the persons, things, and values that form one pole of this opposition are without coherence and shape if severed from that to which they are the supposed alternatives." Compare Stanley Fish, "One more time" in Olson and Worsham (eds.), *Postmodern sophistry*, 269: "I am never in the business of denying the existence of valued forms of behavior ... rather, I deny that the bare abstraction (tolerance, mutual respect, freedom of speech) can do real work without adding to it the leaven or alloy of the very thing thought to compromise it—intolerance, disrespect, regulation."

significant strands of postmodernist thought. These disagreements arise whenever postmodernists purport to find consequences of their philosophical analysis outside the precincts of philosophy itself. One example of this is the claim of "vulgar postmodernism"[129] that anti-foundationalism results in the loss of authoritative moral values or access to objective reality in everyday contexts. We have already seen Fish argue that anti-foundationalism does not have any relativistic consequences, and he insists that more sophisticated *non*-vulgar postmodernists realize this:

> Well, that certainly sounds bad – no truths, no knowledge, no reality, no morality, no judgments, no objectivity – and if postmodernists are saying that, they are not so much dangerous as silly. Postmodernists, however, say no such thing, and what they do say, if it is understood at all, is unlikely to provoke either the anger or the alarm of our modern Paul Reveres. Most of the time, it is not understood.[130]

What concerns us most here, however, is the claim by some postmodernists that their philosophical analysis has positive *political* consequences and requires the adoption of a particular type of political program. Fish agrees with Francois Cusset that political postmodernism grew particularly vigorously when the French theorists were transplanted into the different cultural soil of America:

> For [its detractors and supporters] what was important about French theory in America was its political implications, and one of Cusset's main contentions – and here I completely agree with him – is that it doesn't have any ... Cusset drives the lesson home: "Deconstruction thus contains within itself ... an endless metatheoretical regression that can no longer be brought to a stop by any practical decision or effective political engagement. In order to use it as a basis for subversion ... the American solution was ... to divert it ... to split it off from itself." American academics "forced deconstruction against itself to produce a political 'supplement' and in so doing substituted for 'Derrida's patient philological deconstruction' a 'bellicose drama.'" ... The result is the story Cusset tells about the past 40 years. A bunch of people threatening all kinds of subversion by means that couldn't possibly produce it, and a bunch on the other side taking them at their word and waging cultural war.[131]

---

[129] *Save*, 125.

[130] Ibid., 138–9. See too 134–5. Larry Alexander makes the same point when he writes that "[t]he most sophisticated postmodernists, however, realize that nothing substantive, and surely nothing normative, follows from the postmodern point of view," and he gives Fish as an example of such a sophisticated postmodernist. Larry Alexander, "Academic freedom," 77 *University of Colorado Law Review* (2006) 893.

[131] Fish, "French theory."

A number of the political projects that postmodernist theorists claim to derive from anti-foundationalism differ from the critical theory project discussed earlier. For example, Fish describes Judith Butler as eschewing the goal of overthrowing the dominant ideology and deliberately creating new structures designed to advance the interests of some previously oppressed group. Instead, her goal is limited to the negative work of deconstructing and destabilizing whatever power structures currently exist.

> If you ask which institutions will be the object of this critical perspective, the answer seems to be any and all institutions; and if you ask "Break with which past?" the answer seems to be any past. The insurrectionary moment is welcomed and courted not for what it specifically brings about but for what it brings about in general, the "overthrowing" of "established codes of legitimacy," whatever they happen to be . . . This indifference to outcomes is signaled when Butler describes the "political future" deconstructive thinking will make possible as "unanticipated" . . . Not constrained and controlled by hegemonic purposes, but driven only by the purpose to unsettle the ordinary and the sedimented, deconstructive thinking will bring us to a brave new world of whose outlines we are necessarily (and happily) ignorant.[132]

Fish's first critique of this program is that it is not really politics at all, instead it is philosophy. Butler's project substitutes "for the project of implementing your agenda the project of submitting your agenda, whatever it might be, to the searching criticism of deconstructive interrogation."[133] Rather than being a "politics of rethinking," he says, it substitutes rethinking for politics. If Butler would insist that her project *is* political, because it is grounded in a faith that ultimately "rethinking or revaluing or counter-appropriating will lead to a better world populated by better persons,"[134] Fish replies that she has simply reinvented one pillar of liberalism. Her politics of rethinking is characterized by the same valorizing of an unguided process, rather than the institutionalizing of some substantive conception of the good, that we find in the "fabled marketplace of ideas."[135]

> The politics of rethinking turns out to be pretty much indistinguishable from the politics of classical liberalism, with its insistence that nothing be foreclosed and everything be left open to revision and its disinclination to allow any commitment or value to be regarded as sacrosanct. The politics of rethinking turns out, in short, to be the antipolitics – suspicious of

---

[132] *Trouble*, 136, 137.   [133] Ibid., 137.   [134] Ibid.   [135] Ibid.

closure and downright hostile to the notion of anyone winning – that has been with us at least since Mill's *On Liberty*.[136]

And just as Fish argued earlier that a contestable substance will always be found beneath liberalism's supposedly neutral procedures and principles, so he now points out that Butler is not "really indifferent to how issues [are] resolved so long as the process remain[s] radically open." Instead, he shows how her analysis of free speech exhibits "quite specific ideas about how certain First Amendment disputes should be adjudicated."[137] She purports to endorse a deconstructionist political process, rather than some particular content, but standing apart from content is not possible for necessarily embedded human beings, according to Fish. This is why he says, in a related context, that

> radical culture – understood as the culture of oppositional action, not opposition in particular contexts, but just *opposition* as a principle – cannot be lived ... [I]t demands from a wholly situated creature a mode of action or thought (or writing) that is free from the entanglements of situations and the lines of demarcation they declare; it demands that a consciousness that has shape only by virtue of the distinctions and boundary lines that are its content float free of those lines and boundaries and remain forever unsettled.[138]

The context in which Fish made these remarks was a critique of another postmodernist political program. The postmodernist reasoning here was that if any human experience depends upon a socially constructed background being already in place, and these backgrounds always change over time as a result of material factors and political/rhetorical efforts, then we must practice politics in a way that acknowledges that underlying contingency and provisionality. This means that we must not aim for the institutionalization of some particular conception of the good. We must not make any appeals to universality or absoluteness and should instead adopt "the more flexible and multidirectional mode of being that seems called for by everything we have recently learned about the historicity of our situatedness; we should classify less, remember more, refuse less, and be forever open in a manner befitting a creature always in process."[139] But we have already seen why Fish rejects this political program as impossible: accepting the truth of anti-foundationalism does not release you from your non-philosophical beliefs, or enable you to hold them more tentatively and less absolutely, or allow you to be more open to other beliefs.

---

[136] Ibid., 138.   [137] Ibid.   [138] *No free speech*, 251.   [139] Ibid., 250–1.

The trouble with this advice is that it is impossible to follow. While openness to revision and transformation may characterize a human history in which firmly drawn boundaries can be shown to have been repeatedly blurred and abandoned, openness to revision and transformation are not methodological programs any individual can determinedly and self-consciously enact.[140]

The final postmodernist political program that I will consider is multiculturalism. The postmodern reasoning here is that if any human reality is socially constructed, then the way reality is constructed for my group enjoys no higher epistemological status than the way it is constructed for another group. It follows that no group should try to enforce its values and practices on any other group. But for selves constituted by embeddedness, Fish argues, the resolution to be tolerant can never succeed in the strong form desired by postmodernist multiculturalists. This resolution could only make sense for a person who was not constituted by his commitments but who was instead separate from them – a person whose deepest commitments did not rise above the status of mere "preferences" or "opinions."[141] But as we have seen in Part I, Fish holds that there are not and could not be such persons.

> The demand that discrimination be eliminated entirely is finally the demand that we live outside (or above or to the side of) the varied and conflicting perspectives that give to each of us a world saturated with goods, goals, aspirations, and obligations. It is the demand that we no longer be human beings – beings defined by partiality – but become as gods, beings who know no particular time or place. This is the dream not only of philosophy but of theology (in relation to whose assumptions it at least makes sense), but until we are the beneficiaries of a revelation or of a god who descends to begin his reign on earth, it must remain just that, a dream, and we will continue to be confined within the traditions and histories that generate our differing senses of what is true and good and worth dying for.[142]

Again, it is important to stress what Fish is *not* saying, so as to avert misunderstandings. He is not saying that toleration and openness are impossible; he is just saying that they can only appear in context-specific

---

[140] Ibid., 251. See too *Doing*, 16; Stanley Fish, "One more time" in Olson and Worsham (eds.), *Postmodern sophistry*, 270–1. See 272–3 for his application of this analysis to the American civil rights movement.

[141] *Trouble*, 41–2, 196.

[142] *No free speech*, 74. See too Fish, "Truth but no consequences," 415; Stanley Fish, "One more time" in Olson and Worsham (eds.), *Postmodern sophistry*, 270.

forms. That is, they cannot be achieved by rejecting or stepping outside all forms of local embeddedness, rather they can only be achieved from *within* some particular form of local embeddedness.

> [T]olerance (or, if you prefer, sympathy) is not a separate ability, a virtue with its own context-independent shape, but is rather a way of relating or attending whose shape depends on the commitments one already feels . . . One cannot *just* be tolerant; one is tolerant (or not) in the measure a given situation, complete with various pressures and with the histories of its participants, allows.[143]

Because toleration and openness will always be given a context-specific shape by the background that comes with that particular form of local embeddedness, any forms of toleration and openness will also *exclude* certain things from their scope. Such exceptions therefore do not negate the existence of toleration or openness, according to Fish, rather they make it possible:

> [M]y argument is not that abstractions like tolerance, impartiality, and mutual respect are *invalidated* by exceptions to them, but that they are *constituted* – made operational and doable – by exceptions. That is, they exist only in the form made available by the (prior) exceptions and do not exist in the strong or pure form often assumed by those who recommend them.[144]

So, just as the liberal neutral principle of religious freedom turned out to marginalize and exclude strong religious believers, so does the multicultural principle of toleration and the celebration of "difference and diversity mandate the exclusion from their circle of views alleging racial superiority or the immorality of homosexuals. Liberal neutrality and multiculturalism are both engines of exclusion trying to fly under inclusive banners."[145] Fish's analysis of toleration thus has the same structure as his analyses of neutrality, impartiality, objectivity, critical self-reflection, and freedom. He does not deny that these things exist, rather he points out that their existence presupposes a contingent, socially constructed background that shapes and limits them, even as it makes them possible.

In the piece where Fish makes his most sustained critique of the possibility of multicultural tolerance, he first identifies a weak version

---

[143] *No free speech*, 217.
[144] Stanley Fish, "One more time" in Olson and Worsham (eds.), *Postmodern sophistry*, 266. See generally 266–70; *No free speech*, 37, 251; *Trouble*, 65–9.
[145] *Trouble*, 44. See too 130–1.

of this goal that he calls "boutique multiculturalism."[146] Boutique multiculturalism, Fish claims, is the type manifested by liberals. It is characterized by a willingness to tolerate some aspects of other cultures, such as their food and music, but not others, such as their treatment of women. It is claimed that the disallowed aspects of the other culture are rejected not because they contradict the partisan values of the majority culture but because they violate more universal human values or rights. Boutique multiculturalism thus relies upon the distinction, critiqued in Part I, between characteristics that are essential to personhood and secondary or contingent features that are not essential to personhood. Cultural differences with respect to the secondary features can be tolerated by liberals, but it is not possible for them to tolerate cultural forms that do not respect the essential core that all humanity supposedly shares. By contrast, postmodern multicultural tolerance is called "strong multiculturalism" by Fish. This approach rejects the core/secondary feature distinction, and instead, it seeks to be tolerant of *all* aspects of the other culture. Indeed, it wants to encourage the flourishing of different cultures and is willing to afford different treatment to achieve this. "If the politics of equal dignity [i.e., liberalism] subordinates local cultural values to the universal value of free rational choice, the politics of difference names as its preferred value the active fostering of the unique distinctiveness of particular cultures."[147]

Fish rejects both of these versions of multiculturalism as impossible, and he argues that there is no alternative to uniculturalism. The liberal is a uniculturalist who fills the core/secondary feature distinction with a content that ensures that her culture's deepest values are categorized as core, and so are protected from challenges from other cultures. As for the postmodern strong multiculturalist, Fish asks: What will she do when some other culture that does not value toleration and diversity acts to assert its own core values and destroy those of its opponents? The strong multiculturalist can act to defend her values of toleration and diversity, in which case she ceases to respect the core values of the other culture (and reveals herself to have been a uniculturalist all along). Alternatively, she does not act, in which case she has accepted that the values of the other culture are trumps and has become a uniculturalist of a different kind.

> In the end neither the boutique multiculturalist nor the strong multiculturalist is able to come to terms with difference, although their inabilities

---

[146] Ibid., ch. 4. See too Olson, *Justifying belief*, 53–7.   [147] *Trouble*, 59.

are asymmetrical. The boutique multiculturalist does not take difference seriously because its marks (quaint clothing, atonal music, curious table manners) are for him matters of lifestyle, and as such they should not be allowed to overwhelm the substratum of rationality that makes us all brothers under the skin. The strong multiculturalist takes difference so seriously as a general principle that he cannot take any particular difference seriously, cannot allow its imperatives their full realization in a political program, for their full realization would inevitably involve the suppression of difference.[148]

Once again, Fish is insisting that there is no way for embedded beings to transcend their embeddedness. They cannot do other than live according to the values that grip and constitute them as a result of their particular form of local embeddedness, and so they cannot be other than uniculturalists. For postmodernists to believe otherwise is to succumb to antifoundationalist theory hope.

Pragmatism

Pragmatism is older than postmodernism and originated in America, rather than Europe (although pragmatism has European forebears and cousins[149]). In the late nineteenth and early twentieth centuries, Charles Peirce, William James, and John Dewey developed a philosophical approach characterized by both an acceptance of anti-foundationalism and a rejection of relativism.

The pragmatists have always been relentless in their criticism of all varieties of absolutism, foundationalism, and fundamentalism. But they have also rejected relativism and extreme skepticism. They have advanced an ideal of "concrete reasonableness." We can distinguish

---

[148] Ibid., 62.

[149] See Thomas Grey, "What good is legal pragmatism?" in Brint and Weaver (eds.), *Pragmatism*, 11 where he describes pragmatism as having two roots: "One is the Enlightenment empiricist positivism of the *philosophes* and the Benthamite radicals that came down from the eighteenth century. The other is the mix of nineteenth-century contributions to the synthesis: [Darwinian] evolutionary biology, [Hegelian] historicism, and Romanticism." See too Richard Rorty, "Pragmatism as polytheism" in Morris Dickstein {ed.}, *The revival of pragmatism. New essays on social thought, law, and culture* (Durham, NC: Duke University Press, 1998), 21 (hereafter cited as Dickstein (ed.), *The revival of pragmatism*). Rorty describes how in 1911 René Berthelot "traced the romantic roots of pragmatism back behind Emerson to Schelling and Hoelderlin, and the utilitarian roots to the influence of Darwin and Spencer. . . . Berthelot was probably the first to call Nietzsche 'a German pragmatist,' and the first to emphasize the resemblance between Nietzsche's perspectivism and the pragmatist theory of truth."

better and worse options, and we should try to support our convictions with the best available evidence and reasons.[150]

The traditional epistemological model, which required us to seek access to a foundational reality free of human distortions, was rejected. Instead, pragmatists claimed, the social practices humans have developed for warranting beliefs in different contexts are all we have and all we need to attain truth and establish facts.

> Dewey, following Peirce, held that the best way human beings had found to fix beliefs – or, as Dewey preferred to call them, "warranted assertions" – was by means of the methods, practices, and values of a community of competent inquirers, the best exemplification of which was the community of modern science. Such communities began their investigations under the stimulus of particular doubts within the context of a body of warranted assertions that they had no good reason to doubt. And they settled such particular doubts with warranted assertions that, like all warranted assertions, were not certain but fallible and subject to revision should fresh doubts about their warrant arise.[151]

There was a redirection of focus away from timeless universals and abstractions and toward consequences for actual human experience.[152] The importance of social/historical contexts and the role of communities of inquirers are both stressed, as is the need to adapt human thinking and practices to achieve success in environments that will be fluid and contingent. Consequently pragmatists urge

> a temper of mind that is open, innovative, experimental, free of imprisoning dogma . . . [T]hought is shaped and tested by its use in the pursuit of human ends . . . We pragmatists keep in the back of our minds the reminder that we are thinking to some end – thinking *instrumentally*. We also keep there a reminder that we are thinking against a background of tacit presuppositions of which we can never be fully aware – thinking *contextually*.[153]

---

[150] Richard Bernstein, "Community in the pragmatic tradition" in Dickstein (ed.), *The revival of pragmatism*, 154.

[151] Robert Westbrook, "Pragmatism and democracy: Reconstructing the logic of John Dewey's faith" in Dickstein (ed.), *The revival of pragmatism*, 131. See too Thomas Grey, "What good is legal pragmatism?" in Brint and Weaver (eds.), *Pragmatism*, 3–14.

[152] James Kloppenberg, "Pragmatism: An old name for some new ways of thinking?" in Dickstein (ed.), *The revival of pragmatism*, 85; Richard Posner, "What has pragmatism to offer law?" in Brint and Weaver (eds.), *Pragmatism*, 35–6.

[153] Thomas Grey, "What good is legal pragmatism?" in Brint and Weaver (eds.), *Pragmatism*, 14–5.

Because pragmatism rejects relativism, it is distinct from any "vulgar postmodernism" of the sort that Fish described earlier. However, its anti-foundationalism means that it could have affinities with sophisticated postmodernism, and these affinities have been stressed by modern "neo-pragmatists," such as Richard Rorty.[154]

Stanley Fish has explicitly identified himself as a philosophical pragmatist,[155] and he has engaged sympathetically with pragmatism in his contributions to *The revival of pragmatism*[156] and *Pragmatism in law and society*.[157] He has also described pragmatism positively in "Truth but no consequences: Why philosophy doesn't matter,"[158] "Theory minimalism,"[159] and in his commentary on Joseph Margolis's recent book, *Pragmatism's advantage*.[160] He endorses many of the key elements of pragmatist thought – the simultaneous acceptance of anti-foundationalism and rejection of relativism, the distrust of transcontextual abstractions and a focus on local contexts, the concern for consequences, the stress on the importance of communities of inquiry (or as Fish will call them, "interpretive communities") and their shared "background of tacit presuppositions." The description of pragmatism he provides here makes clear the affinities between that position and his own:

> If you say that something or someone is wrong, you will often be asked to provide a basis for your judgment that is independent of the social, political, and biographical circumstances in which it was formed. The thesis of this book has been that no such basis is available and that the ordinary resources that come along with your situation, education, and personal history are both all you have and all you need. There is a philosophy, or anti-philosophy, that takes much the same position. It is called pragmatism ... [A] pragmatist believes in the sufficiency of human

---

154 Morris Dickstein, "Pragmatism then and now" in Dickstein (ed.), *The revival of pragmatism*, 11. The legitimacy of Rorty's linkage between classical pragmatism and postmodernism has been questioned by some. See, for example, James Kloppenberg, "Pragmatism: An old name for some new ways of thinking?" in Dickstein (ed.), *The revival of pragmatism*, 95–100 and Robert Westbrook, "Pragmatism and democracy: Reconstructing the logic of John Dewey's faith" in Dickstein (ed.), *The revival of pragmatism*, 128–9.

155 Fish, "Theory Minimalism," 773.

156 Stanley Fish, "Truth and toilets: Pragmatism and the practices of life" in Dickstein (ed.), *The revival of pragmatism*, 418.

157 Stanley Fish, "Almost pragmatism: The jurisprudence of Richard Posner, Richard Rorty, and Ronald Dworkin" in Brint and Weaver (eds.), *Pragmatism*, 47.

158 Fish, "Truth but no consequences," 405–17.   159 Fish, "Theory Minimalism," 773–6.

160 See Stanley Fish, "Pragmatism's Gift" in his *New York Times* Opinionator Blog, March 15, 2010.

practices and is not dismayed when those practices are shown to be grounded in nothing more (or less) than their own traditions and histories. The impossibility of tying our everyday meanings and values to meanings and values less local does not lead the pragmatist to suspect their reality, but to suspect the form of thought that would deny it. When the dream of finding invariant meanings underwritten by God or the structure of rationality is exploded, what remains is not dust and ashes but the solidity *and* plasticity of the world human beings continually make and remake.[161]

However, there is one important aspect of pragmatist and neo-pragmatist thought that Fish rejects and that is its claimed political consequences.[162] An explicit linkage between pragmatist philosophy and a political program was present from the beginning:

> James and Dewey considered their pragmatism inseparable from their commitment to democracy as an ethical ideal. Both believed that their challenges to inherited philosophical dualisms and absolutes, their conception of truth as fluid and culturally created, and their belief that all experience is meaningful were consistent only with democracy, specifically with the principles of social equality and individual autonomy.[163]

As noted earlier, Dewey adopted Peirce's notion of a community of competent inquirers who develop methods and procedures to evaluate competing claims and establish truths. The community of modern science was the prime model of this, but Dewey extended the description to all areas of life. For a community of inquirers to work properly, he believed, the full and free participation of all competent members was necessary. So in dealing with social or political problems, as opposed to scientific ones, the full and free participation of all citizens was

---

[161] *Trouble*, 293–4. See too Fish, "Truth but no consequences," 405–6 where Fish notes the assumption of Habermas "that the norms and standards built into everyday practices are deficient and in need of support from transcontextual norms and standards. This, however, is the very assumption contested so vigorously by the pragmatist/postmodernist thinkers against whom he writes. Their thesis is that the norms and standards to which we have an unreflective recourse most of the time are by and large up to their job, which is not the job of being transcontextual and universal, but the job of helping us in our efforts to cope with and make sense of the exigencies of mortal life and to shape and alter those exigencies in accordance with our human needs."

[162] For a concurring opinion that draws upon Fish for support, see Michael Brint, William G. Weaver, and Meredith Garmon, "What difference does anti-foundationalism make to political theory?" 26 *New Literary History*, (1995) 225.

[163] James Kloppenberg, "Pragmatism: An old name for some new ways of thinking?" in Dickstein (ed.), *The revival of pragmatism*, 100. See generally 100–3.

necessary. Dewey was therefore a strong advocate of participatory or deliberative democracy on epistemological grounds:

> Dewey argued that a community of inquiry should be democratic, not (in this case) on ethical grounds, but on what Putnam terms "cognitive" grounds. That is, the quality of inquiry is affected by the degree to which that community is inclusive or exclusive of all the potential, competent participants in that inquiry and by the democratic or undemocratic character of the norms that guide its practice.[164]

The strong linkage between classical pragmatism and democracy is also maintained by many modern pragmatists, such as Richard Bernstein, Robert Westbrook, Hilary Putnam, and James Kloppenberg.[165]

By contrast, the modern pragmatist Richard Rorty rejects any claim that pragmatism entails democracy or any particular political position. "I do not think that there is an inferential path that leads from the antirepresentationalist view of truth and knowledge common to Nietzsche, James, and Dewey to either democracy or antidemocracy."[166] We have already noted his observation that "[n]o argument leads from a coherence view of truth, an anti-representational view of knowledge, and an anti-formalist view of law and morals, to Dewey's left-looking social prophesies. The Heidegger of *Being and Time* shared all these views, but Heidegger looked rightward and dreamed different dreams."[167] Although he argues that pragmatism does not *require* liberal democracy, Rorty does acknowledge that there has been a strong contingent connection between pragmatism and the progressive political tradition in America.

> [I]n American intellectual life, "pragmatism" has stood for more than just a set of controversial philosophical arguments about truth, knowledge, and theory. It has also stood for a visionary tradition to which, as it happened, a few philosophy professors once made particularly important

---

[164] Robert Westbrook, "Pragmatism and democracy: Reconstructing the logic of John Dewey's faith" in Dickstein (ed.), *The revival of pragmatism*, 131. See too Richard Bernstein, "Community in the pragmatic tradition" in Dickstein (ed.), *The revival of pragmatism*, 149.

[165] Morris Dickstein, "Pragmatism then and now" in Dickstein (ed.), *The revival of pragmatism*, 1, 13; James Kloppenberg, "Pragmatism: An old name for some new ways of thinking?" in Dickstein (ed.), *The revival of pragmatism*, 83, 111.

[166] Richard Rorty, "Pragmatism as polytheism" in Dickstein (ed.), *The revival of pragmatism*, 27. See too 25.

[167] Richard Rorty, "The banality of pragmatism and the poetry of justice" in Brint and Weaver (eds.), *Pragmatism*, 92.

contributions – a tradition to which some judges, lawyers, and law
professors still make important contributions. These are the ones who,
in their opinions, briefs, or articles, enter into what Unger calls "open-
ended disputes about the basic terms of social life."[168]

Rorty himself is sympathetic to this progressive liberal tradition.[169]
In *Contingency, irony, and solidarity*, he describes how an anti-
foundationalist can defend liberal society without trying to find philosophical foundations for it. He suggests that such defenders become
"liberal ironists," who are "never quite able to take themselves seriously
because [they are] always aware that the terms in which they describe
themselves are subject to change, always aware of the contingency and
fragility of their final vocabularies, and thus of themselves."[170] His ideal
liberal society is one

> whose hero is the strong poet and the revolutionary because it recognizes
> that it is what it is, has the morality it has, speaks the language it does, not
> because it approximates the will of God or the nature of man but because
> certain poets and revolutionaries of the past spoke as they did. To see
> one's language, one's conscience, one's morality, and one's highest hopes
> as contingent products, as literalizations of what once were accidentally
> produced metaphors, is to adopt a self-identity which suits one for
> citizenship in such an ideally liberal state ... They would be liberal
> ironists – people who met Schumpeter's criterion of civilization, people
> who combined commitment with a sense of the contingency of their own
> commitment.[171]

Fish, however, rejects any attempt by pragmatists to draw non-
philosophical consequences from their philosophical analysis. He makes
this point by distinguishing between a pragmatist *account* of our situation and a pragmatist *program*.

---

[168] Ibid., 95. See too Morris Dickstein, "Pragmatism then and now" in Dickstein (ed.), *The revival of pragmatism*, 3: "In Dewey's work as a active reformer and prolific theorist, pragmatism became part of the surge of liberalism, progressivism, and social reform in the first decades of the twentieth century."

[169] See James Kloppenberg, "Pragmatism: An old name for some new ways of thinking?" in Dickstein (ed.), *The revival of pragmatism*, 104 where he says Rorty "has repeatedly characterized the culture and institutions of liberal democracy as a precious achievement and endorsed the social democratic program that has been at the heart of pragmatic political activism since the days of James and Dewey."

[170] Rorty, *Contingency, irony, and solidarity*, 73–4. See too xv.

[171] Ibid., 61. See too 84.

A pragmatist *account* of the law speaks to the question of how the law works and gives what I think to be the right answer: the law works not by identifying and then hewing to some overarching set of principles, or logical calculus, or authoritative revelation, but by deploying a set of ramshackle and heterogeneous resources in an effort to reach political resolution of disputes that must be framed (this is the law's requirements and the public's desire) in apolitical and abstract terms (fairness, equality, what justice requires) ... A pragmatist *program* asks the question "what follows from the pragmatist account?" and then gives an answer, but by giving an answer pragmatism is unfaithful to its own first principle (which is to have none) and turns unwittingly into the foundationalism and essentialism it rejects.[172]

There are four related reasons why Fish holds that no pragmatist program can follow from a pragmatist account.[173] First, philosophical pragmatism endorses anti-foundationalism and claims that this epistemology is necessarily rather than contingently true. So if pragmatism is correct, then everyone has always been acting as the pragmatic account describes and could not have been doing otherwise. Hence a pragmatist cannot consistently urge people to act in a more pragmatic fashion. Second, pragmatism's anti-foundationalism claims that human beings are necessarily embedded and constituted by their local embeddedness, as described in Part I. It would be inconsistent to give an account of human beings as necessarily embedded and also to claim that realizing this truth frees human beings to act in a more pragmatic way that was not constrained by their forms of local embeddedness. Third, the autonomy of practices defended at the end of Part I means that positions taken while practicing philosophy have no necessary consequences for other practices and that applies to pragmatist philosophical positions.

> [Y]our philosophical views are independent of your views (and therefore of your practices) in any realm of life other than the very special and rarified realm of doing philosophy. If you believe that your convictions have their source not in ultimate truths or foundations but in contingent traditions of inquiry and are therefore revisable, that belief, in and of itself, will not render you disposed to revise your convictions or turn you into a person who enters into situations provisionally and with epistemic modesty. You can give all the standard answers to all the pragmatist questions

---

[172] *No free speech*, 209. See too 215, 218; Schanck, "Understanding postmodern thought" 2564–6.

[173] For a different account of Fish's arguments for this claim, see Kathryn Abrams, "The unbearable lightness of being Stanley Fish" 47 *Stanford Law Review* (1995) 600–5, 610–1.

and still be an authoritarian in the classroom, a decided conservative in cultural matters, or inclined to the absolutes of theology. (I am, in differing degrees, all three.)[174]

Fourth, on the philosophical pragmatist account, there are no overarching, trans-contextual principles. All purported principles in fact presuppose and advance some local and contestable background commitments. (This is what *The trouble with principle* was devoted to showing.) Therefore, it would be inconsistent to claim that pragmatism can generate some overarching, trans-contextual principle, such as Rorty's "principle of ever more tolerant inquirers" and Posner's "principle of undistorted empirical inquiry."[175]

These criticisms would catch all those who try to connect pragmatist philosophy with democracy[176] or any other political position. The feminist legal scholar Margaret Jane Radin writes that "[t]he best critical spirit of pragmatism recommends that we take our present descriptions [of the world] with humility and openness, and accept their institutional embodiments as provisional and incompletely entrenched."[177] This sounds like the postmodernist injunction, encountered earlier, to embrace, rather than fear, contingency and provisionality in our political practices. Fish's response is that both the postmodernist and the pragmatist injunctions are manifestations of "anti-foundationalist theory hope," and that such hope contradicts the conception of the socially constructed, necessarily embedded self that is part of anti-foundationalism. Necessarily embedded selves remain so even after they have become convinced of the truth of anti-foundationalism. This means that their constituting and enabling background beliefs remain in place and grip them just as tightly as before. Similarly, Fish argues,

> [w]hen Cornel West asks of Richard Rorty, "What are the ethical and political consequences of adopting his neo-pragmatism?" the answer is, "none necessarily," although in certain circumstances the proclaiming of pragmatist views might have political effects of an unpredictable kind. West wonders how an argument like Rorty's can "kick the philosophical props from under bourgeois capitalist societies and require no change in our cultural practices." The explanation is simple: bourgeois capitalist

---

[174] *Trouble*, 300. See too 302–3; *No free speech*, 197, 215; Fish, "Truth but no consequences," 416.

[175] *No free speech*, 218.   [176] *Trouble*, 300–1.

[177] Margaret Jane Radin, "The pragmatist and the feminist" in Brint and Weaver (eds.), *Pragmatism*, 149.

societies are not propped up by philosophy, but by the material conditions of everyday life – by the means of production, by the patterns of domestic relations, by the control and dissemination of information, etc. It is when those conditions are altered or removed that the cultural practices of bourgeois capitalist society will tremble; all that will tremble when the hit parade of theory undergoes a change is the structure of philosophy departments.[178]

Even Rorty himself, who denied that pragmatism entailed democracy, falls into the error of deriving a pragmatist program from a pragmatist account, according to Fish. Rorty still thinks that you can carry your philosophical positions with you into other contexts where your anti-foundationalism can enable you to act as an "ironist" who is aware of the contingency and provisionality of your commitments and so you are no longer as fully gripped by those commitments. Rorty also advances the hope "that if people would only stop trying to come up with a standard of absolute right which could then be used to denigrate the beliefs and efforts of *other* people, they might spend more time sympathetically engaging with those beliefs and learning to appreciate those efforts."[179] They would become better at identifying with others and avoiding cruelty and the humiliation of others. They would be able to sympathize more with the marginalized and efface the line between "us" and "them," thus creating a more expansive sense of solidarity.

> It is Rorty's hope ... that if "pragmatism were taken seriously" – if we conceived of ourselves as creatures clinging together in a foundationless world rather than as philosophers in search of a foundation – we might cease experiencing life as a fight and we would be less likely to confront one another across firmly drawn lines of battle.[180]

Fish admits that this is an attractive vision, but he insists that it does not follow from taking pragmatism seriously. By thinking that it does, Rorty

> confuse[s] a pragmatist account with a pragmatist program and thereby fail[s] to distinguish between pragmatism as a truth we are all living *out* and pragmatism as a truth we might be able to live *by*. We are all living *out* pragmatism because we live in a world bereft of transcendent truths and leakproof logics, (although some may exist in a realm veiled from us) and therefore must make do with the ragtag bag of metaphors, analogies, rules of thumb, inspirational phrases, incantations, and jerry-built "reasons" that keep the conversation going and bring it to temporary, and always revisable, conclusions; but we could only live by pragmatism if

---

[178] *Doing*, 28.   [179] *No free speech*, 216.   [180] Ibid., 218.

we could grasp the pragmatist insight – that there are no universals or self-executing methods or self-declaring texts in sight – and make it into something positive, use an awareness of contingency as a way either of mastering it or perfecting it (in which case it would no longer be contingency), turn ourselves (by design rather than as the creatures of history) into something new.[181]

However, Fish is well aware that his fellow pragmatists seem incapable of grasping that it is inconsistent to derive a pragmatist program from a pragmatist account.[182] He acknowledges that his own

> parsimonious view of pragmatism's imperatives is not one shared by most self-identified pragmatists, who tend to turn the pragmatist withdrawal from strong claims into a strong claim of their own, the claim that pragmatism, if adhered to, leads to forms of behavior that make the world a better place and you a better person: kinder, gentler, more respectful of others, and less likely to hold it against someone that his beliefs are not yours.[183]

---

[181] Ibid., 218. For a similar criticism of Rorty see Fish, "Truth but no consequences," 416ff.

[182] One critic argues that Fish himself fails to respect this distinction, which shows the impossibility of pragmatism as a coherent position. See Sotirios A. Barber, "Stanley Fish and the future of pragmatism in legal theory" 58 *The University of Chicago Law Review* (1991) 1033.

[183] *Trouble*, 299.

5

Political substance

Fish's claim that there is no necessary connection between his philosophical analysis and any substantive political positions

We have seen Fish argue that, because of the autonomy of practices, there is no necessary connection between any philosophical analysis and any substantive political position, and he rigorously applies this claim to his own work:

> [M]y own reticence about the views I hold on the substantive issues glanced at in my writings is not only defensible but required. Owen reports correctly (but in a tone of criticism and complaint) that it is "impossible to determine from his critique of liberalism what Fish is for ... We can say for sure only that he is against liberalism." I receive this not as the statement of a lack, of something missing, but as a report by an acute and informed reader that I have been consistent in my argument and have not made the mistake of drawing from it conclusions (about particular vexed matters) it does not warrant or authorize. Like the antifoundationalism I explicate, I am not – *at least not when I am being that explicator* – in the business of taking positions on substantive disputes; rather, I am in the business of telling those who are in the midst of those disputes that if they seek aid or clarification from some neutral mechanism of adjudication and judgment, they will not find it ... That does not mean, of course, that I do not have substantive views, only that, as Owen's experience demonstrates, you are not going to be able to deduce what they are from what I say about the superiority of antifoundationalism as an argument.[1]

Fish's own substantive political positions

I have italicized an important qualification in the above quotation that acknowledges that although philosophy and politics are autonomous

---

[1] Stanley Fish, "A reply to J. Judd Owen" 93 *The American Political Science Review* (1999) 929 (hereafter cited as Fish, "Reply to Owen"). Emphasis added. See too *Trouble*, 8, 82, 113–4.

practices, there is nothing preventing the same person engaging in each of these distinct practices at different times. Even if we accept that philosophical analysis does not have any necessary implications for politics, does Fish sometimes stop doing philosophical analysis and start doing politics? The answer to that question is yes, but only rarely.[2] Here are some brief sketches of Fish's personal political positions that can be found in his writings:

> I am ... guilty of not being on the left (although the right has no interest in claiming me). I can't see why it matters, but for the record I am what used to be known as a Skip Jackson–Bobby Kennedy democrat – fairly progressive on social issues, fairly conservative on economic issues, and decidedly conservative on foreign policy issues.[3]

> Suppose that you believe (as I in fact do) that policies favoring racial discrimination have no place on the political agenda, and believe too that if a state or the nation should turn in the direction of theocracy, it would be a bad thing.[4]

> I am in favor of affirmative action and gay and lesbian rights; but I do not support abortion rights (although what I would support in this vexed area is not clear to me), and I disfavor speech codes only in those contexts where the good they do (by my lights) will be outweighed by the trouble and litigation they produce.[5]

The first thing to note about these descriptions is that they do not peg Fish to any constant point on the political spectrum. He is substantively "progressive" on some issues and substantively "conservative" on others. However, those of his substantive political beliefs that he actually defends in his writings and other activities tend to fall into the "progressive" category.[6] A number of times he indicates his support for feminism as a social and political movement,[7] and he energetically defends the

---

[2] Stanley Fish, "One more time" in G. Olson and L. Worsham (eds.), *Postmodern sophistry. Stanley Fish and the critical enterprise* (Albany: State University of New York Press, 2004), 288–9 (hereafter cited as Olson and Worsham [eds.], *Postmodern sophistry*). I therefore disagree with Kathryn Abrams when she claims that by taking political positions Fish is undermining his position that no political consequences follow from anti-foundationalism. See Kathryn Abrams, "The unbearable lightness of being Stanley Fish" 47 *Stanford Law Review* (1995) 611–4.

[3] Stanley Fish, "One more time" in Olson and Worsham (eds.), *Postmodern sophistry*, 265.

[4] *Trouble*, 203–4.   [5] Ibid., 285.

[6] See the account of Fish's activities described in Peter Schanck, "Understanding postmodern thought and its implications for statutory interpretation" 65 *Southern California Law Review* (1991) 2556–7 (hereafter cited as Schanck, "Understanding postmodern thought").

[7] *Trouble*, 7; *Doing*, 20–1; *No free speech*, 294–5.

humanities and the universities against the attacks of conservatives in the "culture wars."[8] He is equally energetic in his defense of affirmative action,[9] and because his argument seems to generate tensions with other areas of his work, I will explore his position on this particular issue in more depth.

Fish identifies two groups of people opposing affirmative action. One group is composed of people who hold racist beliefs (even if they will not admit this publicly) and who therefore do not want outcomes in which black people are advantaged. They want outcomes in which white people are advantaged.[10] Another group is composed of liberals[11] who are committed to supposedly neutral principles such as "law and society should be color-blind," and who therefore do not want outcomes in which one race is deliberately targeted for better or worse treatment than any other. Both groups therefore reject any outcome in which white people are deliberately treated less well than black people. However, the liberal group believes that it can reject affirmative action on principled grounds, while simultaneously rejecting the substantive racist beliefs of the first group. Fish's disagreement with the racist group is straightforward – he describes their position as "unpersuasive and repellent"[12] – but his critique of the liberal group is more subtle and interesting. Fish's critique, as noted earlier, is that all liberal neutral principles have a natural tendency to become very abstract as they seek to rise above the local and particular in search of the universal and timeless. But this process of abstraction means that they lose their grip on concrete situations.

> My argument is that when such words and phrases [as "color-blind"] are invoked, it is almost always as part of an effort to deprive moral and legal problems of their histories so that merely formal calculations can then be performed on phenomena that have been flattened out and no longer have their real-world shape.[13]

---

[8] See No free speech, chs. 1–3 and 92–8.

[9] Fish gives a nice summary of the arguments against affirmative action and his responses to them in Trouble, 29–33. For a short account of his position on affirmative action, see Richard Delgado, "Where's my body? Stanley Fish's long goodbye to law" 99 Michigan Law Review (2001) 1371–5.

[10] Fish describes such people in No free speech, ch. 6 ("Bad Company").

[11] Here Fish is not using "liberal" in the sense of someone who is left of center on the existing political spectrum. Instead Fish means "liberal" in the broader sense of someone who is committed to the existence of neutral principles. This description would cover both classical and modern liberals, and Fish argues that it is this commitment that causes all liberals problems when thinking about affirmative action.

[12] No free speech, 75.   [13] Ibid., viii.

Fish argues that the local and particular context that is crucial for understanding the color-blind principle in America is the history of the involuntary transportation and enslavement of black people by white people in that country. If that historical context is kept firmly in mind (or, more accurately, becomes a part of the assumed background that enables the mind), then the color-blind principle will not lose its grip on concrete situations, because it will be understood as working to remedy the systematic and institutionalized racism that for centuries allowed white Americans to oppress and demean black Americans. But, Fish argues, instead of understanding the principle against the background of this concrete history, the natural tendency of liberals is to abstract away from the local circumstances that generated the principle in order to seek a more neutral and universal principle that sits high above any particular historical context. As a consequence, liberals either accept, or are greatly troubled by, claims that the color-blind principle is not specifically directed at American slavery and its effects but instead prohibits the use of any racial categorization to justify different treatment in every imaginable context. The result of this abstraction from history, Fish charges, is that the color-blind principle comes to be understood in a way that blocks affirmative action to remedy the effects of slavery. Indeed, any such action is now categorized as "reverse discrimination" on the grounds that "any action tinged with race-consciousness is equivalent to any other action tinged with race-consciousness, an assertion that makes sense only if historical differences are dissolved in the solvent of a leveling abstraction."[14]

However, Fish's charge that the American liberal color-blind principle has succeeded in abstracting away from the historical context that generated it seems to be in tension with other aspects of his thought that we have encountered earlier. For example, we have seen him argue in Part I that no human thinking is possible without an assumed context, or background, already in place, so how can liberals have principles that are genuinely detached from any historical context?

> If it is the first thesis of historicism that no human gesture can be either produced or received independently of some context of historical understanding, then the one thing a human being . . . cannot be is unhistorical. That is, it is impossible to *not* historicize, impossible to conceive of an event or a text independently of some notion of its origin, genealogical affiliations, generic habitation, etc.[15]

---

[14] *Trouble*, 6–7. See generally 4–7, 24–9, 42–3, 290–1, 310; *No free speech*, viii–ix.
[15] *No free speech*, 259.

Similarly, Fish has argued in Part I that abstract principles can do no work in the world if they are truly abstract. They can only do such work if they have been filled with some partisan substance, even if this is unacknowledged. So if the liberal color-blind principle has the real-world effect of blocking affirmative action, it follows that it cannot be completely abstract and must conceal some partisan substance.

There are two ways for Fish to respond to this objection. One way is to admit that as a philosophical matter, anti-foundationalism teaches us that it is impossible to have a truly abstract political principle that does not assume some particular context or substance. But, politically, it is a good rhetorical move to accuse your opponent of just such excessive abstraction. That is, if you can make the claim stick that your opponent is lost in an unreal world of principles so abstract as to be empty, and consequently is unable to act in a way that takes account of obvious and important facts, then you will have damaged him. We see this move made, for example, when academics are accused of "living in an ivory tower." Fish could claim that his critique of the liberal opponents of affirmative action falls into this category; he is making a rhetorical move against them as a political partisan rather than as a philosopher.

Another response is to stick with the practice of philosophy, rather than the practice of partisan politics, and seek to describe (or deconstruct) the actual background that is being assumed by the liberal opponents of affirmative action when they wield the "color-blind" principle. Following this second strategy, Fish would accept that they must be operating with a background historical context in mind, albeit not the one that Fish (as a political actor) judges to be the correct one. Perhaps, instead of assuming the history of slavery in America as the background context, they are assuming the context of the rise of liberalism in opposition to medieval political and social systems. This history involved rejecting the notion of a natural or God-given hierarchical social order, and embracing the idea of one law that applied to all equally, rather than different laws for different social strata. This history also involved accepting the idea that individuals should be able to rise as far as their talents and efforts will take them, without being held in place by birth and tradition. With this egalitarian and meritocratic narrative forming part of the assumed background, liberals could, without any bad faith, naturally see the color-blind principle as requiring the rejection of affirmative action.[16] This analysis of the liberal principle is consistent with Fish's philosophical anti-foundationalism, because it accepts that some background context is always assumed and in place. However, it does not engage with the political question of which background context *should* be assumed and in place (a question upon which Fish has taken a stand), and how that is to be achieved. I will defer consideration of such questions until the next chapter on political practice.

The objection that some substantive political positions do follow from Fish's philosophical analysis

We have seen Fish emphatically deny that there is any necessary connection between the positions he (or anyone) takes while doing philosophy and the substantive positions he (or anyone) takes while doing politics. However, many of his commentators do not accept this. They are convinced that, whether Fish is aware of it or not, his philosophical analyses have political implications. For example, Reed Way Dasenbrock argues that Fish's philosophical anti-foundationalism must at least have the negative consequence of depriving him of the ability to make absolute and universalistic claims in the areas of morality and politics, and so when Fish does make such claims he is being Machiavellian.[17] The by now familiar reasoning is that if everything is socially constructed, then every claim is valid only within a particular cultural context, and so cannot genuinely be believed by an anti-foundationalist to be absolutely or universally true. This position is echoed by J. Judd Owen when he endorses Sanford Levinson's concern in *Constitutional Faith* that anti-foundationalism may lead to "the death of constitutionalism."

> By this Levinson means the ever more widespread loss of faith that our liberal constitutional principles are grounded in timeless and universally valid truths. Liberals who have been touched by antifoundationalism are less confident, if they do not deny, that liberal institutions are necessarily the best path for all countries, regardless of their history, culture, religion, and so forth.[18]

---

[16] *Trouble*, 206: "There are no cynics in my scenario, only persons whose strongly held beliefs and commitments lead them to understand, and understand sincerely, notions like equality, fairness, and neutrality in one way rather than another."

[17] Reed Way Dasenbrock, "The trouble with (arguing against) principle: Stanley Fish's incomplete Machiavellianism" in Olson and Worsham (eds.), *Postmodern sophistry*, 127–41.

[18] J. Judd Owen, "Church and state in Stanley Fish's antiliberalism" 93 *The American Political Science Review* (1999) 912 (hereafter cited as Owen, "Church and state").

But in his reply to Owen, Fish insists that all those who argue this way have misunderstood the nature of anti-foundationalism:

> What I take to be Owen's mistakes flow in part from his conflating of two assertions that I regard as distinct, and one of which I regard as false. The first (and true) assertion is that our convictions and beliefs cannot be grounded in any independent source of authority and validation, that is, in any neutral principle, impartial algorithm, master interpretive rule, sacred text, unimpeachable authority, and so on. The second (and false) assertion is that our convictions and beliefs are ungrounded. The second assertion would follow from (or necessarily accompany) the first only if the first were understood to deny the availability of all grounds rather than the unavailability of independent grounds.[19]

Fish says to Owen (and Dasenbrock[20]) what we have already seen him assert in Chapter 2 on epistemology: We are not deprived of good and sufficient grounds for our truth claims by anti-foundationalism. Those grounds are made available to us by our already existing traditions and disciplines. You will only think such grounds to be defective or second-best if you think that human beings could experience reality the way that God does. Nor are we deprived of the ability to assert our truth claims in an absolute or universal fashion by anti-foundationalism. All we are deprived of is a mechanism (such as reason, authority, or revelation) by means of which we can compel others to see the truths that we do.

> People confuse relativism with the statement that there is no overarching or neutral or transcendent perspective from the vantage point of which disputes between well-informed antagonists can be settled. That turns out in the minds of many people to be relativism, but it's *not* relativism, because it doesn't say that there are *no* truths or *no* facts of the matter. I firmly believe that there *are* truths and facts of the matter. It says, rather, that there are no mechanisms available for certainly or absolutely settling disputes between persons equally credentialed who have opposing senses of the truth or the facts of the matter ... [One can simultaneously] say, "I believe this to be absolutely true, not just true for me or true because of my education and background," and also say, "I acknowledge that the absolute truth of this may not be able to be demonstrated in ways that

---

At 919, Owen writes that Fish's "antifoundationalism ... weakens our moral commitments, or at any rate gives us pause."

[19] Fish, "Reply to Owen," 925. See too 926–7; *Trouble*, 125, 280–1; Stanley Fish, "Truth but no consequences: Why philosophy doesn't matter" 29 *Critical Inquiry* (2003) 406 (hereafter cited as Fish, "Truth but no consequences").

[20] Stanley Fish, "One more time" in Olson and Worsham (eds.), *Postmodern sophistry*, 274, 286.

would be immediately accepted by all rational beings." . . . They are in no way in tension with one another.[21]

Finally, the fact that no mechanism is available that is guaranteed to make others accept our truths is no reason for us to doubt our truths, Fish argues. "[T]his unavailability is a problem only if one clings to the foundationalist assumption that the only certainty worth having is a certainty ratified by everyone in relation to a norm independent of anyone"[22] – a norm that Fish has argued is neither attainable nor conceivable by necessarily embedded human beings.

So anti-foundationalism does not have the necessary consequence that we must assert our substantive political commitments less absolutely and more tentatively. Dasenbrock and Owen think this consequence would be a bad thing, while postmodernists, as we saw in the previous chapter, think this consequence would be a good thing, but Fish denies that it is a consequence at all. However, Fish laments,

> Owen simply cannot hear this point, in part because his questions and criticisms always presuppose foundationalism's insistence that without foundations of the kind it seeks, knowledge will be shaky and conviction unfounded (either objective foundations or quick-sand). Within this presupposition – which makes its way into his sentences and infects his vocabulary – the alternative to the absence of independent grounds must be relativism and uncertainty. But it is precisely antifoundationalism's argument, as I have already stated several times, that there are other grounds, that these other grounds are always and already ours, and that they are sufficient.[23]

Another challenge to Fish's claim that his philosophical analyses have no necessary implications for politics is made by those who charge Fish with being either a crypto-liberal or conservative. Owen is one who claims that Fish's philosophical position makes him into a kind of liberal:

> [Fish's] antifoundationalism assumes a posture of perfect neutrality with respect to the variety of beliefs. In this respect it mirrors the liberalism it criticizes. The fact that Fish's writing stands above the fray of the conflict among commitments shows that it occupies a space created by liberalism. Fish does not adequately recognize that his antifoundationalism rests entirely on liberal presuppositions. Thus, however antiliberal his aims may be, he remains in the grip of liberalism in subtle yet powerful ways.[24]

---

[21] Interview with Stanley Fish in Gary Olson, *Justifying belief. Stanley Fish and the work of rhetoric* (Albany: State University of New York Press, 2002), 128–9 (hereafter cited as Olson, *Justifying belief*).

[22] Fish, "Reply to Owen," 927.   [23] Ibid.   [24] Owen, "Church and state," 920, 923.

The claim is that from the vantage point of anti-foundationalism, all belief systems have the same epistemological status, and so an anti-foundationalist views them all with neutrality, as a true liberal should.

Fish replies that it is a mistake to think that an anti-foundationalist is, or can be, neutral on the question of which morality or account of reason and truth is the correct one in any particular real-life context. His argument has two parts. First, when anti-foundationalists are developing their position as part of a philosophical practice, they are not concerned with any real-life contexts, because philosophy abstracts away from them. (The discipline of philosophy has its own special enabling context, as we saw in Part I.) So here the anti-foundationalist's silence on real-life contexts does not signify neutrality on the question of which belief system should rule in those contexts but rather a refusal to consider such contexts at all.

> Antifoundationalism is not "above the fray of the conflict among commitments" (a formulation that puts it into a relationship with that conflict), it is in another fray, the fray between it and foundationalism. About that fray it has plenty to say, but about any other fray it is silent (not neutral).[25]

Second, when you cease arguing for anti-foundationalism against foundationalism and leave the philosophy seminar room to enter some other context, the local commitments that enable and structure your performance and perceptions in that other context will be engaged. Because you will be acting as an extension of these partisan beliefs and values, you cannot be neutral in the strong sense liberals desire, and you will have very definite views about which morality or account of reason and truth is the correct one.

> [I]f you were to ask me: "Can you draw a bright line between the moral and the immoral that is not hostage to the morality or comprehensive doctrine of some person or group?" My answer to that question is "no," and from that answer it does follow that on the general (not linked to any actual moral issue) level on which the question is posed, the choice is between alternative moralities. But that is because the choice, as posed, is without content, has not yet been filled in with specifics and therefore provides no moral handles to grasp, one way or the other. (It is not a moral choice, but a choice between the foundationalist and antifoundationalist pictures.) Once the specifics are provided (affirmative action: for or against? assisted suicide: for or against? term limits: for or against? hate

---

[25] Fish, "Reply to Owen," 929.

speech regulation: for or against?), the moral convictions an agent already has will kick in (it is precisely the point of the general question to suspend or bracket them), and that agent will quite readily affirm, and affirm without metaphysical doubts, one pole as the moral one and condemn the other pole as the immoral one.[26]

Other commentators judge that Fish is a crypto-conservative rather than a liberal.[27] It might seem that Fish must be a conservative because he rejects liberalism. But the fact that Fish rejects liberalism as a coherent *philosophical* position does not compel him to take a conservative stand on substantive *political* issues. As we have seen, he has rejected conservative stands in favor of those that would be called liberal or progressive, such as supporting feminism and gay rights. Again, politics and philosophy are autonomous and distinct practices.

It might seem that Fish must be a conservative because he rejects the critical theory project, which was often tied to the hope of progressive social change. Fish sometimes willfully invites this charge:

> I think it is fair to say that I have come out on the "right" end of the spectrum every time, arguing against the liberationist claims often associated with deconstruction and some versions of feminism, against the political pretensions of the New Historicism, against the utopian vision of interdisciplinarity, against the revisionary program of the Critical Legal Studies movement, the left wing of the legal academy.[28]

But the fact that Fish rejects critical theory as a coherent philosophical position does not mean that he rejects the possibility of progressive social change. All it means is that he is rejecting one account of how that change could be brought about. "I do not argue against radical change, but against the possibility that radical change, of either a feared or desired kind, will be brought about by a theory."[29] If progressive social change happens, Fish argues, it will be because those desiring such change have

---

[26] Ibid., 928.

[27] See, for example, Terry Eagleton, "The estate agent: Stanley Fish and his trouble with principles" in Olson and Worsham (eds.), *Postmodern sophistry*, 181; Andrew Goldsmith, "Is there any backbone in this Fish? Interpretive communities, social criticism, and transgressive legal practice" 23 *Law & Social Inquiry* (1998) 373; Allan Hutchinson, "Part of an essay on power and interpretation (with suggestions on how to make bouillabaisse)" 60 *New York University Law Review* (1985) 860–1, 873–4, 881–5. Schanck, "Understanding postmodern thought" 2548 n172 provides a list of other critics making this charge of conservatism. Another such list can be found in John E. Morrison, "Doing Fish: A review of *There's no such thing as free speech*" 43 *UCLA Law Review* (1995) 539 n127.

[28] *No free speech*, 53.   [29] *Doing*, 27.

engaged in the kinds of context-sensitive political practices discussed in the next chapter.

> I'm just saying that if you are looking for ways in which to underwrite your activism, then you're not going to find it in these large abstractions, and you're not going to find it in an argument like mine against these large abstractions. You're going to find it in whatever urgencies and imperatives seem compelling to you in the empirical context that led you to be a political worker in the first place. But people don't see that and they think that I'm arguing for quietism.[30]

Finally, it might seem that Fish must be a conservative because his analysis cannot allow for change, and thus valorizes the status quo. This charge of hermeticism or stasis arises because of Fish's philosophical positions as described in Part I. First, Fish argues that a person is embedded within particular communities (societal, familial, institutional, disciplinary), and becomes a "moving extension" of community commitments. That is, those institution-specific commitments fill and structure the person's consciousness, simultaneously constraining them and enabling them to perform as a competent member of the community. But this picture seems to rule out critical reflection by members of the community on the deep commitments of the community itself.[31] Second, the thesis of the autonomy of practices claims that each practice has its own jobs and enabling background of beliefs, values, organizing categories, etc. It seems to follow that any practice will be resistant, perhaps impervious, to inputs from outside practices with different backgrounds. The result seems to be that a group of people engaged in the same distinctive practice and who share the background that enables that practice will be a closed community, which resists outside influences that might bring about change. But these objections fail because Fish does have a rich account of change.[32] I have already introduced his account when considering how beliefs change at the end of Chapter 2 and when

---

[30] Interview with Stanley Fish in Olson, *Justifying belief*, 139. See too 122–4; *Doing*, 464–5.

[31] See, for example, Richard Weisberg, "Fish takes the bait: Holocaust denial and postmodernist theory" 14 *Law and Literature* (2002) 135. See too *Doing*, 142–5.

[32] See generally *Doing*, ch. 7 ("Change"). Steven Winter argues that it is still not rich enough. See Steven Winter, "Bull Durham and the uses of theory" 42 *Stanford Law Review* (1990) 664–81. For more sympathetic descriptions of Fish's account of change, see Nick Spearing, "Don't go changing: On Richard Weisberg's critique of Stanley Fish and Holocaust denial" 20 *Law and Literature* (2008) 318; Schanck, "Understanding postmodern thought" 2548–54.

considering how interdisciplinary borrowing can produce change at the end of Chapter 3. I will go on to consider legal change in Chapter 11, but for now I will expand the description of Fish's general account of change in order to respond to the charge that he is a political conservative.

What is distinctive about Fish's account is that it explains change not as the result of external influences, as the objection supposes, but as the result of internal processes.

> If prediction and justification are internal to a system of belief, what could possibly be the agent of its alteration? The answer, either surprisingly or inevitably, is belief. It is beliefs that alter beliefs, an assertion that will seem paradoxical only if you assume that beliefs are discrete items in a storehouse or inventory; but beliefs, as I have already said, are components of a structure and exist in relationships of dependence and scope to one another, and among the beliefs internal to any structure will be a belief as to what might be a reason for its own revision.[33]

Reasons for change are thus community-specific. Anti-foundationalism tells us that every practice is shaped and enabled by already-in-place background assumptions, and so reasons for *changing* the practice are also shaped and enabled by those same background assumptions. That is, something will only be seen as a reason for change to members of a community if the background assumptions of the community enable this perception.[34] But there is no reason, on Fish's analysis, to think that such internal, community-specific reasons for change would not be commonly encountered.

It follows from Fish's analysis that when practices (or societies) change, this will never be because some completely foreign material has intruded and compelled those changes. The members of a community of competent practitioners will not see, or will not see as relevant, reasons for change that only have weight or probative value against the different background assumptions that enable a foreign practice. As we have already seen when considering interdisciplinary borrowing, Fish holds that foreign material will only enter and speak to a practice once that "outside" material has been "domesticated" – that is, when it has been given a role that fits with the "definitions, distinctions, conventions, problematics, and urgencies already in place"[35] in the practice.

---

[33] *Trouble*, 281. See too 283; *Doing*, 146; *No free speech*, 188.
[34] *Doing*, 13, 89, 96, 145–9, 154, 190–1, 193–4, 206–7, 460–1.
[35] *No free speech*, 220. See too 22, 238–9; Fish, "Truth but no consequences," 406.

To put the matter in what only seems to be a paradox, when a community is provoked to change by something outside it, that something will already have been inside, in the sense that the angle of its notice – the angle from which it is related to the community's project even before it is seen – will determine its shape, not *after* it has been perceived, but *as* it is perceived. And all of this will follow from the community's understanding of itself as a mode of inquiry responsible to the facts and theorems of some, but not all, other modes of inquiry.[36]

If this domestication of foreign material cannot be achieved, Fish says, then the material will not enter the practice and have any effects. This is the case, for example, when strong religious believers are challenged by atheists:

> Indeed, a challenge from the outside, from someone who lives elsewhere and who is not coming from where you are coming from, would, quite literally, make no sense. Suppose you believe something because the Bible says so, and I reply that the Bible is just a historical document put together at different times and for different purposes by fallible agents just like you and me, and therefore it is not authoritative in a decisive way. My reply will persuade you of nothing save my unregenerate condition; what you have heard is not evidence of your possible error but evidence of my being so mired in error that nothing I might say (at least on this matter) could be taken seriously. This does not mean that your beliefs are not available to challenge and (possible) correction, only that the challenge must come from a person or source you recognize as weighty (a recognition internal to your belief structure and not forced by something from the outside); if the challenge comes from a person or source you discount from the outset – from an atheist if you are a believer or from a fundamentalist Christian if you are not – it will not trouble you in the slightest.[37]

But while this example shows that sometimes a community is unwilling or unable to domesticate foreign material, according to Fish it is common for such domestication to be achieved. This is because an interpretive community, rather than remaining hermetically sealed from and resistant to outside material, typically seeks to take whatever it encounters and turn it into a resource for its own distinctive projects, even if this means using this new material in ways that other communities would disagree with. As long as fidelity to its distinctive task is maintained, Fish says, the practice remains autonomous, even as it incorporates and domesticates new material.

---

[36] *Doing*, 147.   [37] Fish, "Reply to Owen," 926. See too *Trouble*, 268.

> Autonomy . . . requires the incorporation of foreign elements, which once appropriated – seen in the light of the discipline's underlying point or purpose – are no longer foreign. Autonomy is a social or political achievement (rather than something initially given), and it can only maintain itself by reconfiguring itself in the face of the challenges history puts in its way.[38]

And the incorporation of this new material will not just *add* to the resources of the community, it can also *change* what existed before its arrival. Thus Fish would say that he has no problem with explaining change in interpretive communities – they will always be changing as a result of this domestication and incorporation. They are for this reason "engines of change":

> [A]n interpretive community, rather than being an object of which one might ask "how does it change?" is an engine of change. It is an engine of change because its assumptions are not a mechanism for shutting out the world but for organizing it, for seeing phenomena as already related to the interests and goals that make the community what it is. The community, in other words, is always engaged in doing work; the work of transforming the landscape into material for its own project; but that project is then itself transformed by the very work it does. The stylistician who reaches out to absorb Chomsky into the structure of his own concerns is at once extending those concerns and altering them in as much as they will wear a different aspect once Chomsky has been assimilated.[39]

Roberto Unger urges us to adopt a strategy of political change that he calls "internal development,"[40] but Fish would say that there is no need to urge a strategy of internal development because that is the only way social change can ever occur.[41] Fish is not saying that all change can only be gradual and incremental, never sudden and revolutionary. Rather he is saying that even in the event of radical change, what existed before must have made that change a possibility for that community. "[T]he agent of change must already be a component in the field it alters."[42] No change

---

[38] *No free speech*, 22.
[39] *Doing*, 150. See too 146, 463; *No free speech*, 271: "The neoconservative right rails against change in the name of tradition and continuity and doesn't realize or doesn't want to know that change is the means by which continuity is achieved and reachieved. Tradition does not preserve itself by pushing away novelty and difference but by accommodating them, by conscripting them for its project; and since accommodation cannot occur unless that project stretches its shape, the result will be a tradition that is always being maintained and is always being altered *because* it is being maintained."
[40] Fish describes Unger's project in *Doing*, 419, 422–3.   [41] Ibid., 427.
[42] Ibid., 154. See too *Text*, 354–5.

will be a complete rupture with the past, because it will have been enabled by that past. Fish makes this point by considering a number of examples within literary studies.

> But in fact deconstruction is no more or less than a particularly arresting formulation of principles and procedures that have been constitutive of literary and other studies for some time. Indeed, deconstruction would have been literally unthinkable were it not already an article of faith that literary texts are characterized by a plurality of meanings and were it not already the established methodology of literary studies to produce for a supposedly "great text" as many meanings as possible. Deconstruction takes the additional step of attributing these meanings not to the text as a special kind of object, but to signification as a force untethered to any grounding origin, but this step too can be seen to follow from the growing emphasis in this century of hermeneutical thought, with its emphasis on contexts, cultural matrices, and gestalts ... [R]ather than something new which in its newness gives rise to revolutionary practices, deconstruction is a programmatic and tendentious focusing of ways of thinking and working that have already come to be regarded as commonplace and orthodox.[43]

In summary, Fish is able to defend his position that no political substance follows from his philosophical positions. His philosophical position does not require him to be a relativist, or a liberal, or a conservative, nor does it rule out progressive or radical social change. But because philosophy and politics are autonomous practices, he can and sometimes does adopt a partisan political position that has its roots in something other than his anti-foundationalism.

---

[43] *Doing*, 154–5. For other literary examples see *Text*, 354–5, 349–50.

6

Political practice

Fish's different senses of "politics"

There is a preliminary matter that must be dealt with before Fish's remarks on political practice can be addressed. He uses the term "politics" in different senses, and unless this is kept in mind, his readers might be confused by statements that are prima facie inconsistent. He sometimes says, for example, that politics is inescapable, but he also says that academics should not engage in politics when they perform their academic duties. In order to dispel this apparent inconsistency, and also to isolate the sense of politics that is relevant for this chapter, I need to identify two different senses of "politics" in Fish's writings.

There is first a broad sense of "politics" that follows from Fish's philosophical commitment to anti-foundationalism. As we saw in Part I, Fish holds that any human experience presupposes an already-in-place background of shared local commitments. The particular local commitments that occupy this background position do so because they achieved success in a competition with other commitments. There was nothing necessary or natural or inevitable about this success; it was the contingent result of persuasion, ideology, force, economic or institutional power, demographics, etc. Fish describes this state of affairs by saying that the content of the in-place background is the product of "politics," because it is the result of a contest between commitments where there is no neutral method for deciding between them, which all parties must accept as authoritative.[1] Because success in this contest is sociological and contingent, not philosophical and timeless, it is always possible for the victory to be undone by the same forces that established it. A political and rhetorical success achieved in the past can be revisited and reopened, and a frozen politics can become hot and fluid until another victory establishes new background assumptions.

---

[1] See, for example, *No free speech*, 205.

In short, politics ... is not something you can choose or reject: it is the medium (the soup, the air) within whose ever-expanding confines (there is nothing outside it) one makes the kind of choices – so-called principled choices – to which it is rhetorically opposed. The fact that politics is everywhere has no normative *or* antinormative implications; it provides you with no program, nor does it take any away from you; it points you in no direction but only tells you that, whatever direction you find yourself taking, politics will be there, not as a byway or a danger or an impurity but as the very condition of action.[2]

Fish is using this broad sense of politics when he says that science is "political" because, as Kuhn showed in *The structure of scientific revolutions*, it too rests upon community assumptions, which, although "widely shared and firmly in place," are contingent and potentially revisable.[3]

However, Fish also uses "politics" in a less philosophical and more familiar sense to refer to the things done in the hurly-burly of public life by partisans of different conceptions of the good when they contest for control of legislatures, courts, and other powerful institutions. Politics in this narrower sense covers trying to ensure the success of legislation or litigation that will advance the social and economic outcomes you favor, trying to get people elected or placed in positions of power so that they can advance values you endorse, organizing and funding institutions that will work to produce a world that will benefit those you see as deserving, and smite those you see as dangerous, etc. This narrower sense of politics *does* provide you with a program and point you in a particular direction, unlike politics in the broader sense.[4]

With this distinction established, we can resolve the prima facie contradiction noted earlier. Politics in the broad sense is present in all areas of life, because it puts in place the assumed background that is a precondition for any human experience. But politics in the narrow sense is confined to a particular area of life, and it is not always appropriate to engage in it. For example, Fish rejects the position that academics should expand their professional activities beyond their current disciplinary boundaries to include progressive political activity. He argues that academics should not do politics in the narrow sense when they are doing

---

[2] *Trouble*, 126. See too *Doing*, 431.

[3] *No free speech*, 201–2. Fish's reference to Thomas Kuhn is at 202 n2. See too *Doing*, 297–8.

[4] The same two senses of politics in Fish have been noted in Gary Olson, *Justifying belief. Stanley Fish and the work of rhetoric* (Albany: State University of New York Press, 2002), 15–6 (hereafter cited as Olson, *Justifying belief*).

their job, even though doing their job always involves politics in the broad sense:

> It is one thing to say that everything is political when it means no more or less than that any task one prosecutes proceeds within contestable assumptions; it is another thing to say that the inescapably political nature of disciplinary acts in this sense means that one engages in them with specifically political intentions. Were I to offer a reading of *Paradise Lost*, it could be challenged at any point by someone who believed (and could back up his belief with discipline-specific reasons) that his reading was the better one. Each of us would be proceeding in a controversial manner and therefore each of us would be proceeding politically; but neither of us would be proceeding within a political intention because we would both be possessed by the same desire, to get at the truth about *Paradise Lost*. If that were not our desire, if instead either of us pursued an interpretive direction (itself political in the inescapable and trivial sense) because it furthered a political end – passing a piece of legislation, defeating a particular candidate – he would be acting as a politician and no longer be a literary critic.[5]

Here again we see Fish's insistence upon the autonomy of practices, and the impossibility of interdisciplinarity that was described at the end of Part I. Introducing politics in the narrow sense into literary criticism would not expand the scope of the academic discipline, rather it would mean abandoning the literary task and taking up a completely different one, which literary critics are not paid to perform and for which they have no special training.[6]

Fish on political practice

Although Fish claims that his philosophical position entails no substantive political commitments, his philosophical position does lead him to offer a number of general remarks on political practice in the narrower sense. It is important to stress that what Fish is offering us here are not generalizations derived by observing the performance of successful political actors, nor is he coming up with his own novel techniques for successful political practice and urging political actors to employ them. Because his remarks on political practice derive from his philosophical

---

[5] *Professional*, 67–8. See too 131–2. Fish also makes this point in Stanley Fish, "Postmodern warfare," *Harper's Magazine*, July 2002, 39–40 and Stanley Fish, "Why we built the ivory tower," *New York Times*, May 21, 2004, A23.

[6] *Professional*, 82; *No free speech*, 27.

position, they are neither empirical nor prescriptive. Instead they purport to *describe necessary features of any political practice*, whether actual political actors would accept these descriptions of their performance or not. And because they are descriptions of what political actors have necessarily always done, they are not offered as advice to such actors.

Theory plays no role in political success, but theory-talk can play a rhetorical and contingent role in political success

This returns us to a matter that was introduced when examining the role of theory at the end of Part I. We saw then that Fish rejected the strong extra-territorial claims that are often made for philosophy. According to these strong claims, all other practices rest upon philosophical commitments, even if the practitioners are unaware of this. Philosophers are uniquely qualified to stand back from and evaluate these buried philosophical commitments and are thus uniquely qualified to reveal ways in which our non-philosophical practices and institutions could be reformed. Theory thus has a special role in guiding political practice and social change. Fish rejected all such strong claims, and he argued instead for a deflationary account of the role of philosophy or theory, based on his anti-foundationalism and his thesis of the autonomy of practices. In his analysis, philosophy cannot stand outside all commitments and subject them to neutral reasoned critique, because such transcendence is not possible for necessarily embedded beings. All practices presuppose a particular in-place background, and philosophy is no different. It is a distinct practice with its own values, projects, authorities, modes of reasoning, etc. What happens within its precincts, enabled by its distinctive disciplinary background assumptions, does not travel to other practices. These other practices have their own enabling in-place backgrounds and do not wait for guidance or foundations from philosophers. It follows from this deflationary analysis that theory, *qua* theory, will not play any role in the practice of politics.[7]

Many readers of Fish will find such a claim to be counterintuitive.[8] After all, political actors often make reference to the work of political theorists, and many historically important political actors have been

---

[7] Stanley Fish, "Truth but no consequences: Why philosophy doesn't matter" 29 *Critical Inquiry* (2003) 403–4 (hereafter cited as Fish, "Truth but no consequences"); *Doing*, 319–20.

[8] See, for example, Margaret Kohn, "Critical theory and political action" in G. Olson and L. Worsham [eds.], *Postmodern sophistry. Stanley Fish and the critical enterprise* (Albany:

political theorists themselves. Fish's response is to offer a new description of what is happening in such examples. It is not *theory* that is doing political work but instead *theory-talk*:

> This does not mean, however, that theory, or more properly, "theory-talk," cannot do work and, in doing work, have consequences of a nontheoretical (and *therefore* real) kind. The distinction between theory and theory-talk is a distinction between a discourse that stands apart from all practices (and no such discourse exists) and a discourse that is itself a practice and is therefore consequential to the extent that it is influential or respected or widespread. It is a distinction between the claims often made for theory – that it stands in a relationship of governance or independence to practice – and the force that making those claims (which are uncashable) may have acquired as the result of conditions existing in an institution. That is, it may be the case that in a particular discipline engaging in theory-talk and asserting its impossible claims are efficacious and even obligatory strategies, and in that discipline the presence of "theory" will certainly have consequences, but they will be no different from, or more predictable than, the consequences of any form of talk that has acquired cachet and prestige. In short, when theory has consequences, they will be rhetorical, not theoretical.[9]

As we saw at the end of Part I, the autonomy of practices does not bar those performing practice A from borrowing materials from the completely different practice B if it will advance the goals of A to do so. In such borrowing, however, it is the goals and values of practice A that rule, not the role the borrowed materials played in their home practice of B. So when it comes to the practice of politics, engaged political partisans can borrow and use material from the separate practice of philosophy/theory if it will advance the outcomes they desire in a particular context (because theory-talk happens to be valued in that context). Theory-talk can thus have political consequences, but they are not the consequences theorists have typically claimed for themselves. Theory does not drive and guide the process of political action; rather theory-talk is a rhetorical tool wielded by political actors to advance their non-philosophical goals, and in so doing they can use philosophical terminology and arguments in ways that philosophers would not accept. Theory may think it is the

---

State University of New York Press, 2004), 189 (hereafter cited as Olson and Worsham [eds.], *Postmodern sophistry*).

[9] *Doing*, 14–5. See too 28, 337; *No free speech*, 192–3, 198, 288–9; Stanley Fish, "One more time" in Olson and Worsham (eds.), *Postmodern sophistry*, 284–5 where Fish responds to Kohn's concerns.

star on the political stage, but it is really playing a very different role, and a bit part at that.

> [T]heory, even when it participates in change, is not its engine. Like anything else, but no *more* than anything else, theory is a possible resource for change in the hands of someone agile enough to appropriate its vocabulary for a particular agenda. Theory is available as a resource because its terms ... are not self-defining, but receive their meaning only when the background conditions for their application are specified ... It follows then that the person who can stipulate the background conditions in a way that makes the theoretical terms dance to his tune will prevail ... A theoretical success (if there ever were any outside of philosophy departments) would occur when the cogency of an argument, presented abstractly and without having been preshaped by unexamined and challengeable acts of stipulation, leads directly to a change in policy. A rhetorical success occurs when someone who knows where he wants to go gets there by quarrying theories for material than can be folded into the story of whose plausibility he wishes to persuade us. A rhetorical success, in short, is a political success.[10]

More particularly, although Fish insists that anti-foundationalism as a philosophical position has no necessary implications for non-philosophical contexts, he also insists that this does not bar anti-foundationalist theory-talk from being used rhetorically by someone engaged in the completely different practice of politics (in the narrow sense).[11] A political partisan of *any* position is free to use anti-foundationalist theory-talk as a resource to be quarried if it will work in the context at hand to get his objectives realized. For example, some creationists and Holocaust deniers use postmodernist and anti-foundationalist theory-talk to convince others to make space for their viewpoints in educational institutions from which they have been excluded, even though they do not personally believe in the truth of those philosophical positions:

> [W]hat is interesting about [the appearance of postmodernism] in these debates is that those who mouth it don't believe it for a minute; it's just a matter of political tactics. Philip E. Johnson, a leading Intelligent Design advocate, is quite forthright about this: "I'm no postmodernist," he declares in an interview, but "I've learned a lot from reading them." What he's learned, he reports, is how to talk about "hidden assumptions" and "power relationships" and how to use those concepts to cast doubt on the authority of "science educators" and other purveyors of the reigning orthodoxy.[12]

---

[10] *Trouble*, 227–8.   [11] *Save*, 134–5.
[12] Ibid., 125–6. See too *Trouble*, 226, 288–9; Stanley Fish, "One more time" in Olson and Worsham (eds.), *Postmodern sophistry*, 285. Peter Schanck also notes the ability of

So we can find anti-Semites and religious fundamentalists quarrying anti-foundationalist theory-talk for their purposes, but in Chapter 4 we also saw their political opponents using anti-foundationalist theory-talk to convince us to move to a more progressive, multicultural, tolerant, and less absolutist politics. Although Fish disagrees with the political goals of the Holocaust deniers, he does not see anything improper with their strategy of borrowing materials from the different practice of philosophy in order to further those goals, even if the borrowed materials are not used in a way that philosophers would agree with. (However, the propriety of the strategy does not preclude Fish from seeking to combat it.[13])

The creationists and Holocaust deniers provide clear examples of political actors using theory-talk rhetorically, rather than having their political practice directed by a theory, because they do not believe in the anti-foundationalist theory they are quarrying. But what about the different, and probably more common, situation where the political actor *does* believe in the truth of the theory he is using, and moreover would honestly describe his practice as directed by this theory? Fish argues that such a person falls under exactly the same description as the creationist and Holocaust denier – he or she is only using theory-talk rhetorically rather than being guided by theory. He develops this point when considering the prominent feminist theorist Catharine MacKinnon.[14] MacKinnon believes that feminist theory is important for directing feminist political activity, and she is herself active both in contributing to feminist theory and in feminist political action. Fish says she is mistaken in her beliefs about the role of theory and therefore mistaken as to the nature of her own political performance.[15] But this commitment to a false *description* of her political practice need have no effect on the *efficacy* of that practice. In contexts where theory-talk is valued, incorporating feminist theory-talk into your performance as a political actor

---

religious conservatives to utilize postmodern arguments in his "Understanding postmodern thought and its implications for statutory interpretation" 65 *Southern California Law Review* (1991) 2512 n24. On Holocaust deniers who similarly use postmodern arguments to call into question the epistemological stability of historical facts, see Stanley Fish, "Holocaust denial and academic freedom" 32 *Valparaiso University Law Review* (2001) 499 (hereafter cited as Fish, "Holocaust denial").

[13] He suggests that the best political response is to refuse to engage the Holocaust deniers in philosophical debate and to exclude them from history departments because they do not meet well-established and tested professional standards. See Fish, "Holocaust denial," 511.

[14] *Doing*, 16–25.   [15] Ibid., 20, 22.

seeking to advance the condition of women in society will be rhetorically effective in producing the concrete outcomes you desire in that context.

> [T]heory is crucial to feminism because in one of the worlds in which it must make its way – the world of the academy and of Marxist thought – having or being a theory is a mark of seriousness and respectability ... I am not suggesting that [MacKinnon] doesn't believe in her "theory" or in the relationship between it and the power of her discourse (beliefs I would regard as mistaken), only that the claim of theory was an important and effective one to assert even if, as I would contend, it could never be made good ... The point is finally a simple one: theory is not what gives feminism its power, but in the course of exercising its power, theory or theory-talk may well be one of the things feminism thinks to employ.[16]

What does give feminism its power then? Here Fish continues his deflationary account of theory by stressing the importance of non-theoretical factors in political success:

> And how has [the rise of feminism] come about? In innumerable ways; by opportunities grasped, by accident, by vacuums into which feminists rushed, by changes in the demographics of professions, by the 1960s, by the sexual revolution, by the end of the sexual revolution, by the co-optation of feminist themes by Madison Avenue, by presses that have filled their lists with feminist texts, by jokes, by resistances; in short, by more things than any feminist philosophy could dream of or plan for.[17]

It is not theory that changes the world but other factors, he insists, and theory-talk is only called upon to play a supporting bit part if these other factors make a space for it. He thus pours cold water on the hopes of academics that their theoretical work might migrate to the outside world and influence political events there.

> [Feminism, black studies, and gay and lesbian studies are] not, I would contend, evidence that academic work can ripple out to effect changes in the larger society, but that, rather, when changes in the larger society are already occurring, academic work can be linked up to them by agents who find the formulations of that work politically useful. It is a question of the direction of force. Unlike the new historicism and cultural studies, feminism, gay rights activism and the civil rights movement did not originate in the academy, and academic versions of them acquire whatever extra academic influence they may have by virtue of something already in place

---

[16] Ibid., 23.

[17] Ibid., 24–5. Fish's deflationary account of theory often leads him to stress the role of material factors in political success and social change, rather than the role of theory. See ibid., 28 and *Trouble*, 204.

in public life; academic feminism, academic gay rights studies, and academic black studies do not cause something but piggy-back on its prior existence.[18]

Fish is not denying that the efforts of people to advance values and achieve goals can be important in social and political change. It is just that what drives such efforts are not theories but beliefs.[19] As we have already seen in Chapter 3, Fish insists that the deep beliefs that constitute us as human beings are not theories: "Theories are something you can have – you can wield them or hold them at a distance; beliefs have *you*, in the sense that there can be no distance between them and the acts they enable."[20] Political actors are embedded in a thick local context of beliefs and values, and when they act to protect or advance them, they are "doing what comes naturally" for such embedded beings. They do not need theories to direct them, any more than Dennis Martinez needed theories to tell him how to play baseball. They are acting as extensions of their deep substantive beliefs, not being guided by any theory, though they may use theory-talk as a tool to advance those beliefs if the context calls for it.

> Thus we see that even when something is a theory and is consequential – in the sense that espousing it counts for something – it is not consequential in the way theorists claim. Indeed, on the evidence of the examples we have so far considered, the possible relationships between theory and consequences reduce to three: either (1) it *is* a theory but has no consequences because, as a set of directions purged of interest and independent of presuppositions, it cannot be implemented, or (2) it has consequences but is not a theory – rather it is a belief or a conviction, as in the case of the promotion of individual freedom, or (3) it is a theory and does have consequences, but they are political rather than theoretical, as when, for good political reasons, somebody calls himself a textualist or a supplementer.[21]

Arguments that are philosophically defective may still legitimately be used for political purposes

Fish has just described how anti-foundationalism, a philosophical theory he accepts, is available to be quarried by political partisans of any stripe for their rhetorical purposes. He would say the same about a

---

[18] *Professional*, 86. See too 62; *Doing*, 338. See too *Professional*, 37–8, 44–5, 57 where Fish says that if literary scholarship is to have an influence outside the academy, it will require "structural changes" and changes in "material conditions" outside the academy.

[19] See his example of the two legislators in *Doing*, 327–8 where he makes this point.

[20] Ibid., 326.   [21] Ibid., 331.

philosophical theory he rejected. In both cases, the political actor is borrowing theory-talk from philosophy in order to use it in a completely different enterprise. The status such theory-talk has in its home practice, whether incoherent or convincing, has no relevance to its different use in the borrowing practice.

> A demonstration that the reasons usually given for engaging in and maintaining a practice will not hold up under certain kinds of analysis says nothing conclusive about the wisdom of continuing to employ those reasons, which may be valued because of their power (independent of their philosophical cogency) to induce behavior we think desirable.[22]

Because Fish sees philosophy and politics as distinct and separate practices, he holds that when someone is engaged in the practice of advancing a substantive political position, one is not precluded from using arguments that one would judge to be philosophically incoherent if one were instead engaged in the practice of philosophical analysis. Thus Fish would have no problems with both holding that liberalism is philosophically incoherent and also using liberal theory-talk to defend a liberal position he supported on a substantive political issue. After all, liberalism is the dominant political discourse in our culture, and you would be depriving yourself of a valuable rhetorical tool if you did not try to use its vocabulary to achieve your goals.

> As a genuine model for the behavior of either persons or nations, as something you could actually follow and apply, political liberalism is hopeless ... This does not mean that all is lost, for even in its (inevitably) failed and incoherent form, political liberalism, like any other engine of an impossible abstraction, is available to be quarried and manipulated for the kind of partisan effort from which it claims to be distanced. Political liberalism, in short, can be a resource for politics, not for politics in the rarified sense named by chimeras like fairness and mutual respect but for politics as it has always been practiced, and practiced honorably, in the wards and boroughs of ancient Rome, seventeenth-century London, and twentieth-century Chicago.[23]

---

[22] *Trouble*, 114. See too 290–1: "In general, the incoherence of an argument is no bar to, and may even enhance, its political effectiveness"; 160, 273.

[23] Ibid., 12–13. See too 7: "I have labeled the things I see being done with neutral principles 'bad' because they involve outcomes I neither desire nor approve. They are not 'bad' simply because they were generated by the vocabulary of neutral principles, for that vocabulary has also generated outcomes I favor, especially in the areas of civil rights and the expansion of opportunities for women in the workplace and on the athletic field"; 23–4, 72, 295–6.

It would also be appropriate, on Fish's argument, to borrow a piece of liberal theory-talk to advance a substantive political position he favored on one occasion, and to condemn those borrowing the same piece of theory-talk to advance a substantive political position he disagreed with on another occasion:

> The passion I display when debunking the normative claims of neutral principle ideologues is unrelated to the passion I might display when arguing for affirmative action or for minority-enhancing redistricting. To be sure, there might be a contingent relation in a given instance if the outcome I dislike was brought about in part by neutral principle rhetoric; I might then attack the rhetoric as part of my attack on what it was used to do. But I might turn around tomorrow and use the same rhetoric in the service of a cause I believed in. The grounding consideration in both instances (whether I was attacking neutral-principle rhetoric or employing it) would be my convictions and commitments; the means used to advance them would be secondary, and it would be no part of my morality to be consistent in my handling of those means.[24]

Similarly, Fish could, when engaged in partisan politics rather than philosophy, use foundationalist theory-talk (for example an appeal to timeless and universal values that are common to all) if it advanced a substantive outcome he approved of. This need not even be an example of deliberately using a philosophical vocabulary he did not accept in order to achieve a political advantage. As we have seen Fish argue previously, an anti-foundationalist outside the philosophy seminar room is not disabled from making genuine universal and timeless truth claims. One is only disabled from claiming that there is an authoritative method for making others accept the truth of his claims.[25]

These positions will be hard to swallow for many of Fish's readers, who (as he well knows) will see him as advocating a political practice that is cynical, unprincipled, and contradictory. But, in response, Fish would first insist that he is not advocating anything; he only claims to be providing a more accurate description of what successful political actors have always been doing.[26] Second, he would reject any description of these forms of political practice as cynical or unprincipled. On Fish's account, successful political actors are living out and being true to their deep constituting

---

[24] Ibid., 8.
[25] Stanley Fish, "Theory minimalism" 37 *San Diego Law Review* (2000) 774 (hereafter cited as Fish, "Theory minimalism"); Fish, "Truth but no consequences," 416.
[26] *Trouble*, 296.

beliefs. It is fidelity to these deep commitments that makes their actions principled, Fish argues. The choice of means to advance these commitments in various contexts is secondary and tactical only.

> It would not be at all difficult to imagine someone both prolife and antievolution, who triumphantly brandished the latest news from experimental biology in one context and deconstructed it in the other. Nor would this be inconsistency or insincerity; the consistency would reside in a fidelity to the basic goal and sincerity in the obligation to advance that goal by whatever means come to hand.[27]

Third, to those who would insist upon a more traditional understanding of what it is to be consistent, Fish would reply that while such consistency is a professional concern of logicians, it does not follow that it must be a professional concern of those performing different tasks.

> [I]f someone starts commenting, "You act this way in situation A and three weeks ago in situation B I saw you act in ways that would under a general philosophical description be thought of as a contradiction," I answer, "Don't bother me. Give me a break. I am not in the business of organizing my successive actions so that they all conform to or are available to a coherent philosophical account."[28]

For those performing practices such as politics (and, as we shall see in Part III, law), where incompatible goals and rules are endemic and ineliminable, the professional concern is to work successfully with inconsistency, rather than avoid it.

> Were he to have heard Wechsler's question – "Would I reach the same result if the substantive interests were different?" – Machiavelli would have replied by saying something like "I hope not," for such rigidity would sacrifice the values and interests at stake in a particular moment to a formal consistency that valued nothing but itself.[29]

Because neutral principles are impossible, there is always a political contest as to what partisan substance those principles will really contain

As we have seen in Chapter 4, the distinctive goal of liberal political theory is to identify neutral principles that can regulate political life in a way that favors no substantive conception of the good. As Fish described it, liberal political theory

---

[27] Ibid., 289. See too 9, 242; *No free speech*, 117.   [28] *No free speech*, 299.
[29] *Trouble*, 14.

claims to abstract away from the thick texture of particular situations with
their built-in investments, sedimented histories, contemporary urgencies,
and so on, and move toward a conceptual place purified of such particulars and inhabited by large abstractions – fairness, equality, neutrality,
equal opportunity, autonomy, tolerance, diversity, efficiency – hostage to
the presuppositions of no point of view or agenda but capable of pronouncing judgment on any point of view or agenda. When faced with
opposing courses of action or conflicting accounts of what the law
demands, one can ask of the contenders, "Which is most responsive to
the imperative of fairness?" or "which most conduces to the achievement
of equality?" or "which will promote the greatest diversity?"[30]

We have also seen why Fish says that this liberal neutral principle project
must fail – it seeks to transcend the locally embedded condition that Fish
argues is essential for any human existence. He sometimes makes this point
by saying that neutral principles do not exist, by which he means that they
do not exist in the way liberal theory requires. He acknowledges that they
can exist as subjects for philosophical discussion, but then they are what
I called detached theory in Chapter 3 – abstractions emptied of the content
that would enable them to give directions in any context outside the
seminar room. If they *are* able to give directions in such real world contexts,
this is only because they have been filled with the very partisan content they
claim to have transcended. In other words, all neutral principle-talk used in
political practice is really political rhetoric in which one partisan position
seeks to pass itself off as a higher, unbiased perspective. Fish thus rejects the
liberal picture that has the local and the partisan being regulated by higher
principles. Rather it is principles (if they are to do anything in the world)
that are the product of the local and the partisan.

Although transcending the local is impossible, it is still a very effective
rhetorical move if you can convince your audience that you have
achieved it.

> Curiously enough, this is what makes neutral principles so useful
> politically and rhetorically, and gives them the capacity to do bad things.
> It is because they don't have the constraining power claimed for them (they
> neither rule out nor mandate anything) and yet have the *name* of con-
> straints (people think that when you invoke fairness you call for something
> determinate and determinable) that neutral principles can make an argu-
> ment look as though it has a support higher or deeper than the support
> provided by its own substantive thrust. Indeed, the vocabulary of neutral

---

[30] Fish, "Theory minimalism," 762.

principle can be used to disguise substance so that it appears to be the inevitable and nonengineered product of an impersonal logic.[31]

For example, although the strong neutrality claims made for the freedom of religion principle are uncashable, as we saw at the end of the section on liberalism in Chapter 4, this does not prevent liberals from achieving a political success by using such claims rhetorically. That is, liberals only need to convince most religious people that the liberal freedom of religion principle is genuinely neutral, and therefore that they should live according to the partisan strictures that principle establishes. We can say that neutral principles (since they do not exist) can have no consequences for political practice but that neutral principle-*talk* can have consequences if political actors use this vocabulary rhetorically to advance their partisan agenda.[32] Indeed, Fish argues that liberalism has been so successful in using neutral principle-talk in the area of religion that even many of its strong religious opponents are unable to think their way fully outside the strictures of liberal thought. "That is why we see the spectacle of men like McConnell, Carter, and Marsden, who set out to restore the priority of the good over the right, but find the priority of the right – of liberal proceduralism – written in the fleshy tables of their hearts."[33]

Because it is very advantageous politically to have your partisan position accepted as exemplifying neutrality and fairness, there will be a political contest to occupy this role. Each "neutral principle" therefore is

> an object of contest that will enable those who capture it to parade their virtue at the easy expense of their opponents: we're for fairness and you are for biased judgment; we're for merit and you are for special interests; we're for objectivity and you are for playing politics; we're for free speech and you are for censorship and ideological tyranny.[34]

But this is a contest that anybody can enter. If liberalism's opponents can succeed in filling a liberal neutral principle with a substantive content that advances their non-liberal agenda, then liberals can be bamboozled by such a successful appropriation of their own favored vocabulary.

---

[31] *Trouble*, 4. See too *No free speech*, 8.

[32] *Trouble*, 206, 232; Olson, *Justifying belief*, 52.

[33] *Trouble*, 262. The Biblical reference is to 2 Corinthians 3:3, and Fish also uses it at *Doing*, 431. For the details of his critique of the authors mentioned, see *Trouble*, 250–62. For similar criticisms of the ability of other conservative Christians to break free from liberal ideology, see *Trouble*, 187–90 (Conkle, Gamwell, Thiemann), 221–4 (Gedicks), and 240–1 (Smolin).

[34] *No free speech*, 16.

Fish gives a number of examples of this,[35] but the most significant example he provides brings us back to the topic of affirmative action dealt with in the previous chapter. The relevant liberal neutral principle there was that society and law should be "color-blind," but we saw that with different assumed backgrounds in place, this principle could operate either to support affirmative action or reject it. Consequently, those racists opposing affirmative action do not need to advocate openly for their racist beliefs in order to achieve the outcomes they want. Indeed, that would probably be counterproductive for them today. Instead they can operate by stealth, and "speak in code."[36] More particularly, they can endorse the liberal color-blind principle as long as that principle is understood in a way that ignores the history of slavery in favor of some other historical context, and thus operates to prevent black people being helped. In short, racists can appropriate this liberal principle and fill it with a substance that makes it dance to their tune.

> The response of former and present bigots ... is to figure out a way of appropriating the new vocabulary so that it transmits the same old message. The favorite strategy is to find a word or concept that seems invulnerable to challenge – law, equality, merit, neutrality – and then to give it a definition that generates the desired outcome. David Duke has it down pat. Faced with the apparently difficult task of promoting a white-supremacist agenda in an age when white supremacy is no longer respectable as a public pose, he hits upon the solution of defining equality as a relationship between persons with no history ... [T]he equality David Duke champions is designed to perpetuate the *in*equalities produced by a history of repression and exclusion; by refusing to take into account what has happened in the past, the rhetoric of "equality for everyone" assures that the privileges of a few will be continued into the future, and best of all, this policy is able to dress itself in the vocabulary of moral purity.[37]

---

[35] See, for example, *Trouble*, 224–7 (conservative Christians use free speech arguments to get state support for a Christian student magazine); *No free speech*, 102 (use of free speech arguments to defend pornography, campus hate speech, etc).

[36] *No free speech*, ch. 7 ("Speaking in code, or, how to turn bigotry and ignorance into moral principles").

[37] *No free speech*, 91. See too 68–9; *Trouble*, 33, 43. For a competing understanding of equality that is more attentive to concrete histories of oppression, see Michael Walzer, *Spheres of justice* (New York, NY: Basic Books, 1983), xii: "The root meaning of equality is negative; egalitarianism in its origins is an abolitionist politics. It aims at eliminating not all differences but a particular set of differences, and a different set in different times and places. Its targets are always specific: aristocratic privilege, capitalist wealth, bureaucratic power, racial or sexual supremacy. In each of these cases, however, the struggle has

As Fish puts it in the epilogue to *The trouble with principle*, they can "hijack the magic words."[38] To the extent that liberals fail to appreciate this rhetorical move, they can be hoodwinked or bamboozled by racists they disagree with substantively. Liberals believe their color-blind principle to be neutral, and so if it produces an outcome that aids racists, liberals can conclude that this just has to be accepted as a cost of leading a principled life.

> Why don't more people see through it? Because it is performed with the vocabulary of America's civil religion – the vocabulary of equal opportunity, color-blindness, race neutrality, and, above all, individual rights . . . . [The liberals'] mistake is to assume that the words mean what they did in 1960, when in fact they have been repackaged and put in the service of the very agenda they once fought . . . When the goal was to make discrimination illegal, "color-blind" meant removing the obstacles to full citizenship, but "color-blind" now means blind to the effects of what has been done in the past to people because of their color . . . Liberals and progressives have been slow to realize that their preferred vocabulary has been hijacked and that when they respond to once-hallowed phrases they are responding to a ghost now animated by a new machine.[39]

Fish castigates such liberals for failing to see that some substantive politics is always in place when principles do work in the world. There is never a choice between principles and institutional arrangements that are genuinely neutral on the one hand, and those that are shaped by partisan commitments on the other hand. There is only a choice between principles and institutional arrangements that are shaped by your partisan commitments, and those that are shaped by the partisan commitments of your opponents.[40]

The fact that your opponent can win the political contest to fill a neutral principle with the partisan content necessary for it to do work in the world means that you may be faced with a tactical choice. Do you try to supplant your opponent's partisan content with your own, and so get this neutral principle to dance to *your* tune, or do you try to convince people to turn away from neutral principle-talk altogether in favor of another vocabulary that you will better control? There is no general

---

something like the same form. What is at stake is the ability of a group of people to dominate their fellows."
[38] *Trouble*, 309–12. See too 289: "There is also the delicious pleasure of routing the enemy with weapons thought to be in his arsenal rather than in yours."
[39] Ibid., 312.   [40] *No free speech*, 73.

answer to this question; it will depend on the situation you are faced with. If the opponent's use of the principle is very entrenched, it may make sense to introduce a new way of talking about the problem and seek to make this approach the dominant one. In the course of defending affirmative action, Fish suggests that this might be the way to go:

> Sometimes, as in a number of pieces on affirmative action, I explain why proponents of affirmative action should steer clear of engaging in arguments about principle because, as it is now retailed, the language of universalism is owned by their opponents; and while it is possible to contest the vocabulary of that language (fairness, autonomy, merit, and the like) and try to wrest it away from those who have fashioned it to fit their agenda, the kind of lengthy analysis required by the effort would be no match in the public sphere for the snappy sound bites available to the opposition.[41]

Fish notes that there are dangers in seeking to appropriate a vocabulary that has for a long time been in the hands of your opponents – you may find yourself involuntarily adopting some of the background beliefs and values of your opponents,[42] or you may find yourself becoming confused about your own agenda and pursuing lines of argument inimical to your interests.[43] He suggests this is a danger that conservative Christians often fall into when they employ, rather than reject outright, liberal neutral principle-talk. (People with fundamentalist religious beliefs should be concerned to see that God's commands are obeyed, not that everyone is treated neutrally or equally or fairly.[44])

What type of vocabulary could replace neutral principle-talk in the area of affirmative action? An alternative mentioned by Fish is that affirmative action supporters could argue for it "'nakedly,' that is, as deriving from their substantive vision of what is good and desirable rather than from a formal procedural vision in which the question of what is good and desirable has been bracketed."[45] In other words, they could stop trying to present themselves as rising above local partisan beliefs to the realm of neutral principle, and instead base their argument explicitly upon the merits of their local partisan beliefs. Specifically, they could "[a]rgue that civil rights supporters were not working for a color-blind society (even though it might have been rhetorically effective to use that language) but for better conditions for African Americans."[46]

---

[41] Stanley Fish, "One more time" in Olson and Worsham (eds.), Postmodern sophistry, 289.
[42] Trouble, 262.   [43] Ibid., 142, 148.   [44] Ibid., 220–1.   [45] Ibid., 142.
[46] Ibid., 89. See too the interview with Stanley Fish in Olson, Justifying belief, 131.

*Political paralysis can be produced by a false belief in neutral
principles and in the relevance of philosophy to politics*

The conclusion Fish draws from the analysis so far is that the common
distinction between political practice that is principled, and political
practice that is merely pragmatic or prudential, never accurately
described the situation. No political practice is principled in the way
liberal political theory desires, because that would require the transcendence of the local that anti-foundationalism has shown to be impossible.
All political practice is the effort to advance local, deep, and constituting
beliefs and values, even when it involves the rhetorical use of strong
theory-talk and neutral principle-talk. On Fish's account, there is no
alternative mode of political practice available to necessarily embedded
human beings. "In short, the name of the game has always been politics,
even when (indeed, especially when) it is played by stigmatizing politics
as the area to be avoided."[47] Advancing your deep beliefs and values is
the only game in town, so you should play it as well as you can (which
sometimes involves convincing others that your favored course of action
follows from principles that sit outside all local beliefs and values).

However, although there is no other game in town, you can refuse to
play it. You can sit immobile as your political opponents maneuver
around you and advance their beliefs at the expense of yours.
So described, this seems like a stupid thing to do, and it is hard to
understand why anyone would do it. But Fish gives us a couple of
explanations as to how this paralysis can happen. First, political paralysis
can result from a failure to appreciate the autonomy of practices. This
failure can result in a belief (often urged by your opponents who want to
induce this paralysis in you) that political action cannot be taken until
certain philosophical problems have first been completely resolved.
The epistemological problems raised by vulgar postmodernism often
feature here, as we saw when considering the creationists and Holocaust
deniers earlier. You can also end up in this paralyzed state if you believe
that some neutral principle to which you pledge allegiance blocks you
from taking action to secure an outcome you desire.[48] Typically you will

---

[47] *No free speech*, 111. See too Stanley Fish, "One more time" in Olson and Worsham (eds.),
Postmodern sophistry, 270; *Trouble*, 161.

[48] Richard Delgado analogizes such paralysis to damage to the body's proprioceptive
centers: "The plight of the proprioceptively impaired individual is similar to the predica-
ment Fish diagnoses in the person who approaches real-world problems by first asking
what principle commands and ends up paralyzed, disconnected from the very sources of

believe this because your opponents have bamboozled you – they have managed to fill your neutral principle with their own partisan substance, and so managed to get it to support the outcomes they desire. Fish argues that liberals are particularly vulnerable to such bamboozlement because of their firm belief in the existence of neutral principles.

> [I]t is the habit of framing everything in terms of principle that makes people confused about what they really want and renders them vulnerable to certain argumentative ploys. In recent years, liberals have been discombobulated when a practice they abhor is defended by invoking the same principle they had themselves invoked in order to argue for a practice they favor ... The strategy ... is powerful because it renders your own history an obstacle to your present goals and purposes. In the past you have taken a stand and referred it to a principle, and now you are told that by the logic of that very principle you are committed to supporting the agenda of your enemy ... What's a liberal to do? My answer is simple: forget about the principle (and therefore stop being a liberal), which was never what you were interested in the first place, and make an argument for the policy on policy grounds, that is, on the grounds that you think it is good and right.[49]

Fish sees this liberal paralysis exhibited clearly in free speech contexts. Faced with speech (by neo-Nazis, pornographers, racists, etc.) that they profess to abhor, some liberals declare that this speech must nevertheless be tolerated because of the free speech principle. They do this even while they admit that the speech in question has very harmful consequences and even undermines the reasons for valuing free speech in the first place. Fish's detailed analysis of the liberal free speech principle will be dealt with in Part III, but for now we can just note his strong rejection of such self-induced paralysis in the face of a clear danger to one's desired outcomes.

> It is [Amy] Gutmann's desire to be open that is the problem, because it prevents her from taking the true measure of what she regards as an evil. If you wish to strike a blow against beliefs you think pernicious, you will have to do something more than exclaim, "I exclude you from my community of mutual respect." ... Gutmann's instinct to exclude is the right one; it is just that her gesture of exclusion is too tame – it amounts to little more than holding her nose in disgust – and falls far short of

information that could tell him or her what to do." Richard Delgado, "Where's my body? Stanley Fish's long goodbye to law" 99 *Michigan Law Review* (2001) 1382–3. See generally 1381–4.
[49] *Trouble*, 88, 89.

wounding the enemy at its heart. A deeper wound will be inflicted only by methods and weapons her liberalism disdains: by acts of ungenerosity, intolerance, and perhaps even repression, by acts that respond to evil not by tolerating it – in the hope that its energies will simply dissipate in the face of scorn – but by trying to defeat it. This is a lesson liberalism will never learn; it is the lesson liberalism is *pledged* never to learn because underlying liberal thought is the assumption that, given world enough and time (and so long as embarrassing "outlaws" have been discounted in advance), difference and conflict can always be resolved by rational deliberation, where by rational deliberation is meant the kind of deliberation routinely engaged in by one's circle of friends.[50]

In Fish's analysis, such paralysis in the face of political danger is groundless, and so political actors of any stripe should get on with the only affirmative course of political action open to them – using whatever rhetorical and institutional means the context makes available to achieve the outcomes that advance their deep convictions.

Conflict is unavoidable but can be carried out in ways that avoid warfare

To liberal ears, that last sentence will sound like a recipe for the Hobbesian state of nature, the war of all against all.[51] Why stop at rhetoric and institutional structures in the effort to advance your deepest beliefs? Why not use force against those who fundamentally disagree with you? For those in the liberal tradition, individual liberty and peaceful coexistence are paramount values, and that requires protecting individuals from the danger of force. But Fish's anti-foundationalist response to the liberal tradition is that its goal cannot be achieved, and it's a good thing, too. According to Fish, force, or constraint, in some form is not only inescapable, it is crucial for human life.

One form of such valuable and inescapable force was described in Chapter 1. It is the constraint to which all human beings are subject because they are necessarily embedded creatures. Fish makes the argument (in a chapter of *Doing what comes naturally* called "Force") that if human beings were not constrained by the local commitments that come with embeddedness, they could not exist, and he concludes that "you can never get away from your beliefs, which means that you can never get

---

[50] Ibid., 69. See too 41–3, 91, 149, 204–5; Olson, *Justifying belief*, 58–62, 134.

[51] See, for example, Richard Mullender, review of *Trouble* in 28 *Journal of Law and Society* (2001) 621: "Such a world bears alarming similarities to the one presented in the writing of the bellicist and sometime National Socialist Carl Schmitt."

away from force, from the pressure exerted by a partial, non-neutral, nonauthoritative, ungrounded point of view."[52] The inescapability of this form of force means that

> not only is there always a gun at your head; the gun at your head is your head; the interests that seek to compel you are appealing and therefore pressuring only to the extent they already live within you, and indeed are you. In the end we are always self-compelled, coerced by forces – beliefs, convictions, reasons, desires – from which we cannot move one inch away.[53]

It is because humans cannot separate themselves from or escape their deep constituting beliefs and values that Fish believes that humans will act to advance these deep commitments. In so acting, they will often try to constrain other people who have different deep commitments. This constitutes a second form of inescapable force, according to Fish. As long as humans are differently embedded, as they always will be, the contest for supremacy of their different deep commitments cannot be eliminated.[54]

There are a number of clarifications and qualifications that immediately have to be made regarding this claim. First, the fact that you have deep commitments different from someone else does not mean that you will always seek to constrain that person. I will explain why you might not do so when I discuss Fish's analysis of the freedom of speech principle in Chapter 7. Second, if you do act forcefully against someone with different deep commitments than yours, there is an important distinction that Fish draws between hard and soft versions of force.[55] Fish's use of this distinction was inspired by this remark of Oliver Wendell Holmes: "I believe that force, *mitigated so far as may be by good manners*, is the *ultima ratio*, and between two groups that want to make inconsistent kinds of world I see no remedy except force."[56] Killing or imprisoning your opponents would be a hard form of force, while structuring public institutions so that your opponents are excluded and thus rendered less effective would be a soft form of force, or a form of

---

[52] *Doing*, 519. See generally 517–21.   [53] Ibid., 520.

[54] For an interesting challenge to this claim, see John S. Brady, "Incorrigible beliefs and democratic deliberation: A critique of Stanley Fish" 13 *Constellations: An International Journal of Critical & Democratic Theory* (2006) 374.

[55] *No free speech*, 206: "Force, in short, comes in hard and soft versions, and all things being equal, soft is better than hard." See generally 205–6.

[56] Quoted in *No free speech*, 204. Emphasis added.

force "mitigated ... by good manners." We saw an example of this soft form of force in Chapter 4 when Fish described how the liberal public/ private distinction operated to disadvantage and marginalize strong religious believers. Politics in the broad sense described at the beginning of this chapter would be another type of soft force, because efforts to get partisan deep commitments established in the shared background of the interpretive community employ persuasion and rhetoric, and "rhetoric is by definition the forceful presentation of an interested argument – rhetoric is another word for force."[57]

> Force is simply a (pejorative) name for the thrust or assertion of some point of view, and in a world where the urgings of points of view cannot be referred for adjudication to some independent tribunal, force is just another name for what follows naturally from conviction. That is to say, force wears the aspect of anarchy only if one regards it as an empty blind urge, but if one identifies it as *interest aggressively pursued*, force acquires a content and that content is a complex of goals and purposes, underwritten by a vision.[58]

So although there are no neutral principles, procedures, or reasons that can resolve conflict peacefully as liberals hope, this does not mean that conflict cannot be resolved peacefully in other ways that use only soft forms of force.[59] Partisans can sometimes convert their opponents by various context-sensitive acts of persuasion or rhetoric.[60] Or they can bamboozle their opponents into choosing to act in ways that aid the persuader (as the racist opponents of affirmative action did). Or they can use their control of important institutions to block or hinder any actions by their opponents to advance their beliefs (as Fish suggested be done to Holocaust deniers by professional historians). Fish's position is that peaceful resolution of conflict can indeed be achieved, but always as the result of soft force and "inspired adhoccery" at the ground level, rather than hewing to commands on high from neutral principles.[61] For Fish there is no common ground to uncover that can serve as the foundation for peaceful coexistence – common ground is what politics seeks to *construct*, if it can.[62]

---

[57] *Doing*, 517. See too *No free speech*, 204.   [58] *Doing*, 521.
[59] *No free speech*, 10–11; *Doing*, 522; *Trouble*, 255.
[60] Fish, "Truth but no consequences," 413.
[61] *Trouble*, 63–4, 65, 72. See Olson and Worsham (eds.), *Postmodern sophistry*, 130–2, 270–4 for the disagreement between Reed Way Dasenbrock and Fish on the role of "inspired ad-hoccery" in Fish's account of political practice.
[62] *Trouble*, 170; *No free speech*, 35.

Rawls wonders whether, given the deep oppositions that have always divided men along religious, philosophical, and moral lines, "just cooperation among free and equal citizens is possible at all." It isn't. What is possible is cooperation achieved through the give and take of substantive agendas as they vie for the right to be supreme over this or that part of the public landscape. In the course of such struggles, alliances will be formed and for a time at least conflict of a deep kind will be kept at bay. Alliances, however, are temporary, conflict is always just around the corner (Hobbes was right), and when it erupts, all the muted claims of "comprehensive doctrines" will be reasserted, until, for largely pragmatic reasons, those claims are again softened and replaced (temporarily) by the conciliatory words of another vocabulary, perhaps the vocabulary of political liberalism.[63]

So, just as Fish took a deflationary approach to philosophy at the end of Part I, now at the end of Part II he takes a deflationary approach to politics. Just because political conflict cannot be resolved peacefully in the grand principled way liberals desire does not mean it cannot be resolved peacefully in more mundane ways. But for Fish, even when a peaceful *modus vivendi* is achieved, it is a temporary and contingent achievement that can always unravel or be undone.

The main thing I believe is that conflict is manageable only in the short run and that structures of conciliation and harmony are forever fragile and must always be shored up, with uncertain success. I am tempted to turn this into an imperative – perhaps, with a nod to Frederic Jameson, "always politicise" – but the imperative would be unnecessary, for that is what we do all the time, whether we choose to or not.[64]

---

[63] *Trouble*, 12. See too 63; Stanley Fish, "Sharia law and the secular state," *New York Times* Opinionator Blog, October 25, 2010: "[T]he other contributors to this volume are whistling 'Dixie,' at least with respect to the hope declared by Rawls that liberalism in some political form might be able to do justice to the strongly religious citizens of a liberal state. Milbank's fellow essayists cannot negotiate or remove the impasse he delineates, but what they can do, and do with considerable ingenuity and admirable tact, is find ways of blunting and perhaps muffling the conflict between secular and religious imperatives, a conflict that cannot (if Milbank is right, and I think he is) be resolved on the level of theory, but which can perhaps be kept at bay by the ad-hoc, opportunistic, local and stop-gap strategies that are at the heart of politics."

[64] *Trouble*, 15.

PART III

Law

Law played a crucial role in the classical liberal response to absolutist monarchical power and the imposition of religious orthodoxy by the state. The rule of law would replace the arbitrary rule of kings, and it would not enforce any particular religious beliefs. The law would provide a rational framework within which partisans of conflicting viewpoints could peacefully coexist. But for this liberal political vision to be realized, it was necessary that the law have certain characteristics. First, the law must be neutral. It must not advance the partisan moral and political commitments of some privileged group or person. Second, the law must be objective. Its commands had to be clear and compelling. If the law was to constrain the state and its officials, it was crucial that these same officials not be able to twist and distort the law's meaning. Fish describes these liberal requirements this way:

> The law wishes to have a formal existence. That means, first of all, that the law does not wish to be absorbed by, or declared subordinate to, some other – nonlegal – structure of concern ... And second, the law wishes its distinctness to be perspicuous; that is, it desires that the components of its autonomous existence be self-declaring and not be in need of piecing out by some supplementary discourse ... In its long history, the law has perceived many threats to its autonomy, but two seem perennial: morality and interpretation.[1]

These requirements of liberal political theory have generated two familiar jurisprudential positions, legal positivism and legal formalism.

Legal positivism seeks to preserve the neutrality of law by stressing that law and morality are separate things, each of which can exist independently of the other. A strong version of this separation thesis would hold that law not only can exist independently of morality but that it *should* do so. Moral content is contentious, so law in liberal societies should reflect only neutral principles that are made available to

---

[1] *No free speech*, 141.

us by disinterested reason. A weaker version of the separation thesis could admit that the legislature might pass a particular law to advance a partisan moral position but still insist that what makes that law a law is not its moral content but rather the institutional procedures that brought it into being. Any moral content in a law is a purely contingent, non-necessary feature.

Legal formalism seeks to preserve the objectivity of the law by limiting the material available to somebody wanting to understand and apply a legal rule, thus reducing the capacity of that rule applier to twist and distort the meaning of the rule. The textualist version of legal formalism, for example, seeks to limit the rule applier to the established conventional meanings of the words used in the text setting out the rule, and it precludes any reference to subjective authorial intention or background beliefs and purposes. The textualist hope is that by denying the rule applier access to such material, out of which many competing interpretations can be spun, the legal rule will retain its clear and compelling unitary character. Thus, the law will be able to constrain state officials effectively, and it will provide certainty and predictability for ordinary citizens, who will be enabled to plan and coordinate their affairs.

But challenges to these orthodox jurisprudential approaches also arose. The legal realists and critical legal studies are commonly charged with making the claim that the threats to the neutrality and objectivity of laws cannot be evaded successfully. Consequently, law is pervasively political and indeterminate. Because such a position strikes directly at the heart of the liberal political project, these jurisprudential movements faced heated condemnation and opposition from legal positivists and legal formalists. As I shall show, Fish's response to these familiar debates is to resist taking sides with the realists/critical legal studies or the positivists/formalists. Instead he carves out an independent position that, because of its refusal to slot neatly into the conventional oppositions, has not generally been properly appreciated.[2] I will also show how Fish's positions on law follow naturally from his positions on philosophy and politics as described in Parts I and II. I hope that when his analysis of law is understood in this way, its cogency and force will be more apparent.

---

[2] Gary Olson's sympathetic analysis is a rare exception. See Gary Olson, *Justifying belief. Stanley Fish and the work of rhetoric* (Albany: State University of New York Press, 2002), 64–76.

7

Legal positivism

The impossibility of the unconstrained legal actor

Both legal positivism and legal formalism share a common assumption: they both assume that an unconstrained legal actor is a possibility. (It is unsurprising that they share this assumption, because they are both deeply rooted in the liberal tradition, and it is the liberal conception of the self that gives rise to the possibility of an unconstrained legal actor.) Since unconstrained legal actors threaten law's neutrality and objectivity, legal positivists and legal formalists believe that steps need to be taken to constrain them. But it follows from Fish's critique of the liberal conception of the self described in Chapter 1 that any fear of a "rogue" or "activist" judge is groundless.[1] Fish denies that such a neutrality- and objectivity-threatening radically unconstrained subject is possible, because his account of the necessarily embedded self

> is an argument for the situated subject, for the individual who is always constrained by the local or community standards and criteria of which his judgment is an extension ... [Y]ou will always be guided by the rules or rules of thumb that are the content of any settled practice, by the assumed definitions, distinctions, criteria of evidence, measures of adequacy, and such, which not only define the practice but structure the understanding of the agent who thinks of himself as a "competent member." That agent cannot distance himself from these rules, because it is only within them that he can think about alternative courses of action or, indeed, think at all ... [R]ather than unmooring the subject, [this conception of the self] reveals the subject to be always and already tethered to the contextual setting that constitutes him and enables his "rational" acts.[2]

---

[1] For my earlier attempt to deal with Fish's critique, see Michael Robertson, "Does the unconstrained legal actor exist?" 20 *Ratio Juris* (2007) 258.
[2] *Doing*, 323. See too 12; *Text*, 335.

In short, because the self is constituted, structured, and enabled by "community standards and criteria," any action it performs will be constrained by community standards and criteria.

When Fish's general account of the self is applied to legal actors in particular, we reach the position that because lawyers and judges have had their consciousness shaped and enabled by their legal training, this training is not something they think *with*, but something they think *within*, and so they can never find themselves outside its constraints while they are genuinely performing a legal role.[3] A judge deciding a case therefore cannot follow "merely personal" preferences that ignore his legal training, because any preference the judge could have in that institutional setting would be shaped and enabled by the judge's legal education and training, Fish argues.

> When Judge Parker sits down to consider *Mills* v. *Wyman*, he is in no sense "free" to see the facts in any way he pleases; rather his very first look is informed (constrained) by the ways of thinking that now fill his consciousness as a result of his initiation into the professional community of jurists. That is to say, he looks with judicially informed eyes, eyes from whose perspective he cannot distance himself for a single second except to slip into another way of seeing, no less conventional, no less involuntary. At no time is he free to go his "own way," for he is always going in a way marked out by the practice or set of practices of whose defining principles (goals, purposes, interdictions) he is a moving extension, and therefore it would be superfluous of him to submit his behavior to principles other than the ones that already, and necessarily, constrain him.[4]

Fish expands upon this claim in his responses to the legal theorists Ronald Dworkin and Owen Fiss. Because Fish's debates with Dworkin are considered in Chapter 9, here I will focus only upon Fish's response to Fiss.[5]

Fiss is concerned to find a middle ground between the position that a text has its own objective meaning that constrains an interpreter and the position that an interpreter is free to construct his own interpretation of the text. Fiss's tools for doing this are "'disciplining rules' derived from the specific institutional setting of the interpretive activity . . . They thus act as constraints on the interpreter's freedom and direct him to those meanings in the text that are appropriate to a particular institutional

---

[3] Ibid., 386–7. The case of people who are not genuinely performing a legal role will be considered in Chapter 9.

[4] Ibid., 12–13. See too 10–1, 365–6, and *No free speech*, 225–6.

[5] *Doing*, ch. 6 ("Fish v. Fiss").

context."[6] Fish's first move against Fiss is to argue that a "disciplining rule" cannot be understood if you do not already have some prior understanding of the practice it is supposed to regulate. If you have no understanding of law or basketball, the instructions "follow precedents" or "take only good shots" will not be able to guide your practice at all.[7] You must already be "situated in a field of practice . . . [and have] passed through a professional initiation or course of training and become what the sociologists call a 'competent member.'"[8] In short, to understand what a rule is saying, Fish argues, a particular background must already be in place. We can recognize this as an application of his general anti-foundationalist argument from Part I. (There is no foreground without a background.)

But the result of becoming such a competent member, Fish claims (and this is his second move), is that you have no need of the external disciplining rules Fiss is offering. This is not because becoming a competent member has already equipped you with the tools you must utilize to perform the practice, thus making Fiss's tools superfluous. Rather the reason is that a competent member does not need *any* tools to perform the practice, according to Fish. Becoming a competent member has made you into a particular kind of self, a self whose consciousness, perceptions, thoughts, and possible actions are all immediately structured by the background put in place by your training:

> Just as rules can be read only in the context of the practice they supposedly order, so are those who have learned to read them constrained by the assumptions and categories of understanding embodied in that same practice. It is these assumptions and categories that have been internalized in the course of training, a process at the end of which the trainee is not only possessed *of* but possessed *by* a knowledge of the ropes, by a tacit knowledge that tells him not so much what to do, but already has him doing it as a condition of perception and even of thought. The person who looks about and sees, without reflection, a field already organized by problems, impending decisions, possible courses of action, goals, consequences, desiderata, etc., is not free to choose or originate his own meanings because a set of meanings has, in a sense, already chosen him and is working itself out in the actions of perception, interpretation, judgment, etc., he is even now performing. He is, in short, already filled with and constituted by the very meanings that on Fiss's account he is dangerously free to ignore. This amounts finally to no more, or less, than saying that the agent is always and already situated, and that to be situated

---

[6] Ibid., 120.   [7] Ibid., 121–6.   [8] Ibid., 140.

is not to be looking about for constraints, or happily evading them (in the mode, supposedly, of nihilism), but to be already constrained.[9]

So Fish's deflationary conclusion is that the unconstrained legal actor who figures so prominently in legal positivist, legal formalist, and liberal political thinking cannot exist. The unconstrained legal actor is a bogeyman that has excited unreal fears in us for too long.[10]

Fish's position may be unconventional, but he is not alone in asserting it. Anthony Kronman similarly rejects the fear of an unconstrained legal actor and the legal indeterminacy this actor was supposed to generate: "[T]he true judicial craftsman, the judge endowed with horse-sense, knows that his work is constrained even in its most creative aspects and regards the iconoclastic bogey of an utterly free judicial prerogative as a fantasy or myth."[11] The legal realist Karl Llewellyn also saw the judge as constituted and constrained by tradition and training:

> Writing (and thinking, seeing, judging) with a set of legal rules and categories as the tradition-given scaffolding of his expression, the judge finds certain facts legally "material"; he is alert for them. He finds certain other facts legally "immaterial," and dulls his eye ... What he does see he sees not in terms of life, or love, or holes-in-one; not in terms of wage-earning or investment; of stimulus-response, Gestalt-configuration, claustrophobia; but in terms of tradition-molded legal categories *whose existence, shape, and meaning are a part of him as he observes.*[12]

Although the unconstrained legal actor cannot exist, according to Fish, this does not mean that it is pointless to invoke him. Lawyers often have very real disagreements about what the law is and how it should be applied. Currently one of the ways in which lawyers can advance their favored resolution against those offered by other law-constituted (and so law-constrained) parties is to invoke the bogeyman of the unconstrained legal actor. In a liberal political and legal culture, if you can successfully describe your opponents as having willfully abandoned law's constraints, you will have damaged them. The fact that the unconstrained legal actor is an impossibility does not stop it from being a powerful rhetorical tool for as long as this impossibility is not widely appreciated.

---

[9] Ibid., 127–8.   [10] Ibid., 126–7.

[11] Anthony Kronman, *The lost lawyer* (Cambridge, MA; Belknap Press, 1993), 224.

[12] Karl Llewellyn, "Legal tradition and social science method" in Karl Llewellyn *Jurisprudence* (Chicago, IL: University of Chicago Press, 1962) 100. (Emphasis added.)

Fish's rejection of the separation of law and morality/politics

As we noted in Part I, the positivistic form of foundationalism developed out of the Enlightenment's increased confidence in the powers of human reason and the scientific method during the eighteenth century. This confidence spread beyond the natural sciences to other disciplines. For those in the disciplines influenced by positivism, accurate perceptions of empirical facts are the foundation of all genuine knowledge, while metaphysics and other supposed routes to knowledge that do not rely on empirical facts are rejected. *Legal* positivism follows this pattern when it stresses law's character as a matter of empirical fact only and when it rejects the position that valid laws are essentially connected to some nonempirical source such as God or Nature. That is, valid law is created solely by the observable acts of particular identifiable human beings, such as sovereigns or legislatures or judges or other types of officials.[13] It is also characteristic of positivism to draw a sharp distinction between facts and values: facts are objective, while values are subjective; fact claims can be shown to be true or false, while value claims cannot be; no value claim follows from a fact claim. *Legal* positivism also follows this pattern by claiming that because valid law is completely a matter of empirical fact, it is essentially separate from the kinds of value judgments found in morality and politics. While moral considerations might sometimes prompt the lawmakers to create a law, this is a purely contingent matter, and has no relevance to the law's status as a law. A law would still be a law if created by the appropriate human actions, even if its moral content was objectionable, and even if it ignored or bracketed moral considerations altogether.[14] (Indeed, bracketing moral considerations altogether would be seen as a desirable thing for law in liberal societies where law

---

[13] See J. W. Harris, *Legal philosophies* (London: Butterworths, 1980), 16: "This expression [legal positivism] is used in many ways, but most of its adherents would at least subscribe to the following two propositions. First, no element of moral value enters into the definition of law. Secondly, legal provisions are identifiable by empirically observable criteria, such as legislation, decided cases, and custom." See too Brian Tamanaha, "The contemporary relevance of legal positivism" 32 *Australian Journal of Legal Philosophy*" (2007) 23: "Contemporary legal positivist theory adopts two basic theses: 1) what law is and what law ought to be are two separate questions (the separation thesis); and 2) what qualifies as law in any given society is determined by social facts (the social sources thesis)." He cites J. Coleman and B. Leiter, "Legal positivism" in D. Patterson (ed.), *A companion to the philosophy of law and legal theory* (Cambridge, MA: Blackwell, 1996), 241.

[14] Matthew Kramer, *In defense of legal positivism: Law without trimmings* (Oxford University Press, 1999), 2–3.

aspired to be a neutral framework of rules that rose above partisan debates about the good.) Could laws *created* without any essential connection to morality and politics subsequently be *enforced* without the law applier having to make any substantive moral and political judgments of their own? Here the legal positivist can rely on the legal formalist position described in the next chapter to generate an affirmative answer.

As an anti-foundationalist, Fish argued in Part I that any human apprehension of facts is both enabled and structured by an already-in-place socially constructed background. Positivism is therefore rejected as an epistemology: our apprehensions of empirical reality are never direct and unmediated; facts are never "brute" and available to all in the same shape. (Recall the strong religious believer and the secular liberal from Part II.) Fish would apply the same critique to any analysis of law that both made facts central and conceived of facts in a positivistic way. This would apply to legal positivism and legal realism, but since Fish directs his anti-positivist critique most explicitly at legal realism, I shall expand upon it in Chapter 12, which deals with legal realism. What I will deal with in the present chapter are Fish's arguments that the legal positivist separation of law and morality is both impossible and unnecessary.

Fish argues that the legal positivist separation of law and morality is unnecessary because it is based on a mistaken notion of legal autonomy. Legal positivists seek to safeguard law's autonomy by emphasizing a separation between law and the practices believed to threaten its autonomy – morality and politics. Fish, in contrast, has a different account of how law's autonomy is achieved, and on Fish's account, there is no need to attempt the quarantining of law from such "outside" or extraneous material. For Fish, as I explained at the end of Chapter 3, an institution maintains its autonomy by pursuing its distinctive jobs, and it is not inconsistent with autonomy so understood to borrow material from other practices and use this foreign or extraneous material to advance the institution's job. As Fish put it in "Play of surfaces: Theory and the law":

> What I am suggesting is that one needn't choose between a view of the law as autonomous and self-executing and a view in which the legal process is always unfolding in relation to the pressures and needs of its environment; for autonomy should be understood not as a state of hermetic closure but as a state continually achieved and reachieved as the law takes unto itself and makes its own (and in so doing alters the "own" it is continually making) the materials that history and chance put in its way. The law (or any other enterprise) can display autonomy only in the course of stretching its shape in order to accommodate what seems external to it;

autonomy and the status quo are conceivable and achievable only within movement; identity is asserted not in opposition to difference but in perpetual recognition and overcoming of it.[15]

Earlier we have seen Fish claim that "[An interpretive community] is an engine of change because its assumptions are not a mechanism for shutting out the world but for organizing it, for seeing phenomena as already related to the interests and goals that make the community what it is."[16] What Fish is claiming in "Play of surfaces" is that the legal interpretive community is such an engine of change, and so he says in a subsequent article that

> the particular form in which materials from other disciplines enter the law will be determined by the law's sense of its own purpose and of the usefulness to that purpose of "foreign" information ... It is those purposes and not the purposes at the core of the quarried discipline that rule ... Law will take what it needs, and "what it needs" will be determined by *its* informing rationale and not the rationale of philosophy, or literary criticism, or psychology, or economics.[17]

A more powerful challenge to legal positivism comes from Fish's claim that the separation of law and morality/politics is not only unnecessary but is impossible. Again, the argument begins with the anti-foundationalism and conception of the self established in Part I. Since the background that is a precondition for any human experience is acquired as a result of humans being embedded in local contexts, it follows that no such background will be neutral – it will always reflect a partisan and contestable viewpoint. This was why Fish rejected the liberal political theory project in Part II. Similarly, it follows that the background that enables and structures the practice of law will not be neutral. Fish claims that this background will always contain moral and political commitments, and indeed, *competing* moral and political commitments. But this means that legal positivism must be wrong about law and morality being essentially separate. Law can never be essentially separate from morality and politics, Fish concludes, because moral and political commitments are present in the background that structures the surface (or foreground) of law and enables the perception of legal texts and legally relevant facts.

---

[15] *No free speech*, 195. See generally 22, 195–7, 220; *Professional*, 24.

[16] *Doing*, 150. I have already dealt with this claim in Chapters 3 and 5 and will deal with it again in Chapter 11.

[17] *No free speech*, 221–2. Fish makes this statement in response to Richard Posner, who is not a legal positivist, but the point holds more generally.

Fish's analysis has not collapsed the distinction between law and morality/politics, as legal positivists might fear. Recall that Fish has a strong institutional focus, and he sees different institutions as autonomous because they each have their own distinctive jobs to do. Moral commitments might appear in the enabling backgrounds of both legal institutions and religious institutions but that does not make those institutions equivalent, nor does it dissolve the very real differences between their jobs. Fish would agree with legal positivists that to ascertain whether something is a valid law you do not need to determine that it is morally correct according to some religious institution. But this is consistent with holding that all valid laws rest upon some background moral commitments. Fish is just claiming that the moral commitments valid laws rest upon do not require validation from some non-legal source. He is emphasizing the autonomy and distinctiveness of legal and religious institutions, not reinventing natural law.

Legal positivist responses to Fish

Fish has claimed that law cannot be separated from moral commitments, but a legal positivist will want to challenge him on this point by providing examples of law with no taint of moral or political commitments.

Black-letter law

One possible route the legal positivist could take is to focus on technical, black-letter law. But in *Doing what comes naturally* Fish insists that "[t]he content of the law, even when it is a statute that seems to be concerned with only the most technical and mechanical matters (taxes, for example), is always some social, moral, political, or religious vision."[18] In the first two sections of "The law wishes to have a formal existence," we see Fish fleshing this position out by exposing in some detail the hidden moral and political commitments beneath the surface of orthodox contract law.[19] For example, Fish notes that orthodox contract law's requirement for mutual consideration is imposed to let a purely formal feature serve as the test of an intention to be legally bound, rather than a test tied to some substantive and partisan moral judgment. Under the consideration doctrine, that is, the court "will not . . . inquire into whether or not the two parties were equally informed or received

---

[18] *Doing*, 131.   [19] *No free speech*, 141–68.

equivalent benefits from the exchange or were equally powerful actors in the market. To do so would be to reintroduce the very issues – of equity, of the distribution of resources, of fairness, of relative capacity, of *morality* – that consideration is designed to bracket."[20] But Fish then proceeds to show how the legal positivist's desire to keep morality outside contract law's formal workings in this way is impossible and has never been achieved.

> [T]he distinction between legal and moral obligation will not work because any specification of a legal obligation is itself already linked with a morality ... This is spectacularly true of the procedures built around the doctrine of consideration, a doctrine that finally makes sense not as an alternative to morality, but as the very embodiment of the morality of the market, a morality of arm's length dealing between agents without histories, gender, or class affiliation. Whatever one thinks of this conception of transaction and agency, it is hardly one that has bracketed moral questions; rather it has decided them in a particular way, and, moreover, in a way that is neither necessary nor inevitable.[21]

The doctrine of consideration, like orthodox contract law generally, endorses the account of human nature, human motivations, and human obligations that classical liberalism developed – an account that stresses "possessive individualism" and rational self-interested utility maximizers.[22] Later in the article, Fish notes that "[t]he tension between consideration doctrine with its privileging of the autonomous and selfish agent and the doctrine of moral obligation with its acknowledgment of responsibilities always and already in place is a tension between two contestable conceptions of life."[23] This echoes a point he had made earlier in *Doing what comes naturally*:

> When Judge Parker holds for the defendant because no consideration attached to his promise, he speaks from a vision of public life that is

---

[20] Ibid.,157–8.

[21] Ibid., 158–9. On page 159, Fish also notes that: "Historically, the morality of self-interest and with it the requirement of consideration triumphed after a determined effort by Lord Mansfield to make contractual and moral obligations one and the same. The fact that he failed does not mean that morality had been eliminated as an issue in contract law, but that one morality – the morality of discrete, one-shot transactions – become so firmly established that it won the right to call itself 'mere procedure,' and was able to set up a watchdog – called 'consideration' – whose job it was to keep the other moralities at bay."

[22] See, for example, C. B. Macpherson, *The political theory of possessive individualism* (Oxford: Clarendon Press, 1962).

[23] *No free speech*, 163.

anything but neutral and impersonal. In that vision contracting parties begin in what has been called an "equality of distrust" and are presumed to be bargaining for advantage; actions of altruism and simple faith are not recognized except as aberrations that the law will neither respect nor protect.[24]

So even if judges stick rigidly to the requirements of contract's consideration doctrine, they have not escaped the realm of substantive moral judgments. Consideration doctrine is the manifestation in law of particular contestable moral and political commitments.

A similar result can be discerned from an examination of Fish's analysis of Judge Kozinski's ruling in *Trident Centre* v. *Connecticut General Life Insurance Company*.[25] This case involved an attempt by Trident to refinance a loan, but Kozinski was adamant that the loan agreement would not allow it. His view was that Trident's lawyers had simply failed to grasp the objective textual meaning of the contract before them, and he dismissed their arguments on the grounds that the contractual language left no room for the construction they urged. Because Kozinski thought that the text itself was crystal clear, the implication is that Trident's lawyers were either incompetent or they were cynically and deliberately distorting what they knew to be the clear and objective meaning of the text in order to achieve a partisan purpose. Fish proceeds to give a description of what Kozinski was doing in this case that seeks to highlight the crucial role of moral and political background commitments. His description is compressed, and so I will expand it here.

In Fish's analysis, while lawyers will share a background that will make competent practitioners comprehensible to each other (and often incomprehensible to outsiders), the existence of this shared background is compatible with disagreement within the community. Lawyers all understand law to be a social practice with its own particular goals, which are distinct from those of other social practices, such as sport or religion. But law's institution-specific goals can conflict, and different lawyers can deal with those conflicts in different ways. This is what is going on in the *Trident* case, according to Fish's analysis. That case does not involve

[24] *Doing*, 11–12.
[25] *Trident Center* v. *Connecticut General Life Insurance Company* 847 F. 2d. 564 (9th Cir. 1988). Fish's discussion of the case is in *No free speech*, 144–6. For a competing account of Fish's analysis of the *Trident* case, see John Morss, "Who's afraid of the big bad Fish? Rethinking what the law wishes to have" 27 *University of Melbourne Law Review* (2003) 212–4.

one party seeing an objective textual meaning, which is there independently of any community-specific assumptions, and the other party seeing (or claiming to see) a meaning that is not really there. Rather Judge Kozinski and Trident's lawyers each see a meaning that stands out clearly once certain background assumptions are in place about the goals of contract law and the values it is supposed to advance.

> Trident, [Kozinski] complains, is attempting "to obtain judicial sterilization of its intended default," and the reading its lawyers propose is an extension of that attempt rather than a faithful rendering of what the document says. The implication is that his reading is the extension of nothing, proceeds from no purpose except the purpose to be scrupulously literal. But his very next words reveal another, less disinterested purpose: "But defaults are messy things and they are supposed to be ... Fear of these repercussions is strong medicine that keeps debtors from shirking their obligations." And he is, of course, now administering that strong medicine through his reading, a reading that is produced not by the agreement, but by his antecedent determination to enforce contracts whenever he can.[26]

That is, Kozinski's reading of the contract is produced by his already-in-place background conviction that contract law should protect settled expectations arising from promises for which valuable consideration has been given. With that assumption in place (together with others), he sees one clear and compelling meaning in the contractual language. But there are other competing values in contract law that members of the legal interpretive community would acknowledge, such as individual freedom and economic efficiency. These competing values can make contract breaches desirable and legitimate in certain circumstances: "Kaldor-Hicks efficiency assumes a corrective conception of justice; contractual breaches are permissible and even encouraged if, after compensating the non-breaching party, the breaching party still profits from the breach."[27] If the *Trident* contract is read with the background assumption in place that individual free choice and economic efficiency are the most important values for contract law to protect and advance, then a different clear and compelling meaning is produced – the one that Trident's lawyers see. Consequently the real contest is about which values

---

[26] *No free speech*, 145.
[27] Anne Marie Lofaso, "Toward a foundational theory of workers' rights: The autonomous dignified worker" 76 *UMKC Law Review* (2007) 8. She is describing the account given in Robert Cooter and Thomas Ulen, *Law and economics*, 4th ed. (Reading, MA: Addison-Wesley, 2004), 48.

will sit in the background here and generate the clear and compelling meaning. What Kozinski's rhetorical strategies and arguments (and institutional position) are achieving is the dominance of his values over those gripping Trident's lawyers.

Fish concludes that interpretations of contracts rely on deep background assumptions that "include, among other things, beliefs one might want to call 'moral' – dispositions as to the way things are or should be ... It follows, then, that whenever there is a dispute about the plain meaning of a contract, at some level the dispute is between two (or more) visions of what life is or should be like."[28] On the basis of analyses such as this, Fish argues that even technical or black-letter law relies upon a background in which moral and political commitments will be found.

> [A] purely formal system [of law] is not a possibility, and ... any system pretending to that status is already informed by that which it purports to exclude. Value, of both an ethical and political kind, is already inside the gate, and the adherents of the system are either ignorant of its sources or are engaged in a political effort to obscure them in the course of laying claim to a spurious purity.[29]

Neutral legal principles

Another route open to the legal positivist wanting to challenge Fish's analysis is to point to examples of the neutral legal principles that, according to liberal theory, can order society and deliver peaceful coexistence, even when there is no agreement on conceptions of the good. Fish is well aware that in liberal societies there is a strong desire that the law decide cases "from a perspective – sometimes called the forum of principle, the realm of neutral principles, or the view from nowhere – unattached to any local point of view, comprehensive doctrine, partisan agenda, ideological vision, or preferred state of political arrangements."[30] That is, there is a strong desire for law of the kind the legal positivist holds out – law essentially separate from substantive moral and political commitments. But as we saw in Part II, Fish argues that this desire cannot be satisfied, and beneath all so-called neutral principles that do

---

[28] *No free speech*, 154.   [29] Ibid., 143.

[30] Stanley Fish, "Theory minimalism" 37 *San Diego Law Review* (2000) 761. Fish is referring to the position of Herbert Wechsler as described in N. Silber and G. Miller, "Toward 'neutral principles' in the law: Selections from the oral history of Herbert Wechsler" 93 *Columbia Law Review* (1993) 925.

any work in the world will be found a contestable partisan substance: "[E]very principle is an extension of a particular and *contestable* articulation of the world and none proceeds from a universal perspective (a contradiction in terms)."[31] Therefore he also rejects "the dream of procedural justice ... by which I mean what everyone else means: justice which in its unfolding is neutral between competing moralities or lifestyles or visions of the good."[32] In Part II, we saw him back up this claim by revealing how the supposedly neutral liberal freedom of religion principle contains partisan commitments that disadvantage strong religious believers. Now I will analyze his claim that the liberal freedom of speech principle also always conceals some partisan substance.[33]

Fish's analysis of freedom of speech is complex and contentious, and it has produced incomprehension and outrage among many readers. Terry Eagleton, for example, describes him as "a sabre-rattling polemicist given to scandalously provocative pronouncements [such as] free speech is an illusion," and this is not an unrepresentative view.[34] But if we keep in mind the philosophical premises from which Fish starts, his position can be made more comprehensible, and we can see that most of his critics fail to understand what he is up to.[35] One of Fish's surprising claims about free speech derives from his conception of the necessarily embedded self. As we saw when examining Fish's deconstruction of various liberal dichotomies in Part II, he denies that the relationship between freedom and constraint is one of simple opposition. Rather, he claims, the constraint that comes with embeddedness is the precondition for all action, including free actions. Freedom therefore requires constraint. Another

---

[31] *Doing*, 11. See too *No free speech*, ch 10: "Liberalism doesn't exist."

[32] *Trouble*, 75. See too *Doing*, 516.

[33] The following account draws upon Michael Robertson, "Principle, pragmatism, and paralysis: Stanley Fish on free speech" 16 *The Canadian Journal of Law and Jurisprudence* (2003) 287 and Michael Robertson, "Deconstructed to death? Fish on freedom" in G. Olson and L. Worsham (eds.), *Postmodern sophistry. Stanley Fish and the critical enterprise* (Albany: State University of New York Press, 2004), 99–126 (hereafter cited as Olson and Worsham [eds.], *Postmodern sophistry*).

[34] Terry Eagleton, "The estate agent," *The London Review of Books*, March 2, 2000, 11. See too Edward Rothstein, "A provocateur for whom liberal principles are a sham," *New York Times*, January 22, 2000, B11 ("[Fish claims that] the doctrine of free speech is 'conceptually incoherent'"); Peter Berkowitz, "The principle problem," *The Weekly Standard*, March 20, 2000, 29 ("Free speech, he claims, does not exist"). All of these are reviews of *Trouble*, which was published in 1999.

[35] A more sympathetic reading can be found in Stanley Hauerwas and Michael Baxter, "The kingship of Christ: Why freedom of belief is not enough" 42 *DePaul Law Review* (1992–1993) 111–5.

surprising claim is that a commitment to censoring some speech is logically entailed by any commitment to freedom of speech. In liberal societies, he argues, free speech is only valued because it is believed to produce good consequences, such as more truth, better democratic politics, and more individual self-development. But this means that any freedom of speech principle carries with it a commitment to constrain speech that destroys these good things. Alternatively put, constraint of others is required on a consequentialist approach to free speech, but such constraint is properly understood as a manifestation of a genuine commitment to free speech, rather than as a failure of such a commitment. Liberal tolerance will necessarily run out when applying the free speech principle.

> This is not an empirical but a logical inevitability; for if you have what has been called a consequentialist view of the First Amendment – a view that values free speech because of the good effects it will bring about – then you must necessarily be on the lookout for forms of action, including speech action, that threaten to subvert those effects ... And, to continue the logic, at the point you discern such a threat and move against it, you will not be compromising the First Amendment; you will be honoring it by performing the act of censorship that was implicit in it from the beginning.[36]

So free speech is only important because it produces valued consequences, but the consequences that are valued will necessarily reflect the partisan moral and political commitments of the particular community that institutes the free speech regime. It follows on this argument that no free speech principle can be neutral in the way liberal theory requires.

> This ... amounts to saying that any understanding of free speech will be political; for in order to form a consequentialist position, you must choose some consequences – some vision of the way you want the world to be in the future – above others, and that choice, which will also be a choice of the "special cases" you are willing to recognize, will inevitably be opposed by those who would prefer other consequences and recognize other exceptions.[37]

Consider again the reasons liberals typically give for the importance of free speech, i.e., its positive consequences for truth, democratic functioning, and self-expression. These rest upon some fundamental liberal

---

[36] *Trouble*, 115. See too 85–6; *No free speech*, 13–4, 103–4, 123–4.
[37] *No free speech*, 15. See too *Trouble*, 94.

assumptions and values that are not accepted by all people. Liberals believe that a process of free discussion between competing viewpoints is the only sure way to achieve truth. But this belief is not shared by those who believe in the already revealed truth of a divine authority, which does not await validation by mere human reason. Liberals believe that democracy is the only proper form of political order, but this will have no force for those who see democracy as rule by an ignorant mob. Finally, liberals believe that individuals are the fundamental unit of concern, but not everybody accepts that the self-development and self-actualization of individuals is more important than the coherence and survival of the family, tribe, or community of believers. Fish holds that because humans cannot transcend the state of being constituted by local commitments, any freedom of speech regime will be at bottom an attempt to advance some community's particular and contestable partisan commitments, its social vision. No free speech principle can be neutral as between all competing partisan positions. It can never achieve a position above the fray, because it is always one of the contestants within the fray.[38]

We can now unpack the argument that is presented in a startling and compressed form in Fish's book title, *There's no such thing as free speech, and it's a good thing, too.* In its expanded form, Fish's argument is that *if* "free speech" means what the liberals say it means (i.e., the absence of constraints, neutrality as between partisan positions), then free speech does not exist because nothing could have those characteristics. Freedom of speech does exist but only because it is essentially connected with the very qualities (constraint, partisan bias, non-neutrality) that are excluded from the liberal account. It is thus a "good thing" that freedom of speech is not what liberals say it is and that we are constrained in ways that their account ignores; otherwise we would not have freedom of speech at all. Fish's claim "is that constraint of an ideological kind is *generative* of speech and that therefore the very intelligibility of speech ... is radically dependent on what free-speech ideologues would push away."[39] Fish is not arguing against the existence of free speech, as most of his critics suppose, but is offering a different, non-liberal account of the nature of the free speech that does exist. His project is descriptive, not destructive.

One obvious objection at this point is that Fish is wrong to claim that free speech is only valued in liberal societies because it produces certain

---

[38] *No free speech*, 16.   [39] Ibid., 115.

consequences. Some people in liberal societies talk of free speech as a basic human right to which people are entitled because of their nature as autonomous beings.[40] Fish's response to this objection is bold: a non-consequentialist position on free speech cannot explain why free speech should be protected. His argument for this surprising claim begins with the Kantian conception of the self, described in Chapter 1. On Kant's account, the self is defined in terms of an abstract capacity – the capacity to exercise autonomous free choice – rather than the concrete choices actually made by exercising that capacity. These concrete choices are contingent and revisable characteristics of persons; they are not what is essential and enduring. On this view of the self, Fish argues, what is important about free speech is not the actual content of what is said, or the consequences of saying it, but the fact that an autonomous human had the will to say it and was able to do so without constraint.

> In the legal culture, as crystallized in First Amendment jurisprudence, what counts is the moment in which a lone speaker rises and, in defiance of the forces that press in on him, gives utterance to the inner voice of conscience. In [this] scenario . . . the person is reduced, or exalted, to the status of pure mind, a bodiless agent whose paradigmatic act is either of forming an expression or expressing it. Everything else is accidental, in the strict philosophical sense; everything else is dross . . . [T]he point, and the only point, is to preserve the autonomy of individual moral choice. In the contexts informed by high liberal thought, it is not the consequences of an action – its real-world community effects – that matter but the extent to which the action is free, that is, the product of an uncoerced will.[41]

But if what is important about free speech is the fact that an autonomous human had the will to say something and was able to do so without constraint, not the actual content of what is said or the consequences of saying it, then the right of free speech is indistinguishable from the right to make noise, Fish argues.[42] And why should a right to make noise be valued in and of itself?

> The choice is clear; either acknowledge that, like other items in the Constitution, the First Amendment has a purpose and that in the light of that purpose some acts of toleration make sense and some don't; or acknowledge that the free-speech clause has no purpose beyond itself,

---

[40] *Trouble*, 116.   [41] Ibid., 50.

[42] *No free speech*, 106–7. See too Stanley Fish, "One more time" in Olson and Worsham (eds.), *Postmodern Sophistry*, 268–9.

and face the conclusion that there is no compelling – that is, serious – reason for adhering to it.[43]

Another objection challenges Fish's claim that liberal tolerance will necessarily run out when applying the free speech principle. His anti-positivist argument for this claim is that any free speech regime will be based on partisan background commitments, which include moral and political commitments, and so the operation of the free speech principle in any society will always involve constraint of those who are successfully advancing competing and incompatible commitments. But it seems easy to point to examples of liberal societies doing exactly what Fish says they cannot do. In the United States of America, there are vocal supporters of both an Aryan nation and a Christian commonwealth. These people disagree with and even emphatically repudiate fundamental liberal beliefs (e.g., that truth is best reached through the marketplace of ideas) and moral values (e.g., toleration of difference). But the expression of their viewpoints is protected by the First Amendment. Do we not see in such liberal tolerance both a refusal to constrain speech that rejects fundamental liberal premises and also the adoption of a neutral stance with respect to different partisan viewpoints? If Fish is to rebut this objection, he has to provide us with an alternative account of actually existing liberal tolerance that convinces us that it is not the application of a neutral free speech principle.

The essence of Fish's alternative account of existing liberal tolerance is that it is pragmatic in nature, never "principled" in the liberal sense. Recall again Fish's argument in Chapter 1 that partisan commitments are a precondition of existing as a human being. Since partisan commitments cannot be transcended, we saw in Chapter 6 that most human action (I will explain the remainder shortly) consists of people seeking ways to live out and defend their deep partisan commitments in particular circumstances. This applies to instances of liberal tolerance as well, Fish argues – they will typically be the result of a pragmatic judgment as to what will best advance partisan liberal beliefs and values. They will never be the result of an impossible fidelity to a neutral principle that refuses to favor any particular partisan beliefs and values.

But is it plausible to claim that tolerating anti-liberal beliefs and values advances liberal beliefs and values? One response open to Fish is that his consequentialist claim was not that a liberal free speech regime would

---

[43] *No free speech*, 123. For a slightly different version of this argument, see *Trouble*, 86–7.

never tolerate viewpoints that rejected fundamental liberal commitments. Rather the claim was that such viewpoints would be constrained if they were seen as causing serious *harm* to liberal fundamental commitments. If the expression of anti-liberal commitments is not seen as causing such harm, then there is no need to constrain that expression and toleration is the pragmatic response. It is such pragmatic judgments about the likelihood of actual harm being caused to partisan liberal commitments that are described in "Fish's first law of toleration-dynamics ... Toleration is exercised in an inverse proportion to there being anything at stake."[44] Thus "total toleration of speech makes sense only if speech is regarded as inconsequential and unlikely to bring about a result you would find either heartening or distressing."[45] Not only is it safe to tolerate anti-liberal speech that will do no harm to fundamental liberal beliefs and values, such toleration also has a positive benefit. It gives plausibility to the liberal claim that a true system of free speech exhibits viewpoint-neutrality and the absence of constraint. The liberal critics can safely be left standing as free speech Potemkin villages.

Fish points to examples in the First Amendment case law that demonstrate his first law of toleration-dynamics at work. In his dissents in *Abrams* v. *United States*[46] and *Gitlow* v. *New York*,[47] Justice Holmes clearly felt that the speech in question was unlikely to have *any* negative consequences worth noting, let alone serious and immediate ones, and so it should not be restricted. In *Abrams* he said: "Now nobody can suppose that the surreptitious publishing of a silly leaflet by an unknown man, without more, would present any immediate danger that its opinions would hinder the success of the government arms or have any appreciable tendency to do so."[48] In *Gitlow*, he refers to "the admittedly small minority who shared the defendant's views," and describes the speech in question as "the redundant discourse before us."[49] As Laurence Tribe acknowledges, "[o]ne cynical interpretation of Holmes's handiwork might be that speech is protected only as long as it is ineffective."[50] In *Dennis* v. *United States*,[51] the conviction of leaders of the American Communist Party under the Smith Act was upheld by a majority of the

---

[44] *No free speech*, 217.   [45] *Trouble*, 102. See too *No free speech*, 129.
[46] 250 U.S. 616 (1919).   [47] 268 U.S. 652 (1925).   [48] 250 U.S. 616 (1919), 628.
[49] 268 U.S. 652 (1925), 673.
[50] Laurence Tribe, *American constitutional law*, 2nd ed. (Mineola, NY: Foundation Press, 1988), 843.
[51] 341 U.S. 494 (1950).

Supreme Court. But Justice Douglas dissented in the tradition of Holmes, and similarly stressed that the speech in question was without any chance of success.

> Communists in this country have never made a respectable or serious showing in any election ... Communism in the world scene is no bogeyman; but communism as a political faction or party in this country plainly is. Communism has been so thoroughly exposed in this country that it has been crippled as a political force. It is inconceivable that those who went up and down this country preaching the doctrine of revolution which petitioners espouse would have any success ... [I]n America they are miserable merchants of unwanted ideas; their wares remain unsold. The fact that their ideas are abhorrent does not make them powerful.[52]

In summary: liberal tolerance is easily and without cost extended to anti-liberal speech with no chance of actually damaging liberal beliefs, values, or institutions.

But not all anti-liberal speech is ineffective and without negative consequences. Sometimes it will do real harm, but even in these circumstances liberal states often tolerate it and do not constrain it. How can Fish explain this free speech neutrality and toleration in terms of pragmatism rather than principle? His main answer is that toleration of harmful speech will still be pragmatically justified if, on balance, the real harm done is outweighed by other benefits to liberal beliefs, or if even greater harms would result from constraining the speech.

> Ask, that is, whether the harms supposedly caused by the offending speech are indeed likely to materialize, and if the answer is "yes," weigh those harms against the harms that may be produced by regulation. In short, you substitute for the categorical question "Is it speech?" (and for the assumption that an affirmative answer is the end of the matter) the three-part question "Given that it is speech, what does it do, do we want it to be done, and is more to be gained or lost by moving to curtail it?"[53]

It is important to note that Fish is not *recommending* such a pragmatic balancing approach over a principled approach. As we have seen, his claim is that the neutral principle approach is an impossibility and that pragmatic balancing is the only game in town.[54] However, it is a game that can be played well or poorly. What he *is* recommending is playing it well and that requires asking the right questions and attending to the right things. Pragmatic balancing will be done poorly if you are deflected

---

[52] 341 U.S. 494 (1950), 588–9.   [53] *No free speech*, 127. See too 111.   [54] Ibid., 126–7.

from the task by focusing on the wrong questions ("is it speech?") or by trying to achieve impossible goals (e.g. fidelity to neutral principle).

Fish says that the Canadian courts play this pragmatic game well when they deal with the right to freedom of expression in section 2 (b) of the Canadian Charter of Rights and Freedoms.[55] But while examples of American judges openly taking a balancing approach to the First Amendment that considers context and consequences can certainly be found (see, for example, the decision of Justice Frankfurter in *Beauharnais* v. *Illinois*[56]), not all judges would accept this as a description of their practice, and this poses a problem for Fish's analysis. Indeed, in the *Beauharnais* case itself, Justices Black and Douglas wrote impassioned dissents in which they defended the principled approach that Fish says does not exist. The dissenters said that if speech does not fall within the scope of a few narrowly conceived exception categories then it must be tolerated, regardless of its context or content or consequences – even if those consequences were very harmful. As Black puts it in *Beauharnais*:

> I think that the First Amendment, with the Fourteenth, "absolutely" forbids such laws without any "ifs" or "buts" or "whereases." Whatever the danger, if any, in such public discussions, it is a danger that the Founders deemed outweighed by the danger incident to the stifling of thought and speech. The Court does not act on this view of the Founders. It calculates what it deems to be the danger of public discussion, holds the scales are tipped on the side of state suppression, and upholds state censorship. This method of decision offers little protection to First Amendment liberties.[57]

In the later cases of *Collin* v. *Smith*,[58] which involved a neo-Nazi march through Skokie, Illinois, and *American Booksellers Association* v. *Hudnut*,[59] which involved an anti-pornography ordinance in Indianapolis, the courts had clearly shifted away from the Frankfurter approach. The laws seeking to constrain the march and the pornography were held to be in violation of the First Amendment. In each of these cases, the court recognized that the tolerated speech would cause harm, but because the harms did not fit within any of the recognized categories of exceptions, they had no constitutional impact. No context-sensitive, pragmatic balancing of the harms caused versus the benefits obtained was

---

[55] See Fish's approval of the approach of the Canadian courts in *No free speech*, 104–5, 108, 127.

[56] 343 U.S. 250 (1951).   [57] 343 U.S. 250 (1951), 275.

[58] 578 F.2d 1197 (7th Cir. 1978).   [59] 771 F.2d 323 (7th Cir. 1985).

countenanced by these courts. How can Fish's analysis deal with such judgments? He has said that hewing to a neutral First Amendment principle, rather than engaging in a pragmatic balancing process, is impossible, but these courts appear to be doing just that.

I think that Fish can offer two descriptions of what is really going on in such cases. His first description is that a balancing process is indeed going on, only in an unacknowledged, and perhaps unnoticed, way, rather than in the open way Frankfurter exemplified. This first response can be seen in his reaction to the statement by Holmes in *Gitlow* that, absent a serious and present danger, the First Amendment requires toleration of those who advocate socialist revolution, even if this would result in them winning political power in the future: "If, in the long run, the beliefs expressed in proletarian dictatorship are destined to be accepted by the dominant forces of the community, the only meaning of free speech is that they should be given their chance and have their way."[60] This statement by Holmes appears to contradict Fish's claim that liberal tolerance typically reflects a judgment that, on balance, partisan liberal commitments will be advanced thereby. Holmes seems to countenance the eventual destruction of liberalism as a cost of adhering to the free speech principle. But Fish says that when liberals declare themselves ready to leave anti-liberal speech alone, even if it has dire long-term consequences, "[o]ne suspects that many who declare themselves willing to risk that prospect do not believe that it is a real one and subscribe (as Holmes seems to at some moments) to some undertheorized form of progressivism rooted in an Enlightenment view of history."[61] In other words, Fish claims that in tolerating such speech liberals are not really acting pursuant to a neutral principle above partisanship but are rather acting pursuant to a characteristically liberal belief that the march of history is on their side.[62] While in the grip of this partisan belief, liberals

---

[60] 268 U.S. 652 (1925), 673.   [61] *Trouble*, 107. See too *No free speech*, 119.

[62] On the general importance to liberalism of a progressivist philosophy of history, see John Gray, "Mill's liberalism and liberalism's posterity" in Guido Pincione and Horacio Spector (eds.), *Rights, equality, and liberty* (Norwell, MA: Kluwer, 2000), 138–9: "[I]t is a notable feature of postwar liberal theory in the English-speaking world ... that it is indeed reliant upon a particular philosophy of history in which the idea of progressive cultural convergence on a universal civilization is central ... This Eurocentric historical philosophy, which identified European hegemony with the advance of the entire species and understood progress as the universal adoption of Western institutions, beliefs and values, was a central element in the Enlightenment project that Mill ... endorsed unequivocally."

can view even very harmful anti-liberal speech with relative equanimity, because they are confident that it cannot win in the end. The toleration is thus the result of a hidden balancing exercise in which the liberals' belief in "progressivism" results in them giving less weight to the negative consequences of the anti-liberal speech than may be prudent.[63]

So sometimes Fish's response to the insistence of judges deciding First Amendment cases that they are not engaging in pragmatic balancing, and are instead being true to a neutral free speech principle, is to find pragmatic balancing going on beneath the surface. But this response will not be adequate for all cases, as Fish is aware. Sometimes the claims of judges that they have not engaged in any pragmatic balancing exercise must be accepted as genuine. In the decisions in *Collin* and *Hudnut*, for example, the courts insisted that they tolerated speech that they knew would cause real harm, not as the result of any pragmatic balancing exercise, but because of fidelity to a neutral free speech principle. In his discussion of these cases, Fish appears to accept that no balancing exercise went on, but he still does not accept that it is correct to describe the decisions as the result of fidelity to a neutral principle. How then would he describe what the courts did? This returns us to the issue of political paralysis induced by a belief in the existence of neutral principles that was discussed in Chapter 6. I think Fish would say that cases like *Collin* and *Hudnut* are the product of neither principle nor pragmatism but rather of a paralysis that prevents the judges from engaging in a pragmatic balancing exercise.

> [T]here is no principled way to do this, but let's remember too that the principle upheld in *not* doing it – in not standing up for substantive justice when speech is productive of harms – is the principle of doing nothing, the principle, as the dissenting judge in *Collin* v. *Smith* put it, of "paralysis."[64]

Recall my earlier point in this chapter that although pragmatic balancing is the only game in town, it is a game that can be played well or poorly. We have already noted one way the game can be played poorly – the decision-maker does a poor job of identifying the goals of free speech in a particular institutional context, and the consequences for those goals of constraining or tolerating the speech in question. Now we come to the

---

[63] Fish questions whether the confidence induced by this liberal belief in progressivism is well-founded. See *Trouble*, 103–4, 107–9.

[64] Ibid., 91. Fish develops this position in ibid., 75ff, 93ff and *No free speech*, 120ff.

most extreme way in which the only game in town can be played badly –
someone refuses to play it at all. Consider the case of soccer players who
stand motionless on the field and watch as their opponents dribble the
ball past them and head for the goal. What are these stationary players
doing? They are not playing a game other than soccer; soccer is the only
game on offer. What they are doing is playing soccer abysmally badly.
Similarly, Fish argues that by refusing to make and act on judgments
about the consequences of allowing or restricting the speech before them,
the judges in cases like *Collin* and *Hudnut* are not engaging in a different
activity from pragmatic balancing (such as the activity of hewing to
neutral principle). The advancement of local partisan commitments is
the only game in town, but these judges have rendered themselves unable
to play that game because they stand immobilized before the mirage of
an impossible fidelity to principle. In short, Fish argues that judges
deciding First Amendment cases can either do pragmatic balancing
or not, but they cannot do something else. The judges who refuse to
engage in pragmatic balancing know that the speech in question
can cause serious harm (i.e., it is "fraught with death"[65]), but sadly (i.e.,
using "the rhetoric of regret"[66]) they conclude that they can do nothing
to constrain it. They find themselves staring into the headlights of
something they know can hurt them but declare themselves unable
to move. Self-induced paralysis is the explanation for the minority of
cases of liberal tolerance in which liberals do not act in a pragmatic
way to advance their deep constituting commitments, and Fish's point is
that there is no coherent reason for such paralysis.

So Fish does not make the implausible claim that *any* speech that
rejects deep liberal commitments will not be tolerated. His argument
acknowledges the existence of liberal tolerance and seeks to understand
its true dynamics. He does not accept the liberal description of such
tolerance as fidelity to a neutral principle of freedom of speech. For Fish,
liberal tolerance is either the result of a pragmatic judgment that, in the
long run, liberal partisan commitments are advanced thereby or it is the
result of paralysis that inhibits the making of any pragmatic judgments at
all. Leaving aside the cases of paralysis, it follows on Fish's analysis that
liberal tolerance will always run out at some point. There will always
be some state of affairs in which, on balance, it will seem to be more
harmful to liberal commitments and valued consequences to allow some

---

[65] *Trouble*, ch. 6.   [66] Ibid., ch. 5

speech to exist, and then, Fish predicts, liberals will stop tolerating and start censoring that speech.

But how can such partisan acts of intolerance not undermine the liberal hope for a law of neutral principles? Fish describes how liberal societies have devised ways of concealing their acts of censorship from themselves so as to keep this hope alive.

> To be sure, the tradition is to some extent aware that what its right hand gives (total freedom of speech) its left hand takes away, but in the face of criticism it invokes a succession of distinctions designed to save its coherence. Basically the strategy is to declare that forms of speech found unworthy or intolerable are not really speech and therefore we do not compromise our free-speech principles by regulating them.[67]

One important example of this strategy at work is the speech/action distinction. This distinction emphasizes that speech – i.e., the expression or advocacy of ideas – is one thing and is protected by the neutral principle, while action is in another category altogether, and is able to be regulated by the general law without any free speech issues being raised. Consequently, what looks to be the constraint of speech is, properly understood, not so, but is instead the constraint of action. This speech/action distinction can allow a powerful "absolutist" position on free speech to be maintained and is eloquently endorsed by Justices Black and Douglas in their approach to the American First Amendment.

> The line between what is permissible and not subject to control and what may be made impermissible and subject to regulation is the line between ideas and overt acts. The example usually given by those who would punish speech is the case of one who falsely shouts fire in a crowded theatre. This is, however, a classic case where speech is brigaded with action ... They are indeed inseparable and a prosecution can be launched for the overt acts actually caused.[68]

Fish's response to the speech/action distinction is scathing. He denounces it as the major device by which First Amendment purists are able to conceal (from themselves as well as others) the fact that they

---

[67] *No free speech*, 125. See too *Trouble*, 95.

[68] Concurring opinion of Justice Douglas in *Brandenburg* v. *Ohio* 395 U.S. 444 (1969), 456–7. See too Roger K Newman, *Hugo Black. A biography*, 2nd ed. (New York, NY: Fordham University Press, 1997), 513 where Justice Black is quoted as saying: "I believe with Jefferson that it is time enough for government to step in to regulate people when they *do* something, not when they *say* something, and I do not believe myself that there is *any* halfway ground if you enforce the protections of the First Amendment."

are constantly engaged in the constraint of speech. The constraint that Fish has declared to be unavoidable is often not seen because it is hidden in plain sight through this recategorization. The constraint is there, but because it is recategorized as applying to action, rather than speech, it seems to fall outside the protection of the First Amendment umbrella.

> Hard-line First Amendment advocates will vigorously protest this account of their sacred text, but the protest is belied by their own activities, for they typically play the regulation game behind their own backs. They insist up front that they read the text without exceptions ("shall make no law") but then smuggle in the exceptions by declaring them not really to be speech or to be speech "brigaded with action." ... A so-called principled analysis is ... ad hoc behind its back; it is continually engaged in saving its own appearances by inventing (and then reinventing as needed) distinctions that hide from itself what is really going on.[69]

Fish claims that the speech/action distinction cannot do the work the free speech purist wants it to do. It cannot serve to separate two distinct categories, because speech can nearly always be redescribed as action and so moved from one side of the line to the other as desired. His argument for this position is based on his rebuttal of the Kantian, non-consequentialist approach to free speech described earlier. There he argued that freedom of speech could only mean more than a right to make noise if the speech was connected with consequences. But if speech can be connected with consequences, then any such speech can be redescribed as *action* seeking to bring those consequences about. Fish cites this passage from Holmes's dissent in *Gitlow* in support of his position:

> It is said that this Manifesto was more than a theory, that it was an incitement. Every idea is an incitement. It offers itself for belief, and, if believed, it is acted on unless some other belief outweighs it, or some failure of energy stifles the movement at its birth. The only difference between the expression of an opinion and an incitement in the narrower sense is the speaker's enthusiasm for the result.[70]

As Fish puts it in his own words:

> There is no speech that is free of consequences – no speech, that is, whose impact can be confined to the sterilized and weightless atmosphere of a philosophy seminar (assumed as a model for the entire world by free speech ideologues). And because there is no speech free of consequences, a jurisprudence based on the identification of such a category of

---

[69] *No free speech*, 124, 127.   [70] 268 U.S. 652 (1925), 673, cited in *Trouble*, 106.

speech – a jurisprudence strongly invested in some form, however qualified, of the distinction between speech and action – will be fatally confused and engaged in activities it is incapable of acknowledging or even recognizing. It will be protecting something that doesn't exist, and therefore it will not be doing what it thinks and says it is doing.[71]

Fish concludes that because the speech/action distinction is inherently malleable, it serves not to separate speech from action but to conceal the constraint of speech. If you want to restrict speech, reclassify it as action, while if you do not want to restrict speech, abstract away from its possible consequences and stress its "non-performative" character as pure ideas.[72]

Fish sees the speech/action distinction as just one of a number of devices that liberals use to draw a principled line between protected speech and something falling under a different category that can therefore be legitimately regulated. But he argues that all such distinctions fail:

> [T]he so-called principled drawing of the line by distinctions like that between speech and action, or between content and time-place-manner regulations, or between high- and low-value speech, or between fighting words and words that are merely expressive, will be equally ad hoc and context sensitive; there is no other way to draw a line except in the context of an act of judgment that rests on disputable definitions and stipulations of value. What is a fighting word today may not be one tomorrow and may not be everyone's fighting word even today; what is low-value speech under one set of conditions may become high value under another. Line drawing, in short, will always be a political and contestable action and therefore inseparable from the biases and blindnesses inherent in politics.[73]

Fish points out that the consequences of such supposedly even-handed and principled distinctions always benefit the speech of some groups and constrain the speech of others, as is evidenced by the history of challenges to such regulations.[74] His conclusion is that

---

[71] *Trouble*, 94. Fish's language may court misunderstanding here. He is not claiming that all speech actually has empirical consequences. Rather he is making the conceptual point that any speech only has importance for us (i.e., is not just "noise") because of its linkage with possible consequences. Of course, the possibility of those consequences ensuing may be slight, as with the speech Holmes is commenting upon in the *Gitlow* case. But the ability to redescribe most speech as the action of seeking to achieve certain consequences means that the speech/action distinction is "fatally confused."

[72] *No free speech*, 105–6, 125; *Trouble*, 98–9, 139–40.   [73] *No free speech*, 130–1.

[74] Ibid., 15.

> [c]ensorship is the name you give to censorious acts of which you disapprove; censorious acts that have effects you like will receive another name and be attached to some principle (good order, equality, democratic process) you take them to be protecting or promoting.[75]

Such concealment of constraint through recategorization is what allows free speech purists to have their cake and eat it too. They can pledge allegiance to the free speech principle while they simultaneously engage in the constant constraint of speech that Fish says is inevitable in any free speech regime. It is also what allows the faith in free speech as a neutral liberal principle to endure in liberal societies.

> [P]eople cling to First Amendment pieties because they do not wish to face what they correctly take to be the alternative. That alternative is politics, the realization ... that decisions about what is and is not protected in the realm of expression will rest not on principle or firm doctrine but on the ability of some person to interpret – recharacterize or rewrite – principle and doctrine in ways that lead to the protection of speech they want heard and the regulation of speech they want silenced ... In short, the name of the game has always been politics, even when (indeed, especially when) it is played by stigmatizing politics as the area to be avoided.[76]

So the legal positivist attempt to present the free speech principle as a counterexample to Fish's claim that law cannot be separated from morality and politics fails.

---

[75] *Trouble*, 147.   [76] *No free speech*, 110–1. See too *Trouble*, 72, 124.

8

Legal formalism

The textualist version of legal formalism

The hope of legal formalism is that subjectivity in law can be reduced and objectivity enhanced by limiting the materials an interpreter may consider in understanding and applying the law.[1] The legal formalist believes that the limited domain of materials he or she specifies is all that is needed to generate an objective meaning for the law, while reference to anything outside this domain will only undermine the objective meaning of the law. Legal formalism has been advanced over the past 150 years in two main variants.[2] First there was "classical" legal formalism, which was associated with the work of Harvard Law School's Dean Langdell in the late nineteenth century and Professor Joseph Beale in the early twentieth century.[3] Simply put, the claim of classical legal formalism was that behind the welter of decided cases, a smaller number of broad legal principles were operating. It was the job of the legal scholar to distill these broad principles from the data of the recorded cases, much like a scientist distills general laws from the data of events in the natural world. Once these broad legal principles had been ascertained, conceptual analysis could derive subsidiary rules entailed by them.[4] When a new

---

[1] See *No free speech*, 175 where Fish agrees with Peter Goodrich's observation "that a 'defining feature of all formalism' is the 'rejection of history,' that is, of the circumstantial background that informs the supposedly self-sufficient and self-declaring rule or doctrine."

[2] This chapter draws in part upon Michael Robertson, "The impossibility of textualism and the pervasiveness of rewriting in law" 22 *The Canadian Journal of Law and Jurisprudence* (2009) 381.

[3] See Richard H. Pildes, "Forms of formalism" 66 *University of Chicago Law Review* (1999) 609 ("classical legal formalism"); Elizabeth Mensch, "The history of mainstream legal thought" in David Kairys (ed.), 2nd ed. *The politics of law* (New York, NY: Pantheon, 1990), 13, 18–21 ("classical legal consciousness").

[4] Anthony Kronman, *The lost lawyer* (Cambridge, MA: Harvard University Press, 1993), 173: "Once the basic premises of a particular branch of law have been established, the remaining task is one of ratiocination only. The many subrules that fill out the doctrinal detail on any legal subject can, Langdell assumes, be drawn by implication from its

case arose, the task of the legal decision-maker was to identify a legal rule that was conceptually required by the broad legal principles and that also fit the particular facts of the case. The correct legal result would then be reached by a process of logical deduction.

> [Classical F]ormalist views of law can be pared down to two core notions, conceptual formalism and rule formalism. *Conceptual formalism* was the idea that legal concepts and principles, like property ownership, liberty of contract, and duty in torts, had necessary content and logical interrelations with one another, which could be discerned through reason, constituting a coherent, internally consistent, comprehensive body of law. *Rule formalism* was the idea that judges could reason "mechanistically" from this body of law to discover the right answer in every case.[5]

So for the classical legal formalist, the limited domain of permitted material contained only the basic legal principles and their logically entailed subrules. Correct legal results could be derived from this material alone (after findings of fact) in an objective manner that required no subjective contribution from the decision-maker.

This version of legal formalism had been comprehensively critiqued by Oliver Wendell Holmes and the legal realists by the middle of the twentieth century.[6] The critique was that it was not possible to stay inside the limited domain described by the classical legal formalist. General legal rules or principles (and the application of logic and conceptual analysis to them) would never be sufficient to produce a legal result by themselves. Arriving at a legal result required recourse to matters outside the system of legal principles and rules, such as desirable social outcomes, the costs and benefits of different policies, economics, politics, and morality. In his 1897 paper "The path of the law," Holmes put it this way:

> The language of judicial decision is mainly the language of logic. And the logical method and form flatter that longing for certainty and for repose which is in every human mind. But certainty generally is illusion, and repose is not the destiny of man. Behind the logical form lies a judgment

---

foundational principles, whatever these may be. On this view for example, it is possible to produce a full and accurate account of the law of contracts merely by analysing the elementary notions of mutuality, intention, and consideration on which it rests."

[5] Brian Tamanaha, *Law as a means to an end: Threat to the rule of law* (Cambridge: Cambridge University Press, 2006), 48.

[6] This is described in Stephen Feldman, "Republican revival/interpretive turn" (1992) *Wisconsin Law Review* 683–4 (hereafter cited as Feldman, "Republican revival/interpretive turn").

as to the relative worth and importance of competing legislative grounds, often an inarticulate and unconscious judgment, it is true, and yet the very root and nerve of the whole proceeding. You can give any conclusion a logical form.[7]

Legal decisions were therefore not as objective and self-contained as the classical legal formalist hoped.

However, the demise of classical legal formalism did not mean the demise of legal formalism itself, which, as I noted in the introduction to this Part, responds to deep needs in liberal societies and so is unlikely ever to disappear. Today legal formalism is typically advanced under the banner of textualism. Textualism asserts that if you understand the grammar of the language the text is written in and the conventionally accepted meanings in that language of the words making up the text that is all that you need in order to understand the objective meaning of the text itself. It is not necessary, nor is it desirable, for a law-applier to go outside the limited domain of syntax and semantics to consider external matters such as the author's intention, or the context surrounding the text's production, or more generally the spirit rather than the letter of the law.

Textualism is a response to the fear of the unconstrained legal actor that was critiqued in Chapter 7. The fear is that if an interpreter is able to twist and subvert the objective meanings of legal rules and texts, then the rule of law has been eviscerated, leaving only an empty husk. If legal rules and texts are malleable and subject to manipulation by self-interested interpreters, then the state cannot truly be constrained. If a skilled interpreter can, by the exercise of rhetorical tricks, change the meaning of a legal text or rule to suit the interpreter's needs, then the law can become a concealed delivery device for that interpreter's personal morality and politics. The rule of law will simply be serving as cloak behind which the partisan interests of some actors are being advanced. Interpretation therefore replaces the rule of law with the rule of man just as much as a person who compels you to act by putting a gun to your head does. As Fish describes the reasoning here: "If the gunman is the paradigmatic instance of force outside the law, interpretation is the force that resides within the law, and like the gunman it must be regulated and

---

[7] Oliver Wendell Holmes, "The path of the law" 10 *Harvard Law Review* (1897) 465–6. See too Oliver Wendell Holmes, *The common law*, Mark DeWolf Howe (ed.) (Boston, MA: Little, Brown & Co., 1963. Originally published 1881), 5: "The life of the law has not been logic: it has been experience."

policed lest it subvert the law's claim to enact the dictates of general principles of justice and equity."[8]

H. L. A. Hart in *The concept of law*[9] was particularly concerned to distinguish the rule of law from compulsion by someone wielding superior force, such as an armed gunman. Hart's solution was to make general rules central to law, but this is not enough to eliminate the threat of force, because, as Fish notes, there are still the questions of who gets to make the rules and who gets to interpret the rules. The answers to these questions might reveal that force is still operating in law in more "camouflaged" forms.[10] "The great merit of Hart's analysis," Fish says, "is that it makes clear the close relationship – a relationship so close as to be one of identity – between the threat posed to law by force and the threat posed to law by interpretation."[11] Hart's response to this threat is to embrace the textualist version of legal formalism (with a qualification to be described shortly). Hart believes that language can provide "authoritative marks" that repel interpretation,[12] and this is how the law can provide "determinate rules" that leave no room for the rule-applier to exercise independent choice or judgment.[13] For Hart, Fish claims,

> there must be a mode of communication that is general, not tied to the linguistic system of any particular community; once produced, these general communications must be understandable by anyone, no matter what his individual educational or cultural experience; indeed, this understanding must be so immediate as not to be in need of any further elaboration; in fact, its self-sufficiency shall be so perfect that elaboration or direction – otherwise known as interpretation – will constitute an impiety; the content of this unavoidable and self-sufficient understanding will be a set of marching orders; the hearer or reader will be "required," that is compelled, left without choice, deprived of any opportunity to exercise his creative ingenuity; and unless all of this is the case, unless the framing of such general standards in a fail-safe interpretation-proof mode is a possible achievement, there will be no law.[14]

But the textualist version of legal formalism gives rise to its own difficulties. If legal rules consist of authoritative marks that compel readers, how can disagreement about the meaning of legal rules be so common? Can such pervasive error only be explained as wickedness, as a willful turning away from what one knows to be the correct path?

[8] *Doing*, 505.
[9] H. L. A. Hart, *The concept of law* (Oxford: Oxford University Press, 1961).
[10] *Doing*, 504.   [11] Ibid., 505.   [12] Ibid., 507.   [13] Ibid., 505.   [14] Ibid., 506.

Fish acknowledges that Hart has a more subtle answer to this problem: legal rules consist of both a determinate core and an indeterminate penumbra.[15] When the facts of a particular case fall within the core of the rule, the text of the rule directs the rule-applier in a clear and compelling manner. These are the easy or plain cases where the rule operates formalistically and there is no choice to be exercised. When the facts fall into the penumbra, then the law-applier has to exercise choice and independent judgment. Constraint by the law runs out, and the decision will require recourse to contestable extra-legal material, such as morality and politics. These are the hard cases where disagreement arises. So Hart accepts that the textualist version of formalism is not an adequate explanation for all law-application, but it does explain what happens in cases involving the cores of legal rules, and Hart believes that these are more common than cases involving the penumbras of rules. Hence the rule of law is achieved in his analysis.

Frederick Schauer is good example of a contemporary legal theorist who similarly adopts the textualist version of formalism:

> At the heart of the word "formalism," in many of its numerous uses, lies the concept of decisionmaking according to *rule*. Formalism is the way in which rules achieve their "ruleness" precisely by doing what is supposed to be the failing of formalism: screening off from a decisionmaker factors that a sensitive decisionmaker would otherwise take into account. More-over, it appears that this screening off takes place largely through the force of the language in which rules are written. Thus the tasks performed by rules are tasks for which the primary tool is the specific linguistic formu-lation of a rule.[16]

Schauer believes that "the force of the language" is able to create rules that can be applied formalistically – that is, without reference to "factors that a sensitive decisionmaker would otherwise take into account," such as context or authorial intention – because he accepts the central claim of textualism that syntax and semantics alone can generate meaning:

> Words communicate meaning at least partially independently of the speaker's intention. When the shells wash up on the beach in the shape of C-A-T, I think of small house pets and not of frogs or Oldsmobiles precisely because those marks, themselves, convey meaning independ-ently of what might have been meant by any speaker ... Given that the

---

[15] Ibid., 508.

[16] Frederick Schauer, "Formalism" 97 *Yale Law Journal* (1988) 510 (hereafter cited as Schauer, "Formalism").

meaning of words may be acontextually derived from our understandings
of language, the central question becomes whether enough of these
understandings exist to create the possibility of literal language. In other
words, we must ask whether words have sufficient acontextual import so
that communication can take place among speakers of English in such a
way that at least a certain limited range of meaning, if not one and only
one meaning, will be shared by all or almost all speakers of English. The
answer to this question is clearly "yes."[17]

Schauer goes on to defend the initially surprising claim that it is *good*
that those reading and applying legal texts do not consider "factors that a
sensitive decisionmaker would otherwise take into account." One reason
he gives for this is that such constraint preserves the rule of law. If the
rule of law and not of men is to exist, then it is crucial that judges be
constrained from injecting their own personal values and policy preferences into their decisions. But if judges are authorized to look beyond the
"literal language" or textual meaning of a rule to its underlying purpose
or the authorial intention, there is a fear that they will be able to
construct a purpose or intention that fits best with their own personal
preferences. It is therefore good if the judges are confronted with formalistic legal rules that block their ability to consider matters outside the text
itself, because this achieves the necessary judicial constraint. This may
produce suboptimal results in some cases, but the overall benefit achieved
by the rule of law is higher:

> In sum, it is clearly true that rules get in the way, but this need not always
> be considered a bad thing. It may be a liability to get in the way of wise
> decisionmakers who sensitively consider all of the relevant factors as they
> accurately pursue the good. However, it may be an asset to restrict
> misguided, incompetent, wicked, power-hungry, or simply mistaken deci-
> sionmakers whose own sense of the good might diverge from that of the
> system they serve . . . [F]ormalism is only superficially about rigidity and
> absurdity. More fundamentally, it is about power and its allocation . . .
> Insofar as formalism disables some decisionmakers from considering some
> factors that may appear important to them, it allocates power to some
> decisionmakers and away from others. Formalism therefore achieves its
> value when it is thought desirable to narrow the decisional opportunities
> and the decisional range of a certain class of decisionmakers.[18]

---

[17] Ibid., 527–8.

[18] Ibid., 543–4. This concern of Schauer's is shared by fellow textualists such as U.S.
Supreme Court Justice Antonin Scalia. See Antonin Scalia, "Common-law courts in a
civil-law system: The role of United States Federal Courts in interpreting the Constitution
and laws" in Amy Gutmann (ed.), *A matter of interpretation: Federal courts and the law*

A second reason Schauer gives for holding formalistic legal rules to be good is that they can provide an authoritative resolution of complex, contentious disputes. The resolution, or shutting down, of the dispute by the rule provides social benefits such as certainty, predictability, efficiency, and coordination. But all of these benefits depend upon accepting the textual meaning of the rule as authoritative and not going outside it. Once decision-makers are permitted to consider whether the purpose of the rule is advanced by the literal meaning in some context, they have in effect abandoned what Schauer earlier called "decision-making according to *rule*," with all its benefits, and reintroduced the underlying dispute in all its complexity.[19]

Finally, textualism is more sophisticated than the simple assertion that any properly drafted legal text will have a plain meaning that a competent reader will grasp immediately and beyond which that reader should not go. Textualists acknowledge that sometimes literal meanings are not *immediately* perspicuous. This can occur when the text uses terms with conventional meanings, but the relevant convention is familiar only to a specialized technical community. Thus the reader of the text might have to conduct inquiries into the relevant convention before they can discover the textual meaning.[20] Similarly, some textualists insist that the conventional meanings that are important are those that were in place *when the text was created*, not when it is being read, and so for older texts, such as constitutions, ascertaining the literal meaning might involve difficult historical linguistic investigations.[21] However, the matters that are legitimate to consider on this more subtle textualist account are still confined to semantics or syntax only. You can consult a dictionary, or learn about a specialized trade usage, or investigate past word usage, but the textualist legal formalist denies that it is necessary to consider non-linguistic matters, such as the purpose behind the text or the intention of the author of the text, in order to arrive at the meaning of the text. The textualist legal formalist would deny access to these outside matters to anyone seeking to ascertain the object-ive meaning of a legal text or rule.

(Princeton, NJ: Princeton University Press, 1997), 17–8 (hereafter cited as Scalia, "Common-law courts").

[19] Schauer, "Formalism" 535. See too 537–9.

[20] John Manning, "What divides textualists from purposivists?" 106 *Columbia Law Review* (2006) 92.

[21] See, for example, Scalia, "Common-Law Courts."

Fish's critiques of textualism

It is the textualist, rather than the classical, version of legal formalism that Fish wishes to critique, as is clear from his description of the formalist position:

> [I]n the pejorative sense it usually bears in these discussions, interpretation is the name for what happens when the meanings embedded in an object or text are set aside in favor of the meanings demanded by some angled, partisan object ... It follows then that, in order to check the imperial ambitions of particular moralities, some point of resistance to interpretation must be found, and that is why the doctrine of formalism has proved so attractive. Formalism is the thesis that it is possible to put down marks so self-sufficiently perspicuous that they repel interpretation; it is the thesis that one can write sentences of such precision and simplicity that their meanings leap off the page in a way no one – no matter what his situation or point of view – can ignore.[22]

The anti-foundationalist argument against formalism

Fish's broadest argument against formalism flows from his anti-foundationalism as described in Chapter 2.[23] In essence, Fish's anti-foundationalist epistemology claimed that whatever we apprehend in the foreground of consciousness is always both enabled and structured by an unnoticed and already-in-place background. But the legal formalists failed to appreciate the crucial role of this background, for in effect they command us to attend only to the foreground – the legal rule or text – and exclude everything in the background that makes the existence of that rule or text possible. Fish's critique is that the legal formalist distinction between a limited domain of material that can deliver legal objectivity and a body of material outside that domain that threatens legal objectivity cannot be maintained because the outside materials the formalist wants to exclude are preconditions for the existence of the very things that he wants to defend. Attempting to exclude this material is thus like the familiar cartoon character in a tree who is attempting to saw off the branch he is sitting on.

---

[22] *No free speech*, 142–3. For a more extended description of formalism by Fish, see *Doing*, 1–6.

[23] See *Doing*, 5 where Fish notes "the intimate relationship between formalism as a thesis in the philosophy of language and foundationalism as a thesis about the core constituents of human life."

Fish first advanced this anti-formalist argument against textualism in Part II of his 1980 book *Is there a text in this class?* He stressed there that the apprehension of textual meaning cannot be explained by reference to the limited domain of syntax and semantics alone. Rather the apprehension of textual meaning depends upon a much larger set of background beliefs, values, categories, etc., being already in place when the reader encounters the text.[24] In *Doing what comes naturally* he made the point this way:

> The moral is not that there are no such things as texts or acts, but that our ability to point to them or perform them depends on prearticulations and demarcations they cannot contain; and it is only so long as such pre-articulations and demarcations are in place – and in a place we cannot locate because it locates and defines us – that texts and acts will have the immediate palpability they seem always to have. The mistake is to confuse that palpability – the immediacy with which shapes make themselves available *within* local and historical conditions of intelligibility – with something inherent in those shapes, for that is the mistake of claiming for interpretively produced entities the status of being constraints on interpretation.[25]

In *There's no such thing as free speech, and it's a good thing, too*, Fish makes his anti-foundationalist-inspired anti-formalist argument again and again in an effort to convince his reader that without the "outside" or "external" material the textualist wants to prevent the legal actor from considering, there could be no objective law at all:

> [A]n instrument that seems clear and unambiguous on its face seems so because "extrinsic evidence" – information about the conditions of its production including the situation and state of mind of the contracting parties, etc. – is already in place and assumed as a background; that which [formalism] is designed to exclude is already, and necessarily, invoked the moment writing becomes intelligible.[26]

> The underlying point here has to do with the distinction – assumed but never examined in these contexts – between inside and outside, between what the document contains, and what is external to it. What becomes clear is that the determination of what is "inside" will always be a function of whatever "outside" has already been assumed.[27]

> [E]fficacious formalisms – marks and sounds that declare meanings to which all relevant parties attest – are always the products of the forces – desire,

---

[24] *Text*, chs. 11–6.   [25] *Doing*, 300. See generally chs. 6, 13, 21.
[26] *No free speech*, 146.   [27] Ibid., 148.

will, intentions, circumstances, interpretation – they are meant to hold in check.[28]

It is important to emphasize that in these passages Fish is not denying the existence of legal texts with meanings that are clear and compelling and understood by all in the same way – i.e., objective legal meanings, as required by the liberal vision. It is quite consistent with Fish's analysis to accept, as he does, that we can have

> a situation in which for all competent members of a community the utterance of certain words will be understood in an absolutely uniform way. That *does* happen. It is a possible historical contingent experience. When that does happen you have, as far as I'm concerned, a linguistic condition that it might be perfectly appropriate to characterize as the condition of literalism. That is, at that moment you can with some justice say that these words, when uttered in this community, will mean only this one thing. The mistake is to think that it is the property of the words that produces this rather than a set of uniform interpretive assumptions that so fill the minds and consciousness of members that they will, upon receiving a certain set of words, immediately hear them in a certain way.[29]

What Fish does reject is the textualist account of how these objective or literal meanings come to exist, and he seeks to provide a more adequate explanation of them. His anti-foundationalist explanation is that a shared background can produce a shared foreground. That is, a group of people similarly trained and engaged in similar practices will share background beliefs, values, and organizing categories, and this shared background explains why the members of the group will often see the same clear and compelling meaning in a text. Consequently,

> when you come to the end of the anti-formalist road, what you will find waiting for you is formalism; that is, you will find meanings that are perspicuous for you, given your membership in what I have called an interpretive community, and so long as you inhabit that community (and if not that one, then in some other), those meanings will be immediately conveyed by public structures of language and image to which you and your peers can confidently point.[30]

Fish would reject the charge that his explanation makes textual meaning multiple and subjective, because he would deny that the background

---

[28] Ibid., 152.   [29] Ibid., 301. See too *Doing*, 122, 358, 359.
[30] *Trouble*, 294–5. See too *Doing*, 26.

that delivers the apprehension of textual meaning is unique and idiosyncratic.[31] Instead, it is social and shared, and this is how it can provide
the objectivity law requires.

> The notion of "interpretive communities" was originally introduced as an
> answer to a question that had long seemed crucial to literary studies.
> What is the source of interpretive authority: the text or the reader? Those
> who answered "the text" were embarrassed by the fact of disagreement.
> Why, if the text contains its own meaning and constrains its own inter-
> pretation, do so many interpreters disagree about that meaning? Those
> who answered "the reader" were embarrassed by the fact of agreement.
> Why, if meaning is created by the individual reader from the perspective
> of his own experience and interpretive desires, is there so much that
> interpreters agree about? What was required was an explanation that
> could account for both agreement and disagreement, and that explanation
> was found in the idea of an interpretive community, not so much a group
> of individuals who shared a point of view, but a point of view or way of
> organizing experience that shared individuals in the sense that its
> assumed distinctions, categories of understanding, and stipulations of
> relevance and irrelevance were the content of the consciousness of com-
> munity members who were therefore no longer individuals, but, insofar as
> they were embedded in the community's enterprise, community property.
> It followed that such community-constituted interpreters would, in their
> turn, constitute, more or less in agreement, the same text, although the
> sameness would not be attributable to the self-identity of the text, but to
> the communal nature of the interpretive act.[32]

In the same way that a shared, already-in-place background explains
the experience of clear and compelling meanings, Fish argues, it is also
this background (rather than some defect in the text itself) that explains
the experience of ambiguity in a text. "[L]anguage has neither fixity nor
ambiguity as a property; to assert either is to be a textualist."[33] The role of
the shared background in generating ambiguity is brought out by Fish
when he considers the differences in the assumed backgrounds of the
interpretive community engaged in the academic discipline of literary
studies and the interpretive community engaged in the professional

---

[31] If the background *is* unique and idiosyncratic, and the textual meaning it delivers is
apprehended only by one person, we may have the condition of madness.

[32] *Doing*, 141. For a helpful elaboration of what he means by "interpretive community," see
Stanley Fish, "One more time" in G. Olson and L. Worsham (eds.), *Postmodern sophistry.
Stanley Fish and the critical enterprise* (Albany: State University of New York Press,
2004), 274–9 (hereafter cited as Olson and Worsham [eds.], *Postmodern sophistry*).

[33] Stanley Fish, "There is no textualist position" 42 *San Diego Law Review* (2005) 636
(hereafter cited as Fish, "There is no textualist position"). See too *Doing*, 301.

practice of law. It is these different backgrounds, he argues, rather than any inherent difference in the texts they study, that account for the fact that literary critics typically find (and value) multiple meanings or ambiguity in their texts while lawyers do not.

> [I]n literary studies, at least in the context of a modernist aesthetic . . . the rule is that a critic must learn to read in a way that *multiplies* crises, and must never give a remedy in the sense of a single and unequivocal answer to the question, "What does this poem or novel or play mean?" . . . Legal rules might be written in verse or take the form of narratives or parables (as they have in some cultures); but so long as the underlying rationales of the enterprise were in place, so long as it was understood (at a level too deep to require articulation) that judges give remedies and avoid crises, those texts would be explicated so as to yield the determinate or settled result the law requires.[34]

Fish's description of how textual meaning is apprehended also explains how the accepted understanding of a text can change over time as the background beliefs of the interpretive community change,[35] and it explains too how the members of different interpretive communities with different in-place backgrounds can see very different meanings in the same text. For example, when a community is engaged in a special-ized trade, words that might have one clear meaning for outsiders can come to have a different clear meaning for the insiders embedded within the trade practice. Fish describes how in one legal decision, "the shipment term 'June-Aug.' in an agreement was to be read as excluding delivery in August; and in another case the introduction of trade usage led the court to hold that an order for thirty-six-inch steel was satisfied by the delivery of steel measuring thirty-seven inches."[36] In another decision the key question was "'what is chicken?' There the dispute is

---

[34] *Doing*, 137–8. See too 54, 303–5; *Professional*, 15–6. For examples of Fish explaining ambiguity in other contexts, see *Doing*, 129 and Stanley Fish, "The intentionalist thesis once more" in G. Huscroft and B. Miller (eds.), *The challenge of originalism. Theories of constitutional interpretation* (Cambridge: Cambridge University Press, 2011), 99, 112–3 (hereafter cited as Huscroft and Miller [eds.], *The challenge of originalism*).

[35] See, for example, Cass Sunstein, *The second bill of rights* (New York, NY: Basic Books, 2004), 123: "In 1900 it was clear that the Constitution permitted racial segregation. By 1970, it was universally agreed that racial segregation was forbidden. In 1960, the Constitution permitted sex discrimination. By 1990, it was clear that sex discrimination was almost always forbidden. In 1930, the Constitution allowed government to suppress political dissent if it had a bad or dangerous tendency. By 1970, it was clear that the government could almost never suppress political dissent."

[36] *No free speech*, 148.

between the ordinary man-in-the-street definition of chicken and the definition of 'chicken' prevalent in the industry."[37] As Fish put it in a different context: "All language is code-like, and what we have here is not a tension between ordinary, literal meaning and code meaning, but a tension between two forms of code meaning, one of which is shared by a larger public."[38]

Finally, it is important to stress that Fish did not see textual meaning emerging as the result of a two-stage process. Readers do not first see a bare text and then access their background beliefs and combine the two components so as to generate an interpreted meaning. This would give the text an existence prior to and independent of any background beliefs, which Fish denies is possible:

> [I]nterpretation is not a two-stage process in which the interpreter first picks out a "context-independent textual meaning" and then, if he chooses, consults this or that context; rather, it is within some or other context – of assumptions, concerns, priorities, expectations – that what an interpreter sees as the "semantic meaning" emerges, and therefore he is never in the position of being able to focus on that meaning independently of background or "supplemental" considerations.[39]

Such a two-stage process would be analogous to the foundationalist epistemology discussed in Chapter 2 according to which we first perceive unmediated or brute facts about the world and then go on to interpret them. Fish's anti-foundationalism causes him to see perceiving the empirical world and perceiving textual meaning as having the same structure. In each case, whatever we see is always mediated by the background already in place, and that background gives what we see its immediately apprehended shape. If the background changes, a different fact or meaning is immediately apprehended.

---

[37] Stanley Fish, "The intentionalist thesis once more" in Huscroft and Miller (eds.), *The challenge of originalism*, 118. This 1960 case (*Frigaliment Importing Co. v. B. N. S. International Sales Corp.*) is also usefully discussed in Walter Benn Michaels, "Against formalism: Chickens and rocks" in L. Michaels and C. Ricks (eds.), *The state of the language* (Berkeley: University of California Press, 1980), 412–4.

[38] Fish, "There is no textualist position," 638. See too Stanley Fish, "Intention is all there is: A critical analysis of Aharon Barak's *Purposive interpretation in law*" 29 *Cardozo Law Review* (2008) 1123 (hereafter cited as Fish, "Intention is all there is"); Stanley Fish, "The intentionalist thesis once more" in Huscroft and Miller (eds.), *The challenge of originalism*, 101–3.

[39] *Doing*, 329. See too 133; *Text*, 310, 313.

When he wrote *Is there a text in this class?*, Fish was developing his account of textual meaning in the context of literary studies, and so most of his supporting examples were drawn from that discipline. Significantly, however, he did use one legal example, the case of *Riggs v. Palmer* (involving the ability of a person to inherit under the will of a person he murdered) that Ronald Dworkin made famous:

> If it is assumed that the purpose of probate is to ensure the orderly devolution of property at all costs, then the statute in this case will have the plain meaning urged by the defendant; but if it is assumed that no law ever operates in favor of someone who would profit by his crime, then the "same" statute will have a meaning that is different, but no less plain. In either case the statute will have been literally construed, and what the court will have done is prefer one literal construction to another by invoking one purpose (assumed background) rather than another.[40]

In subsequent works devoted to law rather than literature, Fish provided other examples where a clear text with a single meaning is not achieved simply by the judicious choice of words with single conventional meanings.[41] His constant point is that clear and objective legal meanings are the products of complex assumed contexts or backgrounds that extend beyond the limited domain of semantics and syntax:

> If there are debates about what the Constitution means, it is not because it is a certain kind of text, but because for persons reading (constituting) it within the assumption of different circumstances, different meanings will seem obvious and inescapable. By "circumstances" I mean, among other things, the very sense one has of what the Constitution is for. Is it an instrument for enforcing the intentions of the framers? Is it a device for assuring the openness of the political process? Is it a blueprint for the exfoliation of a continually evolving set of fundamental values? Depending on the interpreter's view of what the Constitution is for, he will be inclined to ask different questions, to consider different bodies of information as sources of evidence, to regard different lines of inquiry as relevant or irrelevant, and, finally, to reach different determinations of what the Constitution "plainly" means.[42]

Fish applies his anti-foundationalist-inspired critique of formalism to Hart's position as set out in *The concept of law*.[43] As noted in the previous section of this chapter, Hart relies upon textualism to explain

---

[40] *Text*, 280. Fish's full analysis of the case can be found at pages 278–80. Note that this analysis has the same structure as the analysis of the *Trident* case described in Chapter 7.

[41] *Doing*, 123, 138, 513; *No free speech*, 154–6.

[42] *Doing*, 129. See too *No free speech*, 183–4.   [43] *Doing*, ch. 21 ("Force").

the constraining power of the cores of legal rules. But Fish's response to Hart is that "[w]hatever is invoked as a constraint on interpretation will turn out upon further examination to have been the product of interpretation."[44] That is, all of Hart's core textual meanings only exist because of an already-in-place background that is shared by the members of the legal interpretive community and that is made and remade by acts of persuasion.

> The question is not whether there are in fact plain cases – there surely are – but, rather, of what is their plainness a condition and a property? Hart's answer must be that a plain case is inherently plain, plain in and of itself, plain independently of the interpretive activities it can then be said to direct. But it takes only a little reflection to see that the truth is exactly the reverse ... Plainness, in short, is not a property of the case itself – there is no case itself – but of an interpretive history in the course of which one interpretive agenda – complete with stipulative definitions, assumed distinctions, canons of evidence, etc. – has subdued another. That history is then closed, but can always be reopened ... So that while there will always be paradigmatically plain cases – Hart is absolutely right to put them at the center of the adjudicative process – far from providing a stay against the forces of interpretation, they will be precisely the result of interpretation's force; for they will have been written and rewritten by interpretive efforts.[45]

So plain cases are possible not because of constraints imposed by the text itself (there is no "text itself" according to Fish), but because of constraints imposed by the shared background of the members of an interpretive community. What about hard cases then? Unlike Hart, who must offer different explanations for plain and hard cases, Fish offers a unified explanation. In hard cases too, he says, the shared background of the interpretive community is still operating to constrain the law-appliers, only instead of producing agreement it now produces disagreement that has a particular "enterprise-specific" [46] or "discipline-specific"[47] shape.[48] So while on Hart's account the constraints of the law run out in hard or penumbral cases, on Fish's account the constraints of the law are always operating, whether the case

---

[44] Ibid., 512.   [45] Ibid., 513.   [46] *Doing*, 130.

[47] Stanley Fish, "Interpretation is not a theoretical issue" 11 *Yale Journal of Law and the Humanities* (1999) 514 (hereafter cited as Fish, "Interpretation is not a theoretical issue").

[48] I shall return in more detail to the situation of disagreement within the one interpretive community in Chapter 9.

is easy or hard, core or penumbra. As he argued in the previous chapter, the unconstrained legal actor does not exist.

The intentionalist argument against textualism

Fish's anti-foundationalist argument against textualism, described above, stressed the importance of an already-in-place background in producing an apprehension of textual meaning, a background that was more extensive and complex than just syntax and semantics. His second argument against textualism, to which I now turn, is that we can know *a priori* that this background will include an assumption that the text was produced by an author who intended it to mean something. This second argument is part of a position that Fish calls "intentionalism." Intentionalism is less intuitive than textualism, and fewer people defend it. In the legal context, the main advocates of intentionalism are Steven Knapp and Walter Benn Michaels,[49] Larry Alexander and Saikrishna Prakash,[50] and Stanley Fish.[51] Intentionalism takes aim squarely at the central claim of textualism that you can ascertain the meaning of a text without considering authorial intention at all. According to Fish, for a meaningful text to exist the reader must be assuming that it was produced by an author and that the author intended it to mean something. Therefore you can never do without an author and authorial intention in the way textualism claims:

> Words alone, without an animating intention, do not have power, do not have semantic shape, are not yet language; and when someone tells you (as a textualist always will) that he or she is able to construe words apart from intention and then proceeds (triumphantly) to do so, what

[49] Walter Benn Michaels, "Against formalism: The autonomous text in legal and literary interpretation" 1 *Poetics Today* (1979) 23; Steven Knapp and Walter Benn Michaels, "Against theory" in W. J. T. Mitchell (ed.), *Against theory. Literary studies and the new pragmatism* (Chicago, IL: University of Chicago Press, 1985), 11 (hereafter cited as Knapp and Michaels, "Against theory"); Steven Knapp and Walter Benn Michaels, "Not a matter of interpretation" 42 *San Diego Law Review* (2005) 651.

[50] Larry Alexander and Saikrishna Prakash, "'Is that English you're speaking?' Why intention free interpretation is an impossibility" 41 *San Diego Law Review* (2004) 967 (hereafter cited as Alexander and Prakash, "Is that English you're speaking?").

[51] *No free speech*, ch. 12; Fish, "Interpretation is not a theoretical issue," 509; Fish, "There is no textualist position," 629; Fish, "Intention is all there is," 1109; Stanley Fish, "The intentionalist thesis once more" in Huscroft and Miller (eds.), *The challenge of originalism*, 99.

he or she will really have done is assumed an intention without being aware of having done so.[52]

There is also another part of Fish's intentionalist position, namely the claim that interpretation is always the task of ascertaining the actual authorial intention or meaning, but I will defer consideration of this claim until the next section of this chapter.

If intentionalism is correct, all self-proclaimed textualists are deeply confused about their own practice. Even though textualists insist that they are ignoring authorial intention and are only relying on conventional word meanings as set out in dictionaries and on established rules of grammar, they must actually be assuming an author with an intention whenever they see a meaningful text.

> I have stipulated that there are public meanings; you can find them in any standard dictionary. But the fact of public meanings does not tell you what any particular utterance means, for a speaker/writer is not obliged to deploy them and in the absence of evidence that he or she intends such an obligation they have no necessary relevance. In other words, while there are public meanings, they are of no interpretive help without an additional step – the step of forming an intention – they cannot supply.[53]

Textualists, naturally, would deny that they are doing this, and to support this denial they rely upon two strategies.

Texts without authors

One textualist strategy involves thought experiments in which English words appear in situations where it seems obvious that *no author* is involved. Schauer's example of shells being washed up on the beach in the shape C-A-T falls into this strategy. The argument is that because these shapes form English words that we can read in the absence of any author, this proves that words can have a textual meaning independently of any authorial intention. These thought experiments have a lot of intuitive power. It seems obvious that we can read the imagined texts, even though they were produced in a random, accidental, and authorless way. The intentionalist has the burden of showing that in any such imagined situation, some authorial intention is necessarily assumed. Although there are a number of arguments that can be brought to bear

---

[52] Fish, "There is no textualist position," 632–3. See too 635.

[53] Stanley Fish, "The intentionalist thesis once more" in Huscroft and Miller (eds.), *The challenge of originalism*, 108. See too *No free speech*, 299–300.

here,[54] the main intentionalist counterargument is that the textualist has not conducted his thought experiment carefully enough. If one genuinely *did* succeeded in making the author disappear, then the text would disappear too, leaving only random marks without sense.

Knapp and Michaels considered the thought experiment of a person walking on a beach and seeing a stanza of Wordsworth's poetry written in the sand. As the waves wash up the beach and recede, another stanza appears in the sand. Is this an example of a text that is meaningful without an author? They say no:

> You will either be ascribing these marks to some agent capable of intentions (the living sea, the haunting Wordsworth, etc.) or you will count them as nonintentional effects of mechanical processes (erosion, percolation, etc.). But in the second case – where the marks now seem to be accidents – will they still seem to be words? ... As long as you thought the marks were poetry, you were assuming their intentional character. You had no idea who the author was, and this may have tricked you into thinking that positing an author was irrelevant to your ability to read the stanza. But in fact you had, without realizing it, already posited an author. It was only with the mysterious arrival of the second stanza that your tacit assumption (e.g. someone writing with a stick) was challenged and you realized that you had made one. Only now, when positing an author seems impossible, do you genuinely imagine the marks as authorless. But to deprive them of an author is to convert them into accidental likenesses of language. They are not, after all, an example of intentionless meaning; as soon as they become intentionless they become meaningless as well.[55]

The textualist claim is that because we can understand the words in such thought experiments, this proves that we do not need authorial intention to understand the meaning of a text. The intentionalist counterclaim is that we are only able to understand the words produced in these thought experiments – we are only able to see them as words at all – because we have assumed that they were produced by an author with a certain intention. As Fish puts it:

> [I]n order to hear sense in arbitrarily produced sounds and marks we have to hear those sounds and marks within the assumption that they have been produced by some purposeful agent; that is, we have to hear them *as not arbitrarily produced*, even if to do so we must attribute purpose and

---

[54] See Michael Robertson, "The impossibility of textualism and the pervasiveness of rewriting in law" 22 *The Canadian Journal of Law and Jurisprudence* (2009) 388–91.
[55] Knapp and Michaels, "Against theory," 16.

intention to the waves or to the wind or to the great spirit that rolls
through all things.[56]

Fish also agrees with Knapp and Michaels that if you really do succeed in
expunging from your mind the belief that the marks before you were
produced deliberately by some author in order to communicate some
meaning, the result will be that you experience them as meaningless,
rather than as words.

> Suppose you're looking at a rock formation and see in it what seems to be
> the word "help." You look more closely and decide that, no, what you are
> seeing is an effect of erosion, random marks that just happen to resemble
> an English word. The moment you decide that nature caused the effect,
> you will have lost all interest in interpreting the formation, because you
> no longer believe that it has been produced intentionally, and therefore
> you no longer believe that it's a word, a bearer of meaning. It may look
> like a word – it may even seem to be more regularly formed as such than
> the scratchings of someone who is lost – but in the absence of the
> assumption that what you're looking at is a vehicle of intention, you will
> not regard it as language.[57]

Who might be the assumed authors of the unusual texts in these thought
experiments? In Knapp and Michaels's wave poem example, the first
assumed author is, naturally enough, an unknown person who earlier
wrote the words in the sand with a stick. But that assumption is both
revealed and demolished by the appearance of the second stanza. Who
might the author be now? One might conclude that the words are being
produced by an unknown person who is using unfamiliar technology
that enables him to generate words at a distance. Or one might turn
away from human authors and, as Knapp and Michaels suggest, conclude
that the author was Wordsworth's ghost, communicating from the other
side, or that the sea itself was trying to communicate a message. This is
an important point to which I shall return in the next section of this
chapter: intentionalism places no *a priori* limits on who or what the

---

[56] *No free speech*, 182. See too Alexander and Prakash, "Is that English you're speaking?"
976: "Without an author, real or hypothetical, intending to convey a meaning through
these marks, our seemingly grand Constitution [generated by a monkey hitting a key-
board] is nothing but a randomly generated mass of inked shapes that merely resembles a
text . . . Our simple point is that one cannot look at the marks on a page and understand
those marks to be a text (that is, a meaningful writing) without assuming that an author
made those marks intending to convey a meaning by them."

[57] Stanley Fish, "Intentional Neglect," *New York Times*, July 19, 2005, A 21. See too Fish,
"There is no textualist position," 632; *Doing*, 295–6; Fish, "Intention is all there is," 1111.

intentional agent producing the text is. That agent need not be a human being or collection of human beings. One can even stipulate or hypothesize an author other than the actual author. One can also ascribe to the actual author an intention other than the one you know the author really had. This aspect of the intentionalist argument is only that *some* agent with an intention must be assumed as author or we will not perceive a meaningful text. "[L]exical items and grammatical structures by themselves will yield no meaning – will not even be seen as lexical items and grammatical structures – until they are seen as having been produced by some intentional agent."[58]

The distinction between textual meaning and author's meaning

The second strategy used by textualists to support their position is to consider situations where an actual author is admitted (unlike the thought experiments just discussed) but to insist that a distinction can always be drawn in these situations between the textual (or literal or sentence) meaning and the author's (or intended or speaker's) meaning. Because there are two distinct meanings possible, textualists argue, you can take the textual meaning as definitive and ignore the author's meaning if you have good reasons to do so. It is then claimed that there are often good reasons to prefer the textual meaning to the author's meaning in the interpretation of legislation and in the interpretation of contracts.

The intentionalists' response is to deny the possibility of a distinction between textual meaning and author's meaning for the same reasons that they denied the possibility of an authorless text. Their claim is that in any situation where a text or an utterance is apprehended as meaningful, it will always be because some authorial intention has already been assumed. Without such an assumption, they say, there would not be a meaningful text at all. Therefore there can never be a bare textual meaning that could be preferred to authorial meaning – all there ever can be are competing assumptions about the authorial meaning.

> No act of reading can stop at the plain-meaning of a document, because that meaning itself will have emerged in the light of some stipulation of intentional circumstances, or purposes held by agents situated in real world situations. The difference between ways of reading will not be between a reading that takes communicative intent into account and a reading that doesn't, but between readings that proceed in the light of

---

[58] Fish, "There is no textualist position," 635.

differently assumed communicative intents. Formalist or literalist or "four corners" interpretation is not inadvisable ... it is impossible.[59]

To defend their claim, intentionalists need to provide alternative descriptions of what is really going on in the textualists' second strategy that expose the assumptions about authorial intention that are being made.

Fish does this when he considers the utterance: "Go through the light," which he reports was made by his father while Fish was driving them toward an intersection. He describes how a textualist would see this utterance as having a literal meaning ("Don't stop, just barrel on through"), which was generated by the conventional meanings of the words actually used, but would also identify a different meaning ("As soon as the light turns green, drive straight ahead; don't turn either left or right"), which his father intended but did not express adequately by the words he actually used. "This account of the matter is in line with the distinction (standard in mainstream philosophy of language) between sentence meaning and speaker's meaning, between the meaning an utterance has by virtue of the lexical items and syntactical structures that make it up, and the meaning a speaker may have intended but not achieved."[60] Fish, however, asserts that in order to understand his father's utterance as meaning "Don't stop, just barrel on through," he does not turn away from speaker's meaning to sentence meaning. Rather he substitutes one speaker's meaning for another speaker's meaning. That is, he assumes a different authorial intention; he assumes that a different set of concerns is animating his father and causing him to make the utterance.

> But were I to hear my father say that, it would not be because I heard his words apart from any intention within which they were uttered, but because I heard the words within the assumption of an intention different from the one I would have had to assume in order to hear him telling me to go straight ahead and not make any turns. The question here is, with which of two possible purposes (there could be many more) did my father produce these words? ... The choice is not between what my father said and what he meant, but between two specifications of what he meant. Did he mean (intend) to give directions to a son so hopelessly professorial that he could not be trusted to know where he was going, or did he mean (intend) to instruct that son to break the law, perhaps because he was late for an appointment, perhaps because he suddenly felt a pain in his chest, or perhaps because he enjoyed flouting authority and taking minor risks?[61]

---

[59] *No free speech*, 208.   [60] Fish, "There is no textualist position," 629.
[61] Ibid., 631.

According to intentionalists, textualists are not and could not be looking only at contract or statutory language (sentence meaning) and ignoring authorial intention (speaker's meaning), regardless of what they profess themselves to be doing. When textualists claim to be attending to syntax and semantics alone, they are misdescribing their practice, because the practice they claim to be performing is impossible. Textualists may be ignoring the actual intentions of the author (the legislature or the drafter of the contract) and may be assuming instead that the author intended the words used to have their most conventional dictionary meanings. Or textualists may be assuming an author other than the actual author, such as "the reasonable man." But whichever path they are following, it is not textualism, because an author with intentions is being assumed, not ignored in favor of semantics and syntax alone.

However, it is important to stress that this new description of the practice of textualists does not imply any criticism of the practice itself. There may be good reasons to move from actual to hypothetical authors in law or to ascribe non-actual intentions to actual authors, such as the rule of law reasons that Schauer advanced earlier. Alexander and Prakash argue that the real dispute between textualists and intentionalists cannot be over whether authorial intention is necessary, because it is. The real dispute is over "whether interpreters should look to the intentions of actual authors or hypothetical ones, and when, if we are to look for actual authorial intent, policy considerations (such as rule of law concerns) should lead us to ignore certain evidence of that intent."[62] This is another important matter to which I shall return in the next section of this chapter.

In summary, Fish's anti-foundationalist and intentionalist arguments bring us to the conclusion that the textualist version of formalism is impossible, and so it cannot provide the hoped-for route to legal objectivity and the preservation of clear and compelling meanings for legal texts. This is not to say that legal objectivity and clear and compelling meanings are impossible, only that their existence must be explained in some other way, which Fish has attempted to do. Fish is aware that his explanation will not satisfy most formalists/textualists, because it does not seem to make clear and compelling textual meaning rest upon a secure enough foundation. "[M]y conclusion will not be that the law fails to have a formal existence but that, in a sense I shall explain,

---

[62] Alexander and Prakash, "Is that English you're speaking?" 968–9.

it always succeeds, although the nature of that success – it is a political/rhetorical achievement – renders it bitter to the formalist taste."[63] After all, if apprehended meaning depends upon what sits in the background, then if you can change what sits in the background you can change the apprehended meaning. This malleability is precisely what formalist/textualists fear, and I shall consider Fish's response to this fear in Chapter 11.

More on Fish's intentionalism

Fish's intentionalism consists of two distinct claims, which he tends to present bundled together under the one name. Fish's first claim is that no text or utterance (or similar things such as "paintings, gestures, [and] facial expressions"[64]) will be experienced as meaningful unless we assume that it was produced by some intentional agent. This claim identifies an author with an intention as a necessary precondition for the existence of communicative phenomena in general.[65] I will hereafter call this aspect of intentionalism "the author claim."

> The crucial point is that one cannot read *or* reread independently of intention, independently, that is, of the assumption that one is dealing with marks or sounds produced by an intentional being, a being situated in some enterprise in relation to which he has a purpose or a point of view. This is ... an assumption without which the construing of sense could not occur. One cannot understand an utterance without *at the same time* hearing or reading it as the utterance of someone with more or less specific concerns, interests and desires, someone with an intention.[66]

Fish's second intentionalist claim is that interpretation can only be the activity of ascertaining the actual intention of the actual author who

---

[63] *No free speech*, 144.

[64] Stanley Fish, "The intentionalist thesis once more" in Huscroft and Miller (eds.), *The challenge of originalism*, 105. See too Fish, "Intention is all there is," 1113.

[65] Fish's analysis thus has no application to non-communicative phenomena. See Stanley Fish, "The intentionalist thesis once more" in Huscroft and Miller (eds.), *The challenge of originalism*, 105: "There are of course meanings just found in nature, what philosophers from Augustine to H. P. Grice call 'natural meanings'; as in 'if there's smoke, that means there's a fire' or 'tracks with a certain shape meant there's a bear in the vicinity.' These signs and others like them are signs of physical processes; they are not signs that some agent is trying to communicate something to you." Similarly, the data from a chemistry experiment are not communicative phenomena and so are not subject to interpretation although the scientist will seek to analyze, explain, and understand their significance.

[66] *Doing*, 99–100.

produced the text or utterance (or similar things). I will hereafter call this aspect of intentionalism "the interpretation claim."

> To interpret something is to determine what its author (or authors) intend. Whether I am offering a reading of Milton's *Paradise Lost* or of *Shaw* v. *Reno*, I am in the business of specifying, as fully and accurately as I can, what it is the author was getting at, meant to say, desired to communicate, had in mind, etc.[67]

Although Fish does not emphasize that there are two distinct claims contained within intentionalism, he implicitly acknowledges this separateness by providing different arguments for each claim. Arguments for the author claim and some objections to it were considered in the previous section. Arguments for the interpretation claim and some objections to it will be considered in this section.

Fish's interpretation claim – interpretation can only be the attempt to ascertain the actual intention of the actual author of the text or utterance, etc. – is narrower than and distinct from the author claim, which only states that without the assumption of *some* authorial intention a text or utterance will not be experienced as meaningful and will instead be experienced as meaningless marks or sounds. The author claim will still be satisfied if the reader turns away from the actual author and actual intention in favor of a fictional author or fictional intention, but the interpretation claim will not.

It is certainly the case that a reader *can* turn away from the actual intention of the author in favor of a fictional intention. Fish notes that "because it is not words alone but words as tokens of an intention that mean, a space can be opened up in which someone with a mind to can endow another's words with an intention he knows the speaker or writer not to have had."[68] We might do this in a spirit of generosity, so as to make the text or utterance "the best it can be," regardless of the author's actual intention. Or we might do this with more malicious intent, as when we knowingly ascribe a fictitious intention to an author in order to harm him. Fish offers the example of a university administrator who decides to treat as genuine a resignation threat that he knows was intended only as a negotiating ploy.[69]

---

[67] Fish, "Interpretation is not a theoretical issue," 509. See too Stanley Fish, "The intentionalist thesis once more" in Huscroft and Miller (eds.), *The challenge of originalism*, 115; Fish, "Intention is all there is," 1112.

[68] Fish, "There is no textualist position," 633.   [69] Ibid., 633–4.

It is also possible to assume a completely fictitious author of a text. We can do this in the absence of an actual author, as in the next two examples.

> Suppose, for example, my method of interpreting a text consists of taking every third word of it and seeing what patterns of significance then emerged. There are at least three understandings within which I might be proceeding: (1) I might believe that the author, in writing the text, employed a code that I have now discovered; (2) I might believe that the author (unbeknownst to him) was controlled (through brainwashing, injection, diabolic possession) by a superior force employing the same code (that force would then *be* the author); or (3) I might believe neither (1) nor (2) nor any version of them but simply want to see what I could make of the text by subjecting it to this procedure. Under the first and second understandings I am interpreting; under the third I am playing with the text.[70]

If such playing with the text with understanding (3) in place generated the sequence "the weather is fine today," the author claim would insist that Fish could only perceive that sequence as a meaningful English sentence (rather than a random collection of marks that accidentally resembles an English sentence) if he imagined a fictional author intentionally producing that sequence. (He cannot suppose that there is an actual author of the sentence, because he has rejected all versions of understandings [1] and [2].) Similarly, in "There is no textualist position" Fish discusses the example raised by Walter Sinnott-Armstrong of a lightning strike that produces marks on a tree that look like the word "Stop."[71] Drivers generally obey, but one does not, resulting in an accident, and a lawsuit ensues. Fish insists that the marks caused by the lightning are meaningless, because they have no author, but he acknowledges that it might be sensible for the court to "give legal weight to a long-standing and effect-producing mistake."[72] However, he says, if the court did this, it "would be doing law, not philosophy of language . . . and it could come to its decision without ever pronouncing on whether or not the marks meant 'stop.'"[73] But if in the course of its judgment the court *did* hold that the marks meant "stop," the author claim holds that the court would have to imagine or hypothesize a fictitious author who intentionally produced the written command to stop.

---

[70] *No free speech*, 185.   [71] Fish, "There is no textualist position," 640–2.
[72] Ibid., 642.   [73] Ibid.

Finally, even when there is an actual author of a text, and we know who it is, it is possible to imagine how it would read if somebody else had authored it. "If you are not concerned with the meaning a speaker or writer puts into a text, nothing bars you from finding in it whatever you like, perhaps by imagining the text as spoken by someone other than the author (what would Mark Twain or Elvis have meant by these words?)."[74] Lawyers do this when they ignore the beliefs and expectations of the actual author of a legal document and assume that a fictional author, "the reasonable man" (who has a different bundle of beliefs and expectations assigned to him), produced it. In his critique of Aharon Barak, Fish describes the "reasonable testator," who is a version of the reasonable man, and who "is built not on the person and history of the real testator, but on an idealized fiction."[75]

Given that Fish acknowledges that we can make counterfactual assumptions about authorial identity and/or authorial intention, and we have just seen that such assumptions can be part of a creative engagement with a text that produces interesting and useful results, why should such activities not be categorized as forms of interpretation? It is natural to object here that Fish is just stipulating a narrow meaning for "interpretation" that others are not required to respect. He can certainly resolve to give a word a particular meaning in his own writings, but he cannot impose this on others by fiat. A version of this objection is made by Steven Smith, who accepts Fish's author claim while rejecting his interpretation claim:

> My own view, for what it is worth, is something of a hybrid. Legal interpreters are looking for semantic meaning, I think, and semantic meanings are always the meanings intended by authors. Up to this point, I agree with Alexander, Prakash, Fish, Campos, and Kay . . . However, we can and often do interpret texts to ascertain the semantic intentions not of the flesh-and-blood historical authors, but rather of constructed or hypo-thetical authors. This method is problematic to be sure . . . but it is *possible* – and it is practiced. So in a sense, we have power to choose which authors to look to. And this choice might be described as a sort of choice among "meanings."[76]

---

[74] Stanley Fish, "The intentionalist thesis once more" in Huscroft and Miller (eds.), *The challenge of originalism*, 119.

[75] Fish, "Intention is all there is," 1132.

[76] Seven D. Smith, "That old-time originalism" in Huscroft and Miller (eds.), *The challenge of originalism*, 242.

Fish is well aware of this objection to his interpretation claim: "At this point someone always objects ... who are you to say what is and is not interpretive? Aren't you just foisting (or attempting to foist) a stipulative definition on us?"[77] But Fish emphatically denies that he is just stipulating a private use of the term "interpretation." Instead he offers an argument for the interpretation claim that he says everyone else is compelled to accept if they want to retain interpretation as a rational activity that should be taken seriously:

> For interpretation to be a rational activity and not a form of what H. L. A. Hart called "scorer's discretion," there must be an object prior to and independent of the interpreter's activities, an object in relation to which you can marshal and assess evidence and measure progress. The text cannot be that object because until an intention has been posited for it, it is radically unstable, it doesn't stand still. The desire of the interpreter cannot be that object because it is a moving and ever changing target; it doesn't stand still. The only object of interpretation that makes it a rational activity rather than a free-for-all is the intention of the author. Which is not to say that the intention of the author is immediately and perspicuously available; it is, rather, what the interpreter seeks. It is the lodestar that at once guides the interpreter's efforts and is their goal. It keeps the game honest.[78]

The first step in Fish's argument is that interpretation must have some independent thing as its object, some thing that is fixed in advance of the interpretive process and that it is the goal of the interpretive process to discover and describe accurately. It is only if such an independent object of interpretation exists that there will be a standard against which competing interpretations can be judged to be right or wrong, better or worse. The interpretation claim "is the answer to the question 'What must be the case – what must we presuppose – if notions like agreement, disagreement, error, correction, and revision – are to make any sense?'"[79] Without such an independent object of interpretation, Fish argues, the process becomes a free-for-all, with people able to try and read the text in any way they want, without any constraints. There would no longer be any grounds to consider one interpretation better than another, and instead, there would just be a sequence of readings limited only by the ingenuity of the interpreter and the gullibility of the audience. There

---

[77] Fish, "Intention is all there is," 1133. See too Stanley Fish, "The intentionalist thesis once more" in Huscroft and Miller (eds.), *The challenge of originalism*, 104–5.
[78] Fish, "Intention is all there is," 1138 n98. See too 1114.
[79] Fish, "There is no textualist position," 647.

are an infinite number of fictitious authors and fictitious authorial intentions that might be assumed. The process would cease to have any real purpose other than the display of ingenuity and rhetorical power; it would cease to make sense as a rational inquiry into the truth of some matter. (Here we see clearly the invalidity of any charge that Fish is a kind of textual relativist who is unwilling to say that one interpretation is better than another).[80]

At this point, I need to flag the problem that this first step in the argument for Fish's interpretation claim appears to be inconsistent with positions Fish has argued for strongly elsewhere in his corpus. Talk of an independent object of interpretation that exists prior to any interpretive efforts, and that those efforts seek to discover and describe, sounds like the foundationalism Fish rejected in Chapter 2. Talk of a free-for-all with readers striving to make the text mean whatever they want sounds like a resuscitation of the unconstrained legal actor that Fish argued was an illusion in Chapter 7. I will return to these prima facie contradictions at the end of this chapter.

The second step Fish takes to defend his interpretation claim is to argue that all but one of the available candidates to provide the required independent object of interpretation fail to do so.

> [T]raditionally, three answers have been given to the question, "what is the meaning of a text?": a text means what its author intends; a text means what its language, reasonably construed according to accepted usage, says it does; a text means what its interpreters take it to mean. My argument throughout has been that the second and third answers don't work.[81]

The second answer is textualism, the claim that the words in a text have already established meanings (recorded in dictionaries) and these word-meanings, together with rules of grammar, generate a fixed and stable objective meaning. But as we saw in the previous section, textualism is eliminated as a viable position by the author claim – in the absence of authorial intention you will not have a text with an objective meaning, only random marks. The third answer claims that textual meaning is determined by an interpretive community. It asserts that

---

[80] Ronald Dworkin makes this charge in "My reply to Stanley Fish (and Walter Benn Michaels): Please don't talk about objectivity anymore" in W. J. T. Mitchell (ed.), *The politics of interpretation* (Chicago IL: University of Chicago Press, 1983), 289–95 (hereafter cited as Dworkin, "My reply to Stanley Fish").

[81] Fish, "Intention is all there is," 1138 n98. See too Fish, "There is no textualist position," 644–5 for a more extended description of the answers that do not work according to Fish.

the question of meaning is settled by the community of interpreters and
not by the intention of any author: marks can acquire a meaning even if
no one intended it, so long as the meaning is agreed on by those who
encounter them: "What gives the marks their meanings are the ways in
which they are understood by the community, not the way in which they
are produced." This might be called the "interpreters (or readers) decide"
principle, and it is one frequently encountered in the literature . . . This
position . . . is supported by the reception-history of texts, a history in
which the specification of a text's meaning undergoes repeated revision at
the hands of subsequent generations of readers; it is the intentions of
those readers, says Shusterman, rather than the intentions of the author
"that continue to guide and shape understanding . . . far beyond . . .
authorial control."[82]

This third answer is one embraced by some modern movements in
literary theory:

> There is another answer to the question that is neither textualist nor
> intentionalist. It asserts that a text means what its interpreters and ratifiers
> say it means. It is not authors and their intentions, or texts and their
> properties, but interpreters and their activities that determine meaning.
> Sometimes this thesis grows out of a post-structuralist account of mean-
> ing as always other than itself, always being grafted and then regrafted
> onto new contexts where it takes on ever new forms. Meaning, it is said,
> often by followers of Derrida, cannot be controlled by the intention of any
> author and is always being abandoned to an "essential drift" that renders
> it forever indeterminate.[83]

Indeed, this third answer is often attributed to Fish himself,[84] since it
seems to follow from the importance he gave to interpretive communities
in his earlier work.[85] If that attribution is correct, then Fish has fallen into
a contradiction. The meaning of a text cannot both be what the author
intended and also what the readers agree it is.

In his contribution to *Postmodern sophistry*, Fish squashed this poten-
tial contradiction. He clarified his position on interpretive communities

[82] Fish, "There is no textualist position," 642.
[83] Stanley Fish, "The intentionalist thesis once more" in Huscroft and Miller (eds.), *The
challenge of originalism*, 113.
[84] See, for example, Dennis Patterson, *Law and truth* (Oxford: Oxford University Press,
1996), ch. 6 ("Law as an interpretive community: The case of Stanley Fish"); Torben Spaak,
"Relativism in legal thinking: Stanley Fish and the concept of an interpretative community" 21 *Ratio Juris* (2008) 160–3; Georgia Chrysostomides, "Doing the unnatural –
Stanley Fish's theory of interpretation" (2000) *UCL Jurisprudence Review* 172–3.
[85] Fish sometimes gives good grounds for this attribution. See, for example, *Text*, 16 where
Fish seems to adopt the thesis that community agreement determines textual meaning.

in response to criticisms of it, and in doing so he showed how this position fits with his intentionalism.[86] The interpretation claim gives an answer to the general or theoretical question "what is the meaning of a text?" – a text means what its author(s) intended it to mean – while an interpretive community is a tool used to explain the history of attempts by readers to ascertain the textual meaning generated by such authorial intention. That is, an interpretive community is a tool used in an empirical investigation as to why a particular text comes to be seen as having a particular meaning by a particular group at a particular time. This investigation will explain the apprehended meaning by focusing upon elements of the background understandings, etc., shared by the members of that particular group.

> The interpretive community is a device of interrogation, and what it promises and delivers is a method. Once a question [about why a group has accepted or discarded a particular textual interpretation] has been framed, the interpretive community thesis tells you that in order to answer it you should attend to the relevant background conditions – assumed definitions, notions of evidence, locations of reputable archives, storehouses of legitimate arguments, lists of exemplary achievements, lists of achievements for which one will be rewarded, lists of authoritative practitioners, senses of what we do around here and what it is not our business to do – within which the relevant actors perform.[87]

Even if all of the members of an interpretive community agree on what the text means at one time, the meaning of the text is not defined by that agreement, Fish insists. It is possible for everyone in an interpretive community to agree on what a text means, he says, but for everyone to be wrong, because what the text *really* means is what the author of the text intended it to mean.

> Much of the criticism directed at the interpretive community idea flows from a misconception of the claims I make for it, which are not norma- tive, but sociological. That is, I do not employ it to answer questions like what does *Paradise Lost* mean or is this or that reading of *Paradise Lost* true. I employ it to explain how a particular reading of the poem gained the ascendancy and became the leading candidate (perhaps the entirely triumphant candidate) for the designation of "true one," but I neither identify that institutional success with the emergence of the real meaning or of "the truth," nor do I assert that the question of truth is foreclosed by

---

[86] Stanley Fish, "One more time" in Olson and Worsham (eds.), *Postmodern sophistry*, 274–9.
[87] Ibid., 276

the judgments the community has produced ... What it can provide is a
satisfactory account of how meanings have made their way, and the
question of whether or not those meanings were the right ones remains
open; an interpretive community analysis cannot answer it or even
approach it; it's not that kind of exercise.[88]

Now we can see why Fish rejects the third answer to the question "what
is the meaning of a text?" described earlier and why it is consistent of him
to do so. The "interpreters (or readers) decide" position would not
provide the "object prior to and independent of the interpreter's activities"
that interpretation must have if it is to be a rational activity. Instead the
"interpreters (or readers) decide" position would make *the true meaning*
of a text always susceptible to alteration by the powerful persuasive or
rhetorical acts of members of the interpretive community. Fish certainly
allows that community apprehensions of textual meaning can be changed
by powerful persuasive acts, as the reception-history of texts shows, but, as
he argued in *Postmodern sophistry*, this does not affect the claim that the
true meaning of the text does not change. Different apprehensions of
textual meaning within an interpretive community provide "an account of
the career of *communication*, not of *meaning*. The meaning remains what
it is, even if determinations of what it is proliferate."[89] Indeed, the conduct
of those striving to dislodge a previous interpretation and put a new one
in its place implicitly accepts that the true meaning is fixed independently
of community agreement. Fish argues:

> A reader who does that believes that he or she has (at long last) discovered
> the true meaning of the text, the meaning its author intended. If that were
> not the case, successive interpreters would not bother to argue that a
> previous reading was wrong, or that the evidence adduced for a rival
> interpretation was unpersuasive, or that new evidence has finally solved
> the puzzle. If the point is just to be more ingenious than the last guy, why
> not get right to it and skip all the disagreement and demonstration stuff?
> The whole process, along with the notions of "same" text, only makes
> sense if there is something everyone is after.[90]

Other objections to Fish's interpretation claim have been raised by
Natalie Stoljar, as Fish describes in "There is no textualist position":

---

[88] Ibid., 277.

[89] Stanley Fish, "The intentionalist thesis once more" in Huscroft and Miller (eds.), *The
challenge of originalism*, 113. Emphasis added.

[90] Fish, "There is no textualist position," 643. See too 644; Stanley Fish, "The intentionalist
thesis once more" in Huscroft and Miller (eds.), *The challenge of originalism*, 113.

First, she says, there is the "epistemological objection": because evidence of intention "is often equivocal, incomplete, or obscure, it will be difficult for an interpreter to offer convincing justification for the claim that a certain interpretation corresponds to an author's actual intention." ... A second standard objection – Stoljar calls it the "non-existence objection" – is a relative of the first. It says that in the case of groups like legislatures, "individuals within the majority have different aims and intentions in mind. How should the individual intentions be combined to form a group intention that is plausibly the intention 'behind' the legislation?"[91]

With regards to the "epistemological objection," it is important to remember that the argument for Fish's interpretation claim is conceptual in nature, not empirical. That is, it purports to identify what must necessarily be the case for interpretation to be a rational activity rather than an exercise in frivolity. As a conceptual argument, it is untouched by empirical problems such as those raised in Stoljar's first objection. Even if it turns out to be difficult or impossible to determine what the author's intention was in creating a particular text, utterance, or similar thing, that does not affect the claim that interpretation is necessarily the activity of seeking to ascertain that intention, Fish insists.

> Yes, it is often the case, as many have pointed out, that intention is obscure and hard to discern, either because the evidence of it is wanting or contradictory, or because the intending agent is a committee or a congress, or because the intending agent has been dead for 300 years, or because the intending agent is mentally ill or a multiple personality. All of these speak to the fact that in many cases and for many reasons it may prove impossible to figure out what the intention is, but that does not change the prior fact that figuring out what the intention is is the interpreter's job, irrespective or whether or not he or she succeeds in doing it.[92]

Because they are conceptual rather than empirical claims, neither the author claim nor the interpretation claim provides a *method* for interpreting anything.[93] Although the upshot of the claims is that

---

[91] Fish, "There is no textualist position," 646 and 648 citing Natalie Stoljar, "Survey article: Interpretation, indeterminacy and authority: Some recent controversies in the philosophy of law" 11 *Journal of Political Philosophy* (2003) 470.

[92] Stanley Fish, "The intentionalist thesis once more" in Huscroft and Miller (eds.), *The challenge of originalism*, 116. See too Fish, "Intention is all there is," 1115; Fish, "There is no textualist position," 636.

[93] Fish, "There is no textualist position," 643–4, 646, 647; Fish, "Intention is all there is," 1114, 1144; Stanley Fish, "The intentionalist thesis once more" in Huscroft and Miller (eds.), *The challenge of originalism*, 100, 115.

interpretation necessarily is seeking to ascertain the actual author's real intention, this knowledge does not help you in the slightest in figuring out who the author is or what that author intended. For example, neither claim allows you to assume that the actual author is a human being. Also, neither claim allows you to assume that the actual author intended a single clear meaning. Some authors might deliberately intend to create ambiguity or multiple meanings to achieve a literary effect or to satisfy different groups of readers.[94] Again, neither claim allows you to assume that the actual author is the best authority on what the intention behind the text etc. was. Authors can have unconscious intentions as well as conscious intentions, and can later change their minds about what their intention was when they originally produced the text or utterance. That is, authors have to interpret their own works just as other people do, and may sometimes be unsure about what they meant.[95]

So Fish does not minimize the very real difficulties that can arise in attempting to interpret a text or utterance, and he does not hold out the author claim or the interpretation claim as a method for resolving those difficulties. But neither do his two claims make successful communication into an unlikely phenomenon. Successful communication first requires that the sender and the recipient of the communication belong to the same interpretive community. That is, they share an already-in-place background of assumptions, values, goals, etc., of the sort that Fish described in Part I. This is not a rare and precarious situation but a common one for human beings who become who they are through being socialized into different communities, as we have also seen in Part I.

> [T]he reason why I can speak and presume to be understood by someone like Abrams is that I speak to him *from within* a set of interests and concerns, and it is relation to those interests and concerns that I assume he will hear my words. If what follows is communication or understanding, it will not be because he and I share a language, in the sense of knowing the meanings of individual words, and the rules for combining

---

94 Though even here the ambiguity is shaped by an intention. Stanley Fish, "The intentionalist thesis once more" in Huscroft and Miller (eds.), *The challenge of originalism*, 113: "As Steven Smith observes, 'legislators may sometimes choose to be deliberately ambiguous or vague, but they will communicate their favored ambiguity as precisely as possible,' for 'they will want the courts and the public to have the blessing and burden of *their* preferred ambiguity, not someone else's ambiguity.'"

95 See *No free speech*, 183; Fish, "Interpretation is not a theoretical issue," 510; Stanley Fish, "The intentionalist thesis once more" in Huscroft and Miller (eds.), *The challenge of originalism*, 110–1.

them, but because a way of thinking, a form of life, shares us, and implicates us in a world of already-in-place objects, purposes, goals, procedures, values, and so on; and it is to the features of that world that any words we utter will be heard as necessarily referring.[96]

Next, the recipient of the communication has to determine what meaning the sender intended his words, etc., to have, and although this can sometimes be difficult, normally it will not be. Authors of texts or utterances can intend the words they use to have any meaning, and so it is true that an author can choose to use meanings known only to a small number of people.[97] Although private languages and secret codes are certainly possible in Fish's account (we saw a larger version of a private code when considering trade usage), their use is not typical. People who want to achieve successful communication in everyday contexts will typically intend by their words the common meanings that are already established and recorded in dictionaries.

> Words, wholly conventional as they are, can bear any meaning at all, although in this or that real world context – drafting legislation, giving directions, ordering pizza – you might be well advised (it is advice, not a law deriving from the true order of things) to mean by your words what most people would assume (it is an assumption based on expectations and habit, not on language's natural limits) you to mean. What this means (and its hard to get away from the word), is that while a speaker or writer can resolve to respect the meanings words conventionally have in ordinary usage, that resolve is a *part* of his intention, not a constraint on it. "Public language" – word-meaning correlations known to and accepted by a great many people most of the time – is a resource for speakers and writers (it allows them to predict the response of one, very large, population), not a limitation on what they can mean by the words they employ.[98]

---

[96] *Text*, 303–4. See too *Professional*, 14. Ronald Dworkin makes a similar point in *Law's empire* (Cambridge, MA: Belknap Press, 1986), 63–4 (hereafter cited as Dworkin, *Law's empire*): "They must, to be sure, agree about a great deal in order to share a social practice ... They must understand the world in sufficiently similar ways and have interests and convictions sufficiently similar to recognize sense in each other's claims, to treat these *as* claims rather than just noises. That means not just using the same dictionary, but sharing what Wittgenstein called a form of life sufficiently concrete so that the one can recognize sense and purpose in what the other says and does, see what sort of beliefs and motives would make sense of his diction, gesture, tone, and so forth." It is significant, I believe, that both Fish and Dworkin use Wittgenstein's term "form of life."

[97] Fish, "Intention is all there is," 1123.

[98] Ibid., 1124. See too Stanley Fish, "The intentionalist thesis once more" in Huscroft and Miller (eds.), *The challenge of originalism*, 103.

Stoljar's second "non-existence objection" to the interpretation claim assumes that Fish requires us to identify some human being(s) as the author, and she then points out that multiple human authorship can pose a problem if the humans making up the group author have different intentions. In his response to Stoljar's objection in "There is no textualist position," Fish seeks to deal with it on its own terms, and so he considers various situations of multiple human authorship.[99] But it was equally open to him to point out to critics like Stoljar that their assumption that his interpretation claim requires human author(s) with intentions is based on an incorrect understanding of the author claim. Elsewhere Fish has stressed that the author claim does not

> tell you who or what the author is. That is, again, an empirical, not a theoretical question, and there are no *a priori* limits as to what answer it will receive. St. Paul declares "not me, but my master in me"; that is, I am a mouthpiece for the intention of another. Freud tells us that it is the unconscious that speaks in fractured and non-linear ways that can be uncovered only by an analysis that may prove interminable. Some historians argue that it is the spirit of the age, the *zeitgeist*, that speaks, filling and structuring the minds of politicians, preachers, poets, and the proverbial man in the street. Wordsworth believes in a great spirit that rolls through all things including, one presumes, the cortical things with which intentions are formed.[100]

Recall that in the "wave poem" thought experiment described by Knapp and Michaels, the assumed author of the verses (once we were forced to abandon the belief that that author was a human being who had earlier written the first verse in the sand with a stick) shifted to "the living sea, the haunting Wordsworth, etc."[101] Ronald Dworkin sought to inflict damage on intentionalists by pointing out that "[w]e can read Hamlet in a psychodynamic way without supposing that Shakespeare either did or could have intended that we do so."[102] However, Fish replies that "[i]f we are convinced that the [true] meaning of Hamlet is psychodynamic but that Shakespeare intended no such meaning, then we are attributing the meaning to an intentional agent other than Shakespeare, perhaps to the spirit of the age, to some transhistorical truth about

---

[99] Fish, "There is no textualist position," 648.

[100] Stanley Fish, "The intentionalist thesis once more" in Huscroft and Miller (eds.), *The challenge of originalism*, 114–5. See too 105–6; Fish, "Interpretation is not a theoretical issue," 511; Fish, "Intention is all there is," 1111; *Doing*, 119.

[101] Knapp and Michaels, "Against theory," 16.

[102] Dworkin, "My reply to Stanley Fish," 310.

human nature, or to the intentional structure of language ... [O]ne can conceive of intention as something other than the possession of a 'particular historical person.'"[103]

Once we realize that Fish's author claim does not require us to find a *human* author, and that a ghost, or God, or an abstraction can satisfy the requirement for an author just as well, a new route becomes available to rebut Stoljar's second objection that the intention claim is unable to deal with the multiple and conflicting states of mind of the human legislators who voted to enact a statute. It is open to an intentionalist to respond that the actual author of the statute is not a group of human beings at all but is an institution, the legislature, understood as something that is not reducible to the individual legislators currently elected to it.[104] As it happens, Dworkin develops just such an institutional approach to legislation in Chapter 9 of *Law's empire*. In that chapter, Dworkin invents a new ideal judge, Hermes, to advance "the speaker's meaning theory of legislation" against the approach of Hercules,[105] but eventually Hermes comes to see "that official statements of purpose, made in the canonical form established by the practice of legislative history, should be treated as themselves acts of the state personified."[106]

> So long as we think legislative intention is a matter of what someone has in mind and means to communicate by a vote, we must take as primary the mental states of particular people because institutions do not have minds, and then we must worry about how to consolidate individual intentions into a collective, fictitious group intention. But Hermes abandoned the search for mental states when he decided that a legislator's pertinent intention is a matter of his overall convictions, organized by constructive interpretation, not his particular hopes or expectations or discrete concrete opinions. *Constructive interpretation can be directed to the record of institutions and practices as well as individuals, and Hermes has no reason not to attribute convictions directly to the legislature itself.*[107]

Dworkin believes that his analysis is superior to "the speaker's meaning theory of legislation" because it is not vulnerable to the types of problems

---

[103] *Doing*, 119.

[104] This raises the debate between those committed to "methodological individualism" and those who take an organizational or "systems approach" to complex things such as legislatures and corporations, but intentionalists can appear on either side of that debate.

[105] Dworkin, *Law's empire*, 314–5, 317.   [106] Ibid., 343.

[107] Ibid., 335–6. Emphasis added.

Stoljar identified in her second objection.[108] But he fails to see that his "speaker's meaning theory of legislation," because it assumes that the speaker is a human being or group of human beings, is not the same as Fish's intentionalism. Fish's intentionalism imposes no such requirement (it places "no *a priori* limits" on who or what the author is) and is completely compatible with making an institution, rather than human beings, the actual author of a statute. A supporter of Fish's intentionalism can do just what Dworkin does, namely attribute intentions "directly to the legislature itself." The interpreter's task is then to ascertain what this institutional author actually intended by any particular enactment by looking to such things as "official statements of purpose, made in the canonical form established by the practice of legislative history."

Interestingly, Fish himself takes a different approach to the authorship of legislation. He tries to develop a position intermediate between a human author and an institutional author. He wants to identify human individuals as the authors, but he stresses that their intentions can only be understood in terms of their institutional roles:

> Imagine, for example, a group of legislators, people charged with the task of framing laws. Imagine further that they are considering the law of campaign finance regulations. They produce a text and you want to know what it means. You don't read it through the lens of what you may happen to know about their psychological and neurological profiles. You read it through the lens of a set of intentions – institutional not psychological – they could possibly have had given the legal history of the issue and their place in the system, the intentions (or purposes) of tightening campaign finance regulations, or loosening them, or modifying them or eliminating them or all of the above. (A complicated piece of legislation might defer to many constituencies and preferences in the course of its unfolding.) The "actual" author, then, *is* the author-as-institutional-actor, at least for legal purposes; the other sense of "actual" – tied to psychology and physiology – is irrelevant, not to the legal point.[109]

In "Intention is all there is," Fish notes other objections to the interpretation claim that are posed by Aharon Barak:

---

[108] Dworkin had earlier raised the same objection as Stoljar's regarding legislation in Ronald Dworkin, "Law as interpretation" 60 *Texas Law Review* (1982) 547 (hereafter cited as Dworkin, "Law as interpretation"). Another form of this "non-existence objection" can be found at 541–2 where Dworkin says that interpretation of his chain novel "must be interpretation in a non-intention-bound style, because, at least for all novelists after the second, there is no single author whose intentions any interpreter can, by the rules of the project, regard as decisive."

[109] Fish, "Intention is all there is," 1131. See too 1131 n80; 1144.

Barak believes that purposive interpretation is [a] better answer [to the question "what is the meaning of a text?"] because its scope and ambitions are much larger than the narrow goal of specifying the intentions of the author. Purposive intention, he claims, "facilitates viewing the text as part of the totality of the system as a whole and helps the text and its interpreter fulfil their roles in a democracy." In short, purposive interpretation answers more questions than mere intentionalism (which often cannot even answer its own question).[110]

A second objection raised by Barak is that

"[Intentionalism] fails to view the text being interpreted as a creature of a changing environment," and therefore it "freezes the meaning of a text to the historical point in time of its creation, rendering it irrelevant to the meaning of the text in a modern democracy."[111]

Although Fish did not mention him by name in his recent articles on intentionalism (perhaps to avoid reigniting their old quarrel which shall be described in the next chapter), Dworkin also raised a number of objections to the position that interpretation means ascertaining what the author(s) of the text intended.[112] In the 1982 paper "Law as interpretation," which first sparked his debate with Fish, Dworkin stated:

The idea of interpretation cannot serve as a general account of the nature or truth of propositions of law, however, unless it is cut loose from these associations with the speaker's meaning or intention. Otherwise it becomes simply one version of the positivist's thesis that propositions of law describe decisions made by people or institutions in the past. If interpretation is to form the basis of a different and more plausible theory about propositions of law, then we must develop a more inclusive account of what interpretation is.[113]

In essence, Dworkin's objections to Fish's interpretation claim anticipate those of Barak – it offers an account of interpretation that is too narrow and too static. As we shall see, Dworkin's "more inclusive account of what interpretation is" holds that the legal interpreter cannot just confine his attention to a particular statute or judgment, and ask what its author(s) intended when it was created. Instead the legal interpreter (exemplified by Hercules) must consider the entire legal institutional history in order to ascertain which set of moral and political principles

---

[110] Ibid., 1144.   [111] Ibid., 1145.

[112] See Dworkin, "Law as interpretation" 536–40, 546–8; Dworkin, "My reply to Stanley Fish," 308–13; Dworkin, Law's empire, ch 2.

[113] Dworkin, "Law as interpretation" 529.

make the most sense of that history. Then law as integrity requires that
the interpreter be guided by these background moral and political principles in deciding what meaning the statute or precedent currently before
him has and how it is to be applied. The job of the interpreter, on
Dworkin's account, is to make the legal text "the best it can be"[114]
by making it cohere with, and extend, the background moral and political
principles that best explain the legal institutional history. Interpretation
for Dworkin is therefore an expansive creative process, not an empirical
investigation into facts about past authorial intention. For Dworkin, the
most interesting and important aspects of interpretation are to be found
outside the narrow boundaries drawn by intentionalists. Also, while
for intentionalists the meaning of a text is fixed for all time by an author's
original intention, Dworkin would accept that if the legal institutional
history and its background moral and political principles change over
time, then the demands of integrity or coherence will require changes
in what particular cases and statutes mean, regardless of the original
authorial intention.[115]

In order to explain how Fish responds to these objections of Dworkin
and Barak, I first need to introduce a final element of Fish's intentionalist
analysis. In this section, I have already separated out the interpretation
claim and the author claim and have examined the argument Fish gives
in support of the interpretation claim. If that argument is successful, then
interpretation is an activity with a precise and narrow focus: it is seeking
to ascertain the actual intention of the actual author of the text or
utterance (or similar communicative phenomenon). But as I noted
earlier, we can do things with texts other than interpret them. We can
also assume a fictional author and/or a fictional intention. If those
activities are not interpreting, what are they? Fish says these activities
constitute *rewriting*:

> But what if getting it right is not a priority for you? What if you are just
> trying, in Richard Rorty's words, to beat the text into a shape useful to
> your purposes? You do not care what the author meant by the text; you

---

[114] Ibid., 531–2, 543–4, 546, Dworkin, *Law's empire*, 52.
[115] Dworkin, *Law's empire*, 348: "Hercules interprets not just the statute's text but its life, the
process that begins before it becomes law and extends far beyond that moment. He aims
to make the best he can of this continuing story, and his interpretation therefore changes
as the story develops"; ibid., 350: "Hercules interprets history in motion, because the story
he must make as good as it can be is the whole story through his decision and beyond.
He does not amend out-of-date statutes to suit new times, as the metaphysics of speaker's
meaning would suggest. He recognizes what the old statutes have since become."

just want to make it mean what you need it to mean . . . One understands the strategy and the desire behind it; but the strategy is political, not interpretive. It is a strategy of rewriting. Rewriting is always what is being done when the interpreter's desire for an outcome takes precedence over the search for meaning. Rewriting is what is authorized by those who say that interpreters determine what a text means. Rewriting is what is urged by those who say that the constitution is a living document or a living tree and should be read in the light of present concerns. Even if the goals are arguably laudable, the moment you prefer their achievement to the task of specifying the author's intention, you have ceased to be an interpreter and have become instead an agent of power.[116]

I will argue in Chapter 10 that rewriting turns out to be a very important part of law in Fish's analysis, but it is a practice about which he displays ambivalence (which I will attempt to explain soon). On the one hand, his descriptions of what people are doing when they move away from interpretation have a negative flavor. Fish described the alternative to interpretation as "a free-for-all"[117] and as a "weightless and irresponsible affair."[118] The contrast drawn seems to be between a better practice and a worse practice, rather than between two separate but equal practices. On the other hand, Fish acknowledges that in the practice of law, shifting from interpreting a text to rewriting a text can sometimes be the right thing to do – that is, rewriting now becomes the rational and sensible thing to do. In "Intention is all there is," Fish agrees with Barak's general observation that

> the tasks law is asked to perform are complex and varied, and it would be unrealistic to assume either that they could all be accomplished by specifying the intention of some author or that, if information about the author's intention is lacking, they should be left undone. This doesn't mean, however, that interpretive avenues other than the search for intention should be explored; rather it means that interpretation is not always what you want to be doing when you're trying to bring resolution to a legal problem.[119]

In "There is no textualist position," for example, Fish notes that in literary studies there is no time pressure to ascertain what the author of a literary text intended it to mean. "But there are fields of endeavor where

---

[116] Stanley Fish, "The intentionalist thesis once more" in Huscroft and Miller (eds.), *The challenge of originalism*, 114.

[117] Fish, "Intention is all there is," 1138 n98.   [118] Ibid., 1143.

[119] Ibid., 1145. See too Fish, "There is no textualist position," 637–40 where he discusses similar claims by the legal writers Greenawalt, Vermeule, and Rickless.

this is not a tolerable situation – disputes must be settled promptly, for if they are not the entire business grinds to a halt – and law is one of them."[120] Adrian Vermeule says that to avoid the business of law grinding to a halt because the investigation into authorial intention is too time-consuming or expensive, the law will sometimes create a "stopping rule" that "provides a justification for considering less than all probative information bearing on legislative intentions."[121] What such a stopping rule does is authorize the substitution of a fictional intention instead of the actual intention of the author of the legal text – it is an instance of rewriting in law. Fish's response to stopping rules in law nicely exhibits his ambivalence toward rewriting. He first notes that such a rule "provides a justification for abandoning the search for meaning when the going gets too tough or too expensive; and one wonders if the calculation underlying the justification – efficiency should trump figuring out what the law means – would be welcomed if it were baldly stated."[122] But immediately after this negative observation on rewriting in law, Fish moves to acknowledge that it is often necessary and good:

> I am not inveighing against the employment of so-called stopping rules. They are not at all unusual . . . and it is always possible to argue that they are necessary if the stability and predictability of the law are to be maintained. My only point is that stopping rules are not rules of interpretation, but rules that tell you when the effort to interpret should cease and something else should take over. I am perfectly willing to concede that in some instances (maybe many), the search for meaning is either so difficult that keeping at it paralyzes the system or so subversive of the purposes law is supposed to fulfill that insisting on it would be perverse. I would just say that acknowledging the obstacles to the specification of meaning, or the unwisdom in some cases of bothering about meaning at all, does not change the fact that the answer to the question "what does a text mean?" is that a text means what its author intends it to mean.[123]

We have already encountered other examples of rewriting in law besides Vermeule's stopping rules. In the previous section of this chapter, we saw that textualists were not really attending only to word meaning, as they claim, because if they were not assuming an authorial intention, no text would exist. What they were really doing was ascribing an intention to the author other than the actual intention; they were assuming an intention by the author to use the words of the text in their most

---

[120] Fish, "There is no textualist position," 637.   [121] Ibid., 639.   [122] Ibid.
[123] Ibid., 640. See too Fish, "Intention is all there is," 1129.

conventional dictionary meanings. In other words, they were rewriting. Fish acknowledges that such an assumption might be a good rule of thumb with which to begin the interpretive process, a rule of thumb that might need to be abandoned if we come to believe that it does not reflect the actual author's real intentions.[124] But a rule of thumb is not what the textualist is endorsing. The textualist wants to insist that we must always proceed on the basis that the author intended the words to have their most conventional dictionary meanings, regardless of the actual authorial intention. And textualists can have good rule of law reasons for doing so, as we saw Schauer argue. If their arguments have power, we will have found again that rewriting in law can be justified over interpretation.

Rewriting in law can also involve assuming a fictional author instead of the actual author. As noted earlier, lawyers do this when they substitute the "reasonable man" or the "reasonable testator" for the actual author of a legal text. Fish makes this point briefly in "There is no textualist position,"[125] and he expands upon it in "Intention is all there is." In responding to a situation where the wishes of an actual testator cannot be determined, Fish acknowledges that it may be justified for the law to rely upon a fictional construct, the reasonable testator:

> [P]ositing a fictional author in place of a real one and inquiring into his or her (non-existent) intentions . . . might be a rational activity in the sense that you could explain why you did it: the law's business has to be done; it would be nice if we had enough information to determine what she had in mind, but since we don't the next best thing is to presume that she wanted to be fair and egalitarian and reasonable and proceed from there. That's rational, and certainly more so than flipping a coin (which *is* rational at the beginning of a football game), but it is not interpretive.[126]

Now that I have explained the interpretation/rewriting distinction, we can return to the objections raised by Dworkin and Barak that Fish's account of interpretation is too narrow and too static. They felt that Fish's restricted understanding of interpretation as ascertaining the actual authorial intention excluded most of the interesting and important jobs that lawyers had to do. We now see that Fish could respond to these objectors that if they find that interpretation is too narrow and static in a particular legal context, then they have the option of engaging in

---

[124] Fish, "Intention is all there is," 1126–7; Stanley Fish, "The intentionalist thesis once more" in Huscroft and Miller (eds.), *The challenge of originalism*, 103.

[125] Fish, "There is no textualist position," 644–5.

[126] Fish, "Intention is all there is," 1133.

rewriting instead. As we have just seen, Fish acknowledges that rewriting is often justified and rational in law (although we have also seen that he can be ambivalent about this). So he is not ruling out of court any of the more expansive and creative activities that Dworkin and Barak favor with respect to legal materials; he only insists that they be conceptualized correctly. He is criticizing Dworkin's and Barak's descriptions of their practices, not their practices themselves.[127]

Finally, I must deal with the prima facie contradictions in Fish's position that I flagged earlier when describing his arguments for the interpretation claim. In advancing this claim, Fish argued that "for interpretation to be a rational activity and not a form of what H. L. A. Hart called 'scorer's discretion,' there must be an object prior to and independent of the interpreter's activities, an object in relation to which you can marshal and assess evidence and measure progress."[128] I noted that talk of an independent object of interpretation that exists prior to any interpretive efforts, and that those efforts seek to discover and describe, sounds like the foundationalism Fish rejected in Part I. But this objection misses the mark because Fish is only insisting here that interpreters must be seeking to ascertain the truth about a matter of fact. There has to be a right answer – what the actual author actually intended – that is being sought and that can serve as the basis for evaluating different interpretive efforts. This goal distinguishes interpretation from other activities in which there is not some matter of fact that has to be ascertained, such as rewriting. However, a commitment to facts, right answers, and objective truths does not make one a foundationalist. As we saw in Chapter 2, Fish insists that anti-foundationalism does not throw doubt upon our ability to achieve any of these things. For embedded humans, local contexts will provide the enterprise-specific practices and criteria by which objective truths can be attained, and Fish insists that these truths are not rendered less certain by the bare possibility that they might change in the future or by the certainty that others differently embedded will not see them.

The second prima facie contradiction is not so easily resolved, however. Fish has argued that if one stops interpreting, and starts rewriting instead, then one is no longer constrained; instead one is engaged in "a free-for-all." But this reintroduces the specter of the unconstrained

---

[127] I shall offer a more extensive account of how Dworkin's project fits with Fish's intentionalism in the next chapter after I have explained Dworkin's project in more detail.
[128] Fish, "Intention is all there is," 1138 n98.

legal actor that Fish argued was illusory in Chapter 7. Fish argued then that because the consciousness of a competent legal practitioner has been shaped and enabled by his legal training, it was not possible for that practitioner to act professionally in a way that was unconstrained by the in-place background provided by that legal training. But, crucially, we have seen Fish acknowledge that rewriting is a legitimate part of the practice of a competent legal professional. It follows that rewriting is internal to the practice of law; it is part of "doing what comes naturally" for an embedded legal practitioner. It is true that rewriting in law is not constrained by the need to describe correctly an empirical fact, as interpretation is, but that does not mean that the legal rewriter is in a position to "make it up wholesale," as Dworkin nicely put it.[129] A lawyer will still be constrained by the structuring effect of the already-in-place background that enables the competent legal practitioner to perform all aspects of his or her professional role. A legal rewriter cannot be unconstrained for the same reasons that an unconstrained legal actor cannot exist. A legal rewriter will therefore never be in "a free-for-all," but will always be acting to advance the goals and values and jobs of the legal system, or at least an arguable conception of them. This can be seen in the examples of legal rewriting discussed earlier, such as "stopping rules" and "the reasonable testator." These rewritings had rational explanations that stressed the advancement of law-specific goals; they were nothing like a frivolous free-for-all.

I do not see how this problem can be explained away; I think Fish has slipped into a genuine although uncharacteristic inconsistency here. But I will now suggest two possible explanations for why this has happened. One explanation would refer to the admitted influence in his writing of what Fish has called "the 'angle of lean,' the direction you are facing as you begin your discursive task."[130] In his three most recent pieces on intentionalism, he is very concerned to make interpretation into a rational activity, an activity that has a single correct answer, an activity that is constrained by the need to accurately state a fact about the world. In stressing these features of interpretation, he might have leaned too far and overstated the extent to which a non-interpretive activity like rewriting is *un*constrained. My second explanation would describe the contradiction as the result of Fish's own professional training as a scholar of English literature. In English literature, unlike law, there is no

---

[129] Dworkin, "Law as interpretation" 546.   [130] *Doing*, 32.

place within the professional practice for deliberate rewriting of an author's work. It is never a justified activity, and so if it happens, it will be seen by those embedded within the practice as something foreign or external to what they do, something unconstrained by their enterprise-specific background and protocols, and hence "a free-for-all" or a "weightless and irresponsible affair." (Of course, it will not really be unconstrained; it will simply be constrained by the enabling background of a practice *other than* English literature.[131]) I suspect that this negative attitude toward rewriting found in the study of English literature some-times influences the way Fish sees rewriting in law. Although, when pressed, he will admit that rewriting is a legitimate part of legal practice (and therefore, I would argue, always enabled and shaped by the enterprise-specific background shared by lawyers), at other times the English literature attitude to rewriting bleeds through, and he talks of rewriting in law as an unconstrained free-for-all. Hence the ambivalence that I noted earlier.

---

[131] For example, the rewriting of literature can be part of a political practice. See *Professional*, 66–7 where Fish describes the use of Milton's poetry by G. Wilson Knight during World War II to "provide comfort and inspiration to a nation beleaguered by evil forces; he is *not* going to claim that the meanings he finds are the meanings Milton intended: only that the meanings he finds are helpful to the British people in a moment of present crisis." Accordingly, the battle of Christ against Satan was read as the battle of Winston Churchill against Hitler. But now Knight's rewriting of Milton "is barely remembered and has had no lasting effect on Milton criticism. It could not have had because it was not a critical, but a hortatory, effort and once the occasion provoking it had passed from the scene (once World War II was won) it ceased to be of interest and the tradition returned, with scarcely a ripple, to its former ways."

9

The Fish/Dworkin debate

Ronald Dworkin and Stanley Fish engaged in a spirited debate spanning a decade.[1] Dworkin's 1982 article, "Law as interpretation,"[2] started it off, prompting Fish's response, "Working on the chain gang: Interpretation in law and literature."[3] Dworkin quickly shot back with "My reply to Stanley Fish (and Walter Benn Michaels): Please don't talk about objectivity anymore,"[4] but Fish parried with "Wrong again."[5] After this initial flurry of punches, the combatants took a few deep breaths before Dworkin targeted Fish again in his 1986 book, *Law's empire*.[6] Fish came back strongly with two articles, "Still wrong after all

---

[1] For accounts of the Fish/Dworkin debate, see Judith M. Schelly, "Interpretation in law: The Dworkin-Fish debate (or, soccer amongst the Gahuku-Gama)" 73 *California Law Review* (1985) 158; Marianne Sadowski, "Language is not life: The chain enterprise, interpretive communities, and the Dworkin/Fish debate" 33 *Connecticut Law Review* (2001) 1099 (hereafter cited as Sadowski, "Language is not life"); Leonard Kaplan, "Without foundation: Stanley Fish and the legal academy" 16 *Law & Social Inquiry* (1991) 597–602; Allan Hutchinson, "Part of an essay on power and interpretation (with suggestions on how to make bouillabaisse)" 60 *New York University Law Review* (1985) 862–6.

[2] Ronald Dworkin, "Law as interpretation" 60 *Texas Law Review* (1982) 527 (hereafter cited as Dworkin, "Law as interpretation"). Originally published in 9 *Critical Inquiry* (1982) 179. Subsequently included in Ronald Dworkin, *A matter of principle* (Cambridge, MA: Harvard University Press, 1985) as ch. 6.

[3] Stanley Fish, "Working on the chain gang: Interpretation in law and literature" 60 *Texas Law Review* (1982) 551. Originally published in 9 *Critical Inquiry* (1982) 201. Subsequently included in *Doing* as ch. 4.

[4] Ronald Dworkin, "My reply to Stanley Fish (and Walter Benn Michaels): Please don't talk about objectivity anymore" in W. J. T. Mitchell (ed.), *The politics of interpretation* (Chicago IL: University of Chicago Press, 1983), 287 (hereafter cited as Dworkin: "My reply to Stanley Fish"). Subsequently included in Ronald Dworkin, *A matter of principle* (Cambridge, MA: Harvard University Press, 1985) as ch. 7.

[5] Stanley Fish, "Wrong again" 62 *Texas Law Review* (1983) 299. Subsequently included in *Doing* as ch. 5.

[6] Ronald Dworkin, *Law's empire* (Cambridge, MA: Belknap Press, 1986) (hereafter cited as Dworkin, *Law's empire*).

these years"[7] and "Dennis Martinez and the uses of theory."[8] A longer
break followed before the two met for their final exchange in the pages
of a 1991 book, *Pragmatism in law and society*.[9] Fish's piece was called
"Almost pragmatism: The jurisprudence of Richard Posner, Richard
Rorty, and Ronald Dworkin"[10] while Dworkin had the final word in
"Pragmatism, right answers, and true banality."[11]

Their exchanges were often testy, which is surprising given that they
had a lot in common jurisprudentially.[12] They both claim that law is not
just a matter of rules and that an adequate understanding of law must
look to what sits unnoticed in the background and generates the rules.
Moreover, they both find political and moral content in that background
and neither sees this as a defect in the law. Rather they see background
moral and political commitments as necessary for the law's existence,
and consequently they both reject the separation thesis of legal positivism
(described in Chapter 7). Additionally, each of them insists that law is
inescapably interpretive, and so they both reject the legal formalist and
textualist accounts offered by others.

But notwithstanding this commonality, Fish and Dworkin disagreed
strongly over the correct account of what interpretation in law involves
and also over the correct account of how legal actors are constrained.
These disagreements about law stem from deeper philosophical disagreements regarding the matters covered in Part I – conceptions of the self,

---

[7] Stanley Fish, "Still wrong after all these years" 6 *Law and Philosophy* (1987) 401.
Subsequently included in *Doing* as ch. 16.

[8] Stanley Fish, "Dennis Martinez and the uses of theory" 96 *Yale Law Journal* (1987) 1773.
Subsequently included in *Doing* as ch. 17.

[9] Michael Brint and William Weaver (eds.), *Pragmatism in law and society* (Boulder, CO;
Westview Press, 1991) (hereafter cited as Brint and Weaver [eds.], *Pragmatism*).

[10] Stanley Fish, "Almost pragmatism: The jurisprudence of Richard Posner, Richard Rorty,
and Ronald Dworkin" in Brint and Weaver (eds.), *Pragmatism*, 47. Subsequently
included in *No free speech* as ch. 13.

[11] Ronald Dworkin, "Pragmatism, right answers, and true banality" in Brint and Weaver
(eds.), *Pragmatism*, 359.

[12] For accounts that find similarities between Fish and Dworkin other than those
I emphasize, see Gary Wihl, "Fish and Dworkin on the work of interpretation in a
democracy" in G. Olson and L. Worsham (eds.), *Postmodern sophistry. Stanley Fish
and the critical enterprise* (Albany: State University of New York Press, 2004), 75
(hereafter cited as Olson and Worsham [eds.], *Postmodern sophistry*); Arthur Glass,
"Dworkin, Fish and legal practice" 10 *Bulletin of the Australian Society of Legal Philosophy* (1986) 208 (hereafter cited as Glass, "Dworkin, Fish and legal practice"); Michael
Moore, "The interpretive turn in modern theory: A turn for the worse?" 41 *Stanford Law
Review* (1989) 908 (hereafter cited as Moore, "The interpretive turn").

epistemology, and the role of philosophy. Unfortunately, their debate did not foreground these philosophical disagreements sufficiently, and consequently the two protagonists talked past each other to a large extent. Indeed, I do not think that Dworkin ever achieved a clear understanding of what Fish was urging upon him, and this accounts for the incredulity and vexation that is often palpable in his responses to Fish. However, this failure to understand Fish's position meant that Dworkin's critiques often failed to inflict damage on his opponent, and I believe that Fish emerges from their debate as the winner.

Fish's critique of Dworkin's fear of an unconstrained legal actor

Dworkin argues that legal rules are always the expression of background moral and political principles, and so in deciding a new case, a judge has to consult this background carefully to find out how to respond. But this raises all of the familiar liberal fears about threats to law's neutrality and objectivity. If a judge is permitted – indeed, required – to move outside the legal rules to consider morality and politics, how can the law fail to become subjective and uncertain as different judges pursue the moral and political principles that appeal to them? The fear of the unconstrained legal actor looms large here, and Dworkin feels compelled to find a way to bring him under control.

Dworkin's solution is that while judges must consider moral and political principles, they are not free to advance those that appeal to them personally. Instead one must ascertain which set of principles make the most sense of the actual institutional history of the law (enacted legislation and decided cases). Whether or not the judge approves of the principles so identified, they are the ones the judge must follow in deciding the case before the court so as to maintain the overall coherence of the law. This coherence requirement is what Dworkin means by "law as integrity."[13]

> Law as integrity asks judges to assume, so far as this is possible, that the law is structured by a coherent set of principles about justice and fairness and procedural due process, and it asks them to enforce these in the fresh cases that come before them, so that each person's situation is fair and just according to the same standards. That style of adjudication respects the ambition integrity assumes, the ambition to be a community of principle.[14]

[13] Dworkin, *Law's empire*, ch. 7 ("Integrity in Law").

[14] Ibid., 243. See too 225: "The adjudicative principle of integrity instructs judges to identify legal rights and duties, so far as possible, on the assumption that they were all created by a

In this way, Dworkin allows the legal actor to consider morality and politics while simultaneously constraining this actor and providing an objective test for which principles are to apply. In theory, there is one correct answer to the question of which principles fit best with, or make the most sense of, the legal institutional history. It may be that only his superhuman construct, Hercules, could reliably come up with this answer, but all human legal actors should seek to emulate Hercules as far as they are able, and the constraint imposed by law as integrity is what turns aside subjectivity and preserves law's neutrality and objectivity. As Fish describes it:

> The idea is that the continuity of legal practice is not something one can spot on its surface, but is something one can grasp only by seeing through the practice to the underlying and abstract assumptions of which particular decisions and statutes are the intended instantiations. That is the interpreter's task: to construct or reconstruct that abstract shape and then to characterize and decide the present case in a way that makes of it a confirmation or extension of that same shape. Such an interpreter is creative without being willful since he is guided by something independent of him, and he is also constrained without being slavishly so since the something that guides him is something he must construct.[15]

Fish rejects Dworkin's account of how legal constraint can and should be achieved because Fish is committed to a conception of the self that both supplies a different form of constraint and also declares Dworkin's form of constraint to be impossible. (The conception of the self that Fish champions was described in Chapter 1, and its application to law was described in Chapter 7.) Dworkin accepts the standard liberal account of the self as a rational will in need of constraint, but Fish argues that the self is constituted by local embeddedness and so can never stand outside the constraints that come with embeddedness or be in need of extra constraints. Dworkin saddles himself with the task of ensuring that a radically free self is constrained by the moral and political background of the law, and this is why he urges legal actors to accept "law as integrity" and to emulate Hercules. But Fish's position is that there is no need to impose upon legal actors any constraints in addition to those that already enable their thinking and acting.

single author – the community personified – expressing a coherent conception of justice and fairness . . . According to law as integrity, propositions of law are true if they figure in or follow from the principles of justice, fairness, and procedural due process that provide the best constructive interpretation of the community's legal practice."

[15] *Doing*, 363. See too the description (with supporting references) of Dworkin's position that Fish provides at 356–7.

Although Dworkin sees (in a way that legal positivists and formalists do not) that a background of moral and political commitments is crucial to law, Fish would argue that he does not pursue that insight far enough. Dworkin insists that because the background is important, lawyers and judges have to be urged to pay close attention to it and to self-consciously base their decisions upon it. Fish insists that because the institutional background both structures and enables the consciousness of legal actors, they can never *not* be relying on it, so there is no need to urge them to do so. Dworkin does not realize that the background he points to is even more important than he supposes, because he does not see the connection between the enabling background of an institutional practice and the constitution of the self. Fish would argue that if Dworkin had made that connection, then he would have been freed from the illusory fear of an unconstrained legal actor.

In the course of his debate with Dworkin, Fish pursues this main critique in finer detail. In response to Dworkin's fear that a lawyer or judge will act according to personal preferences, and not according to law as integrity, Fish seeks to demonstrate (i) that no competent legal practitioner could act in a way that did not attend to institutional history, and (ii) that no content can be given to the idea of a competent legal practitioner acting according to purely personal preferences in a legal context.

No competent legal practitioner could act in a way that did not attend to institutional history

The unconstrained legal actor is alive and well and causing trouble in Chapters 4–7 of *Law's empire* where Dworkin calls him a "pragmatist." Not only is this pragmatist an unconstrained legal actor, but he also acts without shame or subterfuge and claims that his lack of constraint is a good thing.

> A pragmatist, as Dworkin defines him, would be one who does not take into account "any form of consistency with the past." Not bound by any sense of obligation to history, he would "stand ready to revise his practice" and "the scope of what counts as legal rights" in the light of his judgment as to which course of action best serves the community's future. His actions would comprise "a set of discrete decisions" which he would be "free to make or amend one by one, with nothing but a strategic interest in the rest," with "no underlying commitment to any . . . fundamental public conception of justice."[16]

[16] Ibid., 360. The passages in quotation marks are taken from Dworkin, *Law's empire*.

Fish's argument that a legal actor who does not attend to, or submit to constraint by, legal institutional history is not possible begins in "Wrong again" when he notes "the law's conservatism, which will not allow a case to remain unrelated to the past, and so assures that the past, in the form of the history of decisions, will be continually rewritten."[17] In other words, one element of the institutional background that all legal actors will have absorbed in the course of their training is that the present case must relate to the past cases, and therefore one mark of their competence is that they will always be able to construct an account of how it does so. They will achieve this account by describing the past in such a way that it relates to the present (even if other lawyers or judges can provide competing accounts). The institutional history will never be ignored by a competent lawyer; instead it will be rewritten, Fish claims. In "Still wrong after all these years," Fish expands this point:

> What this means is that "law as integrity" is not the name of a *special* practice engaged in only by gifted or Herculean judges, but the name of a practice engaged in "naturally" – without any additional prompting – by any judge whose ways of conceiving his field of action are judicial, that is, by any judge. The moment he sees a case *as* a case, a judge is already seeing it as an item in a judicial history, and at the same moment he is already in the act of fashioning (with a view to later telling) a story in which his exposition of the case exists in a seamless continuity with his exposition (and understanding) of the enterprise as a whole.[18]

Dworkin's position, says Fish,

> rests on a distinction between legal practice as a set of discrete acts and legal practice as a continually unfolding story about such principles as justice, fairness, and equality. But the distinction is a false one, for it is not possible (except in a positivist world of isolated brute phenomena) to conceive of a legal act apart from just that story and those principles ... If one were to construe a case without any such regard or strong sense of the judicial field as both a structure and an ongoing narrative, the result would not be a case at all, but a set of facts and meanings that would touch only accidentally and intermittently on legal emphases and concerns.[19]

Here we have again the anti-foundationalist point from Part I that there is no foreground without a background. That is, in order to perceive any legal material *as* legal material, the legal actor must *already* be perceiving it against the institutional background that Dworkin urges the legal actor to find and self-consciously apply. Dworkin's urgings are therefore

---

[17] *Doing*, 94.   [18] Ibid., 367–8.   [19] Ibid., 363. See generally 363–4.

unnecessary and superfluous, according to Fish: "[I]f pragmatism is not an option for practice because the history it supposedly ignores is an ingredient of any judge's understanding, then law as integrity, which enjoins us to maintain a continuity with history, enjoins us to something we are already doing."[20]

As Fish puts it later in "Dennis Martinez and the uses of theory": "[A]t the moment when a judge sees a case in a certain way – as falling into this category, or requiring that kind of investigation – there would be no point in his consulting institutional history, because it is that history – not consulted but thoroughly internalized – that already constrains what he sees."[21] So Fish's conclusion is that it is impossible for a competent legal actor to be acting with disregard for institutional history, as Dworkin's pragmatist is supposed to be able to do, because this history is a precondition of the competent legal actor perceiving the objects of his professional concern.

No content can be given to the idea of a competent legal practitioner acting according to purely personal preferences in a legal context

Fish's position is that any preferences a legal actor could have will have been shaped by legal institutional history. So, in response to Dworkin's claim in Chapter 5 of *Law's empire* that a legal pragmatist would ignore the constraints of legal history and produce "a set of discrete decisions," Fish asks:

> My question simply is, could there be such a person performing such actions, and my answer is, no. What, for example, would a "discrete decision" be like? If we are to take Dworkin at his word, it would be a decision that turned on a judgment of what was best for the community's future irrespective of the history of decisions, statutes and invoking of precedents that preceded it. *But where would one's sense of 'best' come from if not from that very history, which, because it formed the basis of the agent's education, would be the content of his judgment?*[22]

Fish expands this point when he critiques Dworkin's analysis of the *McLoughlin* case in the same chapter of *Law's empire*. In that case, the

---

[20] Ibid., 361. See too 360.

[21] Ibid., 387. See too 389 where Fish rejects the "suggestion that institutional history was something the agent consults in the process of making a decision" in favor of a position in which "the shape institutional decisionmaking must take is immediately obvious to the agent for whom institutional history is the very ground of consciousness."

[22] Ibid., 360. Emphasis added

issue was whether compensation should be given for emotional injury. Fish responded to Dworkin's fear that the judge might turn out to be an unconstrained legal actor who is influenced by his personal preference (against awarding compensation) instead of abiding by law as integrity and doing what was required by the legal institutional history (awarding compensation) by asking:

> But are the two kinds of reasons [personal ones and institutional ones] really so different? How does a judge come to "think it is unjust to require compensation for any emotional injury"? Indeed, what makes a judge *capable* of having such a thought? *It will be available to him only because his very ways of thinking have been formed by that institutional history in which notions like compensation, categories like emotional vs. physical injury, and distinctions between just and unjust were assumed and in place. In short, the so-called personal reason is no less institutional and attentive to history than the reason that derives from a commitment to "integrity," and, indeed, the very notion of a "personal" reason that a judge might assert against his obligation to the history of past decisions is finally incoherent.* Any reason that finds its way into the judge's calculations will be perforce a *legal* one, and therefore one whose very existence is a function of that history (that is, of some view of it) – a history he could not possibly discount even if he declared himself to be doing so.[23]

Fish returns to this argument in "Almost pragmatism: The jurisprudence of Richard Posner, Richard Rorty, and Ronald Dworkin" when he considers Dworkin's claim in "Hard cases" that "[i]f a judge accepts the settled practices of his legal system ... then he must, according to the doctrine of political responsibility, accept some general political theory that justifies those practices."[24] Implicit in this claim is the possibility that a judge could *refuse* to accept the settled practices of his legal system. That is, he could instead pursue preferences, values, and goals that do not have their origin in his legal training. Fish questions whether this is really a possibility or an incoherent idea by asking: What would it look like if a judge made the refusal Dworkin contemplates?

> Would it mean that he or she would not recognize the authority of the Supreme Court ... or would decide a case without reference to any other case that had already been decided, or would decide a case by opening, at random, to a page in the Bible or *Hamlet* and taking direction from the first phrase that leapt to the eyes or would simply refuse to decide?

---

[23] Ibid., 365–6. Second emphasis added.

[24] Ronald Dworkin, *Taking rights seriously* (London: Duckworth, 1977) 105, quoted in *No free speech*, 225.

The question is rhetorical in the technical sense that it enumerates kinds of action that would be *unthinkable* for anyone self-identified as a judge ... If one asks, "what does a judge do?" among the answers are, "a judge thinks about cases by inserting them into a history of previous cases that turn on similar problems," or "a judge operates with a sense of his or her place in a hierarchical structure that is itself responsible to other hierarchical structures (a legislature, a Justice Department)," or "a judge is someone who, in the performance of his or her duty, consults certain specified materials which (at least in our tradition) do *not* include (except as occasional embellishments) the Scriptures or the plays of Shakespeare" or even more simply, "a judge is someone who decides." It must be emphasized that these are not things a judge does in addition to, or in the way of a constraint on, his membership in a profession. They are the *content* of that membership; there is no special effort required to recall them, and no danger that a practitioner, short of amnesia, will forget them.[25]

Because Dworkin believes (erroneously, according to Fish) that an unconstrained legal actor is a possibility, he searches both for something that will constrain the freewheeling legal actor from going in the wrong direction and also for something that will point the wayward legal actor in the right direction. In the next section of this chapter, we will see Dworkin arguing that the shape of the legal institutional history itself forms an external constraint on any acceptable interpretation of that history that a legal actor might try to offer. In the section after that, we will see Dworkin arguing that a philosophical investigation by a judge into the moral and political principles behind the legal rules (as exemplified by Hercules) can generate a theory that will guide judicial conduct in the right direction. In both of these sections, we will see Fish arguing that the necessarily embedded self needs neither external constraints nor recourse to a guiding theory in order to be able to perform competently.

Fish's critique of Dworkin's hope for an independent constraint upon interpretation

In "Wrong again," we find Fish noting that the fear of a radically free interpreter has a counterpart, namely the hope that something pre-interpretive and objective can be found that will constrain the interpreter.

If one conceives of the interpreter as free to choose his beliefs and therefore to choose his interpretations, then one must always imagine a

---

[25] *No free speech*, 225. See too *Doing*, 10–3, 92–3.

constraint on that choice so it won't be irresponsible or whimsical. And, of course, the reverse holds: anyone who is in search of constraints, or thinks it crucial to identify them, must at the same time imagine an interpreter who needs the constraint because he stands apart from any tethering structure or gestalt. In the positivist picture of things the uninterpreted text (or rule or distinction) and the unsituated (or weakly situated) subject are constitutive of one another.[26]

It is this hope of finding some preinterpretive and objective constraint to impose on his legal interpreters that, Fish claims in "Working on the chain gang," sends Dworkin down a dead-end path toward positivism, formalism, textualism, and foundationalism:

> [Dworkin] repeatedly makes two related and mutually reinforcing assumptions: he assumes that history in the form of a chain of decisions has, at some level, the status of a brute fact; and he assumes that wayward or arbitrary behavior in relation to that fact is an institutional possibility. Together these two assumptions give him his project, the project of explaining how a free and potentially irresponsible agent is held in check by the self-executing constraints of an independent text.[27]

This foundationalist/positivist/formalist/textualist side of Dworkin is clearly on display, Fish claims, in Dworkin's account of how a judge deciding a case is like the current author contributing a chapter to a "chain novel." In "Law as interpretation," Dworkin argued that a novelist contributing his chapter later in the chain will be more constrained than a novelist beginning the sequence. This was because the later novelist no longer had the option of striking out on his own but instead had to extend the group enterprise in the direction laid down by the earlier contributors. The longer the chain, the more constrained the author at the end of it was. Dworkin claimed that the judge deciding a case today was in a similar position. He is obliged to decide the case in a way that fitted with the past decisions made by a long chain of earlier judges considering similar situations. He could not strike out in his own direction because, if he was to comply with the coherence requirement of law as integrity, he was constrained to apply the principles that made the most sense of that history or chain of decisions. Dworkin returned to this analysis subsequently in *Law's empire*:

> Just as a chain novelist must find, if he can, some coherent view of character and theme such that a hypothetical single author with that view could have written at least the bulk of the novel so far, Hercules must find,

[26] *Doing*, 115.   [27] Ibid., 95.

if he can, some coherent theory about legal rights to compensation for emotional injury such that a single political official with that theory could have reached most of the results the precedents report.[28]

First in "Working on the chain gang" and later in "Wrong again," Fish replied that although Dworkin denies that law can be understood as a brute social fact (in legal positivist fashion), and urges instead an interpretive account of law, he nevertheless understands proper legal interpretation to be constrained by something external to the interpretive process itself. That is, he conceives of the legal institutional history as having its own inherent shape or character that limits what an interpreter who seeks to understand and continue it (as opposed to change it) can do. But, as we will see, this amounts to an appeal to a different kind of preinterpretive, positivistic, brute fact about the world, and so is a version of the foundationalist epistemology we saw Fish reject in Chapter 2, and of the illusory hope of formalism/textualism we saw Fish reject in Chapter 8.

As an example of how interpreters such as chain novelists and judges can be constrained by something external to the interpretive process itself, Dworkin offers the fact that Agatha Christie's crime mystery novels cannot properly be interpreted as philosophical novels:

> [I]t does not follow, from the aesthetic hypothesis, that because a philosophical novel is aesthetically more valuable than a mystery story, an Agatha Christie novel is really a treatise on the meaning of death. This interpretation fails, not only because an Agatha Christie novel, taken to be a treatise on death, is a poor treatise less valuable than a good mystery, but because the interpretation makes the novel a shambles. All but one or two sentences would be irrelevant to the supposed theme; and the organization, style, and figures would be appropriate not to a philosophical novel but to an entirely different genre.[29]

Dworkin's claim is that the raw textual material just will not allow such an interpretation to be made; he asserts that this raw material has its own independent shape that rules out at least some interpretations and so forms an external constraint on acts of interpretation. As he put it later in *Law's empire*:

> Convictions about fit will provide a rough threshold requirement that an interpretation of some part of the law must meet if it is to be eligible at all .... That threshold will eliminate interpretations that some judges

---

[28] Dworkin, *Law's empire*, 240. See generally 228–38.
[29] Dworkin, "Law as interpretation" 532.

would otherwise prefer, so *the brute facts of legal history* will in this way limit the role any judge's personal convictions of justice can play in his decisions. Different judges will set this threshold differently. But anyone who accepts law as integrity must accept that the actual political history of his community will sometimes check his other political convictions in his overall interpretive judgment.[30]

Fish replies that this shows how Dworkin "makes the positivist assumption that at some level the novel is available in an uninterpreted shape; that is, in a shape that determines which interpretations of it will be appropriate."[31]

> I do not have to saddle Dworkin with the thesis that a text demands a single reading or assignment of genre in order to convict him of textual positivism. So long as he believes that there are some ways, some generic identifications, that a work rules out ... then he is as much a positivist as anyone would want or not want him to be ... [T]hat just makes Dworkin a positivist of the pluralist variety, one who doesn't believe that a text constrains a single interpretation, but believes that the text constrains the range of interpretations it will receive without becoming a shambles.[32]

In Fish's analysis, an apprehension of the character of an Agatha Christie novel (or of a chain novel, or of a string of precedents) is never produced or constrained by the independent shape of its subject matter. Rather textual features are apprehended because of the background assumptions that readers bring to the text, as described in Chapter 8. Textual features such as "organization, style, and figures" are not independent constraints on interpretation, as Dworkin supposes, but are themselves products of interpretation: "organization, style, and figure are interpretive facts – facts which, rather than setting limits to the elaboration of a reading, emerge and become established in the course of that very elaboration."[33] In the same way, the history of the chain novel, or the history of a string of precedents, cannot serve as an external constraint upon any present act of interpretation, for any such history is itself the product of a present act of interpretation.

---

[30] Dworkin, *Law's empire*, 255, emphasis added. See too 52: "[C]onstructive interpretation is a matter of imposing purpose on an object or practice in order to make of it the best possible example of the form or genre to which it is taken to belong. It does not follow, even from that rough account, that an interpreter can make of a practice or work of art anything he would have wanted it to be ... *For the history or shape of a practice or object constrains the available interpretations of it*" (emphasis added.).

[31] *Doing*, 105.   [32] Ibid., 113.   [33] Ibid., 105–6.

[O]ne doesn't just find a history; rather one views a body of materials with the assumption that it is organized by judicial concerns. It is that assumption which gives shape to the materials, a shape that can *then* be described as being "found." ... To see a present-day case as similar to a chain of earlier ones is to reconceive that chain by finding in it an applicability that has not always been apparent. Paradoxically, one can be faithful to legal history only by revising it, by redescribing it in such a way as to accommodate and render manageable the issues raised by the present ... All histories are invented in the weak sense that they are not simply "discovered," but assembled under the pressure of some present urgency.[34]

It is because Dworkin misunderstands the nature of the constraints that are genuinely operating on legal actors and chain novelists that he incorrectly claims that the first novelist in the chain, or the judge deciding a case of first instance, is unconstrained, or free to strike out on their own. The true situation, Fish responds, it that any such actor is constrained by being embedded in the interpretive community of novelists or jurists. It is this form of embeddedness, with its background beliefs, goals, categories, values, etc., that enables the actor, that is, that makes available to them a range of possible and desirable ways to proceed in the project of novel writing or judicial decision-making.[35] Similarly, Dworkin is wrong to claim that later participants in the process are more constrained, Fish argues. These later participants, as members of the same interpretive community, are constrained in just the same way and to the same extent as the first participant.[36] Indeed, it is only because they share the same forms of constraint (or embeddedness) that they can understand each other and engage in a common project.[37]

It follows on Fish's analysis that if the already-in-place background that both enables and structures the participants in a particular enterprise were different, then what they are constrained by that background to see would be different, too. He gives an example from literary studies of how such a shift in the assumed background of the interpretive community of Miltonists produced a change in what they saw when they read *Paradise Lost*, and he then argues:

My point is that what *has* happened to *Paradise Lost could* happen to Agatha Christie, and if it did, if in the course of criticism and commentary, not only the theme, but the style, organization, and even genre of her novel were recharacterized, then it could not be said [as Dworkin

---

[34] Ibid., 93–4.   [35] Ibid., 88–9.   [36] Ibid., 89–90.   [37] See *Professional*, 14.

does] that interpretation will have made the novel a "shambles" because interpretation will have remade the novel.[38]

Fish makes this point in a bravura fashion by turning Dworkin's own example against him. Not only could Agatha Christie's novels be read as philosophical works if the right background were in place, but he describes how such a background *is already in place* within literary studies, and so Fish can point to examples where the characterization of Christie's novels that Dworkin declares to be impossible has already been advanced![39]

Finally, Fish goes on to argue that the same analysis applies to all of the distinctions that Dworkin seizes upon in an attempt to draw an objective (i.e., not interpretation-dependent) line between acceptable and unacceptable interpretations of a novel or an institutional history – explaining vs. changing, finding vs. inventing, continuing vs. beginning anew.[40] All of these distinctions are quite real and exercise a constraining effect. At any time there will certainly be readings of any text that will be deemed unacceptable. Fish agrees with Dworkin that currently *Hamlet* cannot be understood to be about a man of action. But the present shape of each of these distinctions is perspicuous and can be confidently applied by some group only because a background of shared assumptions is already in place. If that background changes, the shape of the distinction (and so what falls on each side of the line) changes, too. "This does not mean that the distinction has no force whatsoever, only that its force is felt from *within* interpretive conditions that give certain objects and shapes a real but constructed – and therefore unsettleable – stability."[41] Again, rather than being external constraints on interpretation, as Dworkin hopes, these distinctions are revealed to be interpretive products. Dworkin's foundationalist and formalist hopes fail, but for Fish this has no consequences for law because they were never necessary in the first place.

Fish's critique of Dworkin's hope that philosophy can provide coherence and guidance for law

As I have noted previously, philosophy has traditionally claimed a role as "the master art underlying all the other arts,"[42] and Dworkin is one who

---

[38] *Doing*, 106–7. Later he makes the same point using the example of *A Christmas carol*. See *Doing*, 108–9.

[39] *Doing*, 95–7. See especially the works listed at 96 n13.   [40] Ibid., 107–9.

[41] Ibid., 107.   [42] *No free speech*, 228.

accepts that claim with respect to law. "[F]rom its very beginning," Fish notes, *Law's empire* "is an argument for the necessity of philosophy and for the superiority of that judge who is the most philosophical."[43] As Dworkin himself put it:

> Any practical legal argument, no matter how detailed and limited, assumes the kind of abstract foundation jurisprudence offers, and when rival foundations compete, a legal argument assumes one and rejects others. So any judge's opinion is itself a piece of legal philosophy, even when the philosophy is hidden and the visible argument is dominated by citation and lists of facts. Jurisprudence is the general part of adjudication, silent prologue to any decision at law.[44]

Philosophical analysis is what Hercules engages in (and it is him all judges should emulate) to ascertain the set of background moral and political principles that make the most sense of the legal institutional history. The philosophical task is to throw light upon the foundations that sit below and generate the surface of legal practice. Once philosophy has exposed the relevant background principles, the judges and lawyers can apply them to particular cases in a way that maintains law's integrity. Beyond that immediately practical function, there is an even more rarefied role for philosophy in law according to Dworkin:

> The law we have, the actual concrete law for us, is fixed by inclusive integrity. This is law for the judge, the law he is obliged to declare and enforce. Present law, however, contains another law, which marks out its ambitions for itself; this purer law is defined by pure integrity. It consists in the principles of justice that offer the best justification of the present law seen from the perspective of no institution in particular and thus abstracting from all the constraints of fairness and process that inclusive integrity requires ... The courts are the capitals of law's empire, and judges are its princes, but not its seers and prophets. It falls to philosophers, if they are willing, to work out law's ambitions for itself, the purer form of law within and beyond the law we have.[45]

Fish has two arguments against Dworkin's grand hopes for philosophy in law. The first argument draws again upon his conception of the self described in Chapter 1: a competent practitioner – one who is embedded within a particular local institutional context, and whose consciousness has been enabled and structured by absorbing the background assumptions, goals, and values of that institution – does not need any additional guidance to know how to perform properly. This enabling background is

---

[43] *Doing*, 368. See too 385.   [44] Dworkin, *Law's empire*, 90.   [45] Ibid., 406–7.

not something one thinks *with*, but something one thinks *within*; one does not consciously advert to it the way one would with a worked-out philo-sophical theory.[46] "The internalized 'know-how' or knowledge of 'the ropes' that practice brings is sufficient unto the day and no theoretical apparatus is needed to do what practice is already doing, that is, providing the embedded agent with a sense of relevancies, obligations, directions for action, criteria, etc."[47] This is the point of Fish's analysis in "Dennis Martinez and the uses of theory" of the non-response given by the pitcher to a journalist who asked him what (theoretical) guidance his manager had just given him.[48] As an embedded practitioner, Dennis Martinez needs no theory to tell him how to perform competently. Similarly, trained lawyers need no theory (or help from Hercules) to tell them how to perform competently. Fish says that Dworkin sometimes comes close to grasping this but that ultimately it eludes him:

> Often Dworkin will begin by talking as if he imagines the agent ... embedded within a practice in the sense that his every action is an extension of it; but he soon slides into imagining the agent – at least when he is expert – as happily distanced from practice's flow ... Dworkin's inability to grasp the implications of an enriched notion of practice – even when he gestures in the direction of that notion – is at one with his inability to understand what it would mean to be an agent embedded in that practice, an agent who need not look to something in order to determine where he is or where he might now go because that determination is built into, comes along with, his already-in-place sense of being a competent member of the enterprise.[49]

Fish's second argument against Dworkin draws upon his deflationary approach to the claims of philosophy. We have already seen in Chapter 3 that Fish's anti-foundationalism leads him to emphasize the autonomy of practices. This means that each practice has its own enabling background and so it cannot speak to other practices with different enabling back-grounds. (This is why Fish made the surprising claim that interdiscipli-narity is impossible.) Philosophy and law are autonomous practices with their own distinctive projects, values, and modes of reasoning. It follows from this argument that any hope that philosophy can reform or guide law is illusory.

We can see an example of this argument applied in the context of the Fish/Dworkin debate when Fish claims in "Still wrong after all these years" that Dworkin's deepest concerns, such as eliminating the threat of

---

[46] *Doing*, 386–7.   [47] Ibid., 388.   [48] Ibid., 372–4.   [49] Ibid., 387–8.

"external skepticism" (i.e., relativism) and advancing the merits of "law as integrity," belong to the practice of philosophy, and accordingly have nothing to contribute to the separate practice of law. Those concerns of Dworkin, Fish says, are:

> stand-ins for the general claim of philosophy to be a model of reflection that exists on a level superior to, and revelatory of, mere practice. But, in fact, "external skepticism" and "law as integrity" are themselves practices – philosophical practices, practices of speculation that emerge from the special context of academic philosophy where the constructing of a "perspective of no institution in particular" is the first order of business – and the mistake is to assume that as philosophical practices they have anything to say about practices internal to disciplines other than philosophy.[50]

In "Dennis Martinez and the uses of theory," we see a more concrete application to law of the thesis of the autonomy of practices. Fish offers us two examples – the baseball player Martinez and an industrial research and development team – to make the point that performing a practice and offering a theory about that practice are two entirely different practices with no necessary relationship between them. You can do one without being able to do the other. The lesson is then applied to law: "[J]udging or doing judging is one thing and giving accounts or theories of judging is another, and ... as practices they are independent."[51] If theorizing about judging is a separate practice that does not inform the giving of actual judgments, then Dworkin's hopes for philosophy to guide law lie in ruins: "[B]y asking to be judged on the basis of that high aspiration – the aspiration to be a philosopher-king – Dworkin risks emptying his enterprise of any value or significance because as an epistemological recommendation it has nothing to offer us."[52] Philosophy would seem to be a wheel that is not connected to anything in the mechanism that produces legal decisions.

> Another way to make my point would be to say that when judges do what they do, they do not do it in accordance with or at the behest of some systematic and coherent account of law and its relation to morality and society. Judging, in short, cannot be understood as an activity in the course of which practitioners regularly repair for guidance to an underlying set of rules and principles.[53]

---

[50] Ibid., 371.   [51] *Doing*, 378.   [52] Ibid., 391. See too *No free speech*, 230.
[53] *Doing*, 384. See too *No free speech*, 219, 226–7.

But this seems questionable, because as Fish himself acknowledges, to be successful in the delivering of legal judgments you often have to be able to incorporate theoretical claims and arguments into the decision. The passage quoted above continues:

> [A]s a practice judging is one of those that includes as a part of its repertoire self-conscious reflection on itself, and therefore it seems counterintuitive to say that such self-reflection – such theorizing – is not to some extent at least constitutive of what it is reflecting on: but that is just what I will be asserting, and asserting in direct opposition to what is assumed by almost everyone in the legal academy, irrespective of doctrinal or political affiliation.[54]

In advancing this counterintuitive claim, Fish draws upon a distinction he made back in Part I: interdisciplinarity vs. interdisciplinary borrowing. Interdisciplinarity, Fish said, is impossible, but interdisciplinary borrowing is very possible and occurs routinely. Applying this distinction to the present context, it is impossible to combine the practices of philosophy and law into one unified interdisciplinary practice because the two practices have different enabling backgrounds. But it is certainly possible for law to borrow philosophical theory-talk and use it where it will work to advance the projects, values, and assumptions of *law* rather than philosophy. That is, although a philosophical theory is not being used to generate and guide the legal decision, philosophical theory-talk can be used *rhetorically* to sell that decision to the legal audience being asked to consume it. (If lawyers view such talk as a positive rather than a negative factor in the performance of their professional practice.)[55] This is why Fish says that Dworkin can most fruitfully be read as giving rhetorical advice on how to present your judgments, rather than (as Dworkin himself believes) as giving advice on how to generate your judgments.[56]

> Of course, Dworkin would not accept my praise of him as a rhetorician, as someone who is telling us what kinds of stances and poses will best effect our polemical ends. He is not content with giving good rhetorical advice; he wants that advice to link up with a deep epistemological truth of which it is the reflection. He wants the observation that (at least in the current scene) you are more likely to be persuasive if you present yourself as

---

[54] *Doing*, 378–9. Fish is acknowledging that Dworkin is not alone in giving philosophy a guiding role in law. In "Dennis Martinez and the uses of theory," Fish also critiques Michael Moore and Roberto Unger for buying into this claim.
[55] *Doing*, 377–8, 388–90. See too *No free speech*, 198, 227–8.   [56] *Doing*, 390–2.

having first built and then followed a theory to be heard as a description of and a recipe for responsible decision-making. He wants to think of himself as telling us not simply how to dress, but how to be.[57]

How does Fish's analysis of Dworkin fit with Fish's intentionalism?

Fish gave the same reply to Dworkin's formalist/textualist desire for an independent constraint upon interpretation that he gave to Hart: "Whatever is invoked as a constraint on interpretation will turn out upon further examination to have been the product of interpretation."[58] But in Chapter 8 we saw Fish argue that interpretation, if it is to be a rational activity, must be constrained by the need to ascertain the truth about something that is what it is independently of the activity of any interpreters. Prima facie, this seems contradictory. Fish appears to be committed to the position that independent constraints on interpretation are both necessary and impossible. Here resolution of the problem requires separating out two different senses of "interpretation" in Fish's work, just as we had to separate out two different senses of "politics" in Chapter 6.

The broad sense of interpretation in Fish's work is employed when Fish is developing his anti-foundationalist position. Fish argued in Part I that any thought and perception we can have is enabled and structured by an already-in-place background of beliefs, values, categories, etc. Fish sometimes expresses this position by saying that everything humans can experience is an interpretation. That is, the background that mediates all of our experience of the world is socially constructed; it is contingent and contestable. On this broad sense of interpretation, even an objective fact or a clear and compelling literal meaning is an interpretation:

> A meaning that seems to leap off the page, propelled by its own self-sufficiency, is a meaning that flows from interpretive assumptions so deeply embedded that they have become invisible ... The moral is clear: someone who stands on a literal or explicit meaning in fact stands on an interpretation, albeit an interpretation so firmly in place that it is impossible (at least for the time being) not to take as literal and unassailable the meanings it subtends.[59]

The narrow sense of interpretation in Fish's work is employed when Fish is developing his intentionalist position. Here interpretation of a text or

---

[57] Ibid., 391.   [58] Ibid., 512.   [59] Ibid., 359.

utterance means seeking to ascertain the actual intention of the actual author(s). Thus, interpretation in the narrow sense is constrained by the goal of discovering a fact about the world, but that fact about the world, like all facts, is a product of interpretation in the broad, anti-foundationalist, sense. When Fish writes that "[w]hatever is invoked as a constraint on interpretation will turn out upon further examination to have been the product of interpretation," a clearer restatement of his claim would be that whatever is invoked as a constraint on interpretation in the narrow sense will turn out upon further examination to have been the product of interpretation in the broad sense. Although Fish and Dworkin both accept and seek to explain genuine constraints upon interpreters of texts, Fish's criticisms of Dworkin are, first, that he wrongly looks to facts about texts or institutional history, rather than to facts about authorial intention to constrain interpreters of texts or utterances, and, second, that he wrongly believes that any facts constraining interpreters of texts or utterances can exist in advance of interpretation in the broad sense.

Even if this distinction is accepted, it is still open to someone to object that Fish's narrow sense of interpretation is *too* narrow and uninteresting. This is the objection that Dworkin and Barak made in Chapter 8. I suggested in that chapter that Fish could reply that if they wanted to do something grander, they were free to do so, only they must not call it "interpretation," and must acknowledge instead that it was a form of rewriting. Now that I have considered Dworkin's broader position in greater detail, I can give a more extended answer to the question of how Dworkin's project should be viewed from the standpoint of Fish's intentionalism. I see three possibilities:

(1) We have seen when considering legislation that Fish's intentionalism allows for non-human entities to be authors, and he can similarly posit non-human intending agents in legal contexts other than legislation. So, for example, Fish writes that

> one can attribute intentionality to a long-established practice or professional culture and argue, for example, that the law embodies an intention and that individual lawyers and judges take on the law's intentions when they set out to do a job of legal work.[60]

---

[60] Stanley Fish "Interpretation is not a theoretical issue" 11 *Yale Journal of Law and the Humanities* (1999) 511 (hereafter cited as Fish, "Interpretation is not a theoretical issue").

Conceiving of the law as an abstract entity with intentions is what lawyers do when they personify "the common law" and talk as if it were a thing developing itself (or "working itself pure") through the decided cases. Similarly the common law is sometimes described as the real author or source of a principle gradually revealed in a series of cases over decades or years, rather than the individual judges who decided those cases but who may not have fully grasped the nature of the process they were a part of. Dworkin may be holding that an abstract entity, such as the common law, or the community, is the *actual author* of the principles that Hercules uncovers, rather than human judges and legislators. On this explanation, Hercules is a genuine interpreter according to Fish's intentionalist analysis.

(2) Dworkin may be holding that an abstract entity, such as the common law, or the community, should be assumed to be the *fictional author* of the principles that Hercules uncovers, rather than human judges and legislators. "The adjudicative principle of integrity instructs judges to identify legal rights and duties, so far as possible, on the assumption that they were all created by a single author – the community personified – expressing a coherent conception of justice and fairness."[61] On this explanation, Hercules is a rewriter rather than an interpreter because he is turning away from the actual author(s) and assuming a fictional author of the principles that he finds.

Although Fish does not refer to Dworkin by name in his most recent publications on intentionalism, some of the passages in which he describes Barak as a rewriter seem to capture Dworkin's position as well. Barak talks of "detaching yourself from any obligation to a text's author, in the name of the system" (or "the highest level of the system's aspiration"[62]) and of "viewing the text as part of the totality of the system as a whole" or considering which "resolution best fits with the values of the system."[63] What Barak is describing sounds very much like Dworkin's project. The legal interpreter cannot just confine his attention to a particular statute or judgment and ask what its author(s) intended when it was created. Instead the legal interpreter (exemplified for

---

[61] Dworkin, *Law's empire*, 225.

[62] Stanley Fish, "Intention is all there is: A critical analysis of Aharon Barak's *Purposive interpretation in law*" 29 *Cardozo Law Review* (2008) 1128 (hereafter cited as Fish, "Intention is all there is").

[63] Ibid., 1144.

Dworkin by Hercules) must consider the entire legal institutional history (i.e., Barak's "the system as a whole") in order to ascertain which set of moral and political principles make the most sense of that history (i.e., Barak's "the values of the system").

(3) There is a third possible way of describing what Dworkin is doing that makes him neither an interpreter nor a rewriter in Fish's analysis. I noted in Chapter 8 that Fish's account of interpretation is only concerned with phenomena that communicate meaning. Texts and utterances are what he focuses on, although he also mentions "paintings, gestures, [and] facial expressions." He explicitly disavows any interest in mere "physical processes," such as tracks left by an animal or smoke from a distant fire. A track may mean that a bear has been here, and that may be a significant finding, but the track does not *communicate meaning*, Fish insists. The bear is not trying to send you a message.[64] I expanded this disavowal to claim that his analysis would not be concerned with the data from scientific experiments, which also can have significance, but which do not communicate meaning. The data may indicate that you should avoid too much salt in your diet, but the data themselves are not a form of communication. One can seek to analyze, explain, or understand significant non-communicative physical phenomena, but one cannot seek to interpret (or rewrite) them in Fish's analysis. This point takes on more significance if we accept that some forms of human behavior are non-communicative as well and so are also the kinds of things that one seeks to analyze, explain, or understand rather than interpret. Thus a social anthropologist might seek to analyze the behavior of a group of people by positing a set of values or goals that would make the most sense of that behavior. In doing this, the anthropologist need not be claiming that those exhibiting that behavior were aware of those values and goals or that they intended their behavior to communicate those values and goals. For many, the behavior might be completely habitual, and they might not be able to provide any reasons for doing it (perhaps because the reasons originated in the past of the culture and have been forgotten). Or the performers of the behavior might, if asked to explain their behavior, refer to a set of values and goals other than those hypothesized by the anthropologist. This need

---

[64] Stanley Fish, "The intentionalist thesis once more" in G. Huscroft and B. Miller (eds.), *The challenge of originalism. Theories of constitutional interpretation* (Cambridge: Cambridge University Press, 2011), 105.

not unsettle the social anthropologist, because these people might be mistaken or lack insight into their practices. The anthropologist could be confident that he has come up with a more adequate account that explains the behavior of the group in the most elegant manner. Such a scientist would not be interpreting the group's behavior, according to Fish's analysis; he is engaged in a different kind of project entirely.

Can what Hercules does in Dworkin's project be analogized to what the social anthropologist I have just described does?[65] In deciding a case, Hercules is initially interested in explaining a pattern of institutional behavior (legal history) in the most elegant way. To do so, he shows how it could have been generated by a set of values or goals or principles that Hercules himself comes up with. Hercules, like the social anthropologist, is not interested in whether any of the actual people who engaged in this institutional behavior had these values, etc., in mind or were acting with the intention of advancing them. Neither one treats the behavior that they are studying as communicative, and so neither one is concerned with authors. Instead each is concerned to find the solution to an intellectual puzzle: what hypothetical set of values, etc., would most elegantly explain this pattern? On this description, Hercules is neither an interpreter nor a rewriter according to Fish's analysis. He is like a scientist, coming up with explanations for data based on hypothetical constructs.

I do not need to declare which of these three descriptions fits Dworkin's project the best (although I favor explanation 3), because the important point is that whatever Hercules is doing – interpreting, rewriting, or an activity that is neither – Fish is not saying Hercules should not do it. Fish would only object when Dworkin calls what Hercules is doing "interpretation" when it is not.

Dworkin's critique of Fish's rejection of unconstrained legal actors

To Fish's earlier claims that no competent legal practitioner could act in a way that did not attend to institutional history and that no content can be given to the idea of a competent legal practitioner acting according to purely personal preferences in a legal context, Dworkin replies that

---

[65] Dworkin does discuss such an anthropologist trying to understand the practice of courtesy in ch. 2 of Dworkin, *Law's empire*.

it is perfectly possible to imagine a judge who decides to act as a pure act-utilitarian, which rebuts both of Fish's claims:

> I distinguished, using the chain novel as a model, between two assignments a judge might take up: he might try to find the best justification of the statutes and past judicial decisions that are part of the prior law and carry the principles of that justification forward in deciding new cases, or he might ignore the past record of statutes and decisions and decide cases "on a clean slate" instead. How could a judge, Fish asks, possibly decide a case by striking out in a new direction of his own? We need not strain for an answer. A judge might say, or at least think, that though the correct interpretation of past decisions, or the correct interpretation of a statute, requires a decision for the defendant, he is deciding for the plaintiff because that would make the community better off on the whole.[66]

Richard Posner is a judge who gives a description of the judging process that seems to confirm Dworkin's point. In his accounts of what pragmatism has to offer law, Posner argues that while some judges, concerned to uphold the rule of law, will try to achieve maximum consistency with past decisions, "a pragmatist judge always tries to do the best he can for the present and the future, unchecked by any felt *duty* to secure consistency in principle with what other officials have done in the past."[67] Posner denies that this means that a pragmatist judge can completely ignore past decisions, but a pragmatist judge need feel no qualms about reworking and rewriting this material in the service of just and sensible present outcomes. Posner argues that judges must consciously adapt the law to a changing world, and they must consciously use the available forms of legal rhetoric and reasoning to advance valuable social goals. He argues that the law should be concerned with "the sensible, the socially apt, the efficient, the fair rule."[68]

> The pragmatist thinks that concepts should be subservient to human need and therefore wants law to adjust its categories to fit the practices of the nonlegal community ... In approaching an issue that has been posed as one of statutory "interpretation," pragmatists will ask which of the possible resolutions has the best consequences ... [P]ragmatists are not interested in the authenticity of a suggested interpretation as an

---

[66] Dworkin, "My Reply to Stanley Fish," 305.
[67] Richard Posner, "Pragmatic adjudication" in Morris Dickstein (ed.), *The revival of pragmatism. New essays on social thought, law, and culture* (Durham, NC: Duke University Press, 1998), 237.
[68] Richard Posner, "What has pragmatism to offer law?" in Brint and Weaver (eds.), *Pragmatism*, 38.

expression of the intent of legislators or of the framers of constitutions. They are interested in using the legislative or constitutional text as a resource in the fashioning of a pragmatically attractive result.[69]

I will describe two responses that Fish could make to Dworkin's critique here, but I will also argue that they are not of equal strength.

The first, and weaker, response is that an act-utilitarian judge is not really acting and thinking outside the constraint provided by his legal training. That is, utilitarian reasoning is not completely foreign to judicial reasoning (which is often concerned with consequences and the public good), and so an act-utilitarian judge could plausibly still be described as "thinking within" the training a competent legal practitioner receives. However, Dworkin anticipates that Fish will use this strategy against his objection, and he moves to block it:

> Presumably Fish would say that a judge who decides in this [utilitarian] way does not think himself totally free from judicial practice and convention, because he offers, in his claim that the community would be better off were he to ignore precedent or the statute, the kind of reason that is at least conventionally associated with political decisions.[70]

But if Fish takes that line, Dworkin counters, his strategy leaves him unable to distinguish between the two different forms of judicial practice that Dworkin described. If a formalist judge and a pragmatist judge like Posner could both be described as "thinking within" the legal tradition, then their conduct would be equally legitimate on Fish's account. However, for Dworkin, a jurisprudence that cannot register the fundamental difference between these two judicial approaches reveals its bankruptcy and must be rejected.[71]

I take the nub of Dworkin's objection here to be that Fish's strategy, if pushed too far, ultimately undermines Fish's own position. Fish's claim is that a person acting as a judge is always constrained by the background he acquired in the course of his legal training and practice, because this background both enables and structures his performance as a competent practitioner. It follows that the shape of this constraint must *exclude* some ways of thinking, arguing, justifying, etc., that belong to other, non-legal practices. But if, with enough ingenuity, anything can be redescribed as "thinking within" the constraints established by legal training, then it turns out that nothing is excluded. That means that the constraints claimed by Fish do not really exist, and so the possibility of the

---

[69] Ibid., 39.   [70] Dworkin, "My Reply to Stanley Fish," 305.   [71] Ibid., 305–6.

unconstrained legal actor reemerges. Fish seems to court this objection
in "Wrong again" when he imagines a chain novelist being told "to strike
out in a new direction." In order to know how to do that, Fish says, the
novelist would first have to interpret in what direction the novel is
currently going – only then could he know what direction would count
as new. But this means that "he is as constrained by the chain in the act of
departing from it as he would be in the act of continuing it."[72] Here Fish
seems to be arguing that any attempt to reject x can be redescribed as
being constrained by x, and this threatens to make Fish's constraint so
capacious that it could contain anything.

But Fish does not need to expand the scope of his constraint claim in
this dangerously expansive way in order to rebut Dworkin's counterexample. He has a different and stronger argument available. Rather than
attempting to redescribe *every* decision made by a judge (even a pure
act-utilitarian one) as exhibiting the constraints put in place by legal
training, he could admit that someone occupying the institutional position of a judge could act in accordance with the training put in place by a
non-legal practice. Can such an admission be made by Fish? We need not
strain for an answer: yes it can. Fish acknowledges that all of us are
multiply embedded: "[E]ach of us is a member of not one but innumerable interpretive communities in relation to which different kinds of
beliefs are operating with different weight and force."[73] A judge may also
be a member of a community of strong religious believers and the
community of amateur and professional philosophers, for example.
So might it happen that the role a judge plays in one of these non-legal
communities *influences* the way he performs in his role as a judge?
It seems intuitive to say yes, but according to Fish's thesis of the autonomy
of practices (advanced in Chapter 3) the answer is no.[74] Different practices have different and incompatible enabling backgrounds. (Again, this
is why Fish declared interdisciplinarity to be impossible.) The practice
you are currently engaged in will generally determine which background

---

[72] *Doing*, 110.   [73] Ibid., 30.

[74] See, for example, *Trouble*, 301–2: "My reading style, in short, is a *professional* practice,
something I picked up in the course of an apprenticeship designed to prepare me for
performances in the classroom and learned journals; its relationship to any of my other
performances (as a father, citizen, consumer, dean) is entirely contingent and in my case
almost nonexistent." But note *Doing*, 31 where Fish seems to take a weaker position: "I
am never merely a teacher or a parent or a homeowner, for when I am playing any one of
these roles I am registering to some extent the obligations and urgencies that attend the
playing of the others."

is the one enabling and structuring your thoughts, perceptions, and actions. Goals and reasons that would speak to you in a different context, when you were engaged in a different practice, will not be operative so long as you are performing the current practice.

> It follows, then, that it is a mistake to oppose preference to principle. Rather, what opposition there is will be between preferences that are appropriate to a given enterprise and preferences that are appropriate to another enterprise; and, more often than not, there is no choice to be made between them since the choice has *already* been made the moment you see yourself as being engaged in one enterprise rather than another. I may be a judge deciding a case involving voter fraud who "personally" prefers one political party to another (it would be hard to imagine a judge of whom this would not be true), but if I am thinking of myself as a judge, I automatically conceive of my task as a judicial one and comport myself accordingly ... The conflict, then, is never between preference and principle, but between preferences that represent different principles, and if I am deeply enough embedded in some principled enterprise, the conflict will never be actualized because some preferences simply will not come into play.[75]

But imagine a judge who one day experiences a sudden and profound religious conversion, and who thereafter feels compelled to pursue religious goals and values and modes of reasoning in any context he finds himself in, including his judicial role. This state of affairs does not contradict Fish's autonomy of practices; it is not a situation in which different practices have merged or influenced each other. Rather it is a situation in which for this person one practice, religion, has completely taken over the territory formerly occupied by another practice, law. In such a situation, the person acting as a judge is an imposter, a person pretending to be a judge. He can no longer be described as "thinking within" the tradition of lawyers, for he is now acting as an embedded member of a completely different interpretive community.

Might not Dworkin's act-utilitarian judge be seen as analogous to the judge just described? That is, Dworkin's act-utilitarian judge can be seen as someone who is acting as the extension of a philosophical practice, not a legal one.[76] This reasoning could be extended to the description of

---

[75] *Doing*, 366–7. See too *Professional*, 138; Fish, "Intention is all there is," 1136.

[76] On Fish's conception of the self, it would not be as easy or commonplace as Dworkin supposes for a judge to cease acting as the extension of a legal practice and start acting as the extension of some other practice. A Kantian self might be able to change beliefs unproblematically (like changing clothes), but as we have seen in Part I, for Fish deep

pragmatist judicial practice provided earlier by Richard Posner. Posner might be describing his practice as an embedded member of a community other than the legal one – in Posner's case the community of economists.[77] (I think it more likely that Posner is a judge who simply misdescribes his own practice, because as an embedded member of the interpretive community of lawyers, he could not be acting in a way that did not attend to institutional history for the reasons given at the beginning of this chapter.) Once Dworkin's counterexample is understood as involving a person who is not embedded within the interpretive community of lawyers, Fish can start to undermine it more effectively. He can point out that such a religious or utilitarian or economic actor does not breathe new life into the "unconstrained legal actor," for this actor is neither unconstrained nor legal. The person who acts according to religious or utilitarian or economic reasoning might.be free of the constraints imposed by legal training but only because they are now completely constrained by whatever constitutes them as a competent performer of a completely different practice.

However, this new non-legal form of constraint will afford scant comfort to liberals concerned to uphold the rule of law. Liberals want judges to be constrained by *law*, not by some other practice or tradition. A person occupying the role of judge who is only constrained in his decisions by religion or political philosophy or economics is just as bad for them as a judge not constrained by anything. But how much danger does such a non-law constrained actor really pose to liberal rule of law values? If the person occupying the institutional position of judge openly decides cases without any reference to legal authorities and legal modes of reasoning, and instead decides only by references to the Bible or Bentham's collected works, this person will quickly be removed from that institutional position, probably on the grounds of mental ill-health.[78] As Fish put it earlier, it is "unthinkable" for a judge to decide in that way,[79] so a person who does will not be allowed to remain a judge. A judge deciding on the basis of the Bible or Bentham alone would be like the judge deciding on the basis of hair color in the following passage:

beliefs constitute the self, and are not accidental or secondary qualities of an underlying self. This is why religious conversions where those deep beliefs change are sometimes described as being "born again"—the result is a new self.

[77] I will return to the topic of law and economics and Richard Posner in Chapter 12.

[78] Stanley Fish, "On legal autonomy" 44 *Mercer Law Review* (1993) 738.

[79] *No free speech*, 225.

> A judge who decided a case on the basis of whether or not the defendant had red hair would not be striking out in a new [judicial] direction; he would simply not be acting as a judge, because he could give no reasons for his decision that would be seen *as* reasons by competent members of the legal community. (Even in so extreme a case it would not be accurate to describe the judge as striking out in a new direction; rather he would be continuing the direction of an enterprise – perhaps a bizarre one – *other* than the judicial.)[80]

What if the non-law constrained actor is more cunning and conceals the fact that they are "continuing the direction of an enterprise . . . *other* than the judicial"? That is, they still seek to advance the goals and values that animate their religious or utilitarian practice but do so by making public reference only to legal authorities and by employing only legal modes of reasoning. This more subtle version of Dworkin's utilitarian judge would not justify their decisions openly on the grounds "that it would make the community better off on the whole." Rather they would try to come up with an account of decided cases, legislation, and legal principles that allowed them to reach the result they desired for utilitarian reasons. (Richard Posner's account of a pragmatic judge had him "using the legislative or constitutional text as a resource in the fashioning of a pragmatically attractive result.") Dworkin would disapprove of this conduct, because he believes that the judge should not be "inventing" an account of the legal institutional history in order to justify a desired outcome. Instead, the judge should be "interpreting" or coming up with the account of the legal institutional history that makes the most sense of it and then extrapolating from that account to reach the outcome. As we have seen earlier in this chapter, Fish rejects Dworkin's position because it presupposes that legal institutional history has some pre-interpretive shape that constrains interpreters (rather than the background assumptions of a community constraining interpreters), and thus Dworkin veers toward positivism and formalism. Fish would say that if the utilitarian or religious practitioner occupying the institutional position of judge was successful in translating his moral reasons into legal reasons, *and* was successful in persuading other members of the legal interpretive community that these legal reasons justified the outcome, then this rhetorical success is not improper.[81]

---

[80] *Doing*, 92–3.

[81] For an example of such a successful argument, see Fish's discussion of *Rosenberger v. Rector* in *Trouble*, 224ff.

A natural objection to Fish's claim in the last sentence is that it allows morality to invade and subordinate the law in exactly the way liberals fear. Fish has two responses to this objection. First, since Fish (like Dworkin) holds that morality and politics sit in the background of all law anyway, this judge has not improperly injected a foreign element into the law. Rather the judge has succeeded, by using law-approved techniques, in replacing one background morality with another. "If that alteration were effected, it would not be because the structure of the law had been made to bend to the pressure of some moral or political perspective, but because a structure already moral and political had been given another moral and political shape."[82] Second, this process is not one in which law has been rendered subordinate to morality; rather law remains in the driver's seat. This can be seen when we consider what would happen if the judge cannot formulate a justifying argument for their desired religious or utilitarian outcome using only law-specific categories, histories, authorities, goals, principles, values, etc., or cannot convince other members of the legal interpretive community to accept the judge's argument as persuasive. If that happens, the cunning judge has to abandon their favored outcome or risk exposure and expulsion. The religious judge who is unable to translate their religious reasons into acceptable legal reasons would thus be like the academic feminist Fish describes in the following passage:

> An academic who is also a feminist is not two persons but one – an academic-who-is-also-a-feminist. That is, when her feminism weighs upon her, it takes the form specific to her situation; it is feminism-as-an-academic-might-be-concerned-with-it ... Nor is that relationship itself stable: a feminist academic may have worked out a modus vivendi that allows her to satisfy and even make capital of her "divided" loyalties, only to find in a moment of crisis that the two loyalties cannot both be satisfied and that, for the present at least, she must shut herself off from considerations to which she would otherwise be attuned.[83]

Similarly, the cunning judge's religion can only play a role if it can "take the form specific to her situation," and if it cannot take such a form, then she must "shut herself off from considerations to which she would otherwise be attuned." By shutting herself off in this way, the judge is submitting herself to law's standards and requirements, not those of religion. By accepting the requirement that her religious goals must be

---

[82] *Doing*, 131.   [83] Ibid., 31–2.

justified using law-specific tools, the cunning judge is hoist by her own petard, because her cunning has brought her back within the legal fold. The autonomy of practices says that you cannot serve two masters, and this actor is serving law.

> A judge hearing *McLoughlin* might be inclined to decide against the plaintiff because she reminds him of a hated stepmother or because she belongs to an ethnic group he reviles. But think of what he would have to do in order to "work" such "reasons" into his decision. He could not, of course, simply declare them, because they are not, at least in our culture, legal reasons and would be immediately stigmatized as inappropriate. Instead, he would be obliged to find recognizably legal reasons that could lead to an outcome in harmony with his prejudices; but if he did that he would not be ruled by those prejudices, but by the institutional requirement that only certain kinds of arguments – arguments drawn from the history of [legal] concerns and decisions – be employed.[84]

Once again, Fish has reached the position that the fears of liberals like Dworkin are groundless. The completely unconstrained legal actor cannot exist, and the non-law constrained actor can do no harm.

Dworkin's critique of Fish's analogizing judging to the instinctive performances of athletes

Dworkin takes Fish to task for this, as do Owen Fiss,[85] Michael Moore,[86] Steven Winter,[87] Andrew Goldsmith,[88] and Hamish Stewart.[89] In making

---

[84] Ibid., 366. See too 93: "[I]f in deciding a case a judge *is* able to give such [lawyerly] reasons, then the direction he strikes out in will not be new because it will have been implicit in the enterprise as a direction one could conceive of and argue for. That does not mean that his decision will be above criticism, but that it will be criticized, if it is criticized, for having gone in one judicial direction rather than another, neither direction being 'new' in a sense that would give substance to Dworkin's fears."

[85] See Owen Fiss, "Conventionalism" 58 *Southern California Law Review* (1985) 187.

[86] Moore, "The interpretive turn" 914–6.

[87] See Steven Winter, "Bull Durham and the uses of theory" 42 *Stanford Law Review* (1990) 688–91.

[88] Andrew Goldsmith, "Is there any backbone in this Fish? Interpretive communities, social criticism, and transgressive legal practice" 23 *Law & Social Inquiry* (1998) 397–9 (hereafter cited as Goldsmith, "Backbone").

[89] Stewart does not mention baseball, but the gist of his criticism is the same: "In Fish's view, the constraints of practice are so severe that they eliminate thought itself: any idea one has, any reason one offers for a conclusion, is fully determined by the practice. Thus, judgment, in the sense of serious reflection on different ways of resolving a problem, is not possible." Hamish Stewart, "Is judgment inscrutable?" 11 *The Canadian Journal of Law and Jurisprudence* (1998) 439. See too 422–6, 436–7.

this objection, Dworkin is responding to the position Fish advanced in "Dennis Martinez and the uses of theory," which I have described in this chapter and in Chapter 3. Fish's position was that a competent practitioner, whether they are a baseball player or a judge, has no need of a theory to tell them what to do, because in becoming an embedded member of a particular community they have already acquired the background that will enable and shape their actions. In his final contribution to their debate, "Pragmatism, right answers, and true banality," Dworkin takes issue with this claim:

> [Fish] wants . . . to picture lawyers and judges as like natural, unreflective athletes: instinctive craftsmen who react unthinkingly to legal problems, deciding as they have been trained to do, as no one trained in that way can *help* but do, obeying the ancient practices of their profession because it would be unthinkable to do otherwise . . . This is an exceptionally poor description of legal practice. Fish's account leaves no room for puzzle or progress or controversy or revolution.[90]

> Fish's crucial assumption that an interpretive practice cannot be self-conscious and reflexive . . . is undefended, counterintuitive, pervasive, and crippling. The force of the assumption is consistently down-market: It makes interpretive practice seem unreflective and automatic . . . [I]t leaves actual interpretive practice flat and passive, robbed of the reflective, introspective, argumentative tone that is, in fact, essential to its character.[91]

Not only does Dworkin insist that Fish is wrong to think that judging is "unreflective and automatic," he also argues that Fish is wrong to think that all athletic performances fit this description:

> Even in baseball, moreover, theory has more to do with practice than Fish acknowledges. The last player who hit .400, fifty years ago, was the greatest hitter of modern times, and he built a theory before every pitch.[92]

As we saw in Chapter 2, Fish's anti-foundationalist claim endorsed a form of social constructivism. He held that because all humans are necessarily locally embedded, they are never without a background of socially acquired beliefs. etc., that structure and enable their perceptions, thinking, and acting. But it is a mistake to conclude from the fact that human experience of the world is always structured by a background in this way that Fish holds that (i) there can be no disagreement among

---

[90] Ronald Dworkin, "Pragmatism, right answers, and true banality" in Brint and Weaver (eds.), *Pragmatism*, 387.
[91] Ibid., 380.   [92] Ibid., 382.

members of the same interpretive community, or that (ii) human experience will always be "unreflective and automatic," as Dworkin supposes Fish to be claiming.

Many of Fish's critics think that the constraint imposed by membership in the legal interpretive community must be so all-embracing that it transforms legal actors into robots marching in lockstep and incapable of disagreement.[93] Some critics argue that Fish can only explain disagreements between people by placing them in different interpretive communities, which results in such a multiplication of interpretive communities that the concept's power as an explanatory tool is lost.[94] But Fish does not make uniform agreement crucial to the notion of an interpretive community.[95] As he put it in *Postmodern sophistry*:

> [A]greement might be a (temporary and contingent) feature of a community's landscape at a particular time, but what makes something a community for my purposes is not whether its members agree or disagree, but whether there is an in-place set of assumptions about what the project is (recovering the past, sequencing a gene, interpreting literary works), what the resources are for implementing it, what the obstacles are to its implementation, what past performances are exemplary and tutelary, what workers are currently in the forefront of the effort, what marks one as a participant in the game. Within these assumptions there is plenty of room and opportunity for disagreement; but those who have not internalized them will be able neither to agree or disagree because they will not have – could not have – a sense of what is at stake.[96]

---

[93] Sadowski, "Language is not life" 1125–35; Georgia Chryostomides, "Doing the unnatural – Stanley Fish's theory of interpretation" (2000) *UCL Jurisprudence Review* 176–8, 183–4 (hereafter cited as Chrysostomides, "Doing the unnatural"); Goldsmith, "Backbone" 385–91; Allan C. Hutchinson, *Dwelling on the threshold. Critical essays on modern legal thought* (Toronto: Carswell, 1988), 142–63; Glass, "Dworkin, Fish and legal practice" 216–7; Drucilla Cornell, "'Convention' and critique" 7 *Cardozo Law Review* (1986) 681–2, 686–8; David Luban, "Fish v. Fish or, some realism about idealism" 7 *Cardozo Law Review* (1986) 694.

[94] Chrysostomides, "Doing the unnatural" 171–2; Dennis Patterson, "You made me do it: My reply to Stanley Fish" 72 *Texas Law Review* (1993) 73–4, 76 n48; Dennis Patterson, *Law and Truth* (Oxford: Oxford University Press, 1996), 123–6; Torben Spaak, "Relativism in legal thinking: Stanley Fish and the concept of an interpretative community" 21 *Ratio Juris* (2008) 163.

[95] Some commentators acknowledge this. See Daryl Levinson, "The consequences of Fish on the consequences of theory" 80 *Virginia Law Review* (1994) 1686.

[96] Stanley Fish, "One more time" in Olson and Worsham (eds.), *Postmodern sophistry*, 278. See too *Doing*, 149, 367.

It is true that on Fish's account the already-in-place background will sometimes deliver obvious facts, or clear textual meanings, or self-evident courses of action – Dennis Martinez provides an example of this. But it is just as possible on Fish's account that the background will deliver disputed factual claims, or ambiguous textual meanings, or conflicting possible courses of action. In short, anti-foundationalism does not rule out uncertainty, ambiguity, or conflicting choices, it only claims that these things will always be "enterprise-specific"[97] or "discipline-specific."[98] That is, the uncertainty, ambiguity, or conflicting choices all take forms that are given shape and significance by the particular background in place.[99] As Fish put it: "This doesn't mean that everything is understood, but that even what is puzzling and mysterious is so in ways specific to some elaborated system of thought."[100]

In attempting to resolve this enterprise-specific uncertainty, ambiguity, or choice, Fish acknowledges that the embedded practitioner will often have to engage in reflection and evaluation that takes time. "When I use phrases like 'without reflection' and 'immediately' and 'obviously' I do not mean to preclude self-conscious deliberation on the part of situated agents; it is just that such deliberations always occur within ways of thinking that are themselves the ground of consciousness, not its object."[101] That is, the embedded practitioner will employ investigative strategies and criteria of evaluation that are themselves enabled and structured by the background in place and so are just as enterprise-specific as the doubts and ambiguities they respond to. Therefore, for Fish, those engaging in such extended deliberation and self-reflection are "doing what comes naturally" for an embedded practitioner just as much as Dennis Martinez was in his unreflective athletic performance. They are all acting within and as extensions of a socially constructed background.[102]

Take the example of an experienced chess player pondering their next move in the middle of a game. Such a person does not make their moves

---

[97] *Doing*, 130.   [98] Fish, "Interpretation is not a theoretical issue," 514.

[99] Interview with Stanley Fish in Gary Olson, *Justifying belief. Stanley Fish and the work of rhetoric* (Albany: State University of New York Press, 2002), 124 (hereafter cited as Olson, *Justifying belief*).

[100] *Doing*, 16.

[101] Ibid., 128 n19. See too the interview with Stanley Fish in Olson, *Justifying belief*, 123.

[102] Dworkin is not the only critic of Fish who does not grasp this point. See James Seaton, "The two branches of the law and literature movement: A critique of Stanley Fish" 15 *Legal Studies Forum* (1991) 69–70; Chrysostomides, "Doing the unnatural" 179–82.

in an "unreflective and automatic" fashion, instead they engage in difficult and extended deliberations. But the chess player's deliberations are all shaped and enabled by the in-place background they acquired in the course of becoming a competent member of the community of chess players. Their current deliberations do not explicitly advert to this background (i.e., they do not remind themselves how the pieces move or remind themselves that the point of the game is to attack the opponent's king) but range within the enterprise-specific space this background opens up. The different moves one could now make, the possible long-range strategies one could pursue, the risks attendant upon each of these choices, and the criteria used to evaluate them all depend upon and are extensions of a specific background of assumptions, norms, goals, etc., put in place by their socialization into the interpretive community of chess players. Someone who did not share that background could not understand those deliberations or engage in them. Similarly, when a lawyer is uncertain how to resolve a legal issue, their uncertainty is very different from that of a layperson asked to resolve the same issue. The lawyer's uncertainty is enterprise-specific, because the competing possibilities seen are all generated by legal authorities, categories, and principles. The layperson would be operating with a completely different background and would see very different possibilities. It might be a difficult and lengthy process for the lawyer to decide which resolution was best, but they would do so by applying a law-specific understanding of "best" – an understanding that reflects law's goals, fears, hopes, and values. The point of both examples is that being locally embedded does not entail seeing only one option and performing it without thought; it can mean seeing a number of enterprise-specific options and having to evaluate them by using enterprise-specific criteria in an extended process of deliberation.

Finally, in response to Dworkin's claim that some successful baseball players achieve their results not by acting unreflectively and instinctively but by following an explicitly worked-out theory, Fish seizes upon a book co-authored by the famous hitter Ted Williams, called *The science of hitting*.[103] Fish notes that Williams claims that the theory of hitting advanced by Ty Cobb was impossible to put into practice, even though Cobb was "the smartest hitter of all." Thus Cobb's theory could not have

---

[103] *No free speech*, 228–30, 303–4. For a debate with Fish about the significance of this text, see Brook Thomas, "Stanley Fish and the uses of baseball: The return of the natural" 2 *Yale Journal of Law and the Humanities* (1990) 65ff.

been directing his practice, contrary to Dworkin's hope. What then does it mean to be a "smart" (i.e., reflective, non-instinctual) baseball player if it does not mean constructing and applying a theory? Fish answers that it means becoming

> *attentive* to the situation. The shape of your attentiveness is situation specific and dependent, so that . . . insofar as one is ever critically reflective, one is critically reflective *within* the routines of a practice. One's critical reflectiveness is in fact a function of, its shape is a function of, the routines of the practice. What most people want from critical reflectiveness is precisely a distance on the practice rather than what we might call a heightened degree of attention while performing that practice.[104]

Fish has the smart or reflective player thinking about what happened the previous times they were up to bat and what pitch they are likely to face now given the situation on the field, etc. Such a player is not acting in an "unreflective and automatic" fashion, but neither is the player ceasing to be an embedded practitioner in the way a strong theorist would have to be. Their reflectiveness is situational, or enterprise-specific, and Fish would argue that the same is true for judges too.

[104] *No free speech*, 304.

10

Fish's positive account of law

Law's disorder

Fish advances an account of legal reasoning that emphasizes its disorderly nature rather than its logical and systemic nature.

> [T]he law works not by identifying and then hewing to some overarching set of principles, or logical calculus, or authoritative revelation, but by deploying a set of ramshackle and heterogeneous resources in an effort to reach political resolution of disputes that must be framed (this is the law's requirements and the public's desire) in apolitical and abstract terms (fairness, equality, what justice requires).[1]

He endorses the similar accounts of legal reasoning provided by others, such as Richard Posner in *The problems of jurisprudence*.[2] As Fish describes it, Posner's account of how law works accepts that the legal system is "no system at all, but a ramshackle nonstructure made up of bits of everything and held together (when it is held together) by transitory political purposes."[3] Posner emphasizes the importance in law of practical reason, a form of reasoning that he describes as "a grab bag that includes anecdote, introspection, imagination, common sense, empathy, imputation of motives, speaker's authority, metaphor, analogy, precedent, custom, memory, 'experience.'"[4] Fish comments that:

---

[1] *No free speech*, 209. See too 222.
[2] Richard Posner, *The problems of jurisprudence* (Cambridge, MA: Harvard University Press, 1990). Fish describes Posner's account of how law works at *No free speech*, 200–8 and concludes: "[I]t is perhaps superfluous for me to say that I agree with him on almost every point." Fish also endorses the account of law offered by Gerald Burns, which he quotes approvingly at *No free speech*, 193: "[The law] is not a system working itself pure but a play of surfaces, a heterogeneous cultural practice that cannot be formally reduced but needs to be studied locally in terms of its position and effects within specific social and political situations."
[3] *No free speech*, 203. [4] Quoted in ibid., 203.

It is that untidiness that makes practical reasoning what it is, not a self-enclosed mode of algorithmic or mechanical calculation, but an ever-changing collection of rules of thumb, doctrines, proverbs, precedents, folk-tales, prejudices, aspirations, goals, fears, and, above all, beliefs.[5]

The critical legal studies (CLS) account of how law works, as Fish describes it, also sounds very like his own:

[L]egal reasoning is not a formal mechanism for determining outcomes in a neutral fashion but is rather a ramshackle ad hoc affair whose ill-fitting joints are soldered together by suspect rhetorical gestures, leaps of illogic, and special pleadings tricked up as general rules, all in the service of a decidedly partisan agenda that wants to wrap itself in the mantle and majesty of THE LAW.[6]

Fish and CLS agree too on the reasons why law's disorder cannot be remedied. They both point to the in-place background that structures the surface (or foreground) of law, and they note that this background contains moral and political commitments. We saw Fish make this point when he rejected the legal positivist separation of law and morality/politics in Chapter 7: "The content of the law, even when it is a statute that seems to be concerned with only the most technical and mechanical matters (taxes, for example), is always some social, moral, political, or religious vision."[7] Roberto Unger makes the same point in *The critical legal studies movement* when he writes that "every branch of doctrine must rely tacitly if not explicitly upon some picture of the forms of human association that are right and realistic in the areas of social life with which it deals."[8] Moreover, CLS and Fish agree that there are conflicts and contests between these background moral and political commitments. Roberto Unger developed this argument at length using the example of contract law in *The critical legal studies movement*,[9] and Fish also used contract law to make this point in Chapter 7.

These conflicts cannot be resolved, Fish argued in Part II, because there is no escape from the contest between incompatible and

---

[5] Ibid., 203. See too *Trouble*, 52 where Fish describes the legal canon, "which is neither stable nor homogeneous but is rather a rag-tag and shifting collection of quotations, precedents, statements of principle, talismanic phrases, charismatic practitioners, exemplary accomplishments, all of which carry authority in the sense that you can be fairly certain that by deploying them your agenda will be advanced."

[6] *No free speech*, 21.   [7] *Doing*, 131.

[8] Roberto Unger, *The critical legal studies movement* (Cambridge, MA: Harvard University Press, 1983), 8.

[9] Ibid., 57–90.

incommensurable commitments into a higher realm of liberal neutral principles. No meta-principle is available to rationally resolve or balance these incompatible commitments. The very rationality that would perform this operation is itself the product of contestable local commitments, Fish argued. Because these competing "visions of what life is or should be like"[10] cannot be unified or reconciled, the tensions and contradictions they engender at the surface of legal doctrine cannot be reconciled either. Consequently it is impossible for lawyers to remedy the "contradictions that fissure legal doctrine,"[11] and the law will always be a disorderly collection of heterogeneous elements that will resist the efforts by people like Dworkin to tidy it up and make it coherent and consistent.

Thus far, Fish and CLS have offered similar descriptions of how the law works, but they differ when it comes to evaluating this state of affairs. Fish notes that CLS considers law's ineradicable disorder to be a "farce"[12] or "insidious"[13] or "a shameful fact"[14] or "a scandal."[15] As we shall see in Chapter 12, this is because CLS sees law's disorder as operating ideologically to facilitate the oppression of some groups in society. But Fish parts company with CLS here because he argues that law's disorder is desirable and functional. As I shall explain in more detail in the next section of this chapter, Fish holds that law's disorder enables law to perform successfully the incompatible tasks assigned to it in a liberal society.[16] His central question is not: "How can the law be made philosophically coherent?" nor is it: "Is the law implicated in maintaining the dominance of one social group over another?" Instead he asks: "What are the jobs that a liberal society assigns to law, and how does law succeed in doing them?" In summary, while Fish acknowledges that CLS's emphasis on the disorder of law "has an obvious relationship to the position I have been elaborating,"[17] he emphatically rejects

> the CLS-style conclusion that the law is a sham or an elitist conspiracy, and assert[s] instead that these very features of the law, even though they are in tension with the law's "official story," are what enables the law to perform its task, the task of advertising its actions as following faithfully

---

[10] *No free speech*, 154.   [11] Ibid., 168.   [12] Ibid., 156.   [13] Ibid., 168.
[14] Ibid., 169.   [15] Ibid., 176.
[16] In *Doing*, 23 he offered a similar explanation for the success of feminism: "Indeed, it could well be that the 'looseness' of feminist practice, its eclectic and even ramshackle character, is essential to its success, to its ability to intervene in situations linked only by the fact that in them women's interests are seen to be at stake."
[17] *No free speech*, 21.

from general principles of justice, due process, impartiality, and so on while at the same time tailoring and remaking these principles in accordance with the pressures exerted by present-day exigencies. The law, in short, is always in the business of constructing the foundations on which it claims to rest and in the business too of effacing all signs of that construction so that its outcomes can be described as the end products of an inexorable and rule-based necessity.[18]

Law's jobs

I have noted Fish's claim that the law is assigned incompatible jobs in liberal societies, and now it is time to look more closely at what these jobs are. In passages quoted in the previous section, Fish describes law's task as "advertising its actions as following faithfully from general principles of justice, due process, impartiality, and so on while at the same time tailoring and remaking these principles in accordance with the pressures exerted by present-day exigencies," and as "reach[ing] political resolution of disputes that must be framed (this is the law's requirements and the public's desire) in apolitical and abstract terms (fairness, equality, what justice requires)." Clearly, there is not a single task here but two tasks that pull in opposing directions. Stated at a high level of generality, the basic incompatibility Fish identifies is between a rule of law job and a substantive justice job.[19] These jobs pull in opposing directions, because while the rule of law job stresses the goals of certainty, consistency, predictability, and continuity with the past, the justice job stresses the goals of flexibility, context-sensitivity, an ability to adapt to new realities, and the importance of achieving fair and sensible results. Each of these jobs reflects competing "visions of what life is or should be like" operating in the background shared by members of the legal interpretive community.

The rule of law job is an extension of the political and social vision at the heart of liberalism and is responsible for the law's wish "to have a formal existence."[20] Liberalism's central concern is protecting individual liberty and constraining the state, which is seen as the major threat to

---

[18] Ibid. See the same claim being made at 168–9.

[19] For a fuller account of the two jobs, see Michael Robertson, "Telling the law's two stories" 20 *The Canadian Journal of Law and Jurisprudence* (2007) 430–3 (hereafter cited as Robertson, "Telling the law's two stories"). For a critique of Fish's attempts to describe law's jobs and values, see Daryl Levinson, "The consequences of Fish on the consequences of theory" 80 *Virginia Law Review* (1994) 1682–91.

[20] See *No free speech*, ch. 11 ("The Law wishes to have a formal existence").

individual liberty. If laws are to constrain state actors, the laws must have clear and compelling meanings that are resistant to self-interested manipulation by those same state actors. This means that the rule of law job requires stable legal rules that are not amenable to change by legal interpreters. It is this requirement that Fish is identifying when he notes that "formalism ... provides the law with a palpable manifestation of its basic claim to be perdurable and general; that is, not shifting and changing, but standing as a point of reference in relation to which change can be assessed and controlled."[21] Similarly, a goal of liberalism is to prevent the exercise of arbitrary power by the state. Achieving this goal requires that the law apply general rules impartially and uniformly across a wide range of different contexts. Law is seen as defective and dangerous if it is too responsive to local circumstances and concerns, too particular, too ad hoc – this raises the fear of arbitrariness. It is this goal that Fish is identifying when he talks of law's "desire to identify a perspective larger and more stable than the perspective of local and individual concerns."[22] Finally, the rule of law in liberal societies seeks to identify principles and procedures that are neutral. Such principles and procedures, because they stand outside the competition between particular local conceptions of the good, are able to order society without partisan bias. It is this aspect of law's job in liberal societies that Fish is referring to in the following passage: "Law emerges because people desire predictability, stability, equal protection, the reign of justice, etc., and because they want to believe that it is possible to secure these things by instituting a set of impartial procedures."[23]

The substantive justice job is an extension of a different political and social vision that is less focused on individual liberty, constraining the state and achieving neutrality, and is more focused on resolving disputes in a way that respects community standards of reasonableness and morality and that also maximizes community benefits. It incorporates some religious and communitarian elements that liberalism displaced but did not eliminate. The substantive justice job is therefore very context-sensitive; achieving it requires the judge to be attuned to the requirements of community morality and to the broader social consequences in the circumstances of the present case. This directs the judge toward the

---

[21] *No free speech*, 143. See too *Doing*, 137: "The maintenance of continuity is a prime judicial obligation because without continuity the rule of law cannot claim to be stable and rooted in durable principles."

[22] *No free speech*, 142.   [23] Ibid., 213.

local and particular, rather than the abstract and general. Similarly, the justice job requires laws that are flexible enough to adapt to new circumstances if required – that is, laws that can be changed by legal interpreters. Finally, as we saw in Part II, Fish holds that the liberal search for neutral principles and impartial procedures is impossible because humans cannot rise above, or transcend, or hold at arm's length their local commitments in a comprehensive manner so as to arrive at a viewpoint that is uncontaminated by any partisan bias.[24] We have seen Fish flesh this surprising claim out with respect to the liberal principles of freedom of religion in Chapter 4 and freedom of speech in Chapter 7. Consequently, law is always at bottom local and substantive, rather than principled and general in the strong sense required by liberalism.[25] It is therefore impossible to jettison or ignore the perspective of the justice job, a perspective that is rooted in local and contestable conceptions of what is fair, sensible, and proper.

The claim that law is committed to achieving two incompatible jobs may seem outrageous to those who prize consistency and coherence, but, as Steven Smith has noted, there is a risk

> that philosophical analysis will fail to appreciate, and may even undermine, the puzzling capacity of humans *in practice* to embrace and live with both sides of an antinomy, or at least with what seem on an intellectual level to be divergent or incompatible positions or perspectives ... Such antinomies abound in law. Should criminal law be animated by consequentialist concerns of deterrence or by more deontological concerns of retribution? Should tort law be governed by considerations of economic efficiency or corrective justice? Should public law be understood and promoted by individualist or communitarian commitments? When considered on a theoretical level, such questions may present what appear to our finite and language-limited minds to be radically dissimilar or even incompatible alternatives. And yet it seems that in practice, and particularly in the practice of law, humans manage to embrace such incompatible alternatives in ways that arguably are more productive and beneficial than the single-minded commitment to either alternative would be.[26]

Fish makes the same point when he acknowledges that the pursuit of its incompatible jobs might make law a failure from a philosophical perspective, but he then goes on to ask: [W]hy should law submit itself to the

---

[24] See generally ibid., ch. 10 ("Liberalism doesn't exist") and *Trouble*.   [25] *Doing*, 516.

[26] Steven D. Smith, "That old-time originalism" in G. Huscroft and B. Miller (eds.), *The challenge of originalism. Theories of constitutional interpretation* (Cambridge: Cambridge University Press, 2011), 223, 238–9.

judgment and values of a foreign practice like philosophy?[27] Fish's position is that law has found ways of using the disorderliness described in the previous section to manage the tensions between its incompatible jobs, and thus to preserve its legitimacy and mana as an important social institution. (Nor is he alone in taking this position. Elsewhere I have considered the work of other legal theorists who take seriously the idea that the law is productively and beneficially committed to achieving incompatible jobs.[28]) Consequently, judged by how well it performs its assigned institutional functions (or responds to the desires behind its creation), law is a spectacular success according to Fish, and this achievement should not be dimmed by viewing it through the lens of some other practice's standards.

> By the standards applied to determinate and principled procedures, the law fails miserably (this is the charge made by Critical Legal Studies); but by the pragmatist standard – unsatisfactory as a standard to formalists and objectivists, as well as to deconstructors – the law gets passing and even high marks because it *works*.[29]

The existence of these two competing law jobs is longstanding in liberal societies, so what strategies have been adopted to deal with the conflict? One possible response is to abandon one of the two jobs in order to eliminate any messy contest between them at the heart of law. On this approach, one of the law jobs is argued to be the true or proper job of the law, and the other is denigrated as a dereliction of law's real task or as an impossible dream. There are legal formalists and legal positivists who argue strongly that the rule of law job is law's only real job, while some legal realists argued to the contrary that the substantive justice job was law's only real job. Richard Posner argues strongly for the primacy of his version of the substantive justice job and denigrates the desires behind the rule of law job, but Fish chides him for his monism:

> [Posner] writes deprecatingly of the delusions, pretensions, and false understandings with which actors in the legal culture deceive themselves.

---

[27] *Doing*, 397–8; *Professional*, 103.

[28] See my descriptions of the work of Thurman Arnold, Oren Perez, Anthony Kronman, and Karl Llewellyn in Robertson, "Telling the law's two stories" 433–2.

[29] *No free speech*, 209. See too 169: "Law, however, is not philosophical (except when it borrows philosophy's arguments for its own purposes) but pragmatic, and from the pragmatic standpoint, the inconsistency of doctrine is what enables law to work"; ibid., 178: "Once contingency (or ad-hocness or makeshiftness or rhetoricity) is recognized as constitutive of the law's life, its many and various instantiations can be explored without apology and without any larger (that is, grandly philosophical) rationale."

But the results of success in this struggle, should he or anyone else achieve it, would not be a cleaned-up conceptual universe, but a universe deprived of the props that must be in place if the law is to be possessed of a persuasive rationale. In short, law will only work – not in the realist or economic sense but in the sense answerable to the desires that impel its establishment – if the metaphysical entities Posner would remove are retained; and if the history of our life with law tells us anything, it is that they *will* be retained, no matter what analysis of either an economic or deconstructive kind is able to show.[30]

Another possible response is to retain both jobs, but to avoid a messy contest between them by providing a separate territory for each.[31] This is the approach H. L. A. Hart took in chapter 7 of *The concept of law*.[32] He saw the legal formalists as describing what happened when the facts of a legal dispute fell within the core of a rule (the rule of law job prevailed), and the legal realists as describing what happened when the facts fell within the fuzzy penumbra of a rule (the substantive justice job was able to prevail). Both law jobs are acknowledged on this approach, but they do not conflict because their performance is required in completely different contexts. Moreover, Hart believed, the separate territories of the two jobs were not equal in size. In the typical case, he thought, the facts would fall within the core of a rule. Penumbral cases were less common in everyday life though they might be more common in the higher courts.

A third response rejects both of the first two responses. It denies that one of the law jobs can be eliminated, thus leaving the other job in occupation of the entire territory of the law, and it also denies that each of the law jobs can be assigned a separate territory to avoid clashes between them. It therefore accepts the existence of clashes of moral and political commitments at the heart of law, and CLS, Dworkin, and Fish can each be understood as arguing for different versions of this third response. CLS and Fish argue that the resulting pervasive tensions and contradictions in law can never be tidied up in a philosophically satisfying way, whereas Dworkin believes that Hercules shows the way to

---

[30] Ibid., 213.

[31] The creation of separate institutions (the courts of common law and equity) to pursue the different law jobs was achieved in preliberal societies. Thurman Arnold noted that "[t]he court of equity is gone, but with its disappearance arises the administrative or quasi-judicial court endowed with the freedom of action which the old court of equity had." Thurman Arnold, *The symbols of government* (New York, NY: Harcourt, Brace & World, 1962. Originally published 1935), 64.

[32] H. L. A. Hart, *The concept of law* (Oxford: Oxford University Press, 1961).

achieve this. Fish differs from CLS by holding that the pervasive tensions and contradictions in law are functional, rather than problems.

Law's two stories

In Fish's analysis, as I have described it so far, each of the law jobs is capable of making territorial claims over any part of the legal field. That is, whenever a legal dispute arises, it will be possible to argue that its resolution requires performing either the rule of law job or the substantive justice job. The contest between law's two basic jobs is therefore not resolved logically but rhetorically. Two stories about what the law should do will compete to be the most plausible and persuasive.

Sometimes one story will win without facing strong competition from the other. In some situations, the demands of the rule of law or the demands of justice can seem overwhelmingly obvious. Dworkin says that this was the case in *Riggs* v. *Palmer* (rejecting the ability of a person to inherit under the valid will of a person he murdered) where the substantive justice job trumped the rule of law job. In most situations, however, there is more scope for a genuine contest between the two law jobs, but the rule of law job has a built-in advantage in any rhetorical contest because it is the dominant story in our liberal culture. The values and goals it advances are more closely tied to the liberal social vision than those of the substantive justice job. Consequently, it is the story that will resonate most strongly and seem most obvious and intuitive, and this has an effect on the way in which the substantive justice job is typically advanced.

Sometimes the substantive justice job can be advocated for openly. As Fish put it in *The trouble with principle*, "[i]f the system should prove resistant to an outcome desired by the majority, formulas of flexibility will be invoked, but with an insistence that in their apparent irregularity they are true to the core values of the enterprise . . . [Y]ou say, 'After all, we must always keep in mind what equity or justice requires.'"[33] But it can be a risky strategy for a legal actor to assert baldly that justice requires a particular resolution in the present dispute and that rule of law concerns are to be discounted. Such a claim risks being denigrated as ad hoc and unprincipled. This difficulty does not mean that the substantive justice story is invariably silenced, but it does mean that it is often more effective to employ more indirect rhetorical strategies to advance the substantive justice job.

---

[33] *Trouble*, 51.

One indirect strategy is to do the substantive justice job but to describe what you are doing as falling under the rule of law story. I will call this the camouflage strategy. The camouflage strategy can be pursued by selecting from among the competing existing rules the one that delivers the result that substantive justice requires. Or it can be pursued by manipulating a formal rule so that it delivers the result that substantive justice requires. A second strategy is to admit that you are doing the substantive justice job in the particular case, and not the rule of law job, but to insist that this does not generate a serious clash between the two jobs. That is, both stories are told at the same time, but they are told as if they really constituted one unified story. I will call this the stereo strategy. Fish describes the stereo strategy this way:

> [Y]ou tell two stories at the same time, one in which the freedom of contracting parties is proclaimed and protected and another in which that freedom is denied as a possibility and undermined by almost everything courts do. But in order to make them come out right, you tell the two stories as if they were one, as if, rather than eroding the supposedly formal basis of contract law, the second story merely refines it at the edges and leaves its primary assertions (which are also assertions of the law's stability) intact.[34]

Both of these strategies are on display in the second part of "The Law wishes to have a formal existence"[35] where Fish seeks to convince us that contract law has developed ways of using its surface disorder to do the substantive justice job – achieving context-sensitive results that are attentive to the demands of morality and community expectations – while at the same time presenting this performance as consistent with the requirements of the rule of law job. He is therefore adamant that the contradictions and tensions within contract law are a good thing.

> Rather than being an embarrassment, the presence in contract doctrine of contradictory versions of the enterprise is an opportunity. It is in the spaces opened by the juxtaposition of apparently irreconcilable impulses – to be purely formal and intuitively moral – that the law is able to exercise its resourcefulness ... In order to be what it claims to be ... contract law must uphold a view of transaction in which its features are purely formal; but in order to be what it wants to be – sensitive to our always changing intuitions about how people ought to behave – contract law must continually smuggle in everything it claims to exclude.[36]

---

[34] *No free speech*, 163–4.   [35] Ibid., 156–68.

[36] Ibid., 161, 163. See too Professional, 103: "It is by virtue of the contradictions it harbors that contract law is able to exhibit the flexibility required by the double obligation to

He points out that even when judges acknowledge the requirements of the formal consideration doctrine, they have shown great creativity and skill in finding consideration to be present (when initially it seemed to be absent) in order to reach a morally satisfying result in the particular circumstances of the case before them.

> As the case history shows ... judges have no difficulty recharacterizing the shape of consideration so that it supports the conclusion they wish to reach. Indeed, directions for performing this interpretive feat are built into contract doctrine itself, which turns out in my analysis to be as porous and plastic as poetry or abstract art.[37]

He offers an extended analysis of the majority's reasoning in the case of *Webb* v. *McGowin* to demonstrate this.[38] What we see here is a fine example of the camouflage strategy in operation. Consideration is found and the formal rule satisfied, but the judges have been performing heroic work to make sure that the formal rule would deliver the just result. Interestingly, Fish reports that one of the judges opted for the stereo strategy rather than the camouflage strategy:

> In a brief but revealing concurring opinion, Judge William H. Samford further pulls back a curtain that had never really been closed. He admits that the opinion he now joins is "not free from doubt" and acknowledges that according to "the strict letter of the rule" Webb's recovery would be barred, but then he simply declares the "principle" the court has been following, a principle whose articulations he attributes to Chief Justice Marshall when he said "I do not think that law ought to be separated from justice."[39]

Fish's final point is that the substantive justice job can also be achieved by the use of other rules and devices that already exist and sit beside consideration doctrine within orthodox contract law. There is, for example, the "contract implied in law," which Fish describes as

> a judgment by a court that a party *ought* to have had a certain intention or performed in a certain way and for the purposes of justice and equity that intention or performance will now be imputed to him along with the obligations that follow. The notion of a contract implied in law springs all the bolts that consideration is designed to secure and provides the means for a court to do what, under contract law, a court is not supposed to do, make a new contract in accordance with its conception of morality.[40]

---

adhere to an official morality of contractual autonomy while adjusting its rulings to the reality of a world in which such autonomy has always and already been compromised."
[37] *No free speech*, 21.   [38] Ibid., 164–8.   [39] Ibid., 167.   [40] Ibid., 160.

Fish reports that there are many ways in which contract law comes to contain the competing rules that provide the flexibility that enables the justice job to be done without generating a direct conflict with the rule of law job:

> You develop a taxonomy of contractual kinds, one of which violates the principles of the taxonomy; you produce a document (the *Restatement*) that, in the guise of clarifying the law, presents its contradictions in a form that further institutionalizes them; . . . you develop and expand notions like promissory estoppel, duress, incapacity, unconscionability, and unjust enrichment and then expand them to the point where there is no action that cannot be justified in their terms; you invoke the distinction between public and private, even as you allow public pressures to determine the distinction's boundaries.[41]

Fish goes on to claim that other areas of law will exhibit the same (anti-legal positivist) character as contract law – that is, morality will always be present, but devices will be found to deflect attention away this.

> [T]he first thing a moral tradition must do after having captured the law (or some portion of its territory) is present itself as being beyond or below (it doesn't really matter) morality . . . Just as the winning interpretation of a contract must persuade the court that it is not an interpretation at all but a plain and clear meaning, so the winning morality must persuade the court (or direct the court in the ways of persuading itself) that it is not a morality at all but a perspicuous instance of fidelity to the law's form.[42]

Law is therefore constantly employing "strategies by which it generates outcomes from concerns and perspectives it ostentatiously disavows."[43] This might sound bad, but Fish describes it differently:

> The history of legal doctrine and its applications is a history neither of rationalistic purity nor of incoherence and bad faith, but an almost Ovidian history of transformation under the pressure of enormously complicated social, political, and economic urgencies, a history in which victory – in the shape of *keeping going* – is always being wrested from what looks like certain defeat, and wrested by means of stratagems that are all the more remarkable because, rather than being hidden, they are always fully on display. Not only does the law forge its identity out of the stuff it disdains, it does so in public.[44]

---

[41] Ibid.,163. See too 170 where Fish reports that Clare Dalton gives a similar list of the ways in which the conflict between sections 71 and 90 of the *Second Restatement on Contracts* (one defining contract obligation in terms of consideration and the other dealing with "contracts without consideration") is dealt with.

[42] Ibid., 159.   [43] Ibid., 177.   [44] Ibid., 156.

At this stage it might be hard to see how law is not indeed a history of bad faith. It looks as if the substantive justice job is the only one really being done, while the rule of law story is a kind of "noble lie" that is retained as a mere facade. It is in the next chapter dealing with constraints in the law that we will get a better sense of how the rule of law job can genuinely be achieved on Fish's account.

Law's amazing trick

The previous section described ways in which law is able to exploit the disorder at the surface of legal doctrine caused by law's competing background "social, moral, political, or religious vision[s]"[45] in order to do both of its incompatible law jobs. Law found ways to do the substantive justice job while presenting this achievement in ways that did not negate the rule of law job. The ability of the law to "generate outcomes from concerns and perspectives it ostentatiously disavows"[46] is no minor achievement, Fish insisted. This achievement requires law to find ways to present flexibility and sensitivity to local contexts in a way that is compatible with the rule of law's insistence upon stability and consistency with the history of past decisions. How is this trick achieved? The answer was provided by the legal realist Karl Llewellyn, who insisted that *stare decisis* was really a mechanism that enabled the law to change while still telling a persuasive story about its continuity and stability.[47] A precedent is not ignored or overruled; rather it is reshaped by legitimate techniques with an eye to the needs of the present. Then the past precedent with its new content is declared to compel the result in the present case. Thus the decision can be presented as governed by the neutral application of a rule established in the past, even though it really is a response to current pressures.

Fish echoes Llewellyn's insight. He marvels at the way the law is able to reshape the past, efface the evidence of that reshaping, and then declare itself compelled in the present case by the past it has just transformed. This, he says, is "the story of rhetoric, the art of constructing the (verbal) ground upon which you then confidently walk ... [Harry] Scheiber calls this the law's 'amazing trick,' the trick by which the law rebuilds itself in mid-air without ever touching down."[48]

---

[45] *Doing*, 131.   [46] *No free speech*, 177.
[47] Robertson, "Telling the law's two stories" 440–2.   [48] *No free speech*, 170.

The result is a spectacle that could be described (as the members of the critical legal studies movement tend to do) as farce, but I would describe it differently, as a signal example of the way in which human beings are able to construct a roadway on which they are travelling, even to the extent of "demonstrating" in the course of building it that it was there all the while.[49]

What we have here is yet another version of the camouflage strategy, one in which "change is brought about by a discourse that creates the authorities it invokes"[50] and law's task is that "of simultaneously declaring and fashioning the formal autonomy that constitutes its precarious, powerful being."[51]

This is another way of making the argument that we saw Fish advance in Chapter 9 against Dworkin during their debate over the chain novel. The *ratios* of past cases and the meanings of chains of past cases (i.e., legal institutional history) cannot function as the kind of external constraint upon present legal interpretation that Dworkin desires, because they are themselves products of interpretation and the interpretation that produces them is influenced by the needs of the present case.

> [R]ather than the past controlling the present, the present controls the past by providing the perspective from which the two must be brought into line. The truth about precedent, then, is the opposite of the story we tell about it; precedent is the process by which the past gets produced by the present so that it can then be cited as the producer of the present. It is in this way that the law achieves what Ronald Dworkin calls "articulate consistency," a way of thinking and talking about itself which creates and re-creates the continuity that is so crucial to its largest claim, the claim to have an unchanging center that founds its authority. Articulate consistency is not a fact, but an achievement, something that is forever being wrested out of diverse materials which are then being retroactively declared always to have had its shape.[52]

Fish's "law's amazing trick" analysis also cuts against Hart's account of hard cases. Hart talked of hard cases as arising when the legal materials run out and so recourse must be had to non-legal material. But in Fish's analysis, the legal materials will never run out. The past will always be reworked so that it can command the present, even though that may take great skill and lawyers may disagree about how it should come out (hence "hard"). The facts of a case will not be allowed to exist outside the scope of a past rule; some rule will be stretched to cover it, but this

---

[49] Ibid., 156.   [50] Ibid., 171.   [51] Ibid., 177.   [52] *Doing*, 514–5.

stretching will be redescribed in the rule of law story as finding an existing fit. Here we see an example of two things Fish has mentioned before: We see the legal interpretive community operating as "an engine of change"[53] (assimilating the new material changes the rule), and we also see in operation "the law's conservatism, which will not allow a case to remain unrelated to the past, and so assures that the past, in the form of the history of decisions, will be continually rewritten."[54]

Rewriting in law

Finally, I want to make a connection between this chapter and the discussion of Fish's intentionalism at the end of Chapter 8. We saw there that in his most recent writings defending intentionalism, Fish drew a distinction between interpreting a text and rewriting a text. Interpreting a text, he argued, is seeking to ascertain what the actual author of the text intended that text to mean, while rewriting a text involves doing something else with the text, such as assuming an author of the text other than the actual author, and/or assuming an authorial intention other than the actual authorial intention. Fish acknowledged that there were sometimes good reasons for lawyers to rewrite, rather than to interpret, the texts they dealt with. However, we noted too some ambivalence, because he also can be found saying that rewriting results in a "free-for-all" rather than a rationally defensible activity. In that previous chapter, I sought to give an explanation for Fish's ambivalence that emphasized the influence of his training as a scholar of English literature (where rewriting the text being studied is never appropriate), and I also argued that it was an error for Fish to think that rewriting by lawyers (as opposed to literary scholars) could lead to an unconstrained free-for-all. I concluded that his recent fear of rewriting in law was inconsistent with his earlier position (described in Chapter 7) that the fear of the unconstrained legal actor was groundless.

Now I wish to point out what appears to me to be another inconsistency between Fish's recent fears about rewriting and his other work. If you look at Fish's account of how law really works as I have described it in this chapter, I think it fits much more naturally into the rewriting category than the interpretation category. He has not emphasized that law works by finding out what the authors of statutes and precedents and

[53] Ibid.,150.   [54] Ibid., 94.

contracts intended when these texts were written and then enforcing those past intentions. Instead, he has emphasized that law often works by rewriting legal texts so that the substantive justice job can be done in a way that does not deny the demands of the rule of law job.

Consider these two descriptions, with emphasis added to highlight the ways in which law rewrites the past rather than being governed by the past intentions of legal authors:

> [Law's task is] advertising its actions as following faithfully from general principles of justice, due process, impartiality, and so on while at the same time *tailoring and remaking these principles* in accordance with the pressures exerted by present-day exigencies. The law, in short, is always in the business of *constructing the foundations on which it claims to rest and in the business too of effacing all signs of that construction* so that its outcomes can be described as the end products of an inexorable and rule-based necessity.[55]

> To see a present-day case as similar to a chain of earlier ones is to *reconceive that chain* by finding in it an applicability that has not always been apparent. Paradoxically, *one can be faithful to legal history only by revising it, by redescribing* it in such a way as to accommodate and render manageable the issues raised by the present. This is a function of the law's conservatism, which will not allow a case to remain unrelated to the past, and so assures that *the past, in the form of the history of decisions, will be continually rewritten. In fact, it is the duty of a judge to rewrite it* (which is to say no more than that it is the duty of a judge to decide), and therefore there can be no simply "found" history in relation to which some other history could be said to be "invented." *All histories are invented* in the weak sense that they are not simply "discovered," but assembled under the pressure of some present urgency.[56]

When a chain of past precedents is "reconceived" or "redescribed" or "rewritten" in the ways Fish says, we are ascribing to the authors of the decisions in the chain new intentions that enable the law to decide the present case sensibly; we are not concerned to be governed by their actual intentions. In other words, when lawyers perform "law's amazing trick," when they employ law's contradictions and tensions to achieve flexibility

---

[55] *No free speech*, 21.
[56] *Doing*, 94. See too 367: "That judge, as Dworkin says, will have a reason for deciding in Mrs. McLoughlin's favor. That reason needn't be decisive, however, for the judge may view it as a challenge to the exercising of his judicial skills, or as an invitation either to re-read the chain of decisions in a way that excludes the present case from its scope or to characterize the present case in a way that leads it to be seen as turning on an issue other than the issue linking the chain of decisions."

of response, when they engage in the camouflage and stereo strategies, they are rewriting law rather than interpreting it. They are engaging in a rhetorical performance, rather than simply trying to discover an empirical fact about the world – namely, what a particular author's intentions were when they produced a text.

Moreover, rewriting in law is not just performed to achieve the substantive justice job – rewriting can also be performed to achieve the rule of law job. The rule of law job requires legal texts with accessible, clear, and objective meanings, which in turn allow the law to advance predictability, co-ordination, efficiency, and the constraint of state officials. Interpretation, or searching for the actual intentions of the actual author(s) of the legal text, may not provide what the rule of law requires in certain situations. The text might have been written long ago, or have multiple authors, for example, making interpretation difficult and contentious. There can therefore be good rule of law reasons (which Fish acknowledges) for ignoring the actual intentions of the actual author(s) in these situations, and instead stipulating a different set of intentions for the actual author(s) – e.g., the intention to use words in their most common dictionary meanings. As we saw in Chapter 8, this is what textualists are really doing, rather than (as they describe themselves) attending to syntax and semantics alone to the exclusion of any authorial intention. But this stipulative practice amounts to rewriting, and the same is true for other practices justified by rule of law reasoning, such as imposing stopping rules (which limit the sources of evidence for authorial intention), and turning to non-actual "reasonable" authors or testators.

So my conclusion is that Fish's analysis leads to an insightful and surprising result: rewriting is pervasive in law, and it's a good thing, too, because it is through rewriting that law succeeds in performing both of its incompatible jobs.[57] This result will alarm most lawyers because rewriting of the law is viewed very negatively in our legal culture. Unless it is done by elected legislators, rewriting of the law is generally associated with unbridled judicial activism, ignoring the democratic will of the legislators, and undermining established precedent. Most lawyers feel more comfortable with a description of legal practice that has them merely interpreting laws written by some

---

[57] For more detail, see Michael Robertson, "The impossibility of textualism and the pervasiveness of rewriting in law" 22 *The Canadian Journal of Law and Jurisprudence* (2009) 402–5.

legitimate authority. This result will also alarm Fish himself, I suspect, for although he acknowledges in his recent writings that it is sometimes appropriate for lawyers to rewrite rather than interpret the law, his main emphasis is on the virtues of sticking with interpreting. However, I believe that this emphasis is inconsistent with the analysis and insights of his earlier work for which he has provided reasons that still stand up.

Change and indeterminacy in law

There are two diametrically opposed charges that could be levelled at Fish regarding change in the law. The first charge is that he does not leave any room for change. His legal interpretive community is too hermetically sealed and thus unable to change and evolve. The response to this charge, which involved explaining Fish's positive account of change, was dealt with at the ends of Chapters 2, 3, and 5. The second charge is that he leaves too much room for change and therefore is a kind of indeterminacy theorist.[1] Legal indeterminacy theorists, who are now associated with legal realism and critical legal studies but who have roots going back to the ancient Greek sophists, argue that the apprehension of meaning in legal texts is not the result of compulsion and is instead the result of interpretive choices and the exercise of rhetorical skill. Their argument is that there are typically many choices available to legal interpreters, and so the meaning of legal texts is malleable and indeterminate.[2] It is the charge that Fish is a legal indeterminacy theorist that I will consider in this chapter.

Arguments for the claim that Fish is an indeterminacy theorist

At first sight, Fish seems able to rebut the indeterminacy charge with ease. As we saw when we examined his response to legal formalism in Chapter 8, he holds that a legal text has one fixed and true meaning, namely the meaning its author(s) intended when the text was produced. He explicitly rejected the position that a text means what its readers can be convinced it means. Also, his account of the apprehension of textual meaning did not stress indeterminacy and choice; instead it stressed compulsion and constraint. He explained the existence of shared clear and compelling

---

[1] See, for example, Georgia Chrysostomides, "Doing the unnatural – Stanley Fish's theory of interpretation" (2000) *UCL Jurisprudence Review* 174-6, 184-5.

[2] *No free speech*, 189-90.

meanings as the product of constraint by the background one acquires in becoming a competent member of an "interpretive community."

While his position as described so far keeps Fish out of the indeterminacy theorist camp, trouble lies further down the road. Fish has acknowledged that the in-place background of the interpretive community need not always deliver shared clear and compelling (i.e., objective) textual meanings. It can also deliver textual ambiguity, which introduces choice instead of compulsion. Nor does being a member of the legal interpretive community guarantee that you will see one clear and compelling resolution to a legal dispute. He has acknowledged that the background can make a number of legal resolutions available to you, which also introduces choice. But Fish would respond that the choice that is introduced into law in these ways always remains constrained choice. The ambiguous meanings and the alternative resolutions, just like the single clear and compelling meanings and resolutions, are enabled, shaped, and constrained by the shared in-place background. As he put it earlier, all ambiguity and alternatives are "enterprise-specific."[3] This means they will be limited in scope and will not even be seen by those who do not share the in-place background peculiar to that enterprise.

Fish's analysis so far has consistently pointed to the constraining role of the in-place background of the interpretive community in the communication of meaning, and this constraint has served to rebut the charge that Fish is making an indeterminacy argument for the primacy of choice. But, significantly, Fish has acknowledged that *this constraining background itself can change*, and thus a text can be recontextualized and its perceived meaning changed. We have seen that any shared background will naturally change over time as interpretive communities, which are not hermetically sealed and static things, absorb and assimilate new material in the course of advancing their distinctive projects. We have also seen that the background can change because some members of the interpretive community deliberately seek to change elements of it in order to recharacterize a fact or recontextualize a text. Earlier we saw Trident's lawyers try to change the accepted meaning of a loan contract by changing the background assumption about the goal of contract law. Similarly, and more successfully, the constitutional rights of black Americans were changed in the second half of the twentieth century after negative background assumptions about them were altered by the deliberate acts of civil

---

[3] *Doing*, 130.

rights advocates. Another recontextualizing strategy is to persuade the community to shift to a different background assumption about authorial intention. For example, Fish analyzes John Milton's 1643 arguments for the relaxing of the constraints on divorce in the face of Matthew 19:9, which provides: "Whosoever shall put away his wife, except it be for fornication . . . committeth adultery." Fish describes how Milton's strategy is to provide a different account of what Christ's intention was in uttering these words.[4] Elsewhere Fish describes how the same recontextualizing strategy could be employed to "relax" the Constitutional requirement that the American president be at least 35 years of age:

> What did the writers mean by thirty-five years of age? The commonsensical answer is that by thirty-five years of age they meant thirty-five years of age; but thirty-five is a point on a scale, and the scale is of something; in this case a scale of *maturity* as determined in relation to such matters as life expectancy, the course of education, the balance between vigor and wisdom, etc. When the framers chose to specify thirty-five as the minimal age of the president, they did so against a background of concerns and cultural conditions within which "thirty-five" had a certain meaning; and one could argue (should there for some reason be an effort to "relax" the requirement in either direction) that since those conditions have changed – life expectancy is much higher, the period of vigor much longer, the course of education much extended – the meaning of thirty-five has changed too, and "thirty-five" now means "fifty."[5]

But if the interpretive community's constraining in-place background can be altered by deliberate rhetorical strategies like these, then it seems that Fish is an indeterminacy theorist after all. If these deliberate rhetorical efforts succeed, then the meanings the community perceives in the texts that are the object of its professional concern will change, too.[6]

---

[4] Ibid., 8–9.

[5] Ibid., 358–9. In response to the objection that this strategy blatantly disregards the literal meaning of the text and is an egregious example of judicial activism, Fish would reply that "no one and everyone is guilty of judicial activism if by judicial activism you mean departing from the literal text; there is no literal text to depart from, just in-place stipulations of intention; and when you depart from those, you are not committing a crime; you are offering an alternative stipulation and initiating an argument (this not that is what they meant)." Stanley Fish, "The intentionalist thesis once more" in G. Huscroft and B. Miller (eds.), *The challenge of originalism. Theories of constitutional interpretation* (Cambridge: Cambridge University Press, 2011), 115–6.

[6] See *Doing*, ch. 12 where Fish considers how the perceived meaning of books XI and XII of Milton's *Paradise Lost* changed for the interpretive community of Miltonists between 1942 and 1979. Fish also discusses general changes in the understanding of *Paradise Lost* at *Doing*, 106.

It seems to follow that the meanings communicated by legal texts cannot be fixed and stable and are instead malleable and indeterminate.

Does the ability to recontextualize entail indeterminacy?

Fish does accept that no text can be made *immune* to such recontextualizing efforts, which was the formalist/textualist hope. "All shapes are interpretively produced, and since the conditions of interpretation are themselves unstable – the possibility of seeing something in a 'new light,' and therefore of seeing a *new* something, is ever and unpredictably present – the shapes that seem perspicuous to us now may not seem so or may seem differently so tomorrow."[7] The same historical and rhetorical forces that operated in the past to create the apprehension of clear and compelling meanings can operate in the present to revise those meanings. Since any past clear and compelling meaning was the product of rhetorical forces, we cannot rule out of court any present efforts to change that meaning on the grounds that they violate a preexisting literal or objective meaning. "Literal meaning, rather than being independent of perspective, is a product of perspective (it is the meaning that, given a perspective, will immediately emerge); it is itself an interpretation and cannot therefore be the indisputable ground on which subsequent interpretations securely rest."[8] The formalist/textualist insistence that lawyers cease their recontextualizing efforts and interpretive gymnastics and accept the authority of the objective meaning of the text is thus akin to King Canute's command that the tide not come in. "The very words in which an edict mandating an interpretive straight line was promulgated would themselves be subject to interpretive swerves; interpretation cannot be closed down."[9]

But Fish would not accept that any of the negative consequences associated with the indeterminacy thesis follow from his acknowledgment that no text can be made immune to recontextualization.[10] He has three arguments for this position.

---

[7] *Doing*, 302. See too *Text*, 282–3; *No free speech*, 151.   [8] *Doing*, 185.

[9] *Trouble*, 132.

[10] At *No free speech*, 190 Fish considers weaker and stronger versions of the indeterminacy argument, and accepts the stronger position "that unproblematical instances are unproblematic only within interpretive conditions – specifications of what counts as evidence, arguments as to the weight and shape of precedent, etc. – which, while presently settled, can themselves become the object of dispute and so become problematical." But he immediately draws any sting from the tail of this acceptance by saying that "it is precisely

The bare possibility of a future recontextualization
does not affect a determinate text

The first argument involves the application to texts of a broader point that he has made previously in both Parts I and II: a commitment to anti-foundationalism does not entail a commitment to relativism. Becoming convinced of the truth of anti-foundationalism does not cause, or allow, one to hold their present beliefs more loosely or provisionally. Alternatively put, necessarily embedded beings are not released from their local forms of embeddedness in the slightest degree by becoming aware of their embedded condition and of the fact that they could be differently embedded in the future. It follows that our current apprehensions of clear and compelling textual meanings, which are delivered (indeed, compelled) by the in-place background of a particular interpretive community, are not destabilized in the slightest degree by the knowledge that this background could change.

> It may be that at a general level interpretation and language are radically indeterminate because every interpretation (decision, specification of meaning) rests on a ground that is itself interpretive and therefore challengeable; but since life is lived not at the general level but in local contexts that are stabilized (if only temporarily) by assumptions already and invisibly in place, the inherent indeterminacy of interpretation is without the practical consequences both feared and hoped for it. That is, although the logic of a decision can always be undone by a deconstructive analysis of it or by the elaboration of a more powerful logic, until that happens (and in some cases it may not happen for a very long time, long enough to feel like forever) the decision is as determinate as one would like and has all the consequences of a decision that was absolutely determinate.[11]

Until the relevant interpretive community's background actually does change, the bare possibility that it could change has no consequences – it does not give any logical or psychological grounds to doubt the objectivity of the meanings currently apprehended.

> You may know (in the sense that you have certain answers to some traditional philosophical questions) that the urgencies you feel, the values you resonate to, the facts you affirm, are contextually produced and therefore revisable, but that knowledge neither loosens the hold of those

because I am persuaded by the indeterminacy thesis in its strong form that I agree with Kress when he says that the indeterminacy issue is a 'red herring.'"
[11] *No free speech*, 190–1. See too *Doing*, 153.

urgencies, values, and facts nor provides instructions (or even reasons) for their revision. If instructions and reasons do emerge, they will have been produced by the particular circumstances that give rise to the need for particular actions and not by some abstract conviction of circumstantiality in general.[12]

Actually recontextualizing a text need not produce the experience of indeterminacy

The second argument is that if the background actually does change in the future, this need not produce the experience of textual choice or ambiguity. Instead, it will often result in the experience of a single determinate meaning being replaced by a *different* single determinate meaning. When this happens, the experience is not of the textual meaning changing or becoming indeterminate; rather the experience is of an earlier understanding of the text's meaning being revealed as a mistake, and being replaced by a more accurate account of what the fixed meaning always has been. Rather than "an infinite regress of unstable interpretations" we have "an endless succession of interpretive certainties, a reassuring sequence in which one set of obvious and indisputable facts gives way to another."[13] Recontextualization need not be experienced negatively, as the death of fixed meanings, but positively, as progress toward finally ascertaining those fixed meanings.

> We can't help thinking that our present views are sounder than those we used to have or those professed by others. Not only does one's current position stand in a privileged relation to positions previously held, but previously held positions will always have the status of false or imperfect steps, of wrongly taken directions, of clouded or deflected perceptions. In other words, the idea of progress is inevitable.[14]

There are significant constraints on achieving recontextualization in law

The third argument is that actually altering any currently in-place background that compels the apprehension of particular clear meanings for legal texts will typically be difficult to achieve. It is true that attempting to achieve this is always a possible and proper move for lawyers, in the same

---

[12] *No free speech*, 197.   [13] *Doing*, 196.   [14] *Text*, 361.

way that scoring a goal is always a possible and proper move for soccer players. But the fact that a move is possible and proper does not guarantee that you can perform it at will. Just as opposing soccer players will try to prevent a player scoring, resistance to a lawyer's attempt at a persuasive story that changes elements of the current background will come from other legal actors who remain gripped by the clear and compelling meanings established by an earlier persuasive story. They will typically see what is being argued as outlandish or implausible or as a deliberate distortion of a well-established objective meaning. Overcoming that resistance will require rhetorical skills that may be beyond the lawyer's current abilities (as Trident's lawyers found) and also favorable circumstances.[15] The resistance faced by any recontextualizing effort has an important consequence; currently accepted textual meanings can last a long time. Fish emphasizes the point that a rhetorically achieved shared understanding can endure and be stable for "hundreds of years,"[16] "a long, long, long time,"[17] "a moment or a millennium,"[18] or "for a very long time, long enough to feel like forever."[19] So recontextualizing turns out to be yet another activity conducted in the face of constraints, and these constraints on recontextualization blunt the charge that Fish is an indeterminacy theorist. The stability and determinacy of law is thus quite consistent with Fish's analysis.

Consequences of the constraints on achieving recontextualization in law

Change and the possibility of change are harder to see

The constraints imposed on recontextualization in law turn out to be much greater than they are in other interpretive communities. This is due to the prominence of the rule of law job in our liberal legal culture, as described in the previous chapter. The dominance of this job means that law gives a very high value to certainty, consistency, predictability, and continuity with the past and is correspondingly suspicious of change. Other institutions with different deep background values accept change more readily. For example, the institutions involved with art and fashion

---

[15] For a description of the difficulties faced and the work involved in trying to shift one clear reading to another, see Duncan Kennedy, *Freedom and constraint in adjudication: A critical phenomenology* 36 *Journal of Legal Education* (1986) 518.
[16] *Trouble*, 124.   [17] *No free speech*, 301.   [18] Ibid., 4.   [19] Ibid., 191.

welcome and reward open innovation and departures from established tradition. Fish notes that literary studies reserves its greatest rewards "for those who challenge the assumptions within which ordinary practices go on, not so much in order to eliminate the category of the ordinary but in order to redefine it and reshape its configurations."[20] This is not true of law where, as we have seen, change is typically denied and concealed.

One consequence of the institutional bias against change in the law is that lawyers can become less able to see change, or to see the possibility of achieving change, as compared to the practitioners of other disciplines.

> But no fact is self-evident, and therefore it is a mistake to think of change or its absence as being verifiable by a simple (unmediated) act of empirical observation; rather it is only within the perspective of some interpretive descriptive system that change is or is not a feature. That is to say, the fact of change, like any other fact, is irremediably interpretive; its specification cannot be made independently of the way a community conceives of itself, of the story it tells about itself and lives out in the actions of its members. The enterprise of law, for example, is by definition committed to the ahistoricity of its basic principles, and workers in the field have a stake in seeing the history of their own efforts as the application of those principles to circumstances that are only *apparently* new (i.e. changed). That is why a judge will do almost anything to avoid overturning a precedent . . . In short, the very point of the legal enterprise requires that its practitioners see continuity where others, with less of a stake in the enterprise, might feel free to see change.[21]

Routes of change are limited

Another consequence of the institutional bias against change in law is that the routes by which change can be achieved are limited. But any limitation on the ways in which change can be achieved in law constitutes a constraint upon the achievement of change. For example, we saw in the last chapter why change in law typically has to be achieved indirectly. The law's substantive justice job accepts that it can be necessary to change the law to respond to new realities and to depart from past precedents if they would not deliver a fair result in the unique circumstances of a particular case. But these values clash with the more dominant rule of law values, and so it is often inept to advocate for

---

[20] *Text*, 366.   [21] *Doing*, 157.

the substantive justice job nakedly and directly. We saw that it can be more strategically effective to advance the substantive law job in a way that does not challenge the rule of law story with its demand for stable general rules and continuity with the past. So instead of urging that we do what is just in the present case rather than being constrained by an old precedent, it is often a better move to accept that the old precedent must rule the present case but then rewrite that precedent with an eye to achieving a just resolution of the present case. What Fish earlier called "law's amazing trick" does not involve rejecting or ignoring the past, instead it involves recontextualizing or rewriting past decisions and then effacing all evidence of that rewriting. But this rewriting and effacing trick is called "amazing" because it is difficult to pull off. It requires the application of skills acquired over a long period of professional training and experience. Even skilled professionals cannot always perform the trick when they want to, and when they fail, the goal of achieving change in law by this route is not attained. Therefore, requiring that change be achieved in law not directly but indirectly – e.g., by performing law's amazing trick – is an example of a constraint being imposed on the achievement of change.

Change must be achieved by reworking past rhetorical achievements

Another constraint upon change in law is the requirement not to ignore doctrinal rules and concepts that have established themselves as features of the legal landscape, even if their claims can be shown to be empty. Fish provides a good example of this in his analysis of the parol evidence rule in contract law.[22] Fish describes the parol evidence rule as "a rule that prohibits the introduction of oral evidence in order to alter or vary the meaning of a contract that is deemed to be complete in itself. Obviously it is a rule designed to hold interpretation in check by insisting that it respect a self-sufficient and self-declaring (literal) meaning."[23] He first argues that it is impossible to apply the parol evidence rule in the way its defenders desire because it is a form of textualism, and textualism is impossible as we saw in Chapter 8. But he does not go on to conclude that the parol evidence rule can just be ignored. Even though it cannot be complied with, it exists in the legal landscape as a past rhetorical

---

[22] *No free speech*, 144–53. [23] *Doing*, 4.

achievement, and so it often has to be incorporated into a persuasive story about how a particular case is to be resolved.

> It is certainly the case that *Masterson* v. *Sine*, like *Columbia Nitrogen* and the others, indicates that no matter how carefully a contract is drafted it cannot resist incorporation into a persuasively told story in the course of whose unfolding its significance can be altered from what it had seemed to be. But the cases also indicate that the story so told cannot be any old story; it must be one that fashions its coherence out of materials that it is required to take into account. The important fact about *Masterson* is not that in it the court succeeds in getting around the parol evidence rule, but that it is the parol evidence rule – and not the first chapter of Genesis or the first law of thermodynamics – that it feels obliged to get around. That is, given the constraints of the institutional setting – constraints that help shape the issue being adjudicated – the court could not proceed on its way without raising and dealing with the parol evidence rule ... Consequently, the path to the result it finally reaches is constrained, in part, by the very doctrine that result will fail to honor.[24]

This limitation on the way in which the decision can be reached means that the parol evidence rule is

> constraining even if it is not, in the strict sense, a constraint. In short, the parol evidence rule is of more service to the law's wish to have a formal existence than one might think from these examples. The service it provides, however, is not (as is sometimes claimed) the service of safeguarding a formalism already in place, but the weaker (although more exacting) service of laying down the route by which a formalism can be fashioned.[25]

If achieving substantive justice in the resolution of a particular case requires the incorporation of the (uncashable) parol evidence rule, then the routes to such a resolution are constrained and significant hurdles are placed along the way. Fish makes a similar point about consideration: "[T]he fact that the claim of consideration doctrine to be merely formal cannot finally be upheld is of no practical consequence; it is upheld by the rhetorical structure it has generated, and in order to alter that structure you must appear to be upholding it too. As I have already said, you can only get around consideration doctrine by elaborately honoring it."[26] If change in law has to be achieved not by rejecting, but by "elaborately honoring" even defective existing doctrinal rules and concepts, then there are significant constraints on change in law.

---

[24] *No free speech*, 151.   [25] Ibid., 152. See too 153.   [26] Ibid.,163. See generally 161–3.

Three implications of Fish's analysis

There are three main conclusions that can be drawn from Fish's analysis of legal change presented in this chapter.

Change and tradition in law are not simply opposed

The relationship between change and tradition in law turns out to be more complicated than that of simple opposition, because Fish has described how change is achieved not by ignoring tradition but by reworking and honoring it. In *There's no such thing as free speech*, he makes this point in a political context:

> The neoconservative right rails against change in the name of tradition and continuity and doesn't realize or doesn't want to know that change is the means by which continuity is achieved and reachieved. Tradition does not preserve itself by pushing away novelty and difference but by accommodating them, by conscripting them for its project; and since accommodation cannot occur unless that project stretches its shape, the result will be a tradition that is always being maintained and is always being altered *because* it is being maintained.[27]

He made the same point in describing how an interpretive community is an engine of change "whose work is at the same time assimilative and self-transformative."[28] The interpretive community absorbs new material and turns it into grist for its particular mill, and its practice changes shape as a result of assimilating this new material. But tradition, in the form of the interpretive community's ongoing project or job, is maintained and advanced by these changes: "[T]he transformed practice identifies itself and tells its story in relation to general purposes and goals that have survived and form the basis of a continuity."[29]

A stronger way of making this point is to claim that change can *only* be achieved by working within an existing tradition. All changes that appear to be radical departures from what went before are in fact enabled by that past and are extensions of it.[30] For example, we have seen Fish argue earlier that

---

[27] Ibid., 271.   [28] *Doing*, 152.   [29] Ibid., 153. See too 156.
[30] As Gadamer put it, "[t]his ... does not mean that we are enclosed within a wall of prejudices and only let through the narrow portals those things that can produce a pass saying, 'Nothing new will be said here.' Instead we welcome just that guest who promises something new to our curiosity. But how do we know the guest whom we admit is one who has something new to say to us? Is not our expectation and our readiness to hear the new also necessarily determined by the old that has

in literary studies deconstruction was condemned by some practitioners as an abandonment of the whole prior scholarly tradition. But Fish responded that deconstruction could only arise as a possibility within literary studies because it was an extension of elements of that prior scholarly tradition.[31] Similarly, in this chapter we have seen Fish argue that rhetorical efforts to change the law can only gain traction with competent legal actors if elements of the existing tradition – such as the parol evidence rule and the consideration requirement – are employed, even if these elements are, strictly speaking, uncashable and so have to be reworked. It follows for Fish that law will not be changed by foreign practices like deconstruction or ideology critique, which have their home in other disciplines.

Fish is not an indeterminacy theorist

The second conclusion is that Fish is not an indeterminacy theorist in any sense that need cause alarm. The debate between legal indeterminacy theorists and their legal positivist/formalist opponents can sometimes sound as if there are only two choices: a completely constrained legal actor or a completely free one. But Karl Llewellyn tried to describe a more complex middle ground where legal actors are both free and constrained, and Fish continues along this path. Llewellyn thought that the malleability and inconsistency in law were not as threatening to orthodoxy as they seemed, because they would not enable lawyers and judges to do anything with the law. This was because the craft-training that those legal professionals had undergone embedded them within a tradition and structured their perceptions of what was possible and reasonable to do with legal materials. Some readings of legal texts would be impossible, given the current shape of that tradition, and some would be inescapable for the same reason. Between these poles, trained lawyers could make different judgments, although these differences were always shaped and bounded by this shared tradition and training. The craft-training thus *constrained* the uses that could be made of malleable and inconsistent rules, and produced a reasonable degree of certainty and predictability in the law.[32]

---

already taken possession of us?" Quoted in Stephen Feldman, "Republican revival/ interpretive turn" [1992] *Wisconsin Law Review* 708–9.

[31] *Doing*, 154–5.

[32] For supporting references to Llewellyn's work, see Michael Robertson, "Telling the law's two stories" 20 *The Canadian Journal of Law and Jurisprudence* (2007) 440–2.

Similarly, as we have seen, Fish acknowledges that all apprehensions of clear and compelling textual meaning rest upon an already-in-place, socially produced, contingent background of beliefs, and so if the background changes those apprehensions can change. But he then minimizes the dangers to legal determinacy posed by this possibility. First, until such a change actually occurs, the possibility that it might occur does not destabilize anything. Second, even if it does actually occur, this need not undermine our experience of and faith in determinate texts. Finally, (and here he develops a version of Llewellyn's point) it is very difficult to actually change the elements of the interpretive community's in-place background anyway, because of the multiple constraints upon legal actors. All attempts by legal actors to change elements of the in-place background of the legal interpretive community are constrained by the need to work within the existing tradition, even as it is being altered. As Fish noted, "if practice is through-and-through rhetorical, the components of its present rhetorical structure cannot be inconsequential, even if the consequences can never be as total or stable as hard-core theorists (the only real kind) desire."[33] That is, the constraints he is describing are not the (impossible) inflexible chains that a legal formalist/textualist desires. They do not stop a legal actor from moving at all, but they do shape and limit any such movement. This is why, although he approves of Richard Posner's claim that a reading of a precedent "will not have been logically driven, but driven by the direction in which the judge wanted to go," Fish immediately qualifies this by references to the constraints simultaneously operating on the judge: "This does not mean that the judge can decide in any direction he or she pleases. The routes of choice, indeed the alternative forms in which choice can even appear, are constrained by the present shape of practical reasoning, by what arguments will work, what categories are firmly in place, what distinctions can be confidently invoked."[34] Elsewhere he makes the same point:

> Let me be clear. I am not saying that "anything goes," that interpreters of the Eighth Amendment (or Virgil's *Eclogues*) are presented with a "blank check" to be filled in as they like; only that insofar as the filling in of the check is constrained (and it always will be; Posner's positing of a wholly free interpretive activity is as mistaken – it is the same mistake – as his positing of an interpretive act that is wholly prescribed), the constraints will inhere not in the language of the text (statute or poem) or in the context (unproblematically conceived by Posner as a "higher" and

[33] *No free speech*, 192.   [34] Ibid., 204. See too 169–70.

self-declaring text) in which it is embedded, but in the cultural assumptions within which both texts and contexts take shape for situated agents.[35]

The rule of law is not a sham

The final conclusion to be drawn is that the existence of genuine constraints in the law means that the rule of law story described in the previous chapter is not just a sham, or a "noble lie" that laypeople are fed by legal actors so that they will accept the liberal social order.[36] Because of these genuine constraints, many of the things valued by the rule of law story genuinely exist, such as clear and compelling textual meanings that stay in place for a long, long time. Fish would only insist that objective meanings and stable rules are the products of the very things that the rule of law sets its face against: rhetoric and interpretation.

> [T]he notion of the rhetorical is no longer identified with the ephemeral, the outside, but is reconceived as the medium in which certainties become established, in which formidable traditions emerge, are solidified, and become obstacles (not insurmountable ones, but nevertheless obstacles) to the force of counter-rhetorical arguments.[37]

The rule of law tradition sees rhetoric negatively, as a dangerous force that threatens to undermine secure legal rules and meanings. Accordingly it seeks to exclude rhetoric from the law by means of legal formalist and legal positivist reasoning. But while for orthodox jurisprudence the operation of rhetoric and the telling of persuasive stories constitute a threat to law's objectivity and stability, in Fish's account they are what *produce* the objectivity and stability that genuinely exist. That is, powerful persuasive achievements put in place the background that produces a particular form of compulsion that lasts (sometimes for a very long time) until a more powerful persuasive achievement comes along and displaces the earlier one. So lawyers who describe themselves as compelled by the rule of law, and by clear and compelling literal meanings, are not acting in bad faith or cynically, nor are they deceiving themselves. They genuinely feel compulsion and see determinate texts because of the currently in-place background of the legal interpretive community:

---

[35] *Doing*, 300.

[36] Plato discussed the "noble lie" in *The republic*. See Ian Harden and Norman Lewis, *The noble lie: The British constitution and the rule of law* (London: Hutchinson, 1986).

[37] *No free speech*, 290–1. See too 191, 240, and *Doing*, ch. 20 ("Rhetoric").

Are legal actors then living out a lie, asserting as absolute what they should acknowledge as fragile and transitory? Not at all. Legal actors, like everyone else, live *within* the temporary ascendancies they at once affirm and undo (by endlessly modifying the givens that make action possible), and no analysis of their situation, even the analysis offered here, will remove them from it.[38]

---

[38] *Doing*, 523. See too *No free speech*, 214: "[W]hen judges persuade 'themselves and others that their decisions are dictated by law,' the act of persuasion is not a conscious strategic self-deception, but something that comes with the territory, with the experience of law school, of practice, of a life in the courts, etc. The result is not, as Posner would have it, a 'false sense of constraint,' but a sense inseparable from membership in a community from whose (deep) assumptions one takes one's very identity."

Legal realism and critical legal studies

Legal realism

In Chapter 10, I described two competing jobs that Fish claims law is required to perform in liberal societies. I called them the rule of law job and the substantive justice job. Legal positivists and legal formalists emphasize the rule of law job, but legal realists emphasize the substantive justice job. For legal realists, constraint, certainty, and consistency were not more important legal values than flexibility, sensitivity to context, and fair and sensible results.[1]

Legal realists rejected the classical legal formalist position that law application was a matter of logical entailment and deduction only, with no place for the exercise of choice or discretion by the law-applier. Instead, legal realists stressed the pervasive indeterminacy of law due to its gaps and conflicting rules and principles, and the consequent need for the decision-maker to rely upon moral and political commitments when describing and applying the law. However, legal indeterminacy and the role of morality and politics within law did not dismay the legal realists, in contrast to the legal formalists. Legal realists saw these features as desirable and functional because they enabled the law to do its substantive justice job.

Although they rejected the legal positivists' belief that law and morality could be separated, in other respects the legal realists shared their broadly positivistic outlook. Both positivists and realists rejected natural law and held law to be completely a matter of social fact, or a human product. Legal realists stressed empirical approaches to law, rather than highly abstract and conceptual approaches. Some of the legal realists advocated for interdisciplinary legal study, which would incorporate the insights of disciplines that were more fact-focused, such as sociology and psychology.

---

[1] The condensed description of legal realism that follows is developed more fully in Michael Robertson, "Telling the law's two stories" 20 *The Canadian Journal of Law and Jurisprudence* (2007) 429 (hereafter cited as Robertson, "Telling the law's two stories").

Legal realism is an important jurisprudential movement, but Fish does not devote much attention to it. The only explicit critique he offers is of the broad positivist orientation of the legal realists. He takes as his target Felix Cohen's piece, "Transcendental nonsense and the functional approach."[2] He describes how Cohen disparages legal thinking that is overly abstract and "metaphysical" and that does not "rest on the floor of verifiable fact." Once "statistical methods" have brought us close to the "actual facts of judicial behavior," Fish quotes Cohen as saying, we might be able "to substitute a realistic, rational scientific account of legal happenings for the classical theological jurisprudence of concepts." Fish responds:

> In these quotations (which could have easily been supplemented from the pages of Jerome Frank and other early realists) we see that the basic realist gesture is a double, and perhaps contradictory, one: first dismiss the myth of objectivity as it is embodied in high sounding but empty legal concepts (the rule of law, the neutrality of due process) and then replace it with the myth of the "actual facts" or "exact discourse" or "actual experience" or "a rational scientific account," that is, go from one essentialism, identified with natural law or conceptual logic, to another, identified with the strong empiricism of the social sciences.[3]

Fish's reaction to the legal realists' positivism is to criticise it as a form of the foundationalism we saw him take on in Chapter 2. Fish's anti-foundationalist argument is that empirical facts are not just given to human beings as fixed, preinterpretive things that we must accept as they are. Instead, human beings experience facts in the shape that we do because of the structuring effect of an already-in-place background of beliefs, values, categories, etc. That is, facts are what they are because of the prior interpretive (in a broad sense) or political (in a broad sense) or rhetorical successes of human beings.[4]

> Given the realist insistence on the unavoidability of bias and on the value laden nature of all human activities, the recourse to a brute fact level of uninterpretive data seems, to say the least, questionable, as does the assumption that if we could only divest ourselves of the special vocabulary of the legal culture (no longer fooled by our own words) we could see

---

[2] Felix Cohen, "Transcendental nonsense and the functional approach" 35 *Columbia Law Review* (1935) 808. Fish discusses this article in *No free speech*, 209–11.

[3] *No free speech*, 210.

[4] He is not saying that facts are whatever humans want them to be, or agree that they are. The already-in-place background can deliver firm and unavoidable facts to the interpretive community, facts that the community can find distressing and even destabilizing.

things as they really (independently of any discursive system whatsoever) are. Cohen and Frank are full of scorn for theological thinking and for the operations of faith, but as Pound sees, they are no less captives of a faith, and of the illusion – if that is the word – that attends it. That is, however, not the word, for "illusion" implies the availability of a point of view uncontaminated by metaphysical entities or by an a priori assumption of values, and as the realists (and Posner after them) argue in their better moments, there is no such point of view, no realm of unalloyed non-mediated experience and no neutral observation language that describes it.[5]

In response to the legal realists' interdisciplinary hopes, Fish replied that

> [t]he advocate or jurist who moves from the conceptual apparatus codi-
> fied in law to the apparatus of statistical methods and behaviorist
> psychology has not exchanged the perspective-specific facts of an artificial
> discursive system for real, unvarnished facts; rather he or she has
> exchanged the facts emergent in one discursive system – one contestable
> articulation of the world – for the facts emergent in another. It is not that
> there is no category of the real; it is just that what fills it will always be a
> function of the in-place force of some disciplinary or community vocabu-
> lary; eliminate the special jargon of the law, as the realists urge, and you
> will find yourself not in the clear ground of an epistemological reform
> ("now I see face to face") but in the already occupied ground of some
> other line of work no less special, no less hostage to commitments it can
> neither name or recognize.[6]

The reference to Richard Posner in the course of Fish's criticism of the legal realists is significant because Fish sees Posner as a contemporary legal theorist greatly influenced by the legal realist tradition and making many of the same positivist-inspired mistakes as the legal realists. He writes that Posner's program "takes the form of a pro-scientific, no nonsense empiricism that is obviously related to the tradition of legal realism."[7] The particular form of empirical social science that influences Posner is economics, rather than the "statistical methods and behaviorist psychology" favored by some of the legal realists:

> When Posner says that the goal of every legal doctrine should be a
> practical one, he means (in good realist fashion) that legal doctrine should
> be reconceptualized so as to accord with the nitty-gritty facts of social life,
> and that means reconceptualized in the language of law and economics,
> since in his view the language of law and economics is the language of
> real motives and actual goals. If "the object of pragmatic analysis is to

---

[5] *No free speech*, 210–1.   [6] Ibid., 211.   [7] Ibid., 209.

lead discussion away from issues semantic and metaphysical and toward issues factual and empirical," then by Posner's lights pragmatic analysis and the pragmatic program will succeed when legal concepts and terms have been replaced by economic ones.[8]

As we saw in Chapter 10, Posner describes legal reasoning in a pragmatic, anti-foundationalist way, but he does not similarly describe empirical facts in an anti-foundationalist way. Instead, like the legal realists and legal positivists, he understands empirical facts in a positivistic way, as existing in a bedrock, brute fashion. Given Posner's exposure to and familiarity with anti-foundationalist thinking, Fish says, "he should be immune to the lure of empiricist essentialism, but he is not."[9] Fish's anti-foundationalist critique of Posner's positivism is that we cannot make law more scientific "by attaching ourselves to a bedrock level of social/empirical fact because that level, along with the facts seen as its components, is itself an interpretive construction."[10] Posner's backsliding into foundationalism[11] has led him from a pragmatist account of law to an impossible pragmatist program for law.[12]

Posner's foundationalist view of empirical facts explains his enthusiasm for interdisciplinarity, which he also shares with the legal realists.

> Posner ... thinks that the point of an enterprise is to get at the empirical truth about something; and that enterprises are different only in the sense that they have been assigned (or assigned themselves) different empirical somethings – the mind, the economy, the stars, the planets – to get at the truth of. The trouble with law is that it has not accepted such an assignment in the true empirical spirit ... but instead keeps prating on about "intangibles such as the promotion of human dignity, the securing of justice and fairness, and the importance of complying with the ideals or intentions of the framers of the Constitution."[13]

---

[8] Ibid., 212. [9] Ibid., 211. [10] Ibid., 215.

[11] For another example of Posner backsliding into foundationalism, see "Don't know much about the middle ages: Posner on law and literature" (*Doing*, ch. 13) where Fish took Posner to task for thinking of texts as having fixed, preinterpretive characteristics that allowed them to impose external constraints upon what a human interpreter could properly do with them. In *No free speech*, 208, Fish again charges Posner with taking a foundationalist/formalist approach to textual meaning.

[12] Peter Schanck, "Understanding postmodern thought and its implications for statutory interpretation" 65 *Southern California Law Review* (1991) 2566–70 provides a good description of Fish's critique of Posner on this point. Fish's distinction between a pragmatist account and a pragmatist program was described in Chapter 4.

[13] *No free speech*, 222.

If the law adopted Posner's scientific program, and reformed itself around "the principle of undistorted empirical inquiry,"[14] and stopped "going off into self-indulgent 'theological' flights,"[15] then its fact-based decisions could be improved by taking up the methods and categories developed by other, more rigorously scientific fact-finding disciplines, such as economics. Ultimately, it should be possible to unify all of the different disciplines into one large fact-finding project, to combine the many different angled views of the one bedrock reality.[16]

We have already seen, in Chapter 3, Fish's general arguments against the possibility of the sort of interdisciplinarity Posner favors. Applying these general arguments to Posner's particular interdisciplinary project of law and economics, Fish warns that if the values and categories and projects of law are completely translated into the values and categories and projects of economics, we will not have improved law by making it more empirical; instead we will have lost law as an autonomous discipline. We will have replaced its unique structuring and enabling background with that of some other discipline. So if Posner's project of "demystifying" legal concepts and vocabulary by importing economic concepts and vocabulary were to succeed,

> we will not have escaped semantics (merely verbal entities) and metaphysics (faith-based declarations of what is) but merely attached ourselves to new versions of them. As many commentators have observed, "wealth-maximization," efficiency, Pareto superiority, the Kaldor Hicks test, and the other components of the law and economics position are all hostage to metaphysical assumptions, to controversial visions of the way the world is or should be ... Moreover, and this is the more important point, should the transformation occur, the result would not be a more empirically rooted law, but no law at all. The law, as a separate and distinct area of inquiry and action, would be no more; an enterprise of a certain kind would have disappeared from the world (itself not fixed, but mutable and revisable) of enterprises.[17]

This demonstrates an important point about interdisciplinary borrowing mentioned at the end of Chapter 3 — it is not a risk-free enterprise. Although it will often be the case that the borrowing discipline "domesticates" that which it is importing, we now see that the opposite can also occur. The material invited into discipline A from discipline B to advance discipline A's projects can act as a Trojan horse. Once welcomed in,

[14] Ibid., 218.   [15] Ibid., 223.   [16] Ibid.   [17] Ibid., 212–3. See too 222.

it can facilitate the annexing or colonizing of discipline A by discipline B.[18] Fish made this possibility very clear in his article "On legal autonomy":

> Rather than it being the case that there is an antecedent model or template prior to actual practices, there are ... only actual practices, which maintain their share of the franchise by ceaseless acts of self-promotion that are also and chiefly acts of self-creation. It follows that a diacritically achieved autonomy is an autonomy that can be lost. A practice that ceases to elaborate and defend its internal machinery can perish, can be crowded out at the table of practices either because it allows its vocabulary to be overwhelmed by the vocabulary of a rival or because it seeks to discard its vocabulary on the grounds that it tends to obscure the reality in whose service practitioners labor. (This was the "project" of Legal Realism.)[19]

Fish calls attention to Posner's efforts in his book, *Law and literature*, to help economics colonize law. We have seen that Posner, like the legal realists, believes that legal concepts should be reformulated using the vocabulary and concepts of the empirical social sciences. In "Don't know much about the middle ages: Posner on law and literature,"[20] Fish describes Posner's "determination to hand over academic law to one of [the empirical social sciences] on a silver platter,"[21] and that favored empirical social science for Posner is economics. Fish concludes that in disparaging the possible relevance of literary studies to law in his book, Posner's real purpose is "to clear the field so that the authority of economics in the legal academy can be secured."[22] Of course, Posner has pursued this goal in a more open fashion in the many editions of his book, *Economic analysis of law*.[23] However, Fish doubts very strongly that any such colonization of law by economics (or psychology or literary theory, etc.) will be successful:

> [L]aw will only work – not in the realist or economic sense but in the sense answerable to the desires that impel its establishment – if the metaphysical entities Posner would remove are retained; and if the history of our life with law tells us anything, it is that they *will* be retained, no

---

[18] See J. M. Balkin, "Interdisciplinarity as colonization" 53 *Washington & Lee Law Review* (1996) 949.

[19] Stanley Fish, "On legal autonomy" 44 *Mercer Law Review* (1993) 741. See too *No free speech*, 220; *Professional*, 82; Stanley Fish, "Theory minimalism" 37 *San Diego Law Review* (2000) 766 (hereafter cited as Fish, "Theory minimalism").

[20] *Doing*, ch. 13.   [21] Ibid., 307.   [22] Ibid., 308.

[23] Richard Posner, *Economic analysis of law* (Boston, MA: Little, Brown, 1975).

matter what analysis of either an economic or deconstructive kind is able to show.[24]

Although Fish does not comment explicitly upon the other aspects of the legal realist position briefly described at the beginning of this chapter, we can anticipate what his responses would be, based on the accounts of his position already provided. First, Fish would not enter the legal realist vs. legal positivist dispute about which law job – substantive justice or the rule of law – was the genuine one. As we have seen in Chapter 10, Fish holds that law has to perform both jobs and find ways to tell both of law's stories. Second, as we have seen in Chapter 11, Fish would reject the strong indeterminacy arguments of some of the legal realists.[25] Fish does not accept that the failure of legal formalism leads to the conclusion that law is indeterminate. Although the constraints favored by formalists fail, Fish insists that there are other powerful constraints operating on legal actors, which mean that the law is not radically indeterminate and that the rule of law does genuinely exist. Third, Fish would join with the legal realists in rejecting the legal positivists' separation thesis, but he would not agree with the realists that lawyers have recourse to moral and political commitments in the process of *choosing* how to describe or apply the law. The moral and political commitments that Fish describes as necessarily operating in the law do not inevitably increase choice or discretion or indeterminacy, rather the opposite; they can produce the experience of constraint by clear and compelling meanings. That is, the background, with its moral and political commitments, can result in only one possible legal route or resolution being perceived by a judge. (This was exemplified by Judge Kozinski in the *Trident* case.) So unlike the legal realists, who focus on "hard cases" and the role morality and politics has in resolving them, Fish focuses on "easy cases" and the role morality and politics has in producing them.

---

[24] *No free speech*, 213. See too 214: "Law is centrally about such things as conscience, guilt, personal responsibility, fairness, impartiality, and no analysis imported from some other disciplinary context 'proving' that these things do not exist will remove them from the legal culture, unless of course society decides that a legal culture is a luxury it can afford to do without."

[25] See *Doing*, 87, 91, 95, where Fish ascribes a strong indeterminacy position to the legal realists. As I show in Robertson, "Telling the law's two stories," this is not true of a legal realist like Karl Llewellyn, who is much closer to the position of Fish himself.

Critical legal studies

The goal of critical legal studies (CLS) is to uncover and undo the ways in which law facilitates the unjust domination of some groups by others in society. CLS investigates the ways in which the law contributes to the systematic oppression of employees by employers, of women by men, of people of color by white people, of gay people by straight people, etc. CLS rejects the explanation of law's role in such oppression given by the older tradition of orthodox Marxism. According to this older tradition, law was used as an instrument of force by dominant groups to maintain their privileged position in an unjust social order. In the orthodox Marxist account, the lawmakers were generally members of the dominant economic class, and they passed class-biased laws that were enforced by a state apparatus that included the police, the courts, and the military. CLS was more attracted to the work of neo-Marxist political theorists, such as Antonio Gramsci, who argued that unjust social orders are maintained less by brute force than by ideology.[26] The historians E. P. Thompson and Douglas Hay had explored the thesis that the criminal law in eighteenth-century England maintained unjust social relationships through ideology as well as force, and these studies influenced CLS, too.[27] "Ideology" here refers to the operation of ideas that are widely shared but which operate to benefit the dominant group disproportionately.[28]

Because CLS accepted anti-foundationalism,[29] it accepted that background ideas sitting beneath the surface of the law played a crucial but typically unnoticed role in determining how the institution operated. From here it seemed a natural next step to inquire whether this legal background operated systematically to benefit some social groups at the expense of others. That is, did the unnoticed legal background display a structural political bias, did it operate ideologically? CLS answered that

---

[26] This description of CLS is drawn from Robert Gordon, "New developments in legal theory" in David Kairys (ed.), *The politics of law. A progressive critique* (New York, NY: Pantheon, 1982), ch. 14.

[27] Douglas Hay, "Property, authority, and the criminal law" in Douglas Hay. (eds.), *Albion's fatal tree: Crime and society in eighteenth-century England* (London: Allen Lane, 1975), ch. 1; E. P. Thompson, *Whigs and hunters. The origin of the Black Act* (London: Allen Lane, 1975), Part 3, ch. 10, ("The rule of law").

[28] See Hay, "Property, authority, and the criminal law," 26 n2: "By ideology I mean 'a specific set of ideas designed to vindicate or disguise class interest.'"

[29] It had been influenced in this direction more by modern European philosophical and literary theories, such as postmodernism and deconstructionism, rather than by the older American philosophical pragmatists.

question in the affirmative. More particularly, it found that the assumptions, values, and categories of classical liberalism saturate the enabling background in modern Anglo-American legal systems and that this liberal-inflected background operates ideologically to benefit the dominant groups in the societies with these legal systems. All of the following— the liberal public/private distinction, the liberal stress on individualism and negative liberty, the liberal opposition between civil and political rights vs. social and economic rights, and the liberal emphasis on the state as the main danger to liberty—operate to uphold an unjust status quo in the CLS analysis.[30]

CLS therefore rejects the fundamental liberal claim to have identified neutral principles and procedures that stand outside the partisan fray and that could regulate that fray without unfairness to any group. In response to the liberal neutrality claim, CLS replies that "law is politics." This is not simply a restatement of the legal realist claim that an individual law-applier typically has to exercise choice between competing precedents and principles based on personal political beliefs. The CLS claim finds politics at work even in cases where choice is absent; where the law is perceived by the law-applier to speak with a single clear and compelling voice. Politics is still at work in these cases because they are produced by the background beliefs shared by the legal interpretive community, and those background beliefs contain political commitments. It is because the politics in the background is largely unnoticed that it can do its ideological work so well, CLS argues.

The CLS response to the finding that "law is politics" is to engage in ideology critique, in accordance with the program of critical theory described in Part II. Ideology critique seeks to reveal, or bring to consciousness, the hidden and harmful operation of these background ideas in law, in the expectation that this realization would reduce the power these ideas have over us. We would then be liberated to remake law and society unconstrained by the old hegemonic "structure of the legal imagination."[31] The remade law and society envisaged by the CLS writers gave greater weight to democratic participation, egalitarianism, economic and social rights, and feminism than they felt liberalism did.

---

[30] See, e.g., Morton Horwitz, "Rights" 23 *Harvard Civil Rights/Civil Liberties Law Review* (1988) 393; Kathleen Mahoney, "The limits of liberalism" in Richard Devlin (ed.), *Canadian perspectives on legal theory* (Toronto: Edmond Montgomery Publications, 1991), 57.

[31] Gerald Frug, "A critical theory of law" 1 *Legal Education Review* (1989) 53.

Fish has affinities with many aspects of CLS, but he also has areas of strong disagreement. In Chapter 10, I described how Fish and CLS both agreed that law was not a complete and consistent system of rules. Rather, they held, it was "a set of ramshackle and heterogeneous resources,"[32] an "ad hoc affair whose ill-fitting joints are soldered together by suspect rhetorical gestures, leaps of illogic, and special pleadings tricked up as general rules."[33] Moreover, they both accepted that this disorderliness could not be remedied because it resulted from competing moral and political commitments in the shared background of the legal interpretive community. These tensions mean that law does not operate ideologically in a monolithic fashion. That is, the structuring background of law does not only consist of beliefs and values and goals that benefit the dominant groups in society. Other "visions of what life is or should be like"[34] are present and can have an effect at the surface of legal doctrine, even if they are currently consigned to a minor role. However, the presence of such competing social visions means that a contest with the dominant social vision over which is to shape a particular area of law can never be completely closed down. The fact that such contests and attempts to reshape the background can break out, even after long periods of quiescence, is another reason why law was more a matter of rhetoric than of logic, according to both Fish and CLS.

While Fish and CLS agree on their account of law, they start to come apart when the consequences of this account are drawn. Fish notes that many CLS writers conclude from this description that law is very indeterminate.

> Indeterminacy has become an issue in legal theory because of the asser-
> tion by Critical Legal Studies members that the decisions judges render do
> not follow from the materials (laws, precedents, evidence, etc.) they
> invoke, materials that could be made to yield almost any decision one
> wishes to reach. According to the indeterminacy thesis, judges are not
> constrained by the rules and texts that supposedly ground the legal
> process, and this absence of constraint, as Ken Kress points out, "rais[es]
> the specter that judicial decision making is often or always undemocratic
> and illegitimate."[35]

---

[32] *No free speech*, 209.   [33] Ibid., 21.   [34] Ibid., 154.

[35] Ibid., 189–90. See too 168. Just as Karl Llewellyn was an exception to the general trend for legal realists to argue for a strong legal indeterminacy position, there are some CLS writers who do not follow the general trend either. See, for example, Duncan Kennedy, "Freedom and constraint in adjudication: A critical phenomenology" 36 *Journal of Legal Education* (1986) 518.

CLS theorists argue further that law's indeterminacy is generally a bad thing because the dominant groups in society have the resources to make law's indeterminacy work in their favor. They can, for example, afford to hire the lawyers and pursue the appeals to ensure that the political commitments that advance their interests will maintain their dominant background role, or to engage in sustained efforts to recontextualize any legal texts that are currently understood in ways that block their interests.

But Fish disagrees with CLS here. First, as we have seen in Chapter 11, he does not accept that a CLS account of how law works entails the conclusion that law is pervasively indeterminate. Just because law is a rhetorical product, it does not follow that it is generally malleable or unstable or indeterminate. Successful rhetorical efforts can produce clear and compelling meanings that last (i.e., resist subsequent rhetorical efforts to change them) for a very long time. Also, just because law is a rhetorical product, it does not follow that you can do with law whatever you desire. Legal rhetoric operates within constraints, albeit constraints that are socially constructed and so ultimately rhetorical products as well. Second, as we have seen in Chapter 10, Fish does not agree that a degree of malleability in the law is a bad thing. Recall that Fish's central question is not: "How can the law be made philosophically coherent?" nor is it: "Is the law implicated in maintaining the dominance of one social group over another?" Instead he asks: "What are the jobs that a liberal society assigns to law, and how does law succeed in doing them?" And Fish argued strongly that law's malleability is desirable and functional. It enables law to perform successfully the incompatible tasks assigned to it in a liberal society. It enables law to tell its two stories and to perform its amazing trick.

Another disagreement between Fish and CLS arises from CLS's critique of liberalism. CLS writers sometimes sound as if they have uncovered something scandalous, namely the presence of political bias hidden beneath the surface of supposedly neutral liberal law. But Fish would reply that an anti-foundationalist cannot make this criticism. An anti-foundationalist should accept that the background of any interpretive community will never be neutral in the strong sense desired by liberals because it arises from a local, partisan form of embeddedness, as described in Part I. Since liberal neutrality is not possible, the failure to achieve it cannot be the basis for political criticism.

CLS can avoid this difficulty by shifting from criticizing the presence of politics in law to criticizing the presence of a *particular* politics in law, namely liberal politics. The grounds of the criticism would be that liberal values and categories operate ideologically to oppress social groups that CLS wants to champion. The CLS remedy would be to replace liberal politics in the background of law with a different politics that will aid these groups and disadvantage the currently dominant groups. Fish would not deny the propriety of a project to change elements of the current legal background, but, as we saw in Part II, he demonstrates no personal interest in pursuing it. Fish is not a political radical in any substantive sense, which distinguishes him from CLS writers.[36] His critique of liberalism is philosophical, rather than political. Once he has presented arguments that liberalism is not and cannot be neutral in the sense that it claims to be (and hence "Liberalism doesn't exist" [37] since this neutrality is so central to its identity), his work is done. He agrees with the analysis of CLS writers and others that liberalism embodies a contestable substantive conception of the good and that it is one form of partisan politics contesting in the fray with others, even though it presents itself as standing above the fray.[38] However, Fish would insist that it does not follow from this analysis alone that the substantive conception of the good and the partisan politics advanced by liberals are undesirable and should be replaced. Fish could both insist that liberalism hides a substantive partisan position and is therefore philosophically incoherent and also approve politically of the substantive partisan position advanced by liberalism. His response to the actual substantive politics of liberals, he tells us,

> would depend on whether or not I was sympathetic to the values and agendas they were hawking. If I were unsympathetic, if I belonged to some interest group other than that formed by persons with advanced degrees,

---

[36] "[L]ike the Critics, Fish shows how principles that are presented on their face as neutral or apolitical have controversial, politically laden assumptions about values built into them. But, unlike the Critics, Fish does not seem particularly concerned about whether doctrine disadvantages the disempowered or reinforces a capitalist world view." Hamish Stewart, "Is judgment inscrutable?" 11 *The Canadian Journal of Law and Jurisprudence* (1998) 423. Fish's disinclination to focus on how law upholds unjust power relationships is what Allan Hutchinson criticizes him for in "Part of an essay on power and interpretation (with suggestions on how to make bouillabaisse)" 60 *New York University Law Review* (1985) 850.

[37] *No free speech*, ch. 10.

[38] Fish cites approvingly Ronald Beiner, *What's the matter with liberalism?* (Berkeley: University of California Press, 1992) where this critique of liberalism is advanced. See *Trouble*, 110, 113.

tenured positions, vacation homes in the mountains, second wives, and fancy foreign cars (in fact I don't), I might oppose them tooth and nail.[39]

The main objection Fish has to CLS is that people who claim to be anti-foundationalists have derived a program from their anti-foundationalism and so contradicted their anti-foundationalist premises. The basic mistake was surveyed in Chapter 4 when I dealt with Fish's critique of anti-foundationalist political theories for exhibiting "anti-foundationalist theory-hope." To recap: if anti-foundationalism is correct, and human beings are necessarily locally embedded and reality is always "socially constructed," then realizing this fact cannot alter the situation. Realizing that we are always locally embedded cannot empower you to break free of local embeddedness. Realizing that reality is socially constructed will not enable you to see reality free of the distorting influence of socially constructed categories. Realizing the origins of your deep constituting beliefs will not automatically release you from the grip of those beliefs. Our most fundamental beliefs can certainly change, but adopting an anti-foundationalist epistemology is not a method that is guaranteed to bring about such changes, Fish insists. Adopting a new epistemology need not produce any changes in our beliefs outside the precincts of philosophy. Moreover, any act of critical self-reflection upon the enabling background of some practice must itself be enabled by a background that is not itself currently being reflected upon. Critical self-reflection therefore cannot enable us to stand back from all of the background conditions that enable and structure our lives. Fish concluded that critical theory's project of ideology critique leading to enlightenment and emancipation is a non-starter in politics.

For similar reasons, Fish argues that critical theory in law, as advocated by CLS writers, such as Roberto Unger, Robert Gordon, Duncan Kennedy, Peter Gabel, and Jay Feinman, is a non-starter.[40] The form of ideology critique urged by CLS writers such as Mark Kelman,[41]

---

[39] *Trouble*, 292.
[40] *Doing*, 226–31, ch. 18, 496–8. For responses to Fish's deflationary account of critical theory in law, see Daryl Levinson, "The consequences of Fish on the consequences of theory" 80 *Virginia Law Review* (1994) 1691–8; Steven Winter, "Bull Durham and the uses of theory" 42 *Stanford Law Review* (1990) 639; Andrew Goldsmith, "Is there any backbone in this Fish? Interpretive communities, social criticism, and transgressive legal practice" 23 *Law & Social Inquiry* (1998) 373; Kathryn Abrams, "The unbearable lightness of being Stanley Fish" 47 *Stanford Law Review* (1995) 595.
[41] *Doing*, 393–7.

Peter Goodrich,[42] and Pierre Schlag[43] is to strive constantly to become aware of the unnoticed enabling and structuring ideas in the legal background and then to question whether these ideas deserve to be retained.[44] Fish rejects this project because if "every legal procedure turned into a debunking analysis of its enabling conditions, decisions would never be reached and the law's primary business would never get done."[45] Here we see in operation Fish's autonomy of practices thesis described in Chapter 3. If, before you can apply the law, you must first inquire into the background enabling conditions of the law, you will have been deflected from doing the job of law and will have taken up instead a completely different practice – the practice of philosophy, or deconstruction, or metacritical analysis.

> Imagine the judge or lawyer who makes every point in the company of the demonstration that the point depends upon assumptions that one could always challenge. Imagine, too, that same judge or lawyer on the alert for those moments when his own discourse is in danger of becoming convincing, and meeting that danger by analyzing and laying bare the wholly rhetorical conditions that give force to what he has been saying. It would be too little to say of such a performer that he was falling down on the job of lawyering or judging; he wouldn't be doing that job at all, but some other, the job of literary criticism or of continental philosophizing.[46]

Paradoxically, according to Fish, a practice like law is not enhanced by a greater focus on its enabling background; instead, it is hobbled. The fact that the enabling and structuring backgrounds of practices are not more often examined is therefore not the result of a lack of rigor (as philosophers might believe), nor of ideological bamboozlement (as critical theorists might believe). Rather, being a competent practitioner requires that the enabling background of the practice is forgotten, in the sense that it remains something we think within rather than something we think about. Fish paraphrases Derrida to this effect:

---

[42] *No free speech*, 22, 174–77; *Doing*, 396–7.   [43] Fish, "Theory minimalism," 769–72.

[44] Fish is aware that this type of project is pursued by others besides CLS. In *No free speech*, 172–4, he describes how it is the project of James Boyd White. In parts II and III of his essay "Critical self-consciousness, or, can we know what we're doing?" (*Doing*, ch. 19), he describes how it is the project of the Frankfurt School of political theory. At *Doing*, 442, he describes a program of "critical self consciousness on the left," a program that is "rigorously and relentlessly negative, intent always on exposing or unmasking those arrangements of power that present themselves in reason's garb. As we shall see, the program bears many names – critique, critical theory, negative dialectics, reading against the grain, critical legal studies."

[45] *No free speech*, 171.   [46] *Doing*, 396. See too *No free speech*, 22, 173, 176, 177, 240.

That is to say, the truth one would know has always receded behind
the formulations it makes possible, and therefore those formulations are
always ignorant of themselves and incomplete. Indeed, ignorance, the
forgetting of the enabling conditions of knowledge (conditions that
cannot themselves be known) is constitutive of knowledge itself.[47]

---

[47] *No free speech*, 236. For Fish himself stressing the importance of forgetting, see ibid., 176,
241, 317 n6; *Doing*, 397.

CONCLUSION

As I warned in the introduction to this book, there are significant obstacles to understanding Fish. One is the dispersed nature of his writings on philosophy, politics, and law, but that is the easiest to overcome. I have sought to do so by ranging over Fish's corpus, collecting and arranging his arguments so that their structure and interrelationships become clear. A more obdurate obstacle is the unorthodoxy of the positions that are revealed by this process. I have attempted to make these unorthodox positions clearer and more plausible, but I am very conscious of the reasons why his readers find them hard to accept.

The philosophical positions that I describe in Part I, and which I claim are central to the positions he takes in politics and law, are particularly difficult to grasp. For example, in Chapter 1 Fish argued for a conception of the self as necessarily locally embedded, a self that was constituted by and not separable from the beliefs, goals, and values, etc., acquired in the process of being socialized into various communities and institutions. But this claim is hard to accept because it cuts against much that is venerable and valued in our culture. Many of our important philosophical, political, and jurisprudential projects ask us to transcend our local forms of embeddedness. They urge us to abandon the narrow and parochial viewpoint for one more universal, or to identify neutral principles that stand outside the partisan fray regarding conceptions of the good, or to employ a form of reasoning that is common to all human beings, or to overlook our surface differences in order to emphasize our shared essential humanity. But if Fish is right, all of these long-standing projects are impossible and exist only as rhetorical devices employed to advance some limited, local, partisan commitments. Similarly, if Fish is right that the condition of being constrained (and thus enabled) by a form of local embeddedness cannot be transcended, then the gold standard of freedom as the absence of constraints is devalued. Many readers of Fish immediately hear this as saying that there is no such thing as freedom, and it is hard to appreciate that his point is more subtle.

335

He is not denying that freedom exists, but he is pointing out that constraint turns out to be a precondition for the existence of freedom, and so the liberal conception of freedom is flawed.

There are similar difficulties with accepting Fish's anti-foundationalism (there is no foreground without a background) and social constructivism (the background is a contingent, contestable social product) described in Chapter 2. What follows from this position is the primacy of rhetoric, or the context-sensitive, persuasive techniques by which elements of the background are put in place and defended. In Fish's account, it is rhetoric "all the way down," and there is nothing that can constrain rhetoric that is not itself a product of rhetoric. This is very hard for Fish's readers to accept, because it seems equivalent to the claim that everything is malleable and indeterminate, that the world is ever-shifting, and we have no secure foundation to stand upon. Once these fears are aroused, it becomes hard to appreciate that Fish is making no such claim. Fish's argument is for the social construction of reality, not the social construction of an illusion. Anti-foundationalism does not dissolve the solidity and permanence of everyday life, instead it explains how that genuine solidity and permanence is achieved. Once elements of the background have been put in place by successful rhetorical efforts, they can stay in place, constrain us, and resist replacement for long periods of time.

The autonomy of practices described in Chapter 3 also cuts against most orthodox thinking. It claims that each practice is enabled and structured by its own particular background, and so different practices cannot be combined. For the same reason, each practice must be judged according to its own standards, not those of a different practice. The implications of this position are as hard to accept as they were in the previous two examples. Interdisciplinarity must be rejected as an empty and illusory project, as must any special role for the practice of philosophy. Philosophy, instead of being the master discipline scrutinizing all the other disciplines, is just one discipline among others, with its own distinctive values, goals, and standards. It is not a practice that is specially equipped to evaluate and judge all other practices, and it is without consequences outside its own precincts. (Fish insists that this is true of his own philosophical arguments, too.) But it can strike a reader that after offering this minimalist and deflationary account of philosophy, Fish immediately contradicts it by asserting that philosophy-talk can still legitimately be employed in other practices, such as politics and law. This seems cynical as well as inconsistent when Fish adds that even philosophically incoherent arguments can be so used, but Fish insists that it is perfectly acceptable interdisciplinary borrowing for rhetorical purposes, a practice in which the status of the borrowed item in its home practice is irrelevant. It also seems inconsistent for Fish to hold that when doing philosophy, one can be a committed anti-foundationalist, but when engaging in another practice, the background beliefs and values that enable and structure that non-philosophical practice will be held absolutely, not tentatively or in a qualified way. This position is hard to grasp, but it is central to Fish's thought: the same person who is an anti-foundationalist while doing philosophy will necessarily believe in absolute truths and universal values in a different context, because accepting the philosophical truth that we are necessarily embedded cannot release us from our embedded condition. This is the argument against anti-foundationalist theory-hope, the hope that accepting philosophical anti-foundationalism will enable us to be more tolerant, or ironic, or experimental, or open, or democratic in other areas of life. Fish is rare among anti-foundationalists in his emphatic denial of any such hope. Thus his position is not only hard for foundationalists to grasp, it is also hard for his fellow anti-foundationalists to accept.

Finally, there is an obstacle to understanding Fish that is raised by Fish's analysis itself. Recall, from Chapter 8, Fish's account of how particular meanings are apprehended in texts. It is due, he argued, to the already-in-place background beliefs, etc., of the interpretive community whose members are encountering the text. This has implications for how Fish's texts themselves are perceived. The already-in-place backgrounds of the communities who engage in the practices of philosophy, political theory, or jurisprudence have been accumulating over many centuries. They have elements that originate in the liberalism that began in the seventeenth century and elements that originate in the eighteenth-century Enlightenment. With those backgrounds in place, it is completely understandable that the members of those communities who encounter Fish's texts see them as saying something other than what Fish intended. They are, in fact, constrained by their backgrounds to understand Fish's texts as clearly saying something false and outlandish, to see him as a skeptic and a relativist, for example. The typical reader of Fish will be in the same position Fish describes Stephen Toulmin as being in when faced with the anti-foundationalist claim that

> an intrinsically rational argument is nothing more (or less) than a rhetorical or interested argument that has become so deeply established that its truth seems (for anyone operating in the relevant community) to be self-evident. Toulmin, however, sees something else; he sees confusion,

a blurring of differences and of a distinction that he cannot let go of
because at a basic level it is within its confines that he does his thinking.[1]

Not only do the already-in-place backgrounds of the relevant interpretive
communities virtually assure that Fish will be misunderstood, even by
very intelligent and sophisticated readers, it is also the case that this state
of affairs is not easily altered. Fish himself has insisted that, simply
because a background is socially constructed, it does not follow that it
does not constrain tightly, or that it can be changed at will. (This was
what allowed Fish to hold that the rule of law was not just a "noble lie" in
Chapter 11.) In his philosophical, political, and legal writings, Fish is
trying to change large elements of the relevant in-place backgrounds, but
by his own reasoning this is a very difficult task.

> So from my point of view, there are a lot of people out there making
> mistakes, and I'm just going to tell them that they're making mistakes.
> The mistakes are so deeply ingrained in the very forms of their own
> thought, however, that I'm in no danger of being persuasive, and I'm
> therefore in no danger of running out of occasions on which to make this
> limited ... argument.[2]

Similarly, although I have explicated Fish's writings as clearly as I can,
this alone is unlikely to change the enabling backgrounds of the interpretive communities from which Fish's readers come. Indeed, read with
these backgrounds in place, my own efforts might not produce clarity but
rather the confusion and incomprehension that Toulmin experienced.
My exposition too might be rendered opaque by not honoring distinctions and categories that my readers "cannot let go of" because they
enable and structure their thinking. This is a depressing line of analysis
to be sure, but because Fish succeeded in persuading me to change some
of my background beliefs (even though this process took more than a
decade), I entertain a modest hope that my book might also persuade
some of my readers (eventually).

---

[1] *Doing*, 224.
[2] Interview with Stanley Fish in Gary Olson, *Justifying belief. Stanley Fish and the work of
rhetoric* (Albany: State University of New York Press, 2002), 128. Earlier he was more
optimistic: "In general, people resist what you have to say when it seems to them to have
undesirable or even disastrous consequences ... It has been my strategy to speak to these
fears, one by one, and to remove them by showing that dire consequences do not follow
from the position I espouse and that in fact it is only within that position that one can
account for the phenomena my opponents wish to preserve." *Text*, 369.

Abrams, Kathryn, 140
Abrams v. United States, 196
absolute truth, anti-foundationalism
    and, 28–30
abstract theory, 56–60
    partisanship and, 59–60, 77
activism, of judges, 307
act-utilitarian judges, 275, 277–8
affirmative action, 140
    color-blind society and, 141–4
    neutral principle and, 168, 170
    opposition to, 141–2
    racism and, 141
    reverse discrimination and, 142
Alexander, Larry, 123, 221
"Almost Pragmatism:: The
    Jurisprudence of Richard Posner,
    Richard Rorty, and Ronald
    Dworkin" (Fish), 252, 258
amazing trick of law, for Fish, 301, 313
ambiguity
    in anti-foundationalism, 284
    enterprise-specific, 284
*American Booksellers Association v.
    Hudnut*, 198–9
angle of lean, 2–3
anti-foundationalism, 21–40.
    See also progressive anti-
        foundationalism
    absolute truth and, 28–30
    accumulation of facts and, 22–3
    ambiguity in, 284
    autonomy of practices and, 61–2, 110
    beliefs and, 118, 147
    claims and, 27
    CLS and, 327–8, 332
    conservative direction of, 109

critical theory and, 112–21
    in educational institutions, 33–5
    in everyday life, 31–3
    in Fish/Dworkin debate, 256–7
    forms of force and, 173–4
    interpretation and, 269
    lack of political consequences for,
        108–9
    in law, 35–6
    legal actors and, 256–7
    legal formalism and, 213–21
    local theory and, 53
    logic and, 38–40
    misinterpretations of, 145
    partisanship and, 147–8
    philosophy and, 67, 115
    political consequences of, 140, 146
    positive arguments for, 31–40
    post-modernism and, 21–2
    pragmatism and, 21–2, 63, 135
    recontextualization and, 309
    relativism and, 26–8, 44–5, 68–9,
        145–6
    in science, 36–8
    skepticism and, 26–7
    social constructivism and, 282–3
    textualism and, 213–21
    theories, hope and fear in, 108–12
    theory development, 67–8
    theory talk and, 159–60
anti-Semitism, 160
Arnold, Thurman, 294
author claim
    in intentionalism, 228
    unconscious/conscious intentions,
        238
authority, freedom of religion and, 101

author-less intentionalism, 222–5
  context for, 224
autonomy
  free speech and, 194–5
  for Kant, 8
  of self, 7
autonomy of practices, 60–4, 66, 71
  anti-foundationalism and, 61–2, 110
  critical theory and, 117
  in "Dennis Martinez and the Uses of
    Theory," 267
  in Fish/Dworkin debate, 266–9
  incorporation of new material, 72–3
  institutional tasks and, 60
  interdisciplinarity and, 63–4, 73–5
  for judges, 277
  performance of, 76–7
  political paralysis from, 171
  political practices and, 158
  politics and, 156
  pragmatism and, 135–6
  professional correctness and, 60
  separation of practices in, 71
  at work, 62
autonomy of theory, 64–70

background beliefs, 46
  feminism and, 47
  freedom of religion and, 100
  reason and, 97–8
Barak, Aharon, 231, 242–3
  intentionalism for, 271–2
Beauharnais v. Illinois, 198
Beiner, Ronald, 91
beliefs
  anti-foundationalism and, 118, 147
  capacity for change, 45–7
  critical theory and, 118
  deep, 46–7
  epistemology and, 40–7
  historical emergence of, 45
  knowledge and, 23
  perceptions of facts and, 42–4
  reason and, 43
  the self and, 10, 12
  social change influenced by, 162
  surface, 46
  theories compared to, 162

bias, 20
  freedom of religion and, 104
black-letter law, 186–90
boutique multiculturalism, 2
  postmodernism and, 127–8
  the self and, 8–9
Butler, Judith, 124–5
  politics of thinking for, 124–5

camouflage strategy, for substantive
  justice job, 296–7, 300
Canadian Charter of Rights and
  Freedoms, 198
censorship, 202, 204–5
change. See also social change
  of beliefs, 45–7
  communities as engines of, 152
  as community-specific, 150–1
  critical theory and, 119–20
  embeddedness and, 120
  free speech and, 30–1
  through internal processes, 150
  law as engine of, 185
  for neoconservative right, 152
  political, as internal development,
    152–3
  production of, through vocabulary, 47
change, in law. See also legal
    indeterminacy
  claim of consideration doctrine and,
    314
  community as engine of, 315
  constraints and, 306–7
  craft-training and, 316
  critique of Fish's stance, 305
  institutional bias against, 312–13
  through judicial activism, 307
  legal precedent and, 317–18
  limitations of, 312–13
  opposition to tradition and, 315–16
  parol evidence rule and, 313–14
  political context of, 315
  rhetorical achievements and,
    reworking of, 313–14
  rule of law job and, 311–12
  substantive justice job and, 312–13
  for U.S. Constitution, 307
  visibility of, 311–12

Christie, Agatha, 264
civility, freedom of religion and, 102–4
classical legal formalism, 206–8
  conceptual formalism, 207
  critiques of, 207
  demise of, 208
  principles of, 206
  rule formalism, 207
CLS. *See* critical legal studies
Cobb, Ty, 285–6
Cohen, Felix, 321
Collin v. Smith, 198–200
color-blind society, affirmative action
  and, 141–2
  abstract principles of, 143–4
common law, 271–2, 294
communities
  agreement within, 283
  change influenced by, 150–1
  domestication of foreign material,
    151–2
  embeddedness in, 149–50
  as engine of change in law, 315
  as engines of change, 152
  intentionalism in, 271–2
  interpretation claims influenced by,
    233–4
  substantive justice job and, 291–2
  of worship, 101–2
comprehensive doctrines, 50–1
  force and, 176
The concept of law (Hart), 209,
  219–20, 294. *See also* legal
  formalism
conceptual legal formalism, 207
conflict
  force and, 175–6
  manageability of, 176
  political practice and, 173–6
consciousness
  reflective activity and, 54–5
  the self and, 10, 14
Conservative Christianity, 101–4.
  See also freedom of religion
conservative religions. *See* freedom of
  religion
consideration doctrine, 187, 297, 314
Constitution, U.S.

authors' intentions, 224
change in law for, 307
historical changes to, 217
interpretation of, 36
constraints
  change in law and, 306–7
  on interpretation, 259–64, 269
  for judges, 275–6, 278
  by law, 210
  on legal actors, 317–18
  in legal indeterminacy, 306–8
  liberalism under, 85–6
  Milton on, 307
  non-legal, 278–9
  in parol evidence rule, 314
  of practices, 281
  recategorization of, with freedom of
    speech, 205
  on recontextualization, 310–14
  under rule of law, 318
constructive interpretation, 262
Contingency, irony, and solidarity
  (Rorty), 134
contingent consequences of theory,
  70–8
contract law
  contract implied in law, 297
  contradictions within, 296–8
  formal consideration doctrine and,
    297
  interpretation of, 190
  morality and, 187
  orthodox, 186–8, 297
  parol evidence rule in, 313–14
  protections under, 189–90
  taxonomy for, 298
critical legal studies (CLS), 288–90,
  327–34
  anti-foundationalism and, 327–8,
    332
  disorder of law and, 289–90
  Fish critique of, 329–32
  Frankfurt School and, 333
  goals of, 327
  Gramsci and, 327
  ideology as concept in, 327–8
  legal indeterminacy and, 329–31
  liberalism and, 328, 330–2

critical legal studies (CLS) (cont.)
  literary support of, 332–3
  rejection of orthodox Marxist
    account of law, 327
The critical legal studies movement
  (Unger), 288
Critical social science (Fay), 114–15
critical theory
  anti-foundationalism and, 112–21
  autonomy of practices and, 117
  beliefs and, 118
  change and, 119–20
  components of, 112–13
  critical attitudes, 116–17
  enabling background of, 113
  Fish rejection of, 148–9
  Frankfurt School and, 119
  freedom and, 120–1
  legal studies movement, 119
  political project of, 119
  projects, 113, 115–17
  roots of, 114–15
  the self and, 117–18
  social construction in, 118–19
  structural background of, 113
culture wars, 141
Cusset, Francois, 123

Dalton, Clare, 298
Dasenbrock, Reed Way, 144
deconstruction
  of liberalism, 84–5, 122
  postmodernism and, 122
deep beliefs, 46
  feminism and, 47
Delgado, Richard, 171–2
democracy, pragmatism and,
  133–5
"Dennis Martinez and the Uses of
  Theory" (Fish), 251–2, 257, 266
  autonomy of practices in, 267
  legal analogy in, 281–2
  philosophy's role in law in, 268
Dennis v. United States, 196–7
Derrida, Jacques, 16
Descartes, René, 57
detached theory, 56. *See also* abstract
  theory

Fish critique on, 57–9
  philosophy as, 56
Dewey, John, 129
discrimination, 140
  reverse, 142
distortion problem, 18–19
Doing what comes naturally (Fish),
  3, 64, 186–90, 214
"Don't Know Much About the Middle
  Ages: Posner on Law and
  Literature" (Fish), 325
doubt, 57
Duke, David, 168
Dworkin, Ronald, 55, 180. *See also* Fish/
  Dworkin debate
  on articulate consistency, 300
  commonalities with Fish, 252
  constraints against legal actors for,
    263
  critique of interpretation claim,
    242–5
  critique of judges as analogous to
    athletes, 281–6
  foundationalism for, 260–1
  independent constraints upon
    interpretation for, 259–64
  intentionalism for, 240–1, 271–2
  on judges, 253–4
  law as integrity for, 253
  legal formalism for, 260–1
  philosophy as guide for law,
    264–9
  on philosophy's role in law, 268
  positivism for, 260–2
  on pragmatism of unconstrained
    legal actors, 255
  on pragmatist judges, 274–5
  on principles of liberalism, 90
  on rule of law job, 294–5
  the self for, 254–5, 277–8
  on substantive justice job, 294–5
  textualism for, 219, 260–1
  on unconstrained legal actors,
    252–9, 273–81
Dworkin, Ronald, works of.
  See also Fish/Dworkin debate;
  Law's empire
  "Law as Interpretation," 243

"My Reply to Stanley Fish (and Walter Benn Michaels): Please Don't Talk About Obectivity Anymore," 251
"Pragmatism, Right Answers, and True Banality," 252, 282

Eagleton, Terry, 119, 191
Economic analysis of law (Posner), 325–6
educational institutions, anti-foundationalism in, 33–5
egalitarianism, 168–9
embeddedness
  in communities, 149–50
  free speech and, 191
  of judges, 276
  of legal positivism, 179
  liberalism and, 89–92
  local theory and, 53–4
  pragmatism and, 135
  recontextualization and, 309
  of self, 15
  theory and, 49
epistemology
  beliefs and, 40–7
  facts and, 40–7
  foundationalism as, 16–18
  of pragmatism, 130
  reasons and, 40–7
  secular liberalism and, 43–4
equality, 168–9
exclusion, freedom of religion and, 106–8

facts
  beliefs and, 42–4
  epistemology and, 40–7
fairness, liberalism and, 91–2
faith. *See* beliefs
fallibilism, 101, 106
Fay, Brian, 114–15, 119
Feinman, Jay, 332–3
feminism, 47, 140
  reasons for success of, 289
  theory for, 160
  theory talk and, 160–1
fictional intentionalism, 229–30

First Amendment
  free speech under, 196
  pragmatic balancing with, 200–1
  speech/action distinction and, 202
first law of toleration-dynamics, 196
Fish, Stanley. *See also* anti-foundationalism; autonomy of practices; Fish/Dworkin debate; intentionalism
  advocacy of political practice, 164–5
  on affirmative actions, 140
  amazing trick of law for, 301, 313
  angle of lean for, 2–3
  area of expertise, 1
  author claim for, 228
  on bias, 20
  CLS and, 288–90
  commonalities with Dworkin, 252
  conception of the self, 11–15
  on constraint of legal actors, 252
  on constraints of practices, 281
  critique of, on change in law, 305
  critique of Butler, 124–5
  critique of CLS, 329–32
  critique of detached theory, 57–9
  critique of Dworkin, 55
  critique of foundationalism, 18–21, 23–5
  critique of Habermas, 51
  critique of independent constraints upon interpretation, 259–64
  critique of Kant, 9–11
  critique of legal realism, 322–3
  critique of Posner, 293–4, 322–3
  critique of speech/action distinction, 202–5
  critiques of, 1–2, 4
  critiques of textualism, 213–28
  on discrimination, 140
  on gay and lesbian rights, 140
  interpretation claim for, 228–9, 231–4, 269
  judges as analogous to athletes for, 281–6
  on legal canon, 288
  legal indeterminacy and, 305–8, 316–18
  legal positivist responses, 186–205

Fish, Stanley (cont.)
    on liberalism, 141, 165–6
    Milton's influence on, 21–2, 43, 100
    philosophical influences on, 4
    political positions of, 139–44
    as politically conservative, 140
    pragmatism for, 131–2, 134–6
    on pragmatist judges, 274–5
    progressive politics of, 140
    reading style of, 276
    rejection of critical theory, 148–9
    rejection of unconstrained legal
        actors, 273–81
    on rule of law job, 294–5
    on skepticism, 26–7
    social construction of reality, 24
    social constructivism for, 282–3
    structural style, 2–3
    on substantive justice job, 294–5
    on success of feminism, 289
    writing style, 2
Fish/Dworkin debate
    "Almost Pragmatism:: The
        Jurisprudence of Richard Posner,
        Richard Rorty, and Ronald
        Dworkin," 252, 258
    anti-foundationalism and, 256–7
    autonomy of practice in, 266–9
    common law in, 271–2
    communication of meaning in,
        272–3
    "Dennis Martinez and the Uses of
        Theory," 251–2, 257, 266–8, 281–2
    development of, 251–3
    independent constraints upon
        interpretation in, 259–64
    intentionalism in, 268
    interdisciplinarity in, 268–9
    interpretation differences in, 269–71
    judges as analogous to athletes in,
        281–6
    "Law as Interpretation," 251, 260
    Law's empire in, 239, 241, 251, 255
    literary responses, 251–2
    "My Reply to Stanley Fish (and
        Walter Benn Michaels): Please
        Don't Talk About Obectivity
        Anymore," 251

    on personal preferences of legal
        actors, 257–9
    "Pragmatism, Right Answers, and
        True Banality," 252, 282
    the self and, differences in accounts
        of, 254, 277–8
    "Still Wrong After All These Years,"
        251–2, 256
    unconstrained legal actors in,
        252–9
    "Working on the Chain Gang:
        Interpretation in Law and
        Literature," 251, 260–1
    "Wrong Again," 251, 256, 259–61
Fiss, Owen, 180–2, 281
force
    anti-foundationalism and, 173–4
    comprehensive doctrines and, 176
    definition of, 175
    freedom of speech and, 174–5
    partisanship and, 175
    politics and, 175
formalism. See also legal formalism
    recontextualization and, 308
    rule of law and, 291
foundationalism. See also anti-
        foundationalism
    definition of, 16
    distortion problem and, 18–19
    for Dworkin, 260–1
    as epistemology, 16–18
    Fish critique of, 18–21, 23–5
    legal formalism and, 213
    legal realism as, 321–2
    of liberalism, 83–4
    limitation problem and, 18–19
    objective knowledge and, 17–18, 23
    positivism and, 17, 183
    for Posner, 323
    rejection of, 20
    scientific method and, 18
    theory essentials, 22
    theory talk for, 164
    truth and, 23
Frank, Jerome, 321
Frankfurt School, 114–15
    CLS and, 333
    critical theory and, 119

freedom. *See also* freedom of speech
  critical theory and, 120–1
  liberalism under, 85–6
freedom of religion, 100–8
  atheism and, 151
  authority and, 101
  background beliefs and, 100
  civility and, 102–4
  community of worship and, 101–2
  conservative Christianity under,
    101–4
  exclusion and, 106–8
  freedom of association and, 101–2
  hidden bias and, 104
  under liberalism, 176
  marginalization and, 104–6
  multiculturalism and, 127
  obedience to God's commands,
    102–4
  philosophical critique of, 108
  postmodernism and, 127
  rational deliberation and, 101
  rejection of, 105
  tradition and, 101
freedom of speech, 30–1
  in *Abrams v. United States*, 196
  in *American Booksellers Association
    v. Hudnut*, 198–9
  autonomy and, 194–5
  in *Beauharnais v. Illinois*, 198
  censorship and, 202, 204–5
  in *Collin v. Smith*, 198–200
  consequences of, 192, 203–4
  in *Dennis v. United States*, 196–7
  embeddedness and, 191
  under First Amendment, 196,
    200–1
  forms of force, 174–5
  in *Gitlow v. New York*, 196
  as incoherent concept, 191
  liberalism and, 192–3, 201–2
  partisanship and, 191–3
  political paralysis and, 172–3
  pragmatic balancing for, 200–1
  protected speech and, 204
  recategorization of constraint with,
    205
  regulated speech and, 204
  speech/action distinction and,
    202–5
  tolerance and, 192, 195, 199–202

Gabel, Peter, 332–3
gay and lesbian rights, 140
Geertz, Clifford, 21
general theory, 48
Gitlow v. New York, 196
God, 20
  obedience to, under freedom of
    religion, 102–4
  the Self and, 10–11
Goldsmith, Andrew, 281
Goodrich, Peter, 206, 332–3
Gordon, Robert, 332–3
Gramsci, Antonio, 327
grand theory, 48
Gray, John, 83
Grice, H. P., 228

Habermas, Jürgen, strong theory for, 51
Hale, Robert Lee, 95
Hart, H. L. A., 209, 219–20, 294.
    See also legal formalism
  on hard cases, 300–1
  scorer's discretion and, 232, 248
Hay, Douglas, 327
Heidegger, Martin, 109, 133–4
Hobbes, Thomas, 82–3
Holmes, Oliver Wendell, 207–8
Holocaust denial, 160
How Milton Works (Fish), 3

ideology, as concept
  in CLS, 327
  critique of, 328
indeterminacy. *See* legal indeterminacy
institutional history, law and, 255–7
integrity
  for judges, 253–4
  law as, 253
"Intention is All There Is" (Fish), 245
intentionalism, 221–50.
    See also interpretation claim, in
    intentionalism
  advocates of, 221
  author claim in, 228

intentionalism (cont.)
author meaning and, textual
meaning compared to, 225–8
without authors, 222–5, 270–1
for Barak, 271–2
boundaries of, 244
common law and, 271–2
within communities, 271–2
conceptual assumptions of, 221–2
conscious intentions, 238
Dworkin on, 240–1, 271–2
fictions in, 229–30
in Fish/Dworkin debate, 268
interpretation and, 269–70
lack of limitations under, 224–5
law and, with non-human authors,
270–1
legislative, 227, 237, 241–2
methodological individualism and,
241
multiple states of mind, 241
natural meanings in, 228
public language and, 238–9
public meaning and, 222
rewriting and, 244–7, 301
for Rorty, 244
rule of law job and, 303
textual meaning and, author
meaning compared to, 225–8
textualism compared to, 221, 233
unconscious intentions, 238
U.S. Constitution and, 224
interdisciplinarity, 63–4, 73–5
in Fish/Dworkin debate, 268–9
in legal realism, 322
for Posner, 323
risks of, 324–5
interpretation
anti-foundationalism and, 269
broad sense of, 269
communication of meaning through,
272–3
constructive, 262
of contract law, 190
in Fish/Dworkin debate, 269–71
independent constraints upon,
259–64, 269
intentionalism and, 269–70

by judges, 279
of law, 303
in legal formalism, 218
legal indeterminacy and, 306
narrow sense of, 269–70
rewriting compared to, 246–7, 270
textual features of, 262–3
in textualism, 218, 233
of U.S. Constitution, 36
interpretation claim, in intentionalism
community influences on, 233–6
critiques of, 231–4, 236–7
Dworkin's critique of, 242–5
epistemological objection in, 237
for Fish, 228–9, 231–4, 269
independent constraints upon,
259–64
independent object of, 232–3
non-existence objection to, 240
objections to, 242–3
public language and, 238–9
as rational, 249
rewriting and, 244–7
scorer's discretion and, 248
textualism and, 218, 233
unconstrained legal actors and, 248–9
interpretive communities, 216
Ireland, Paddy, 109
Is There a Text in This Class (Fish),
33–5, 214, 219

James, William, 21, 38–9, 129
Jameson, Frederic, 176
Johnson, Philip E., 159
judges
act of persuasion for, 319
act-utilitarian, 275, 277–8
athletes as analogous to, 281–6
autonomy of practices for, 277
constraints for, 275–6, 278
embeddedness of, 276
formal consideration doctrine and,
297
integrity for, 253–4
interpretation by, 279
moral principles of, 259
personal preferences as influence on,
257–9, 276

philosophy as influence on, 265
political principles of, 259
pragmatism in, 274–5, 279
as unconstrained legal actors, 253–4
judicial activism, 307
Justifying belief (Olson), 60, 149, 155, 173, 178

Kant, Immanuel, 83
autonomy for, 8
conception of the self, 7–11, 194
Fish critique of, 9–11
Kelman, Mark, 332–3
Kennedy, Duncan, 95, 332–3
Kloppenberg, James, 133
Knapp, Steven, 221, 223
Knight, G. Wilson, 250
knowledge
beliefs and, 23
foundations of, 17
objective, 17–18, 23
positivism and, 17
relativism and, 27
skepticism and, 27
Kronman, Anthony, 182
Kuhn, Thomas, 37, 62, 155

language. *See also* intentionalism
of neutral principles, 170
public, for interpretation claims, 238–9
textualism and, 209–11
law. *See also* change, in law; contract law; legal indeterminacy; legal positivism; rule of law; substantive justice job, of law
absolutist monarchic power and, 177
amazing trick of, for Fish, 301, 313
anti-foundationalism in, 35–6
anti-legal positivism in, 298
autonomy of, 184–5
black-letter, 186–90
CLS and, 288–90
common, 271–2, 294
conflicts with consistency in, 292
conservatism of, 302
constitutional interpretation and, 36
constraints by, 210

continuity in, 291
culture of, 326
definition of, 36
disorderly nature of, 287–90
distinctions within, 256
doctrine of consideration and, 187
empirical approaches to, 320
as empirical fact, 183–4
enabling background as influence on, 333–4
enforcement of, 184
as engine of change, 185
equity, 294
as expression of moral principles, 253
as expression of political principles, 253
flexibility of, 301
formalism in, 178
forum of principle perspective, 190
goals of, 177–8
hard cases in, 300–1
institutional functions of, 293
institutional history and, 255–7, 300
integrity in, 253–4
intentionalism with non-human authors, 270–1
interdisciplinarity in, 268–9
interpretation of, 303
jobs of, in liberal societies, 290–5
legal canon, 288
legal doctrine of, 288–9, 298–9
legal texts, 36
liberal requirements of, 177
liberalism and, 177–8
malleability of, 330
morality and, 183–6, 253, 280
neutral principles in, 190–205
objectivity of, 216
orthodox contract, 186–8
orthodox Marxism, 327
philosophy as influence on, 264–9, 292–3
as political, 178
politics and, separation from, 183–6
positivism and, 177–8
Posner on, 287–8
pragmatism of, 293

law (cont.)
    precedent in, 317–18
    principles of, 287
    ratiocination as task for, 206–7
    reasoning mechanisms of, 288
    recontextualization in, 310–14
    rewriting in, 246–7, 301–4
    rhetoric in, 330
    separate institutions within, 294
    as social practice, 188–9
    stopping rule in, 246–7
    tasks of, 290, 302
    technical content of, 288
Law and Literature (Posner), 325
law as integrity, 253
"Law as Interpretation" (Dworkin),
    243, 251, 260
Law's empire (Dworkin), 239, 241, 251,
    255, 260–2
    constructive interpretation in, 262
    philosophy in, 265
    pragmatism in, 257
lawyers. See legal actors
legal actors. See also judges
    anti-foundationalism and, 256–7
    constraints on, 317–18
    craft-training for, 316
    Dworkin on, 252–9
    Fish on, 252
    institutional history and, 255–7
    morality as influence on, 254
    nature of constraints on, 263
    philosophy as influence on, 265
    politics as influence on, 254
    pragmatism of, 255
    under rule of law, compulsion of,
        318–19
    textualism and, 208–9
    uncertainty of, 285
    unconstrained, 179–82, 253–9
legal doctrine, 288–9, 298–9
legal formalism, 178. See also classical
        legal formalism; textualism
    anti-foundationalist argument and,
        213–21
    conceptual, 207
    in Doing what comes naturally, 214
    for Dworkin, 260–1

    foundationalism and, 213
    goals of, 206
    interpretation in, 218
    interpretive communities and, 216
    in Is There a Text in This Class,
        214
    legal indeterminacy and, 305–6
    legal realism as rejection of, 320
    rejection of history in, 206
    rule of law job and, 293–4
    rules and, 210–11
    substantive justice job and, 294
    in There's No Such Thing as Free
        Speech, 214–15
    unconstrained legal actors, 179–82
legal indeterminacy
    CLS and, 329–31
    constraints in, 306–8
    experience of, 310
    Fish and, 305–8, 316–18
    interpretive community and, 306
    legal formalism and, 305–6
    legal realism and, 320
    prejudices and, 315–16
    recontextualization and, 308–14
    theoretical development of, 305
    versions of, 308–9
legal positivism, 177–8, 183
    autonomy in, 184–5
    development of, 183
    legal realism and, 320, 326
    neutral principles in, 190–205
    responses to Fish, 186–205
    rule of law job and, 293
    the self and, 180
    unconstrained legal actors and,
        179–82
legal realism, 320–6
    empirical approaches to law, 320
    Fish critique of, 322–3
    as foundationalism, 321–2
    interdisciplinarity in, 322
    legal indeterminacy and, 320
    legal positivism and, 320, 326
    as movement, 321
    myth of objectivity and, 321
    Posner and, 322–3
    rejection of legal formalism, 320

legislative intention, 241–2
  stopping rule and, 246–7
Levinson, Sanford, 144
liberalism, 50–1, 81–108.
  See also freedom of religion
  abstract principles of, 143–4
  censorship and, 202
  CLS and, 328, 330–2
  color-blind society and, 141–2
  conflict resolution under, 81–2
  deconstruction of, 84–5, 122
  dichotomies of, 84–8
  doctrine of consideration and, 187
  Dworkin on, 90
  fairness and, 91–2
  Fish on, 141, 165–6
  foundationalism of, 83–4
  free market under, 94–5
  free speech and, 192–3, 201–2
  freedom of religion under, 176
  freedom *vs.* constraint under, 85–8,
    120–1
  historical development of, 81
  inconsistencies of, 82–3
  law and, 177–8
  marginalization under, 104–6
  moral agenda of, 91–2
  neutral principles of, 90–3, 165–6
  neutral procedures of, 93–6
  neutral reason in, 96–9
  neutrality of, 89–99
  organizing categories of, 84
  partisanship of, 89
  philosophy and, 163
  political paralysis as result of,
    172–3
  pragmatism and, 134
  progressivism and, 199–200
  protection of religion and, 105
  rejection of, as philosophical
    position, 148
  rule of law job and, 290–1
  theory talk for, 164
  tolerance and, 99
  unconstrained legal actors and,
    179–82
limitation problem, 18–19
Llewellyn, Karl, 182, 299, 316, 329–31

local practices. *See also* autonomy of
    practices
  theory and, 53–5
local theory, 52, 69–70
  anti-foundationalism and, 53
  efficacious, 59
  embeddedness and, 53–5
  philosophy and, 65
  practice of, 65
  strong theory compared to, 52–3
Locke, John, 82–3
logic
  anti-foundationalism and, 38–40
  contingent background beliefs and,
    39–40

MacKinnon, Catharine, 160
Mannheim, Karl, 113
marginalization, freedom of religion
    and, 104–6
Margolis, Joseph, 131
Martinez, Dennis, 54, 76
Masterson v. Sine, 314
meaning
  author's, compared to textual, 225–8
  depth of, with textualism, 212
  through interpretation, 272–3
  natural, in intentionalism, 228
  public, intentionalism and, 222
  through recontextualization, 310
  textual, compared to author's, 225–8
  textualism for, 233
methodological individualism, 241
Michaels, Walter Benn, 221, 223
Mill, John Stuart, 83, 103
Milton, John, 9, 235–6, 250, 263–4
  on legal constraints, 307
Moore, Michael, 268, 281
moral agency, of self, 8
morality
  contract law and, 187
  of judges, 259
  law and, 183–6, 253, 280
  legal actors influenced by, 254
  of unconstrained legal actors, 259
multiculturalism
  boutique, 2, 8–9, 127–8
  postmodernism and, 126–9

multiculturalism (cont.)
  religious freedom and, 127
  strong, 128–9
  tolerance and openness and, 126–7
"My Reply to Stanley Fish (and Walter
    Benn Michaels): Please Don't Talk
    About Obectivity Anymore"
    (Dworkin), 251
myth of objectivity, 321

neutral principle, 2
  affirmative action and, 168, 170
  freedom of religion and, 167
  labeling of, 163
  language of, 170
  in law, 190–205
  legal positivism and, 190–205
  of liberalism, 90–3, 165–6
  political paralysis from, 171–3
  of politics, 165–7
  racism and, 168
  in rule of law, 291
Norris, Christopher, 52

objective knowledge, 17–18, 23
Olson, Gary, 60, 149, 155, 173, 178
"On Legal Autonomy" (Fish), 325
On Liberty (Mill), 103
openness, multiculturalism and, 126–7
orthodox contract law, 186–8
  consideration doctrine in, 297
orthodox Marxist account of law, 327
overarching theory, 48
Owen, J. Judd, 144, 146

Paradise Lost (Milton), 235–6, 263–4
parol evidence rule, 313–14
  constraints in, 314
  in Masterson v. Sine, 314
  textualism and, 313
partisanship
  anti-foundationalism and, 147–8
  force and, 175
  free speech and, 191–3
  of liberalism, 89
  politics and, 165–70
  theory and, 59–60, 77
"The Path of the Law" (Holmes), 207–8

Patterson, Dennis, 27–8
Peirce, Charles, 129
personal preferences
  of judges, 257–9, 276
  legal actors influenced by, 257–9
  legal indeterminacy and, 315–16
  principles compared to, 277
philosophy
  anti-foundationalism and, 67, 115
  deflationary approach to, 266–9
  as detached theory, 56
  doubt in, 57
  for Dworkin, 264–9
  as influence on judges, 265
  as influence on legal actors, 265
  interdisciplinarity in, 268–9
  law influenced by, 264–9, 292–3
  in Law's empire, 265
  liberalism and, 163
  local theory and, 65
  politics and, connections between,
    139, 144–53, 163
  theory talk and, 162–3, 268
"Play of Surfaces: Theory and the Law"
    (Fish), 184–5
pluralism, 106
political change, 152–3
political practice, 156–76
  autonomy of practices and, 158
  conflict and, 173–6
  features of, 156–7
  forms of force and, 175
  lack of cynicism in, 164–5
  neutral principles of, 165–7
  paralysis in, from neutral principles,
    171–3
  partisanship and, 165–70
  philosophically-defective arguments,
    162–5
  theory and, 157–62
political theory. See liberalism
politics
  autonomy of practices and, 156, 158
  broad sense of, 154–5
  as concept, 154–6
  conflict and, 173–6
  forms of force and, 175
  of judges, 259

law as expression of, 253
legal actors influenced by, 254
local commitments and, 154–5
narrow sense of, 155
neutral principle in, 165–7
paralysis in, from neutral principles,
    171–3
partisanship and, 165–70
philosophy and, connections
    between, 139, 144–53, 163
public, 155
science and, 155
separation of law from, 183–6
theory and, 157–62
of unconstrained legal actors, 259
positivism. *See also* legal positivism
characteristic theses of, 17
development of, 183
for Dworkin, 260–2
foundationalism and, 183
knowledge and, 17
Posner, Richard, 274–5, 279, 287–8,
    325–6
Fish critique of, 293–4, 322–3
foundationalism for, 323
interdisciplinarity for, 323
on law, 287–8
legal realism and, 322–3
on precedent, 317–18
on substantive justice job, 293–4
Postmodern Sophistry (Olson), 60–1,
    234–6, 283
postmodernism, 121–9
anti-foundationalism and, 21–2
deconstructionism and, 122
definition of, 121
French theorists and, 122
multiculturalism and, 126–9
political consequences of, 123–4
religious freedom and, 127
strong multiculturalism and, 128
uniculturalism and, 128–9
vulgar, 123
pragmatism, 129–38
account compared to program,
    134–5
anti-foundationalism and, 21–2,
    63, 135

autonomy of practices and, 135–6
community and, 132–3
definition of, 131–2
democracy and, 133–5
development of, 129–30
embeddedness and, 135
epistemology of, 130
for Fish, 131–2, 134–6
in judges, 274–5, 279
of law, 293
in *Law's empire*, 257
liberalism and, 134
political consequences of, 132
relativism and, 131
roots of, 129
for Rorty, 131, 133, 136–8
trans-contextual principles, 132, 136
for unconstrained legal actors, 255
Pragmatism (James), 38–9
"Pragmatism, Right Answers, and True
    Banality" (Dworkin), 252, 282
Pragmatism in Law and Society, 131,
    252
Pragmatism's Advantage (Margolis),
    131
Prakash, Saikrishna, 221
principles, personal preferences
    compared to, 277
The problems of jurisprudence (Posner),
    287–8
Professional Correctness (Fish), 60
progressive anti-foundationalism,
    112–38. *See also* critical theory;
    postmodernism; pragmatism
disadvantaged groups and, 112
Frankfurt School and, 114–15, 119
social constructed reality and, 112
progressivism, 199–200
protected speech, 204
protection of religion, 105
Putnam, Hilary, 133

racism
affirmative action and, 141
neutral principles and, 168
Radin, Margaret Jane, 136
rational self, 7
Rawls, John, 83

Rawls, John (cont.)
    comprehensive doctrines, 50–1
    hypothetical agreement and, 8
    information for self and, 8
    on the self, 7–8
reality
    progressive anti-foundationalism
        and, 112
    social construction of, 24
reason
    background beliefs and, 97–8
    belief and, 43
    epistemology and, 40–7
    in law, 288
    in liberalism, 96–9
reasonable testator, 249
recontextualization
    anti-foundationalism and, 309
    constraints on, 310–14
    embeddedness and, 309
    fixed meanings through, 310
    formalism and, 308
    future possibilities, 309–10
    in law, 310–14
    legal indeterminacy and, 308–14
    textualism and, 308
reflection, consciousness and, 54–5
regulated speech, 204
relativism
    anti-foundationalism and, 26–8,
        44–5, 68–9, 145–6
    knowledge and, 27
    pragmatism and, 131
religion. See also freedom of religion
    in substantive justice job, 291–2
religious fundamentalism, 160.
    See also freedom of religion
reverse discrimination, 142
The Revival of Pragmatism, 131
rewriting
    inconsistency of, 301–2
    intentionalism and, 244–7, 301
    interpretation compared to, 246–7,
        270
    in law, 246–7, 301–4
    of literature, 250
    negative attitudes towards, 249–50
    reasonable testator and, 249

    in rule of law job, 303
    in substantive justice job, 303
    unconstrained legal actors and,
        248–9
rhetoric, in law, 330
Riggs v. Palmer, 219, 295
Rorty, Richard, 63, 88, 109, 134
    on intentionalism, 244
    as neo-pragmatist, 131, 133,
        136–8
rule formalism, 207
rule of law, 290–1
    application of, 295–9
    changes in law and, 311–12
    compulsion of legal actors under,
        318–19
    constraints under, 318
    Dworkin on, 294–5
    Fish on, 294–5
    formalism and, 291
    intentionalism and, 303
    legal formalism and, 293–4
    legal positivism and, 293
    liberalism and, 290–1
    neutral principles in, 291
    as noble lie, 299
    rewriting in, 303
    rhetoric and, 318
    substantive justice job compared to,
        290
    textualism and, 208–9, 211
    validity of, 318–19

Scalia, Antonin, 211–12
Schanck, Peter, 4, 22–3, 70, 140, 148,
        159–60
Schauer, Frederick, 210–12
Schlag, Pierre, 332–3
Schreiber, Harry, 299
science
    anti-foundationalism and, 36–8
    as political, 155
scientific method, 18
    foundationalism and, 18
scorer's discretion, 232
    interpretation claim and, 248
Second Restatement on Contracts, 298
secular liberalism, 43–4

the self
  autonomy of, 7
  beliefs and, 10, 12
  boutique multiculturalism and, 8–9
  consciousness and, 10, 14
  critical theory and, 117–18
  deprivation of, 9
  for Dworkin, 254–5, 277–8
  emancipation of, 19
  embeddedness of, 15
  Fish critique of Kant's conception, 8
  in Fish/Dworkin debate, 254, 277–8
  Fish's conception of, 11–15, 254,
    277–8
  God and, 10–11
  information for, 8
  institutional influences on, 13–14
  Kantian conception of, 7–11, 194
  legal positivism and, 180
  local contexts for, 13
  moral agency of, 8
  rational, 7
  Rawls on, 7–8
  self-consciousness and, 10
  social, 14
  as social construct, 13
  solipsism and, 13–14
  in *A Theory of Justice*, 7–8
  values of, 10
self-consciousness, 10
semantics, textualism and, 227
sham theory, 59
Sinnott-Armstrong, Walter, 230
skepticism
  anti-foundationalism and, 26–7
  knowledge and, 27
Smith, Steven, 231, 238, 292
social change
  beliefs as influence on, 162
  theory as influence on, 157
social construction
  in critical theory, 118–19
  of reality, 24
social constructivism, 282–3
social self, 14
solipsism, 13–14
speech. *See* freedom of speech
speech/action distinction, 202–5

consequences of, 204–5
First Amendment and, 202
Fish critique of, 202–5
malleability of, 204
St. Augustine, 4, 228
stereo strategy, with substantive justice
  job, 296–7
Stewart, Hamish, 281
"Still Wrong After All These Years"
  (Fish), 251–2, 256
Stoljar, Natalie, 236–7
stopping rule, in law, 246–7
strong multiculturalism, 128–9
strong theory, 50
  local theory compared to, 52–3
The Structure of Scientific Revolutions
  (Kuhn), 37, 155
substantive justice job, of law, 291–2
  application of, 295–9
  camouflage strategy for, 296–7, 300
  change in law and, 312–13
  communitarian elements of, 291–2
  contract implied in law and, 297
  dispute resolution under, 291
  Dworkin on, 294–5
  Fish on, 294–5
  flexibility of, 298
  legal formalism and, 294
  orthodox contract law and, 297
  Posner on, 293–4
  religious elements of, 291–2
  rewriting in, 303
  Riggs v. Palmer under, 295
  rule of law compared to, 290
  stereo strategy with, 296–7
  in *The Trouble with Principle*, 295
surface beliefs, 46
syntax, textualism and, 227

textualism, 206–12
  See also intentionalism
  ambiguity of, 216–17
  anti-foundationalist arguments
    against, 213–21
  authoritative resolution of disputes
    through, 212
  without authors, 222–5
  contemporary application of, 210–12

textualism (cont.)
depth of meanings with, 212
difficulties of, 209–10
in *Doing what comes naturally*, 214
for Dworkin, 219, 260–1
established meanings of words and, 233
exceptions to, 210
Fish critiques of, 213–28
hard cases and, 220–1
intentionalism compared to, 221, 233
interpretation in, 218, 233
interpretive communities and, 216
in *Is There a Text in This Class*, 214, 219
language and, 209–11
legal actors and, 208–9
in literary studies, 219
parol evidence rule and, 313
plain cases and, 220–1
purpose of, 208
recontextualization and, 308
rule of law and, 208–9, 211
rules and, 210–11
for Schauer, 210–12
semantics and, 227
sensitivity of decision-maker and, 211
syntax and, 227
in *There's No Such Thing as Free Speech*, 214–15
theory. *See also* critical theory; local theory
abstract, 56–60
anti-foundationalism, hope and fear in, 108–12
of anti-foundationalism, 67–8
autonomy of, 64–70
beliefs compared to, 162
as consequential, 59
as deflationary, 48, 64–5, 161
embeddedness and, 49
in everyday practices, 49
feminist, 160
guidance of other practices and, 55–70
interdisciplinary borrowing, 77

local context limitations and, 50–3
local practices and, 53–5
orthodox claims about, 48–9
partisanship and, 59–60, 77
politics influenced by, 157–62
sham, 59
social change influenced by, 157
status of, 78
strong, 50, 52–3
theory-talk compared to, 158
types of, 48
"Theory Minimalism" (Fish), 67
A Theory of Justice (Rawls), 7–8
theory talk
anti-foundationalism and, 159–60
anti-Semitism and, 160
feminism and, 160–1
for foundationalism, 164
for liberalism, 164
philosophy and, 162–3, 268
political consequences of, 158, 161–2
in political practice, 157–62
religious fundamentalism and, 160
theory compared to, 158
There's No Such Thing as Free Speech (Fish), 193, 214–15, 287, 315
Thomas, Brook, 52
Thompson, E. P., 327
tolerance
first law of toleration-dynamics, 196
free speech and, 192, 195, 199–202
multiculturalism and, 126–7
Toulmin, Stephen, 18
tradition, freedom of religion and, 101
"Transcendental Nonsense and the Functional Approach" (Cohen), 321
Tribe, Laurence, 196
Trident Centre v. Connecticut General Life Insurance Company, 188
The Trouble with Principle (Fish), 3, 169
substantive justice job in, 295
truth. *See also* absolute truth
foundationalism and, 23

unconstrained legal actors, 179–82. *See also* judges

Dworkin on, 252–9, 273–81
institutional history and, 255–7
interpretation claims and, 248–9
judges as, 253–4
morality of, 259
politics of, 259
pragmatism for, 255
rejection of, by Fish, 273–81
rewriting and, 248–9
Unger, Roberto, 152–3, 268, 288, 332–3
uniculturalism, 128–9

vulgar postmodernism, 123

Webb v. McGowin, 297
Weber, Mark, 43
Webster, John, 101
Weinrib, Ernest, 62
West, Cornel, 136–8
White, James Boyd, 333
Williams, Ted, 285–6
Winter, Steven, 39, 281
"Working on the Chain Gang:
    Interpretation in Law and
    Literature" (Fish), 251, 260–1
"Wrong Again" (Fish), 251, 256,
    259–61, 276

Stanley Fish on Philosophy, Politics and Law

Fish's writings on philosophy, politics and law comprise numerous
books and articles produced over many decades. This book
connects those dots in order to reveal the overall structure of his
argument and to demonstrate how his work in politics and law
flows logically from his philosophical stands on the nature of
the self, epistemology and the role of theory. Michael Robertson
considers Fish's political critiques of liberalism, critical theory,
postmodernism and pragmatism before turning to his observations
on political substance and political practice. The detailed analysis
of Fish's jurisprudence explores his relationships to legal positivism,
legal formalism, legal realism and critical legal studies, as well as
his debate with Ronald Dworkin. Gaps and inconsistencies in Fish's
arguments are fully explored, and the author provides a description
of Fish's own positive account of law and deals with the charge that
Fish is an indeterminacy theorist who undermines the rule of law.

MICHAEL ROBERTSON is an associate professor of law in the
Faculty of Law at the University of Otago, New Zealand, where he
teaches courses in jurisprudence, legal theory and law and society.

CAMBRIDGE
UNIVERSITY PRESS
www.cambridge.org

Cover photograph by the author.

Cover designed by Hart McLeod Ltd

ISBN 978-1-107-42737-2

9 781107 427372 >